THE WARNING

THE
WARNING

The Coming Great Crash in the Stock Market

JOSEPH GRANVILLE

FREUNDLICH BOOKS

Copyright © Joseph E. Granville 1985

Library of Congress Cataloging in Publication Data

Granville, Joseph E. (Joseph Ensign), 1923–
The warning.

Includes biliographical references and index
1. Stock—exchange—United States—History.   2. United
States—Economic conditions—1981–   3. Depressions—
1929—United States.   I. Title.
HG4910.G76   1985   332.64′273   85-13107
ISBN 0-88191-034-1

Published by Freundlich Books
80 Madison Avenue
New York, N.Y. 10016

Distributed to the trade by The Scribner Book Companies, Inc.
115 Fifth Avenue
New York, N.Y. 10003

Manufactured in the United States of America

10 9 8 7 6 5 4 3 2 1

FOR KAREN

THE AMERICAN BIRTHRIGHT

The richest heritage, the most precious birthright, is to be an American in this day and age.

For never was a country so happy, so prosperous, so peaceful as America today. Never were man's horizons wider, his opportunities for the finer things of life greater—because never was wealth, upon which these enjoyments depend, so open to attainment as in present day America.

The creation of new wealth in fabulous quantities is America's special faculty. The wide diffusion of this wealth is her greatest discovery. *And anyone may participate.*

Incorporated Investors provides an ideal method. Through its one-class, fully participating shares, Incorporated Investors, designed for this new America, passes on to its stockholders the growth and earnings of the greatest companies in America's expanding fields.

Advertisement of Incorporated Investors
The Wall Street Journal
August 14, 1929

Preface

I had always wanted to do a definitive work on the 1929 crash. For the greater part of my life, texts on the subject frustrated me because they were all written by historians and economists, whereas they should have been written by market technical analysts. Never in history had so many people been misled by fundamental analysis, the anathema of all true market technicians. The trouble in 1929 started in the market itself, not in the economy, and the economists and fundamental analysts were not able to read the stock market. Their forte is the economy, and they completely missed all the market warnings. They wasted their time back then talking about rising corporate earnings, but earnings have little or nothing to do with the stock market. People buy and sell stocks, not earnings. Fundamentalists analyze the economy and companies. Technicians analyze the market and stocks. They are two different worlds. So the great market warnings of 1929 fell mostly on deaf ears because most people were following the economy and corporate earnings.

When I saw precisely the same market signals being flashed in early 1983 as had appeared back in 1929, the opportunity to write *The Warning* was at hand. Wall Street was about to make the same mistakes all over again, stressing the economy and corporate earnings when the market would not be listening to those things. As in 1929, the trouble started in the market itself and was to spread to the economy later. Wall Street had encouraged overconfidence in stocks at the very worst of times, and a scenario of psychological steps was to unfold in a pattern that would be uncannily similar to the events of 1929.

This book is about those steps and the predictable public response to them, following a well-trodden path which threatened financial destruction.

Contents

Introduction

There is a point of stress beyond which everything snaps. A popular story has it that Enrico Caruso could break a wineglass from fifty feet away by reaching a certain pitch with his powerful tenor voice. And I believe that there must be an *identifiable point of stress* in financial markets beyond which lies panic. The point of maximum stress corresponds exactly with that magic moment when everyone wants to sell at the same time. A panic is impossible until a point is reached where it can be shown that most people are bearish on the stock market at the same time.

All through 1983 I had been diligently searching through the history of finance for particular points of maximum stress. When I had isolated them, I tried to formulate criteria so I could predict when financial markets were headed toward them. My research drove me to dire conclusions; the evidence of gloom was so overwhelming that I put myself on record in speeches and interviews, saying *we had entered a bear market in the spring of 1983 which would lead to a major stock market crash.*

The financial markets were heading toward that point of maximum stress, and a milestone was reached on February 3, 1984. On that day any hopes for a continuation of the 1982–83 brief rise were dashed by the opening moves of the great 1983–84 bear market.

Panics have been relatively infrequent since the great one of 1929, but to say that we will never have another one makes as much sense as a similar promise made by the president of the New York Stock Exchange on September 11, 1929.

Many years ago I was impressed with what Bernard Baruch had written in a foreword to a new edition of Charles Mackay's *Extraordinary Popular Delusions and the Madness of Crowds,* originally published in 1841. In reference to the stock market frenzy preceding the 1929 crash, he wrote the following: "All economic movements, by their very nature, are motivated by crowd psychology. Graphs and business ratios are, of course, indispensable in our groping efforts to find dependable rules to guide us in our present world of alarms. Yet I never see a brilliant economic thesis expounding, as though they were geometrical theorems, the mathematics of price movements, that I do not recall Schiller's dictum: 'Anyone, taken as an individual, is tolerably sensible and reasonable—as a member of a crowd, he at once becomes a blockhead.' . . . Without due recognition of crowd thinking (which often seems crowd madness) our theories of economics leave much to be desired. It is a force wholly impalpable—perhaps little amenable to analysis and less to guidance—and yet, knowledge of it is necessary to right judgments on passing events."

Crowd psychology took over in the spring of 1983, and from that point forward the stock market public became its own worst enemy.

Baruch implied that we had a terminal stock market delusion. Here is a quote from his book *The Public Years:* "The prehistoric tribal eruptions from Central Asia, the Crusades, the medieval dance crazes, witch burnings, all these—right down to the Florida boom and the 1929 madness—were phenomena of mass action under impulses which no science has explored. Such impulses have power unexpectedly to affect any static condition or so-called normal trend. For that reason, they have a place in the considerations of thoughtful students of economic affairs. It has always seemed to me that the periodic madnesses which afflict mankind must reflect some deep-rooted trait in human nature—a trait akin to the force that motivates the migration of birds or the rush of the lemmings to the sea. In economics there seems to be a cyclical rhythm to these movements. A bull market will be galloping along and then suddenly, something will occur—trivial or important—to break the continuity of thought. And then panic sets in."[1]

What was it that broke the continuity of thought prior to the great downturn of 1983–84? The cover story[2] for economic recovery was airtight. President Ronald Reagan was associated in people's minds with a rising stock market, lower interest rates, and a booming economy. A trend was set in motion and it developed such an upward velocity that it transformed individuals into a crowd. Knowing that 1984 was an election year, the president played his new role as an economic savior to the hilt and the people loved it, not aware at the time of the great price that was going to have to be paid for the new

---

[1]Bernard Baruch, *The Public Years* (New York: Holt, Rinehart and Winston, 1960), p. 228.
[2]A cover story is one that most people find easiest to believe. Since the stock market tends to follow a law of opposites, all significant changes of trend are preceded by cover stories that entrap the majority into believing that the trend in force has no end in sight. In the order of change that follows, it is the financial markets that sense approaching trouble first while the economic landscape is still serene and beautiful.

free lunch of supply-side economics. While the country was mesmerized with the manual dexterity of Reagonomics and its success in pushing the Dow Jones Industrial Average to all-time record levels in a dizzying spiral of speculation, people failed to see that the architecture of the largest budgetary deficits in history was being put in place, deficits far exceeding the total of all previous administrations combined. But Washington and Wall Street had so effectively brainwashed the country with the great cover story of a robust economy that investors and speculators rationalized that there was no end in sight for the Reagan bull market. What got started in late 1982 became a mania by the spring of 1983.

All manias end in a panic and crash, and the warnings in 1983 inevitably led to the same conclusion. David Dreman's *Contrarian Investment Strategy* contains as good a definition of manias as I have seen anywhere: "All manias, though separated by centuries, have had surprisingly similar characteristics. They started in prosperous economies, where people were looking for new investment opportunities and wanted to believe they existed. Each mania had sound beginnings and was based on a simple but intriguing concept. The rise in prices, in every case, became a self-fulfilling prophecy, attracting more and more people into the speculative vortex. Rumor always played a major role, at first of fortunes made and of good things to come, and later in prophecies of doom. In almost every case, the experts were caught up in the speculation, condoning the price rises and predicting much higher levels in the future. At the height of both the 1961 and the 1967–68 markets, money managers stated that the valuation standards of the past no longer applied—things really were different this time. And on both occasions, the statements were uttered shortly before the end."[3]

Was it any different in 1983? Of course not. And that is what was so intriguing, because the pattern was precisely similar. Didn't Wall Street condone the prices and shout to the housetops that the Dow was headed for 1,500 and higher? Didn't Wall Street say that this bull market was different because it was the great secular rise of the 1980s, with the Dow soaring to over 3,000 by the end of the decade?

Dreman concluded his remarks on manias with the following: "Four general principles seem to emerge from a study of financial speculations. First, an irresistible image of instant wealth is always presented that draws a financial crowd into existence. Second, a social reality is created that blinds most people to the dangers of the mania. Opinions converge and become 'facts.' Experts become leaders approving events and strongly exhorting the crowd on. Overconfidence becomes dominant, and standards of conduct and the experience of many years are quickly forgotten. Third, the Le Bon image of the magic lantern suddenly changes and anxiety replaces overconfidence. The distended

[3]David Dreman, *Contrarian Investment Strategy* (New York: Random House, 1979), p. 80.

bubble breaks with an ensuing panic. And fourth, we do not, as investors, learn from past mistakes—things really do seem very different each time, although in fact each set of circumstances is remarkably similar to the last."

Markets leading toward a panic and crash follow definite patterns. When the Dow Jones Industrial Average turned down in early January 1984, it described a definitive pattern very much like that of 1929 just prior to the great crash. As bad as it was, it was not the real thing. It was simply one of the dress rehearsals seen in 1928. When one studies the day-to-day market action of 1929, one can feel the psychology of the times. At first, there was no struggle. On the surface it appeared that everyone was optimistic. There wasn't a cloud in the sky. The 1983–85 evidence showed so many 1929 parallels that I put myself on record everywhere at every opportunity, the laws of probability assuring me that so much data could not be wrong.

PART ONE

EUPHORIA

1

Flee for Your Life

[MARCH 1983]

I

In the spring of 1983 nobody saw even a hint of the approaching storm. The president of the United States had already made several references to the record highs in the Dow Jones Industrial Average and the economic recovery was getting stronger and stronger. Nobody gave a single thought about selling any stocks. Wall Street was virtually 100 percent bullish. The previous Christmas had been the greatest party Wall Street ever had, and the production bonuses for the brokers were the most generous on record. At what would appear to be absolutely the most improbable time to hear valid market warnings, I appeared on ABC's *Nightline* telecast on March 14 and told the viewers to flee for their lives. Ted Koppel held a copy of *The Granville Market Letter* up to the camera and asked me to explain the title of the March 12 issue, "Flee for Your Life."

I said that the letter told of an earlier warning: During the researching of material for his great book on Vesuvius entitled *Volcano: The Search for Vesuvius,* William Hoffer was intrigued to learn that hundreds of years ago a plaque was erected somewhere in the village of Portici, warning its citizens of the evil of Vesuvius.[1] Inscribed in Latin in 1632, the plaque was all but forgotten by the town. Patiently searching the area, Hoffer discovered the plaque—three rectangular marble panels, eight feet wide and fifteen feet tall. Quoting the English translation of the final lines of this 350-year-old warning:

[1]William Hoffer, *Volcano: The Search for Vesuvius* (New York: Summit Books, 1982), pp. 130–31.

> If you are wise, hear this speaking stone.
> Neglect your domestic concerns, neglect your
> goods and chattels, there is no delaying. Fly.

That 350-year-old plaque was as good a stock market letter as could be written. It said that if you ever hear a rumble like this, flee for your life. Ever since the fall of 1982, the technical rumbles in the stock market, starting as small tremors, steadily increased until, by the spring of 1983, they had become a tumult.

But nobody was listening, even though I was certain that the 1982–83 market rise was ending and, being already equipped with enough 1929 parallels to herald something far more serious than an ordinary bear market, I was ready in the spring of 1983 to predict panic and crash.

PARALLEL 1

Historical
The Kondratieff Wave

Probably more than anything else, I bypassed the August 1982 upturn because of how the market looked against the template of the Kondratieff Wave.[2] I had forgotten a key comment I made back in November 1979: that a stock market crash would be impossible until the market first climbed mightily in preparation for a great swan dive. The upturn from the August 1982 bottom was explosive and abnormal. Between August 1982 and March 1983, I amassed a large number of parallels with 1929. In relation to the 1982 bottom I had made a timing error, but I knew my basic analysis was right. History would forget somebody who missed the 1982 bottom, but would never forget one who called the 1983 top.

[2]I had previously written extensively about Kondratieff's famous paper, *The Long Waves in Economic Life*. Nikolai D. Kondratieff was a Russian economist, born in 1892. While head of the Moscow Business Institute, which he founded in 1920, he wrote his paper in 1926, but it didn't receive worldwide recognition until it was translated from Russian several years after the great 1929 stock market crash. On the basis of French, English, and American economic statistics, Kondratieff produced impressive evidence of a long cycle averaging 54 years. The implication was clear that capitalism would survive the cyclical troughs; and that conclusion led to his arrest on a trumped-up charge by the Stalin government and his being sentenced in 1930 to Siberia, where he died soon thereafter. He is survived by his son, who resides in Moscow today, and his grandson, Yuri Kondratieff, who was until recently the head of U.S.A. Affairs at the Moscow Academy of Sciences. As can be seen above, the Kondratieff cycle gave a clear prediction of the major trouble of 1929 and an equally clear prediction of major trouble in the 1980s. Never believing that such a cycle could be mathematically precise, I did, however, state in my 1976 book, *New Strategy* (p. 250), that the theoretical crash year would be 1983. That was based on using the average 54-year length of the cycle. Actual experience had shown that the length of the cycle could vary between 48 and 60 years. No matter how interpreted, the chart of the cycle left no doubt in my mind that by 1983 any huge rise in the stock market had to be seen as a terminal affair, ending a long up cycle.

My speaking schedule was expanded, and I probably gave more speeches, made more public appearances, and was more exposed to radio and TV interviews during that period when the market was going against me than during any other period I could recall. I wanted to be solidly on record prior to an event that I was certain not only was going to occur but would occur sooner than anyone realized. After all, if one has to make a mistake in the market, always miss a bottom but don't ever miss a top. If one misses a bottom, one gives up profits which he never had. On the other hand, if one misses a top, one gives up all or part of his capital. Since most people never go short, my August 1982 miss caused most people only to miss some profits. Wall Street's failure to warn people of the 1983 top, however, caused most people to lose all or part of their capital.

The 20th Century Business Cycle and Crisis Points
(Calculated Path)

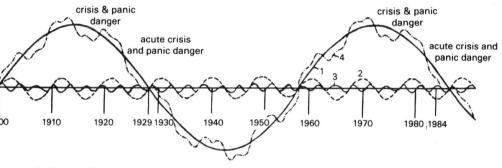

1. Kondratieff
2. Juglar
3. Kitchin
4. Composite of 1, 2, & 3

Source: T.J. Zimmerman
Geschichte der theoretischen
Volkswirtschafts-lehrs
–Dr. P.E. Erdman-unpublished paper

So then I considered the Kondratieff Wave to be a compelling model of my crash thesis and the first of the 1929 parallels.

———————

PARALLEL 2
Market
The Parabolic Rise

A stock market that retraced more than half of the entire previous bear market in a handful of days was unprecedented. I had a match with the 1928–29 market rise, a perfect parabolic curve. The market history of all parabolic or

exponential rises sees them all collapse. That the rise was parabolic underscored its abnormal characteristics and shortened its overall life expectancy.
This constituted the second parallel I had to work with.

Market
Volume Characteristics Identical

Since I knew that the trading markets of 1929 were unprecedented, I was not
daunted by the volume records being set in the 1982–83 period. The volume
upswing was the most certain proof that I had that the 1982–83 upswing was
an ending to a long cycle, not the beginning of a new one. Below are seen the
comparative bar charts of the volume of trading on the New York Stock
Exchange for the periods 1918–29 and 1972–83. Here was the great evidence
of the huge speculative bubble, culminating in the overwhelming euphoria
that was so evident in the spring of 1983.

New York Stock Exchange Trading Volume 1918–1929

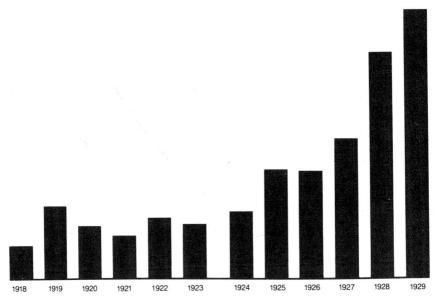

New York Stock Exchange Trading Volume 1972–1983

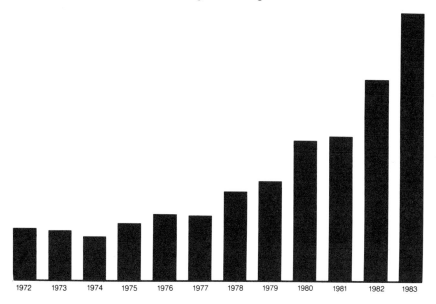

| 1972 | 1973 | 1974 | 1975 | 1976 | 1977 | 1978 | 1979 | 1980 | 1981 | 1982 | 1983 |

With the volume of stock trading soaring to all-time record highs, 1983 was a stock market blowoff year (a year in which bullish activity is red-hot). Not only was the volume a historical record but the *rate of rise* matched a similar volume run-up in the late 1920s. Here are the comparative statistics (in millions of shares):

1918	143.3	1972	4,138.2
1919	318.3	1973	4,053.2
1920	227.6	1974	3,517.7
1921	172.8	1975	4,693.4
1922	260.9	1976	5,360.1
1923	236.5	1977	5,273.8
1924	284.0	1978	7,205.1
1925	459.7	1979	8,155.9
1926	451.9	1980	11,352.3
1927	581.7	1981	11,853.7
1928	930.9	1982	16,458.0
1929	1,124.6	1983	21,589.6

The high volume at the end of a bull market reflects many things, but when the comparison bridges the 54-year Kondratieff span, it reflects a combination of several parabolic rises. For instance, the 1983 volume blowoff reflected the added volume of trading stemming from a record number of margin accounts and margin debt, a record number of stock splits, a record high short interest, record interest in mutual funds, record pension-fund buying, the added market support stemming from Investment Retirement Accounts, as well as record selling by corporate insiders. Moreover, it was a reflection of a new record in the number of shareholders. Most people would rather buy stocks than sell them, and thus record volume also reflected record bullishness and record speculation, all major characteristics of a major bull market top. All these characteristics were in full view by the spring of 1983.

In 1929 there was a similar record upswing, in volume and high-margin debt, a record number of new listings, record short interest, a record number of stock splits, record interest in the new investment trusts, as well as a new high in bullishness and speculation.

PARALLEL 4
Market
Abnormal Characteristics

Something was wrong with the 1982–83 rise from the very start. It was too quickly accepted by the majority as a new and powerful bull market era. Right away it commanded attention on the cover of *Time* magazine. A record amount of money poured into the mutual funds, indicating that the public was back into the market abnormally too soon to equate with normal reinvestment. By January 1983 there had been no normal one-third to two-thirds retracements, and yet third-phase bull market characteristics were being seen, proof positive that everything thus far was abnormal. Everything was speeding up at a dizzying rate and the rapid transition from bull market first phase to second phase to third phase was accomplished in a period of several months, whereas a normal bull market develops in something closer to two years. Low-priced stocks had already recorded a parabolic ascent and I noted heavy insider selling.

I didn't have all the evidence I wanted by early 1983, but it was nevertheless piling up rapidly. Something was wrong.

All these abnormal characteristics underscored the entire upswing as one grand terminal play, which would usher in a severe bear market, panic, and crash. The beginning of a normal bull market is characterized by stock *accumulation* and the beginning of a bear market is characterized by stock *distribution*. Inasmuch as I had detected provable major stock distribution as early as the spring of 1983, and distribution characterizes the start of a bear trend, then a technically genuine rise in the market lasting only a few months was not a normal bull market upswing. It was far too short.

I was bothered by the institutional pattern. Genuine bull markets do not usually begin with institutional buying, but with dumping. Institutions were big buyers at the 1981 top. Their buying in August 1982 underscored the abnormality of the bull market. This led me to believe that the August 1982 upswing would turn out to be one of the shortest bull markets on record.

The abnormal 1982–83 rise had only one parallel in history: 1929. Back in those pages of market history could be found the parallels, the only parallels that matched the current period. There was the new era market, the acute angle of rise that could not be sustained, the unprecedented volume of trading, and euphoria. There was the great stock market clock ticking away, bringing us closer and closer to the most critical portion of the Kondratieff Wave.

PARALLEL 5

Psychological
New Era Thinking

It didn't take Wall Street very long to accept the rapid rise coming off the August 1982 bottom as signaling "a new era." As early as October 30, 1982, I had called attention in my market letter to a Kidder Peabody ad then appearing in *Barron's:*

A NEW ERA FOR COMMON STOCKS?

The sharp, upward spiral of the stock market combined with a record surge in volume supports a new day for common stocks.

That's the thinking of Kidder Peabody's investment strategists. Their conclusions are based on sound reasons. These experts believe the evidence that not only is the economy returning to a traditional low-inflation format, but also interest rates will drop further and will remain down.

With the resulting more rational yield curve, investors can once again look to common stocks for substantial long-term appreciation potential.

Does the recent sharp rise in stock prices mean that uncommitted investors have missed the train? Not at all. Our analysts point out that there are still a wide choice of undervalued situations available. And they believe that this bull market, with corrections, has a long way to go.

It was a good ad and was right as rain for a few more months. But to tell people that it was a new era for stocks offering substantial long-term appreciation potential was no different from similar ads run in *The Wall Street Journal* back in 1929 underscoring the "new era" psychology and stressing that the good stocks had a scarcity value and were being snapped up and being put away in the lock boxes for the long pull.

The new era thinking was also well documented by statements that the Dow 1,000 level would not be broken for many years to come and the still more ridiculous belief by some that the Dow 776 level of August 1982 would never be seen again in our lifetimes. It all smacked of 1929 new era thinking.

PARALLEL 6

Market
Unprecedented Rise

By mid-October 1982 it was obvious that something unprecedented in modern-day markets was taking place. The Dow had leaped out to the wild blue yonder, soaring in uncharted space. The market was certain to get increasingly dangerous, and, like those who ventured into the notorious Bermuda Triangle, many would never return. I wrote as follows in the market letter of October 16, 1982:

"Back in 1977 Dr. Henry N. Southworth of England, in reviewing my work in the British journal *The Chartist,* made a statement that has always stuck in my mind. He stated that many key indicators *malfunction* at critical points in the long waves. As I had stated in the 1976 *New Strategy* book, the most critical of the remaining years in the Kondratieff long wave are the years 1981, 1982, and 1983. It is, therefore, within the context of this most critical period that something totally unexpected occurred, something totally surprising in terms of its extreme parabolic features, both in terms of price amplitude in the Dow as well as the brief period of time in which to achieve it."

PARALLEL 7

Historic
Everybody Going into Everybody Else's Business

By 1983 it was getting increasingly difficult to recognize the difference between a bank, an insurance company, and a brokerage house. They were all getting into each other's business in their great scramble for the public's money. The trend intensified into 1982, but by the spring of 1983 the trend was clear; it was a dangerous one and it paralleled a similar trend in 1929.

PARALLEL 8
Historical
Endless Ways to Get Rich

Wall Street had opened the candy store to a new generation of suckers, offering more new goodies than ever before. The introduction of new options, options on the market indices, new funds, and other enticements to enter the market presented a huge number of devices with which to part the fools from their money. There just wasn't enough money to support all those new markets.

It was no different back in 1929. The new issues were gushing forth at an unprecedented rate, new investment trusts were springing up, one could get into a speculator pool, and there appeared to be no end of ways to get rich.

By March 1983, Wall Street was revved up for the Super Bull Market of the 1980s. President Reagan had already made several references to the soaring stock market as his proof that Reaganomics was working and that the country wanted him to "stay the course." Nobody was making any references to the Reagan "cover-up"; the eight months of recession the administration knew was coming was kept quiet, as was the Federal Deposit Insurance Corporation's problem with bad loans.

I was already talking about the rising budget deficits in the fall of 1982. But who cared about such trivial things when stock prices were going straight up? All through the period from August 1982 to March 1983, I was making increasing references to 1929, but nobody was going to listen to a man who missed the August 1982 bottom. Certain stocks had started breaking, but the public, sworn to the averages, was not going to accept the breaks in Warner Communications, Mattel, Eastman Kodak, and others as important omens. Sure, things were increasingly speculative. Sure, an occasional scandal would be announced. But this was March 1983 and the public had the bit in its teeth. This market was headed for heaven, and nothing was going to stop it.

It was precisely at this time, even while I was on camera with Ted Koppel on March 14, 1983, pleading with the viewers to Flee for Their Lives, that everything began to go wrong in a hurry. It was not seen in the averages, as yet, but it began to show up in many stock price charts. This was probably the time when most people were blind to what was soon to follow. The greatest of all the 1929 parallels was being recorded:

━━━━━━━

Psychological
Nobody Saw It Coming

As in the English panics of the nineteenth century, and as the precursor of all panics—*nobody saw it coming.* Wall Street was as blind to the dangers ahead in the spring of 1983 as was a previous generation of Wall Streeters in 1929. In the incredible blindness in both periods, the common denominator was the total uselessness of fundamental analysis, the very thing that entrapped all the Wall Street pundits, economists, and a broad spectrum of the media: those people who report the stock market every day and are so deeply impressed by fundamentals. As in 1929, everybody was looking at the economy for the answers, and that fact explained, better than all the others, why nobody saw the crash coming. The trouble started in the stock market and much later spread to the economy. That is another parallel in itself and will be listed and discussed in the chapter referring to the January 1984 downturn. The great crash of 1929 took most stocks drastically lower *despite* earnings, dividends, interest rates, and the economy. Those are the things the fundamentalists follow, and *not one of them warned of the coming crash or could explain why the market crashed.*

At this time I had enough evidence to be certain that, as in 1929, anyone who sold out in the spring of 1983 and stayed out would sidestep the great crash and be seen by history to be a winner. This constituted another parallel to be listed later on when supposition became fact. It wasn't necessary by March 1983 to have seen the final peak in the Dow in order to fortify the already existing evidence that most stocks were very close to peaking. I was particularly interested in investor sentiment at that time. It constituted another 1929 parallel:

━━━━━━━

Psychological
Bearish Sentiment at a Minimum

If my bearishness was correctly timed, then it was essential to have the evidence at hand that virtually everybody else was wildly bullish. At major bull market peaks, there is an overwillingness to buy and a greater disinclination to sell. Sure enough, the sentiment figures became seriously lopsided that month, showing how mesmerized the public had become with the bull market, a bull market that was expected by an overwhelming majority to carry well past the November 1984 elections.

This extreme lopsided sentiment was noted in the March 12, 1983, market letter: "And not the least are the extremely bearish sentiment readings coming out from *Investors Intelligence*[3] every week, the increasing rarity of the bear, now threatened with total extinction. Before the species dies out completely, one is on display here in Kansas City, Missouri, almost the very last in a dying species.

"While sentiment figures were not published in 1929, *The Wall Street Journal* gave more than ample evidence that the chorus of bulls that year was so large that any dissenting voices were more than drowned out."

II

On March 25 I appeared on *Crossfire*. Pat Buchanan laced into me for missing the 1982 bottom. I acknowledged the error, but stressed the importance of what to do now, not what one should have done. Unknown to most, March 1983 was very late on the up cycle. I was well armed with what I felt was impressive evidence that the bull move, if not over, was close enough to being over that I wanted to be on record that the time for serious selling was very close. I ran through the major points rapidly, stressing the abnormality of the cycle, the compacting of all three normal bull market phases into one huge rise, the many signs of abnormal stock distribution, individual stock break-downs, and the fact that Wall Street was on the whole fully invested with no place to go except down.

Signs of distribution included stock splits, secondary offerings, insider selling, and sentiment. I was also watching the new issue market carefully. I was beginning to ferret out some key warning areas which were signaling major trouble ahead, new issues, stock splits, and secondary offerings constituting my main signals.

At this time, most analysts had their sights glued to the traditional cycle of three normal up phases, with the bull market terminating two to two and a half years from the bottom. Thus they were looking for Dow levels of 1,250 to 1,350 in 1983 and anywhere from 1,350 to 1,500 or higher in 1984. In keeping with that thinking, most economists were in harmony with it, looking for continued economic recovery in 1983 and a much stronger up-surge in 1984. I saw a warning note in all that. *It was too popular a view.* It was especially questionable because of the unanimous agreement among the economists. I drew attention to a front-page piece that appeared in *The Wall Street Journal* on February 12, 1981. I was under fire at that time for

[3]*Investors Intelligence*, Larchmont, N.Y. 10538. This weekly service, which evaluates seventy investment advisory services, found in March 1983 that only 11 percent of them were bearish.

having issued the January 6, 1981, sell signal at Dow 1,004.69. The piece was headed: "Economists Do Not Agree with Joe Granville." They predicted 990 by August 1981, 1,080 by February 1982, and 1,145 by August 1982. The Dow went in the opposite direction, bottoming at 776 in August 1982, some 369 points under where the economists thought the Dow would be. Their projection showed that they also did not see the economic recession coming. If the economists couldn't see the recession and stock decline coming in 1981, why were their forecasts in March 1983 relied upon so heavily by Wall Street and the investing public? Once again, as in 1981, their unanimous optimism was suspect. Their record increased the odds in favor of the great 1983–84 decline.

III

The common short-term outlook was for a 10 percent correction, a correction that simply refused to materialize. Countering that widespread expectation, there were too many growing signs that the market was fast approaching a major top and that by the time a 10 percent correction did occur the bull market would have to be seen as a bear market. At this point, it was not necessary to depend on something totally unexpected to distort the cycle. The technical indicators offered sufficient proof in their documentation of the growing risks.

The big play from the August 1982 bottom was so self-advertising that it was certain to trigger the Greater Fool Theory, what I would call "the second-generation buyers." Billions of dollars had been wagered on economic recovery and the current signs had justified those bets. All those early bettors were beginning to line up at the cashiers' windows to cash in their winning tickets. The market correctly discounted the future, and the future they had bet on had caught up with reality by March 1983. The first generation of buyers was being paid off. They were selling to a second generation of buyers. In order for that distribution of stocks to be successfully completed, the stage had to be set so as to induce the second generation of buyers to come into the game and hold a hand of cards. This is where the economists always play a key role. They blow the trumpet of the recovery theme, accompanied by the great tuba section of the media. It becomes a virtual symphony and it effectively drowns out all dissenting voices. The great new theme stresses the virtue of long-term stock investment, a theme then picked up by the entire brass section of the stock brokerage industry, which carefully designs its advice to the second generation of stock buyers to make sure that advice always contains one key word: BUY.

The new generation of stock buyers was putty in the hands of Wall Street, so expert when it comes to distributing stocks to the "greater fools." The new buyers bombarded the Street with more buy orders than the Street had ever seen before! They clutched at the new issues then being so widely touted, grabbed at any low-priced stock, and pushed margin debt to new record highs.

But beneath the façade of what seemed to be impregnable strength, cracks were beginning to show up:

PARALLEL 11
Market
Early Stock Breakdown

A growing number of stocks was beginning to break down at this time, stocks such as Warner Communications, Mattel, Bally, Browning Ferris, Baldwin-United, Eastman Kodak, SCA, and Waste Management.

Wall Street brokers, their memories of the great party the previous December still fresh in their minds, threw away all caution and concentrated on production, first, foremost, and always. The brokerage house phones were ringing all over America, the frantic search for new accounts while the getting was good. Certainly no warnings were going out, because people don't buy if a broker warns them not to. Brokers wanted those buy orders, and they got them in wholesale bunches.

IV

PARALLEL 12
Historical
Warnings Fell on Deaf Ears

There had been a storm of warnings about the stock market in 1929, but they were drowned out by public greed, each market reaction being followed by a continuous series of new all-time record highs in the Dow Jones Industrial Average. The Cassandras of that day were laughed off the stage and their comments were replaced by bullish statements which captivated the nation's thinking, until the country was mesmerized into believing that the Coolidge-Hoover prosperity was a permanent plateau. None of the warnings took hold, and the stock market of that day discredited the Cassandras. Even at such points where for a while technical reactions were expected to occur, they did not, and as the Dow made its final spurt in the summer of 1929, even those who had previously expected a technical reaction *finally gave up and announced that there wasn't going to be a correction at all.* It was that thinking that served as the dangerous precedent that coincided with the final breaking of the bubble. That was the general Wall Street thinking by late March 1983.

The market was disregarding documented technical evidence of growing internal weakness. The rising Dow was raising the price for overstaying the market. I was calling attention to the fact that everything was speeding up at a dangerous clip. Already, the market had traversed all three phases of a normal bull market without having recorded a meaningful correction. That is what underscored my contention that history would record the upswing as one uninterrupted and completed bull market. By late March 1983 the third-phase bull market characteristics were already being recorded.

V

Against the background of a market caught up in euphoria, stock splitting was rife. It was adding to the growing paper parade and was distorting the short interest. Stocks in the Dow such as American Express and Procter & Gamble had split, and by late March 1983 General Electric had announced a split. This constituted another 1929 parallel:

━━━━━━━

PARALLEL 13

Market
Stock Splits

This was a key warning of developing major market trouble. The year 1983 was headed toward a record number of stock splits, and that trend was already well discernible by late March 1983. Nothing reflects the euphoric stage of a bull market more effectively than a record number of stock splits. The bigger the record number is, the more certain it is that the stock market has formed a huge bubble that is soon to break. Corporations, playing the stock market game for all it's worth, split their shares when times are good so as to widen the area of ownership through low-cost stock. Splitting a stock is a form of stock distribution, and stock distribution has preceded every bear market in history. Wall Street, in its eagerness to get the public into the market by means of every conceivable ploy, never warns the public about the implications of too many stock splits, but, on the contrary, steps up their bullishness every time a stock splits. The public, in a get-rich-quick mood in periods of rapid and frequent stock splits, always interprets a stock split bullishly, never realizing until it is too late that they have been lured into buying that split stock by the financial press and will be stuck with it in the next bear market. Somebody has to own the stocks in every bear market, and *thus the pressure to make people want to own stocks is at its maximum prior to every bear market.*

With the splitting of stocks, the supply of paper overhanging the market grows. Such a supply of paper was growing so rapidly in 1983 that it was to reach all-time records.

2

Stairway to
the Stars

[APRIL 1983]

I

Probably the most certain of all market warnings of the developing trouble was the fast-rising number of secondary stock offerings. This was a major technical warning because all such previous trends in this indicator leading to record levels had always, without exception, led to severe bear markets. It constituted another 1929 parallel. It was all part of the great distributive process then underway.

PARALLEL 14
Market
Secondary Stock Offerings

An insidious trend began in 1983, and I detected it as early as February. An increasing number of secondary stock distributions began to show up. A primary stock offering is new stock. A secondary offering occurs when an already existing block of stock is up for resale. In other words, *somebody wants out.* What made this trend all the more meaningful was that it was taking place at the same time all of the economists and Wall Street pundits were telling everybody how great everything was going to be. Obviously, something was very wrong. If things were so good, why the fast-rising number of secondary distributions? When comparing data which are not in step with what the economists say—*always trust the data.* Since economists follow economic data, and there are no economic data that precede a stock market series, then the market must be an *internal affair* and must always precede economic data.[1]

Once I was certain that this trend was going to prove to be the most reliable precursor of the stock market crash which was then only a little over a year away, I pounced on each issue of *Barron's Financial Weekly* and looked at the number of secondary distributions. I then checked the listing under "Coming Financing" and discovered serious discrepancies in the way *Barron's* was reporting the weekly number. The true number of secondary stock distributions was far higher than they reported.

In my April 9 market letter I revealed the results of my latest research: "The name of the game is PASS THE TRASH and that is the game currently being played on Wall Street with your money. *The smart money is passing the trash just as fast as the traffic will bear.* That is called *distribution.* The key factor preceding every bear market in history is distribution. The distribution indicators (and there are many) are principally in the areas of coming financing, new offerings filed, and secondary distributions. Every week in *Barron's,* all these offerings are reported in the back pages under the headings of 'Coming Financing,' 'New Offerings Filed,' and 'Distributions and Offerings.' *Right now, the number of secondary offerings is the highest since April 1973.* I have stated here many times that we are not going through a normal cycle. Already the current number of secondary offerings is well beyond bull market *third-phase* characteristics and thus one cannot equate the current market with the first phase of a normal bull market. It has already traversed *all three phases.* "

Not only was the number of secondary distributions by April 1983 increasing rapidly, but it was to grow to approximately 600 by the end of 1983, not only an all-time record but far exceeding the peaks of all previous records. *Barron's* reported only a little over half of them, the remainder having to be ferreted out by reading the small print.

The smart money was piggybacking in this insidious trend of dumping stock on the public. For instance, in the March 21, 1983, issue of *Barron's,* we see a typical listing: Browning Ferris—2,500,000 shares (1,000,000 shares by the company and 1,500,000 shares by *certain shareholders*). The sale by *certain shareholders* is a secondary distribution. In other words, they want out. That was a proposed offering, and by the time it was actually made, the stock was at the bull market peak. In other words, those certain stockholders dumped

---

[1]"Fundamentally the first postulate of the Dow theory appears to be sound, namely, that if the stock market can be forecasted, then the averages must forecast their own future. It would appear from the analysis of other parts of this volume, that no time series yet discovered precedes the stock market averages. Thus, while industrial production appears to depend upon the movement of the stock market behind which it lags about three months, the converse does not appear to be true. Hence, with present data, it would seem that any theory of forecasting market action would necessarily be an internal theory." Harold T. Davis, *The Analysis of Economic Time Series* (Bloomington, Ind.: Cowles Commission, Principia Press, 1941), p. 538.

it on the public at the very worst of times for the public and *the best of times for themselves.*

This went on week after week, most of the statistics buried under the heading "New Offerings Filed." Most of these offerings, with very few exceptions, included a large block of stock "by certain shareholders." In many instances the shareholders were selling more stock than the company. The definition is clear: *Any stock sold in a distribution that does not benefit the company constitutes a secondary offering.* Never in financial history had so many such shareholders sought to dump their paper on an unsuspecting public.

If I hadn't any additional information, what I then knew about the secondary distributions in the spring of 1983 was a sufficient warning of what was to come and approximately where the true stock market stood on the market clock.

I could not understand the bullish posture of *Market Logic,* a well-known advisory service in Fort Lauderdale, Florida. As early as February 1983 they were mildly disturbed by the number of secondary distributions. As the weekly number steadily grew to record proportions, they remained staunchly bullish on the primary trend of the market. Norman Fosback of *Market Logic* wrote the following in his outstanding book *Stock Market Logic:* "A large number of secondaries is bearish for the market because it signifies a lack of confidence in future economic prospects by large shareholders in many companies, and because it adversely alters the market supply-demand relationship."[2]

II

Price is a function of supply, and supply is a function of price. When an imbalance builds up on one side of the equation, the forces reverse and aim toward an equal and opposite imbalance. That explains why every parabolic price rise is followed by an eventual price smash. Applying those principles to several historical examples, we can better understand why gold smashed after a parabolic price rise to $875 an ounce. The rising prices encouraged a search for gold all over the world and eventually the market could find no "greater fools" above $875 an ounce, supply having caught up with price. The same thing happened in silver. Rising prices encouraged an intensive search for new supplies of silver, and the search was successful, supply catching up with price at $50 an ounce. Bunker Hunt had run out of "greater fools" and got caught in an avalanche of supply. The same thing happened in the price of oil. The geometric price rise by OPEC encouraged a tremendous concentrated search for oil all over the world, and the search was successful, the world swimming

[2]Norman G. Fosback, *Stock Market Logic* (Fort Lauderdale, Fla.: Institute for Econometric Research, 1976), p. 101.

in oil by April 1983. Supply caught up with price, and the OPEC price monopoly was weakened. Now we have the current bubble in the stock market to contend with, and the outcome is as mathematically certain as were the price bubbles in gold, silver, and oil. As the Dow average climbed over the past few months, additional supplies of common stock were created to meet the rising demand until, by April 1983, Wall Street was drowning the public in a sea of common stock shares.

III

While the public seemed to be grabbing everything in sight, an increasing number of stocks were starting to collapse. Not only was it Warner Communications, Mattel, Baldwin-United, Eastman Kodak, and Waste Management, but now the list was expanded to include Prime Computer, Paradyne, and NBI.

But the public, totally blind to the increasing number of market warnings, was *afraid of missing out* and Wall Street was quick to capitalize on that fear.

PARALLEL 15
Psychological
Fear of Missing Out

One of the most telling of the 1929 parallels took place on April 6, 1983, and again on June 16, 1983, when the Dow was building the massive top formation. I had just done appearances on ABC's *Nightline* with Ted Koppel and Cable News Network's *Crossfire* with Pat Buchanan and Tom Braden, and would do ABC's *Good Morning America* with David Hartman two months later. On all three of those shows I pleaded with the viewers to Flee for Their Lives! My words mostly fell on deaf ears, because it is human nature that most people become committed to an up trend and all the warnings in the world weren't going to make them let go of their stocks. The biggest fear most people had in April 1983 was *missing out on the bull market*. Merrill Lynch ran a full-page ad in *The Wall Street Journal* on April 6 titled "To Be or Not to Be: Bullish on America." Here is what they said in that ad:

"Have I missed the bull market?" That is the question of the day for many investors.

Is the economy really recovering? Should I be putting money into stocks, or taking profits out?

Merrill Lynch has some thoughts on the subject. We'd like to share them with you and suggest some ways in which we may be able to help you through what is expected to be a volatile but ultimately bullish year.

But don't expect too much too soon.

The economy has been through some pretty rough times, and it's not going to shift into high gear overnight.

Nevertheless, many economic indicators lead us to conclude that this is the right time to be bullish on America.

Lower oil prices should help reduce the inflation rate. Economic growth could actually be enhanced by greater efficiencies forced on business by the recent recession. Once business picks up, unemployment should gradually begin to decline.

Merrill Lynch's market analysts believe that the dramatic advance that took off last August *is only another step in a long-term bull market that could run for several more years.*

The outlook leads to several important investment strategies.

Even though we expect a correction in the market—in part because it has risen so far so fast—we generally recommend holding on to the stock of quality companies with good prospects of earnings growth, and in fact using periods of weakness to build additional long-term equity positions.

In the face of a slow-growth economy overall, the real opportunities may be in selecting *segments of the market* with the most potential.

Currently, the consumer sector looks promising. We believe that housing and autos have seen the worst and appear to be in the early stages of recovery.

Heavy industry and capital goods are now areas that are deeply depressed.

Looking ahead, investments in the recovering or still-growing sectors appear particularly attractive. The fact that so many companies have had to cut costs means that only a small upturn in volume could yield a sizable improvement in profits.

This is not, in our opinion, a get-rich-quick market, but one in which well-chosen equities offer substantial opportunities over the long term.

Four weeks later the bull market was to peak out, the maximum number of new individual stock price highs in 1983 occurring on May 6.

Drexel Burnham ran a full-page ad in *The Wall Street Journal* on June 16, 1983, the very day that the New York Stock Exchange advance/decline line recorded the 1982–83 bull market peak! Their headline was: "Are You Afraid You Missed the Bull Market?" The question was ironically asked on the day the bull market ended.

Now for the parallel: "What stirred Wall Street in the spring of 1929 was something very much like a panic—a panic buying of stocks, *for fear of missing out.* Once the stocks were bought, there was a panicky fear of selling out. It was the kind of emotional vice that keeps people glued to roulette tables or welded to a slot machine."[3]

[3]Geoffrey Perrett, *America in the Twenties* (New York: Simon & Schuster, 1982), p. 375.

IV

The greatest single phenomenon providing the timetable for trouble was culminating in the spring of 1983. I deem it the most troublesome of the 1929 parallels. It is the *new issue boom.* But it went far deeper than that. It encompassed the *entire overissuance of paper* stemming from new issues, debt-equity swaps, convertibles, debentures, preferreds, common stock, and stock splits. It was a virtual unsupportable mountain of paper.

PARALLEL 16

Market
Overissuance of Paper

There is nothing new under the sun. The market pendulum, always swinging from fear to greed on the upstroke and then from greed to fear on the downstroke, ran the full gamut after the August 1982 market bottom. Unlike previous cycles, however, *there was something very wrong about the entire upswing right from the start.* It was too explosive and too all-encompassing to last. More money poured back into the mutual funds than at the start of any previous market upswing, and the overall conversion to the bull side was so complete that the general public fell in love with the market as early as November 1982. Unknown to most, that was putting the cap on the bottle for the spring of 1983.[4] The public appetite for stocks became insatiable, and any and all stocks became fair game for the unwary. Lurking in the shadows, the corporations stood ready not only to satisfy that public appetite for stocks but to glut it with the greatest overissuance of new paper ever thrust into the hands of a greedy and gullible public. Compounding the problem, the debt-equity swap exacerbated the supply imbalance, corporations extinguishing their debt instruments by substituting new stock which the Wall Street investment bankers dumped into greedy public hands, thus swelling the supply of new stock to unprecedented levels. There wasn't enough new investment money to support adequately such a flood of new paper. But rather than turn the faucets off, corporate printing presses continued the endless stream of new stock until the market scales broke under the unbearable weight. Having brought down every bull market in history, the supply of new stock outstripped demand and broke the speculative bubble.

Wall Street, true to form, not only failed to warn the public of the conse-

[4]George Lindsay has demonstrated that when it can be shown that the general public is bullish on the market, 63 to 75 percent of the bull move is over. Thus the November 1982 evidence of such public participation indicated that the bull move off the August 1982 low had a limited life and would be a dying bull by the spring of 1983.

quences of the growing speculative bubble in the spring of 1983, but goaded the public into loading up its portfolios to the very brim at the worst of times. By that fateful time, most stocks had been driven up to their price ceilings. Since one would have had to be seventy-five years old to have been old enough to trade legally in stocks in 1929, the lesson for 1983 was lost on most people. The average investor, born in the 1940s and 1950s, had never seen a major stock market panic and crash and was totally ignorant of how rapidly the weight of the evidence was piling up, singling out 1983 and 1984 as the most critical years in stock market history since 1929.

First and foremost of all the parallels with 1929, the new-issue boom in the spring of 1983 was the major warning of trouble ahead. Every new-issue boom in history had been followed by a bear market in stocks, but Wall Street would not pass that message on to the public because that would have been bad for business. The underwriters were having a heyday, making money as fast as they could while the pickings were easy. As they passed their soon to be worthless merchandise on to an unsuspecting public, the job was made all the more easy by an equally gullible financial media which eagerly, day after day, proclaimed the new highs in the Dow Jones Industrial Average, totally unmindful of the fact that most stocks were topping out in the spring of 1983.

Market gullibility was not limited to the public. It stretched all the way to the President of the United States, who, using the political ammunition of a rising market for all it was worth, kept reminding the public of Wall Street's stamp of approval until a declining Dow made that argument run thin. For convenience, he then stressed the expanding economy as his most successful platform. Just as Treasury Secretary Andrew Mellon expanded upon Hoover's prosperity theme several months before the great crash, Reagan's Secretary of the Treasury, Donald Regan, predicted on June 16, 1983, that the stock market would remain on high ground for the next eighteen months. Unmindful of the fact that most stocks had peaked out at the time of his foolish forecast, Regan, the former head of Merrill Lynch, went on to compound the errors of his bad forecast by stating that stocks were a lot better buy than any we had had in two decades. It was a typical Wall Street con job done with professional flair.

V

Whenever I talk with people who claim to remember the 1929 crash, the first question I ask them is: "Who was E. H. H. Simmons?" If they say they don't know, then I know they don't know much about 1929. E. H. H. Simmons was the president of the New York Stock Exchange, and I have made a close study of all his speeches before, during, and after the great crash. Those speeches gave clues to many of the myths that sprang up after the crash and are still current today.

While most people hadn't the faintest inkling that the market was headed for a crash, certainly E. H. H. Simmons more than qualified to be their leader. Speaking before the New Hampshire Bankers' Association at Manchester, New Hampshire, on May 24, 1929, Simmons addressed the group on the subject of "Speculation in Securities." He praised the positive aspects of current speculation but condemned gambling in all forms: "I would like most emphatically to repeat that wagering or gambling is strictly forbidden on the New York Stock Exchange, and if this were not so, the law would some time in the last century have closed the Stock Exchange completely. In consequence, the phrase 'gambling on the Stock Exchange' is merely an abusive epithet which only displays ignorance, unfairness, and often ill-temper." That statement exposes the naïveté of the man and helps to explain some of his other statements and why he had developed a scenario that supported the permanent-plateau-of-prosperity thinking which was current at the time.

Simmons pointed out that for the first time in our history we had become a creditor nation. All during the nineteenth century, the United States, as a debtor nation, had been buffeted by recurring booms and busts, but now, as a creditor nation, we had an excess of credit and capital and a shortage of stocks; as a debtor nation, we had the opposite situation. In other words, he did not think that stock prices were too high because the excess capital was capable of pushing them still higher. His "bullishness" was well expressed in his May 1929 speech in the following quote: "In my own view of this matter, this vast amount of capital at present invested in stock market loans can only be induced to flow therefrom into security investment by easing credit and refraining from official threats and alarming statements concerning security price levels." He then defended the Exchange as its own most effective policeman when he stated: "Security speculation is not a moral but an economic phenomenon. In practice, its conduct on the New York Stock Exchange is already carefully supervised by the Exchange, and from economic reasons, such speculation is always capable of curing its own excesses. However much one may decry speculative enthusiasm, there is no doubt that it is intimately related to the steady and constructive building up of American business, and the maintenance of high American standards of living. There is no justification whatever for attempting to make security speculation or security speculators a scapegoat for peculiarities in our present situation with regard to credit and capital." Simmons was a bag holder, and it never occurred to him for a moment that the great bubble was soon to burst.

In his speech to the Virginia Bankers' Association on June 20, 1929, Simmons reiterated his bullish thesis of our being a creditor nation and embellished his remarks with his confidence in the Federal Reserve System as the key stabilizer of business.

Then, in a speech to the Indiana Bankers' Association on September 11, 1929, Simmons implied that we had permanently turned a corner and would not have to go through any more panics, such as those of 1907 and 1920. That speech was made eight days after the Dow had peaked on September 3, 1929, never to see that level again for twenty-four years.

The rest is history. The market embarked upon an orderly decline in September 1929 which speeded up into the rout of October and November. Simmons, a widower for nine years, remarried in early October 1929 and spent the next two months in Honolulu, returning to New York on December 2, 1929. In his absence, Richard Whitney presided over the Exchange; Whitney was later elected president of the Exchange in April 1930.

Now for the transformation. Following the greatest financial debacle in history (and Wall Street thought it was over), Simmons suddenly became an expert on the crash. His speech before the Transportation Club of the Pennsylvania Railroad on January 25, 1930, was titled "The Principal Causes of the Stock Market Crisis of 1929." The causes he cited were as follows: (1) The high level of prices which so many leading American share issues had attained. (2) The practice of gauging the value of securities by multiplying their most recently reported net earnings per share by some factor which was deemed to be applicable to the industry in which the company was engaged, such a method leading to price inflation in periods of great industrial activity. On this point, Simmons stated that it was obvious that the high level of share prices the previous August rendered the stock market vulnerable to a considerable price decline. Talk about hindsight vision. Simmons also said here that it seemed strange now that the public failed the previous spring and summer to be more skeptical about the ability of American industry to maintain its tremendous rate of production throughout the winter. (3) Overissuance of stock. Here Simmons makes an interesting point. It wasn't the volume of trading that precipitated the panic but actually the oversupply of new stock:

"Every serious break in the stock market is always attributed to overspeculation, but if we are to ascertain the exact responsibility for the 1929 stock panic, we must consider the actual facts. Many people seem to have the notion that the volume of trading on the Exchange is in itself a sign of unsound and harmful speculative conditions and a necessary precursor to stock panics. This view is, however, not at all supported by the facts. When one studies the volume of share trading on the Stock Exchange during recent years, it becomes at once apparent that the peak of activity occurred not before the crisis of October 1929, but in November 1928. This is all the more striking because of the fact that during 1929, there were added to the list over 350 million additional shares of stock. Naturally, the only accurate way to measure Stock Exchange activity is to consider the proportion of listed shares turned over. Figures in this regard show that through the first half of 1929 share dealings on the New York Stock Exchange were declining both actually and in proportion to share listings. If mere volume of dealings or proportionate velocity of dealings on the Exchange were a cause of the panic, we should have had a panic not last fall, but a year ago."

The next paragraph underscores the basic psychology of all market tops: "For various reasons, some of which I will mention later, *we have had in the stock market an extraordinary willingness to buy and an equally extraordinary unwillingness to sell. It was this lack of equilibrium which really made trouble."*

People today will tell you that we can never have a 1929 again because back then the little guy was trading on 10 percent margins. We have a 50 percent margin requirement today and that is a floor of safety. But here is Simmons again: "Statistics taken off by the Stock Exchange from its members' questionnaires over the first six months of 1929 showed that the margins in customers' accounts averaged 40 percent of the market value of long stocks which they were carrying, and 65 percent on their debit balances with their brokers. I need scarcely point out how enormous these margins were. Never had margins in the New York brokerage business averaged anything like such high figures." He then added to this: "Nevertheless, under conditions of panic and public hysteria, even very large margins may not prove adequate to protect the holders of securities on credit, however much it may assure the safety of financial institutions. This fact has, I think, surprised us all and must be remembered in the future."

Simmons then continues his list of causes with such known events as the Hatry scandal in England, foreign stock liquidation, the income tax on capital gains, the trouble on the Berlin Stock Exchange, the collapse of a large bank in Vienna, and a cabinet crisis in France—all conspiring to put additional pressure on the New York market and, in the view of Simmons, all unpredictable.

He then comes to the fact which, in his judgment, converted an inevitable but orderly declining securities market during September into the panic which was witnessed in October. Here are his words: *"I refer to the colossal output of new stock issues thrust on the market during September and October.* The year 1929 had already proved to be a very active year in the production of new securities. In addition to a record amount of new stock issues publicly offered, the market was called upon to absorb an enormous amount of new stock issued by our leading companies through rights to subscribe."

In 1983 the media were so mesmerized by the new issue market that they went all out to lure the public in at the worst of times. In the April 30, 1983, issue of *Financial World,* the cover was devoted to a herd of bulls and the lead article in the magazine was "New Issues Stampede." The subheadline was: "The herd is off and running toward a new issues record—if all these baby bulls don't trample one another in the rush." But trample each other they did. Quoting *Financial World:* "In retrospect, seasoned observers say that March 4 will be clearly seen as a red-letter day: the day that the first—but by no means the last—crack appeared in the 1983 booming new issues market." But the stream of seduction widened to include over 600 companies raising over $5 billion for an all-time record new issue bubble. And, like all bubbles, it predictably burst. Before it did, it ensnared in its net one of the greatest multitudes of speculator suckers in financial history.

But although the cancer was detected in the early spring of 1983, the patient did not immediately succumb. Continuing to beat the drums, *Fortune* magazine, in its May 30, 1983, issue, ran the new issues market on its cover with an enticing headline: "The New New Issues Market." The author tried to stress a new theme: *This time it is different.* The new issues coming to market have a higher quality, involving bigger and more important companies. Famous last words. When the bubble burst it took down the good, bad, and indifferent. This was but another 1929 parallel. When attempting to keep a bull market going, the cry is always: *This time it is different.* But it was the same formula and it got the same treatment because human nature never changes.

Many people would refuse to gamble at Las Vegas or Atlantic City, and yet they would buy a new issue of stock, not realizing that the odds against investment success are so great that statistically one would have to conclude that all buyers of new issues are out-and-out suckers. Dun & Bradstreet conducted intensive research into what happens to new issues, and their figures should startle all market neophytes. These figures apply to all new issue booms. They discovered that of all new issues floated, 11 percent of them literally disappear, 41 percent go bankrupt, 25 percent today are selling under their initial offering price, 20 percent are barely profitable, and only less than 3 percent prove to be worthwhile holdings. Now, those percentages have held for many, many years, and yet every time there is a new issue boom, the suckers come streaming in with absolutely no idea as to the terrible odds against success. Wall Street isn't going to warn them. The underwriters, of course, are not going to warn them. Only history can warn them, but most people are not going to read history. Remember the English panics of the nineteenth century? Most of them occurred almost ten years apart like clockwork. Yet every ten years the people made the identical mistakes they had made ten years before. Winners have long memories. Losers have no memory at all. When people want something for virtually nothing, they will get virtually nothing. With about three winners out of every hundred issues, the overall returns in the new issue market are close to virtually nothing.

By early 1984, holders of new issues were suffering mammoth declines of from 50 to over 90 percent, but the bulls were still crying that this was merely a correction in an ongoing bull market. One wag remarked that if that was a correction, then somebody must have made one hell of a mistake.

But the key lesson derived from all new issue booms is that *a bear market in stocks has followed every single one of them.* If we didn't know another thing, that fact alone would have enabled us to see the bear market of 1983–84 dead ahead.

V I

I don't think that people ask themselves what happens to all this stock being constantly issued. They don't appreciate the power that corporations have. Corporations can't print money but they can legally print stock certificates. In this case, demand creates supply. When the public has a big appetite for common stocks, the corporations not only satisfy that appetite but glut it. There just wasn't enough money to support adequately the mountain of paper produced in 1983.

By mid-April 1983, *The New York Times* announced that initial stock offerings had set an all-time record in the first quarter. That meant that it exceeded all previous quarters in the issuance of new stock, beating out the hot new issue years of 1960–61 and 1972. To get a still clearer picture of the gigantic mountain of paper being churned out and thrust into the hands of the public who would have to hold it, one also had to look at the record issuance of convertibles, debentures, and preferreds, as well as the torrential stream of common stock. Obviously, all that stock could not maintain a value at the rate it has been created over the years. Cold statistics prove that it all has a limited life and very few stocks get through the filter that separates failure from success.

The important message of a new issue boom is *when* it occurs. The new issue boom of 1960–61 was followed by the crash of 1962. The new issue boom of 1972 was followed by the severe bear market of 1973–74. Millions of people hold worthless stock from years past. Just as the human population is checked by age, disease, starvation, acts of God, and war, the strangulating size of common stock holdings is reduced by disappearance, bankruptcy, and loss.

The new issue boom of the spring of 1983 proved once again that supply always rises to meet price, just as it previously did for gold, silver, and oil.

The most effective method of gauging the approaching market peak was simply to take an ordinary ruler and measure the space allotted to new offerings each day in *The Wall Street Journal.* By April 1983, the length of the listings was exceedingly long, and that only occurs at important market tops.

At this time I called attention to what was happening to convertibles, one of the other sources of adding to the supply of common stocks. One should have been very disturbed by the amount of convertibles offered in the spring of 1983. "When stock prices are high, new issues of convertible stocks are floated to take advantage of investor optimism. If you buy new convertibles, you may pick up a few points quickly, but the long-term prospects are likely to be based on rather enthusiastic projections. Be sure the related stock is not

selling at or near its all-time high."[5] In April 1983, the facts showed that most
of the convertibles being issued revealed that the related common stocks had
had large price run-ups or were close to their highs. "Of 141 New York Stock
Exchange companies which issued convertible stock in the buoyant market of
the late 1960s, the common stock of 70% of these companies fell 25% or
more within the next nine months."[6]

As the supply of stock positioned for a stranglehold, the market was no
longer able to accommodate such a vast amount, and long before sellers could
appear in droves, there first had to be an attrition in the amount of buying.
This was in line with my previous analysis that one does not go from buying
to selling, but from buying to holding to selling. When one becomes 100
percent fully invested, one can no longer add to the volume of trading on the
buying side. That explains why volume has to peak out before the end of a
market rise. It was in the spring of 1983 that we saw a 15-million-share day
in the American Stock Exchange, the very peak of speculative activity. In the
spring of 1983, a riffle through any chart book would have shown that in 95
percent of the cases volume had already peaked out. It was important to keep
in mind that all those who were 100 percent fully invested were stock *holders*,
not stock buyers. The laws of supply and demand dictated that before those
holders could again become stock buyers, they first had to become stock sellers.

I think the biggest problem most people had with the market in the spring
of 1983 was differentiating between a normal bull market and an abnormal
bull market. At this juncture, most market followers thought that between
August 1982 and the spring of 1983 the market was traversing the first phase
in a normal bull market. It produced a raging controversy among technicians.
If one had paid attention to the history of the market, one would have
discovered that no first phase in any bull market had seen that much paper
dumped into the hands of the investing and speculating public. After all, there
are only two things that can change the price of a stock: supply and demand.
If the demand side becomes fully invested, then it has increasingly lost its
influence in raising stock prices still higher. On the other hand, supply was
expanding at an exponential rate. Only one outcome was possible. Forgetting
the blue chip stocks momentarily, the handwriting was clearly on the wall for
the secondary stocks. The market was blowing taps.

Wall Street, of course, was sending out no warnings against the rampant
speculation. Underwriters continued to bring the new issues to market just as
fast as they could while the public's appetite remained unsatisfied.

Why should Wall Street send out warnings and upset the pattern of easy
commissions? I was incensed by the Street's great show of immorality, as well

[5]C. Colburn Hardy, *Dun & Bradstreet's Guide to Your Investments* (New York: Harper & Row,
1983 ed.), p. 44.
[6]Ibid.

as the way the media fanned the flames of the great speculative fever. The word "buy" was universal. It was Wall Street's favorite word, as it always is. Brokers love to tell you to buy, but where was the selling advice when it was most needed? Those runaway markets in April 1983 should have produced at least a modicum of caution.

Receiving little publicity at the time, the Federal Reserve issued a warning against speculation, thus clicking off still another 1929 parallel:

PARALLEL 17

Historic
Federal Reserve Warning Against Speculation

On April 24, 1983, *The New York Times* reported a Federal Reserve warning against speculation. That warning occurred *seven months* before the November peak in the Dow.

On February 7, 1929, the Federal Reserve board issued a statement to the press in which it warned of "the excessive amount of the country's credit absorbed in speculative loans." That warning occurred *seven months* before the September peak in the Dow.

The warning was not picked up and broadcast by the media. The media were too fascinated with reporting the new highs in the Dow Jones, which were setting record levels daily. The typical TV commentator would grab a piece of paper and simply read off what was on it, there being nary a comment about the risks in the market. They were caught up in the daily game, and it was too much fun reporting new highs every day to give a thought about the increasing risks. Those comments were left to Wall Street analysts who were also blinded by the euphoria of the daily new highs.

A veritable sermon had been preached daily to the American people that, because inflation was dead, their money had to go into the stock market. The great mountain of paper had been produced for them to buy and, of course, hold. Then a dangerous thing happened. Wall Street gave up on looking for a 10 percent correction as the Dow, on April 13, broke out to a new high at 1,156.64 and extended its vertical climb. The financial press reported only two market arguments. The first was that there would be no correction, and the second was that there would be a correction of 10 to 15 percent. Nobody breathed a word about a third argument—that the market was headed for a severe bear market, panic, and crash. The discarding of the near-term 10 percent correction argument coincided with the stairway to the stars, an apt description of the very sharp runaway advance in the Dow in that month of April 1983. By the last trading day of April the Dow had soared to 1,226.20.

Cast into the wild blue yonder of uncharted skies, the April 1983 rise in the Dow was a vertical climb of almost 100 points. Thus, unknown to most, that rise produced another 1929 parallel.

Technical
Angle of Rise

Vern Myers, publisher of *Myers Finance & Energy Newsletter,* documented a very important parallel to the 1929 stock market, one which will interest mathematicians. In the spring of 1983 he presented a study comparing the final eleven months of rise in the 1928–29 stock market with the first nine months of the 1982–83 upswing. The two most striking parallels were seen in the *angles of ascent.* The 1928–29 move saw an angle of ascent of 33 degrees. The 1982–83 move saw an angle of ascent of 36.5 degrees. Each of the comparable periods was terminated with one final blowoff month leading to the peak. The blowoff month in 1929 was August and the angle of ascent that month was 58 degrees. A few days later the real bull market ended, as measured by the maximum number of new stock price highs being recorded.

In the spring of 1983 the growing budgetary deficit problem was generally being swept under the rug. In countless interviews I stated that when future historians chronicled the events leading up to the great crash they would look back and recognize that our budgetary deficits were out of control. In the April 16, 1983, market letter I said: "These are not normal times. It is traditional to expect that budget deficits will be by design in a recession but not in a recovery. The very fact that the deficit will total about $400 billion in the 1983–84 period during what the economists project as recovery years is the best evidence you can have that we have totally lost control of the budget. Estimates of future budget deficits are rising, not falling. Now, if we can't reduce the deficits during economic recovery, what then happens if economic recovery falters? This is what the market has not discounted yet, but will start to do shortly when it becomes increasingly apparent that the Administration and the Congress, regardless of all the rhetoric, are simply finding it almost impossible to bring the deficits down."

A little more than a year later, the Grace Commission, under the leadership of J. Peter Grace, reported that the true deficit was closer to $400 billion than the $195 billion the administration claimed. So while Wall Street brokers and the public were caught up in the frenzy of speculative delights, totally oblivious that these were the closing weeks of one of the shortest bull markets in history, the forces were already in motion on a collision course which would impact in 1984–85 and bring down the Reagan administration and produce the worst stock market crash since 1929.

VII

Eight months had gone by since the August 1982 bottom, and I saw the market going through massive distribution. It was very late on the stock market clock. A vast change of ownership had occurred since the volume peaks of the previous fall and stocks were being passed from strong hands to very weak hands, the new buyers being those who would largely be holding their stocks on the next decline, all the way down. I stated at this time that what I saw ahead for the market would prove my contention that the market, on a long-term basis, was for suckers. When the market says get out, simply get out and forget the long term. But Wall Street, not wanting to lose a customer, will always recommend holding on to the stock of quality companies with good prospects of earnings growth and using periods of weakness to build additional long-term equity positions.

In April 1983, the stock market had reached a point where the enormous majority fully expected the big bull market to go on and on. Not a day went by without some analyst or commentator stating that the Dow would go to 1,300 that year and 1,500 the next. The terminal characteristics of all bull markets are the unanimous expectation of higher prices and the belief that all declines are buying opportunities and that the market rise is a certain two steps up, one step down, two steps up, one step down, etc. When caught up in the heat of speculative passion, memories quickly fade. Nobody seemed to suspect that the brief 1982–83 rise was simply the brilliant finis of the nine-year Juglar cycle which had begun in the depths of despair back in 1974 when the Dow Jones Industrial Average had started the cycle at 577. Current thought, without the benefit of the memory of the grander cycle, viewed the compressed 1982–83 speculative explosion as heralding the sunrise of a new and extended cycle rather than the sunset of a super bull market then in its ninth and final year.

PARALLEL 19
Historical
The Nine-Year Cycle

The years preceding the 1929 stock market crash were strangely similar to the years leading up to the great stock market peak of 1983. The table below shows the parallels, and one would have to conclude that that much similarity is beyond luck or coincidence. The unmistakable pattern best explained why the 1982–83 market rise, while violent, had to be brief. It was an ending to a longer cycle rather than the beginning of a new long-term up cycle.

1918	War ends	1972	War ends
1919	Market peaks out	1973	Market peaks out
1920	Teapot Dome scandal	1974	Watergate
1921	Market bottoms	1975	Market bottoms (Dec. 1974)
1922	Market tops (1)	1976	Market tops (1)
1923	Recession	1977	Recession
1924	Market turns up	1978	Market turns up
1925	Up market	1979	Up market
1926	Up market, real estate peaks	1980	Up market, real estate peaks
1927	Recession (2)	1981	Recession (2)
1928	Higher bottom and big rise	1982	Higher bottom and big rise
1929	Market peak (3)	1983	Market peak (3)

Each market bottom was higher and each market top was higher, thus validating the nine-year cycle. But the comparison also points up the Kondratieff Wave, which averages 54 years. In the above comparison I have marked the three phases of the nine-year cycle. In 1983 we were seeing the combined force of the Kondratieff Wave (1929–83) and the Juglar cycle (1974–83) coinciding—1983 had to be *the* critical year.

As in all cycles, we have the laws of triplicity. We divide up the bull market of 1974–76 into three market phases, but it is also seen as the *first phase* of the grander nine-year cycle. We divide up the bull market of 1978–81 into three market phases, but it is also seen as the *second phase* of the grander nine-year cycle. We divide up the bull market of 1982–83 into three market phases, but it is also seen as the *third phase* of the grander nine-year cycle. Particularly revealing was the very fact that the rise of better than 400 points by April 1983 matched third-phase characteristics terminating the grand cycle rather than the start of an orthodox bull market which the majority didn't expect to end until late 1984 or early 1985.

But the warnings seen in the spring of 1983 were then more than sufficient to warrant steps to put one's house in order. A great storm was coming. Jacob Bernstein's key warnings of a major top were reached by April of that critical year:

As prices continue their trend in a given direction they tend to pick up momentum. As more and more news stimulates the price move, there is a concomitant acceleration in price. . . . It is generally believed that the first portion of any price move, called accumulation, occurs as a result of professional buying.

The public begins buying next, and as prices begin their greatest acceleration up
... the public is making its greatest play. . . . Finally, at the top . . . the professional
community is, for the most part, out of its positions since it has slowly but surely
distributed them to the public.

The public perceives nothing but confirmation from the news, no matter what
its actual import may be. Prices shoot up . . . dramatically . . . and there is no
end in sight. In a bullish market climate most news is interpreted as bullish.
When bearish news comes, it is seen as an opportunity to buy on the decline.
. . . And on the day of reckoning, in a bull market, for example, the typical
"buying climax" will come after the following scenario:

1. Very bullish news—possibly the most bullish in months.
2. Record high trading volume for the past few months or years.
3. Record high prices for the past few months or years.
4. Highly bullish public opinion.[7]

All four of those descriptions fit the blowoff April 1983 stock market. In
the heat of the speculative mania then raging and with the Dow making a
vertical climb on a stairway to the stars, those clear warnings were all being
dangerously ignored.

VIII

It had escaped the attention of most that by April 1983 conditions had
reached a point where they were virtually the opposite of 1974. Back in 1974,
when the Dow stood at 577, (1) oil prices were headed higher, (2) inflation
was rearing its ugly head, (3) the United States was going into a recession, and
(4) interest rates were headed higher. In the spring of 1983, 600 points and
nine years later, (1) oil prices were headed lower, (2) the economy was in a
deflationary phase, inflation having cooled off, (3) the economy was in a
recovery phase, and (4) interest rates were headed lower. It became dangerously clear to this writer that if by the spring of 1983 conditions had reached
a point opposite to what they were just prior to a 600-point upswing, how far
could the Dow drop following the proven terminal characteristics of this
nine-year wave? Going into the deflationary Kondratieff cycle, history teaches
us that all the inflationary dollars have to be destroyed, and those dollars were
being rapidly fed into the giant meat grinder called the stock market. It was
all totally exciting but deadly in its implications for the future.

[7]Jacob Bernstein, *The Investor's Quotient* (New York: John Wiley & Sons, 1980), p. 196.

PARALLEL 20
Historical
Immorality

The shortest bull market in history was ending. The degree of immorality on the Street was not as open as it was in the boiler-shop days of the twenties, but it was, nevertheless, there. The very fact that Wall Street would roll out the red carpet for stock buyers but treat sellers as second-class citizens had not changed a bit. Wall Street has no peer when it comes to its expertise in baiting hooks to catch fish. It was immoral to push the low-priced stocks to the limit, knowing that all such moves are followed by bear markets. It was immoral to champion stocks that were splitting, knowing that a record number of splits had to be followed by a bear market. It was immoral not to warn the public about the implications of too much money flowing into the mutual funds and pension funds at the worst of times. It was immoral to allow insiders to piggyback corporate stock offerings, a form of fleecing the public. It was immoral not to blow the whistle on the largest number of secondary stock offerings in history. It was immoral to accept long-term investment money openly when there were no long-term investment opportunities. It was immoral to print and market more stock than the public could healthfully absorb.

If the market was as good as Wall Street was saying it was, why then was big money running for the hills? Along with the number of stock splits, stock distribution was absolutely rampant and Wall Street never breathed a word about it. In his fine book, P. J. Kaufman said, "Accumulation and distribution are the *beginning* phases of a bull or bear market."[8] I underscored the key word *beginning*. Since all the evidence in the spring of 1983 was on the side of stock *distribution*, the conclusion was that the brief bull market stretching back to August 1982 was *ending*. My conclusion that we were seeing third-phase bull characteristics underscored not only the end of the brief eight-month rise in the market but the end of the Juglar nine-year cycle which had started at the 1974 bottom at Dow 577.

The ways to play the market were proliferating rapidly. Here is what *The Wall Street Journal* said in October 1929, while recording that 800 investment trusts had arisen with 751 of them destined to go down the tubes in the market crash and depression that followed: "There have been a bewildering variety of securities, of investment trusts, trading corporations and holding companies which have been issued to investors of late." And then it cautiously proposed: "It may be doubted whether purchasers of these wares have always examined them as carefully as they should. It is a little more than ordinarily important

[8]P. J. Kaufman, *Commodity Trading Systems and Methods* (New York: John Wiley & Sons, 1978), p. 138.

that the principle of *caveat emptor* be borne in mind when considering for investment the stocks of corporations, differing as widely in purpose and structure as these do, from similar investments in the past as well as from one another."

The situation by April 1983 was dangerously similar in that respect. Not only was the flow of money to Wall Street enhanced by pension funds, mutual funds, the Keogh plan, Individual Retirement Accounts, heavy foreign buying, but the whole piece of cake was decorated with the Las Vegas overtones of options, index futures, and index options, and businesses had become so complexly merged that one was not sure whether an insurance company was a bank, a bank a brokerage house, or a brokerage house an insurance company. Takeover mania had so proliferated that it underscored that dangerous symptom of all long-range market peaks—everybody getting into everybody else's business, the important Parallel 7 with 1929. Such complicity and the struggle to attract the investor's dollar were signs of the end of the cycle, not the start of a new one. The market was ripe for the blowoff move.

IX

One of the most interesting of the 1929 parallels began to come into prominence at this time. On the heels of the almost 100-point April run-up, a proliferation of magazine and newspaper articles appeared attesting to the extremity of the speculation and the overpopularity of the stock market.

PARALLEL 21
Historic
Stock Market Boom Articles

Right at the point when historians would see the market in retrospect as in a highly dangerous posture, the most dangerous since the summer of 1929, out came a stream of magazine and newspaper articles strangely reminiscent of those that appeared just before the great crash of 1929. In the spring of 1983 the following appeared:

"Financial Futures: A Hot New Act" (Yla Eason, *The New York Times*, April 24)
"The Stampede to Equity Mutual Funds" (Kenneth N. Gilpin, *The New York Times*, April 24)
"New Issues Stampede" (Diane Harris, *Financial World*, April 30)
"The Rebirth of Equities" (cover story, *Business Week*, May 9)
"What's New about This Boom" (Irwin Ross, *Fortune*, May 30)

In the 1928–29 period, not only were the articles similar but their subject matter and their timing set up still further 1929 parallels:

"The New Era in Wall Street" (John Moddy, *The Atlantic Monthly*, August 1928)

"The World-wide Fever of Speculation" (*The Literary Digest*, June 9, 1928)

"Brokers and Suckers" (Robert Ryan, *The Nation*, August 15, 1928)

"Speculation and the Stock Exchange" (Elizabeth Frazer, *Forum*, September 1928)

"Eyes on the Stock Market" (Merryle Stanley Rukeyser, *The Review of Reviews*, October 1928)

"Wall Street Bids for the Woman Speculator" (*The Literary Digest*, November 17, 1928)

"Have Stocks Struck a Holding Zone?" (Charles A. Dice, *The Magazine of Business*, November 1928)

"The Stock Speculating Mania" (*The Literary Digest*, December 8, 1928)

"The Dance of the Billions" (*The Saturday Evening Post*, December 22, 1928)

"Causes of the Stock Market Boom" (D. W. Ellsworth, *Current History*, December 1928)

"There Is a Tide—The Story of the San Francisco Stock Exchange" (Lucrezia Kemper, *Sunset*, December 1928)

"How to Get Out of the Stock Market" (*The New Republic*, January 2, 1929)

"The Great Bull Market" (*The Saturday Evening Post*, January 12, 1929)

"Riders of the Whirlwind" (John T. Flynn, *Collier's*, January 19, 1929)

"Greatest of Bull Markets" (Will Payne, *World's Work*, January 1929)

"Our Second Largest Stock Market" (Sydney L. Schwartz, *The Review of Reviews*, January 1929)

"With Blue Chips This Time" (Edwin Lefevre, *The Saturday Evening Post*, February 2, 1929)

"Running Past the Signal" (Edwin Lefevre, *The Saturday Evening Post*, February 2, 1929)

"Two and Two Still Make Four" (editorial, *Collier's*, February 9, 1929)

"Bulls on America" (Edwin Lefevre, *The Saturday Evening Post*, February 16, 1929)

"Taming the Great Bull Market" (John T. Flynn, *Forum*, February 1929)

"Is It Safe to Buy on Margin?" (*The Woman's Journal*, February 1929)

"More and Bigger Stock Markets" (*The Literary Digest*, March 2, 1929)

"Stock Market Aristocrats" (*The Literary Digest*, March 2, 1929)

"This Little Pig Went to Market" (Katherine Dayton, *The Saturday Evening Post*, March 23, 1929)

"Behind the Credit Battle" (*The New Republic*, April 10, 1929)

"Who Gains by Speculation?" (Lewis Gorey, *The New Republic*, April 17, 1929)

"The War Against Wall Street Speculation" (*The Literary Digest*, April 13, 1929)

"Men and Markets" (Albert W. Atwood, *The Saturday Evening Post*, April 27, 1929)   .

"The Common Stock Racket" (Frederic Drew Bond, *North American Review*, April 1929)

"Bull Market" (Charles Merz, *Harper's Magazine*, April 1929)

"Ladies of the Ticker" (Eunice Fuller Barnard, *North American Review,* April 1929)

"Speculation" (Garet Garrett, *The Saturday Evening Post,* May 4, 1929)

"The Stock Market" (Uncle Henry, *Collier's,* May 4, 1929)

"By-products of the Bull Market" (William O. Scroggs, *Outlook,* May 8, 1929)

"Another New High" (*World's Work,* May 1929)

"The Conflict over Credit Reaches a Climax" (Alexander Dana Noyes, *Scribner's Magazine,* May 1929)

"The Story of Wall Street" (Mrs. William Laimbeer, *Delineator,* May 1929)

"Mr. Raskob's Poor Man's Investment Trust" (*The Literary Digest,* June 1, 1929)

"A Reformed Speculator" (Will Payne, *The Saturday Evening Post,* August 10, 1929)

"The Brokers Take to the Sea" (*The Literary Digest,* August 31, 1929)

"Everybody Ought to Be Rich" (Samuel Crowther, *Journal of Political Economy,* August 1929)

"What Bull Market?" (*Business Week,* September 7, 1929)

"Wall Street Branches Out" (Charles J. V. Murphy, *Outlook,* September 18, 1929)

X

Overall trading volume continued to rise. The parabolic rise in the trading volume of financial futures soared from 3.9 million contracts in 1978 to 29 million contracts in 1982, and by the spring of 1983 had reached 42 million contracts. That enormous trading in such paper matched the stupendous supply of paper being pumped out in the early months of 1983 and being snatched up by a gullible public. As supplies rose to meet the soaring prices, a stranglehold was developing on the price structure. Trading in all vehicles of investment and speculation had risen to white-hot levels. Warnings against speculation by the Federal Reserve Board were flagrantly disregarded by Wall Street and the banks. While the protagonists of the financial futures game stressed the positive aspects of a method of hedging large stock positions, *The New York Times* referred to the Federal Reserve Board's sternly worded report to bank trust departments stating: "It is difficult to envision a prudent strategy that would involve purchasing stock index futures." The Board had hard evidence that hedging is only a very limited application of the futures and that most of the sharp rise in current activity is due to out-and-out gambling, as was similar speculation on Wall Street just prior to the crash of 1929. The *Times* summed it all up with the question: "Is it Monte Carlo without the music or Las Vegas without the floor show?"

They wouldn't call it gambling at the time, but the size of the bet would have made any high roller pop his eyes. The *tour de force* public entry into the mutual funds after the August 1982 market bottom certainly attested to the all-time record number of 42 million shareholders. It was such a block-buster move that it brought the greatest flood of new money into the mutual funds on record. The stock market charts at the time proved, beyond the shadow of a doubt, that such record influxes of public cash into the mutual funds *occur at or near the end of the line for the bull move*. This constituted another compelling 1929 parallel:

PARALLEL 22

Market
Resurgence of Mutual Funds

Here was the hard evidence that greatly added authority to my predictions that the bull market in 1983 was ending and that the great bear market was about to take over.

The stampede into equity mutual funds was no different from the locust-like multiplication of investment trusts in the 1929 era, and out of the 500 investment trusts then existing, the market crash and depression that followed saw 471 of them completely bite the dust.

As the Dow soared 100 points on the blowoff April 1983 rise, *the market was not responding to valid sell signals*. Here was still another of the 1929 parallels:

PARALLEL 23

Historical
Premature Sell Signals

Ironically, there was no way any technician could avoid seeing many valid market sell signals in 1983 which would have gotten him out of the market long before the Dow peaked on November 29, 1983. Yet the Dow just cut through those signals as if it didn't know they were there. *The disregarding of valid sell signals is a key characteristic of a market upswing preceding a crash.* It was exactly the same back in 1929. There were many technically valid sell signals in 1928 and 1929 that the market seemed to turn a deaf ear to as the Dow rocketed all the way to the September 3 top long after the general market had peaked. William Peter Hamilton, the editor of *The Wall Street Journal*, had published four major market warnings starting as early as 1927. Such earlier warnings were given on January 7, 1927, June 25, 1928, and July 30, 1928. His final warning was given on October 21, 1929. The last warning is well known, but very few are aware of his earlier warnings, which the bull market back then had ignored. A market that seemingly ignores valid sell signals is a dangerous market, and the April 1983 market fit that description very well.

A frequent observation at this time by Wall Street analysts was that there was plenty of money on the sidelines awaiting investment. This was another 1929 parallel:

PARALLEL 24

Historical
Still a Lot of Money on the Sidelines

On April 21, 1983, Newton Zinder was quoted in *The Wall Street Journal* as saying, "There's still a lot of money on the sidelines waiting for a chance to get into the market."

On October 21, 1929, *The Wall Street Journal* carried the following statement: "There is a vast amount of money awaiting investment." Eight days after that statement was made, the market crashed.

The abnormal characteristics of the brief bull market rise since the August 1982 bottom covered several key points: (1) no normal retracements, (2) defiance of the law of gravity, (3) tremendous stock distribution by professionals, (4) super parabolic curve, and (5) an angle of rise duplicating that of 1928–29. Coming at the end of the Juglar nine-year cycle, those abnormal characteristics became normal characteristics for the explosive end of such a cycle. To fit the nine-year cycle, the move had to be a *whirlwind affair.* It also implied that the economic recovery ran a risk of aborting in 1984 and that the key upsetting agent would probably be the rapidly escalating budgetary deficits. Orthodox fiscal policy would allow such deficits to expand during periods of recession and contract during periods of economic expansion. At this time the projection of the deficits stretched all the way to 1989 and beyond and presented overwhelming proof that the whole process was out of control. Already the deficit for 1983 was well above earlier administration estimates, and while the stock market chose to ignore the warnings of that development, it was no different than the warnings back in 1929 that the market also chose to ignore until it was too late.

3

Turbulence

[MAY 1983]

I

The market scored a high in the Dow at 1,226 on the last trading day of April and broke sharply the next trading day on May 2, hitting 1,184 on May 3, attesting to the high volatility of the market as a whole. The drop was pounced upon by the public as a signal to buy, a Pavlovian reflex instigated by the Wall Street distribution machine. Erratic stock action underscored the toppiness of the market. Eastman Kodak on May 4 recorded a morning low at 81¾, only to be gunned all the way up to 87 on very heavy volume. That move was immediately followed by a tidal wave of selling which carried the stock all the way down to 79⅝ at the close on a high volume of 2,599,200 shares. That simply meant that everybody who bought the stock on May 4 took a licking that day, holding the stock at a loss varying from two to eight points. I reported that action as not only a change of pattern for Kodak *but a changing pattern for the entire stock market.*

This was but one more of the terminal characteristics of the eight-month upswing. It was at this time that I applied "Jiler's measured-move technique" in order to determine the fullest probable extent of the Dow's bull market move.[1] The move is in *two* legs, not the traditional three. Applying the Jiler measurements to the August 1982–April 1983 eight-month rise, one would look for one large leg, a consolidation, and then the second and final leg. Taking the initial upside leg as that of August 12, 1982, to November 3 of that year, that would be marked as going from A to B, a distance of 288.57

[1]William L. Jiler, *How Charts Can Help You in the Stock Market* (New York: Commodity Research Publications, 1962), p. 109.

points, the Dow advancing from 776.92 to 1,065.49. The consolidation period, which is B to C, measured from the November 3 peak at Dow 1,065.49 down to the December 16 low of 990.25, a drop of 75.24 points. The C to D leg measured from the December 16, 1982, low of 990.25 and would be expected to rise the equivalent of the first leg of 288.57 points. Adding those 288.57 points to the December 16 level of 990.25, I determined an upside Dow objective of 1,278.82 and published that expectation in my May 7 market letter.

The public was now determined to remain optimistic no matter what happened. The morning after the sharp May 2 break, *USA Today* headlined its market coverage: "Experts Not Worried about Drop." Any historian would have had to be worried after seeing that headline. On October 4, 1929, the day after the worst break of the year up to that time, *The New York Times* headlined it as the worst break of the year and the subheadline was: "Wall Street Remains Optimistic."

It was at this time that a technical landmark was recorded, one that would enable me to home in on one of the most important of all the technical 1929 parallels:

PARALLEL 25

Technical
Market Rise No Longer Genuine

On May 6, 1983, the stock market recorded a peaking in the number of new individual stock price highs. On that day there were 388 new twelve-month highs. Even a schoolboy can figure out that if a bull market is genuine then *there must be a constant expansion in the number of stocks making new highs.* That expansion ended on May 6. From that date forward, the bull market was no longer genuine in terms of the general market.

Most people have a very incomplete knowledge about the 1929 stock market. They look at a chart of the Dow Jones Industrial Average for that fateful year and they see the great peak on September 3. Therefore, they *assume* that was the end of the great bull market, falling into the trap of thinking that the Dow Jones Industrial Average and the market are interchangeable. The truth is that the great bull market of the 1920s ended in December 1928, the month when the maximum number of new stock price highs was achieved. So the advance in the Dow Jones Industrial Average after December 1929 was no longer genuine. The remaining strength in that bull market was confined to a handful of blue chip stocks. The media and Wall Street kept shouting throughout 1929, right up to the time of the Dow peak and even beyond, that the bull market was alive and well. True market technicians knew that the *real* bull market died in December 1928, eight months before the September 1929 break in the Dow.

This was to become much more valuable information later on in 1983 when the market's continuing inability to better these highs would enable me to make a more reliable projection of the most vulnerable period ahead for the Dow. As it turned out, the Dow would peak out almost seven months later and start a steep decline eight months after that, an almost perfect parallel with the peak in new highs in December 1928 that preceded the Dow peak by approximately eight months.

But the public was impervious to the technical landmark that had just been recorded. All the outward appearances seemed to suggest that everything would stay in high gear forever. The true sentiment of the times was well expressed in an article that appeared on May 5 in *The New York Times*. A number of people were interviewed as to their current dealings in the stock market, and the individual stories were absolutely classic in their underscoring of where the market stood in the grand cycle. These were the Johnny-come-latelies who had recently discovered the market and learned how quickly it could disgorge the easy profits. The stories paralleled identical stories told at the time of the 1929 peak.

PARALLEL 26
Historical
The Get-Rich-Quick Stories

Typical was the one about the person who didn't buy Chrysler in 1982 under 10 but loved it in the 20s and would hold it for the long pull. The easy profits built castles in the air. A speculator makes an easy $1,200 profit in a very short period of time. His castles grow very quickly in his mind, and he visualizes being on easy street with $50,000 or $100,000 or more in a few years. After all, Wall Street brokers have told him that the 1980s are the golden years when stocks should be held for the long pull because the upward trend is endemic.

Then, as it always does, the bubble bursts and the castles quickly disappear. The Merrill Lynch bull sees a beautiful oasis ahead, and he walks toward it and the oasis disappears. In May 1983 the public saw a beautiful green oasis of easy profits in the stock market. Ironically, when *they* see it, they discover sadly in retrospect that somebody else saw it first and devoured all the lush greenery long before they could live in their castles. A short-term spectacular rise in the market will always conjure up visions of long-term wealth. The year 1983 went down in history as the year the castles in the air disappeared, a year of a jarring return to reality, which was to start with the new issues market.

All bear markets develop after the third and final phase of a bull market. In every way I could, I had documented that by May 1983 the market was starting an incredible transition—incredible because nobody expected third-phase characteristics to occur so early in a bull market. Only nine months had passed since the August 1982 bottom, but from that point on there would be no turning back. Once bull market third-phase characteristics are in evidence, they don't go away or reverse themselves back to the second phase. Bear markets always start when virtually nobody is looking for one. The entire nation had been brainwashed into expecting that all downturns were buying opportunities. So instead of the market projecting to a normal bull market end by late 1984 or early 1985, the bull market would end in 1983. The public would be holding their newly acquired stocks all the way down as they awaited the carefully advertised continuation of the bull market.

II

By this time, overspeculation was rife on the American Stock Exchange. Taking its cue from the over-the-counter market, the Amex Market Value Index had soared well above its own trendline, and the volume of trading on that exchange had reached the excessive levels associated with all major blow-offs. It was a good time to remember Bernard Baruch's formula for market success: "I always sold too soon." Again I underscored the advice to be out of this market over the next sixty to ninety days. The stock market had been soaring over the previous nine months on a column of hot-air buying, but in recent weeks it had encountered a giant mass of cold air emanating from heavy, concentrated, and continuing stock distribution. The clash of extremely heavy public buying with that of equally heavy professional selling had created market turbulence, resulting in extremely heavy volume and sudden squalls of sharp declines and equally sharp rallies. But the public was missing the key market message: *That market turbulence in May 1983 was reflecting the transition from bull market to bear market.*

Edwin Lefevre must have had a similar market in mind when he penned the following choice paragraph in his 1922 classic, *Reminiscences of a Stock Operator:*

> And there is another thing to remember, and that is that a market does not culminate in one grand blaze of glory. Neither does it end with a sudden reversal of form. A market can and does often cease to be a bull market long before prices generally begin to break. My long expected warning came to me when I noticed that, one after another, those stocks which had been the leaders of the market reacted several points from the top and—for the first time in many months— did not come back. Their race evidently was run, and that clearly necessitated a change in my trading tactics.[2]

[2]Edwin Lefevre, *Reminiscences of a Stock Operator* (Dallas: Books of Wall Street, 1976), p. 181.

While that transition was taking place, however, the Reagan administration was publicizing economic recovery. I described the situation in terms of a horse race. In the summer of 1982, Wall Street bet on a horse called Recovery. It came in. The early bettors were then getting out of their seats and streaming toward the cashiers' windows. The public, waiting to see how Recovery would run its race, then lined up at the betting windows, putting everything they had on a horse called Certain Winner. The only problem was that Certain Winner had never won a race. Meanwhile, those who had made a killing on Recovery were eyeing a two-year-old in the fifth race called Short Sale.

Back in 1979, Merrill Lynch chastised *Business Week* for a cover story titled "Equities Are Dead." The dramatic rise in equity prices since that article was published showed how inaccurate the *Business Week* cover story was. On May 9, at the very peak of the 1982–83 bull market, *Business Week* published a cover story with the intriguing title "The Rebirth of Equities." Since *Business Week* had shown poor timing with its 1979 cover story, why should the timing of the 1983 story, coming out at the very peak of the bull market (maximum stock highs took place on May 6, 1983), be any better?

The *Business Week* article was filled with bad information and trapped the majority at the true market peak. The following paragraph from the article was typical of the euphoric thinking: "Indeed, a growing body of evidence suggests that the current rally may mark the dawning of a new age of equities—a return to an era of generally rising share prices reminiscent of the 1950s and 1960s." Many observers shared the rosy *Business Week* view. "We are witnessing the beginning of a major shift in preference away from tangible assets to financial assets, stocks in particular," said Arnold X. Moskowitz, first vice president and economist for Dean Witter Reynolds. "We are truly in a supercycle," agreed Sidney B. Lurie, an executive vice president at Josephthal & Co. Martin E. Zweig added, "I think the bull market will last most of this decade." Martin D. Sass, president of M. D. Sass Investors Services, said, "We believe that four years into this secular bull market, we will see the Dow industrials double, to 2,400."

But while the Street and the media were mesmerized with their newfound supercycle, a deadlier game was going on. It was the *paper chase*. There was a limit to the demand for stocks. Nobody knew exactly what that limit was, but the evidence was there that there wasn't enough money available to support adequately the ever-growing mountain of paper. Every day more stocks were up for sale, seeking buyers who had a limited amount of buying power. Available investment dollars bought increasingly less of each stock as the paper parade lengthened to the ultimate point where there would be no buyers. The market horse was beginning to choke on its own greed. Corporations glutted that appetite, trying to jam more stock down the public's throats when they were virtually 100 percent fully invested. However, the public had placed their bet on that horse Certain Winner and nothing was going to pry them from their newly acquired stocks. They were cleverly placed so as to ride those stocks all the way down.

It always comes down to supply and demand. If enough paper is placed on the scales, the market has to go down. Most of those new corporations floating the new issues didn't have anything going for them other than the cash they got by selling their shares. A typical new offering might be for 2 million shares, and in the small print it would be announced that 1.4 million would be sold by the company and 600,000 shares by certain shareholders. It seemed so obvious, but apparently it got by the public every time. If the stock was so good, why were the insiders getting out by piggybacking the offering? This technique swelled the number of secondary offerings and was a major factor in pushing that number up to an all-time record high, certain technical evidence that the bull market was fast becoming a basket case. Whatever stock that was sold that did not benefit the company comprised a secondary distribution, and without the public greed for stocks the ploy would have failed. The public was so price-conscious that they were totally unaware of how fast the corporate printing presses were running. That was the supply side of the market equation, and it was fast tilting toward the new bear market.

III

PARALLEL 27
Psychological
This Time It Is Different

Every time a major long-term market top is reached, the bulls tend to rationalize their bullish position by telling themselves that *this time it is different.* They tell themselves that we have the Federal Reserve System, the Securities and Exchange Commission, the Federal Deposit Insurance Corporation, Social Security, etc., so how could the stock market crash? This time things would be different. The government won't let the stock market fall apart. The president of the New York Stock Exchange in 1929 had the same viewpoint, convinced that the days of panics and crashes were forever over.

There is nothing new under the sun, but *Fortune,* in its May 30, 1983, issue didn't agree. The lead article was titled "What's New about This Boom." *Fortune* saw the new issue boom in the spring of 1983 as being *different* from its predecessors. While it stated that all bull markets give private companies the urge and incentive to go public, this new issue boom was different. According to *Fortune,* the companies themselves were different. They saw them as bigger and older than those behind the "new issues" eruption of the 1960s and their owners as more financially astute. They even saw the buyers as a different breed. But the upshot was the same. The collapse of the new issue market in 1983 was a big contributing factor to the developing bear market which started that year. The "new era" thinking caused more people to lose money, regardless of the size or quality of the new offering.

Wall Street brokerage firms bombarded the public with investment advice. The candy store was being overstocked with goodies and soon the Street would be confronted with an inventory problem—too much stock and too few buyers. That, as always, was to lead to a fire sale, a severe marking-down period, which was soon to bring the over-the-counter market to its knees.

With the whirlwind performance of the market over the previous nine months, the public had been exposed to *overcredibility* and, at the worst of times, naïvely placed their belief on the altar of Broad and Wall. The public had forgotten what happens to most professionally managed portfolios. "Over the past decade, more than eighty percent of the professionally managed portfolios in this country have performed worse than the stock market averages. Eighty percent! Four out of five of the allegedly best-managed pools of capital—whether mutual funds, pension funds, endowment funds or trust accounts—are worse off than had they simply bought the stocks which make up the Dow Jones Industrial Average. In short, eighty percent of the brokerage advice, economic analysis, portfolio management and investment committees not only have been worthless, but have lost money."[3] The 1983–84 bear market was to prove that again. By the end of May 1983 the stage was almost set for a major change of scene.

[3]Richard A. Crowell, *Stock Market Strategy* (New York: McGraw-Hill, 1977), p. 1.

4

The Sardines Stink

[JUNE 1983]

I

Addressing a group in Montreal, I told the largely bullish audience that the sardines stank, and gave them the following illustration. A man paid $1 for a can of sardines. He found a buyer at $2. The $2 buyer found a buyer at $3. And so it went in a bullish sardine market until eventually a man paid $98 for the can of sardines. He hoped to find someone who would pay at least $99 for his can of sardines. At the same time, he invited the man who had sold him the sardines to his daughter's wedding. The seller accepted the invitation. The $98 buyer decided to open the sardines at the wedding and serve them to his guests. Upon his doing so, everyone was offended by the awful smell. The buyer turned to the seller guest and said, "These sardines stink." Whereupon the guest said, "These $98 sardines are for selling purposes, not eating purposes."

Stocks had changed hands so many times since the summer of 1982 that by June 1983 they reeked, and the smart money considered them to be untouchable.

By this time I was particularly outspoken on the developing bear market which nobody could see even though internally it was crystal clear that the short bull market was rapidly dying. I stressed the new issues, stock splits, and secondary stock distributions as the most certain evidence that a bear market lay ahead. It was increasingly evident by then that the number of new individual stock price highs had peaked. Overspeculation was at an extreme and already the parallels with 1929 were rapidly growing in number.

━━━━━━━━━

PARALLEL 28

Market
Overspeculation

Overspeculation in 1928 and 1929 is well documented. The parallel with 1982–83 is equally easy to document. As I stood alone in the spring of 1983, viewing the events and markets of that year as constituting a financial bubble of speculation, the overwhelming evidence of the new paper being printed and dumped into the snatching hands of the public was a precise "fix" on where we stood in the grand cycle. The public literally wanted everything, and the lower the price tag, the more they wanted it.

At Williamsburg, the economic summit meeting had just ended on a note of high hopes and many promises. The eyes of the world were upon it, and it was well named—the summit. While I homed in on it at the time as a baited fishhook, nobody saw it that way. It was seen as another in the current series of market lures designed to catch the maximum number of fish right at the top of the bull market.

English panics of the nineteenth century also had demonstrated that *precisely the contrary of that which was expected took place*. At Williamsburg this syndrome of opposites was so clear that it was close to becoming a recognizable law. The media had been quick to underscore the economic summit meeting as having bullish connotations for European countries. They thought that their pleas for lower interest rates and better exchange control would be heeded by the Reagan administration. Anyone who was aware of the stock market's very clear message at that time had to conclude that Williamsburg was a market hook.

The Wall Street Journal told the story well on June 8:

> Last weekend's meeting of many of the world's foreign exchange traders was a gloomy session. Confident that the U.S. dollar was headed down as U.S. interest rates declined, many of them had been taking on heavy commitments in other currencies this year. What's more, they advised their corporate customers to do the same, neatly making sure that practically everybody—except a few sharp American banks—was in the same boat. The boat has now capsized and many traders, mostly European, are struggling to keep their heads above water and/or keep their jobs. The first rule of foreign exchange trading has asserted itself with a vengeance: When everybody goes one way, watch out; the exact opposite is likely to occur. And it did.

PARALLEL 29

Historical
The Williamsburg Economic Summit

In June 1983, I saw the recent Williamsburg economic summit as a hoax on our foreign trading partners. President Reagan sent them home with high hopes that he was going to bring down our budgetary deficits and lower interest rates, thus aiding their currencies. They all went back to their respective countries dumb and happy, about to experience colossal losses based on Reagan's information. Instead of coming down, the dollar soared to new highs and produced massive losses for those who bet on their own currencies.

"In 1929 Montagu Norman, governor of the Bank of England, had visited Washington early that year, hoping to be given a clearer view of monetary conditions. Instead, he had returned home 'baffled,' with an 'even deeper feeling of confusion and obscurity.' "[1]

The Reagan administration made promises it couldn't deliver. There was no way that interest rates could be brought down in the face of out-of-control budgetary deficits which were brought about by its own policies.

By this time *Barron's* had reported 72 secondary offerings since February. My private figures had already grown to over 200 and I knew I was on the track of the biggest stock distribution program in financial history!

My discovery of the insidious practice of piggybacking explained why *Barron's* did not have the true count of the secondary distributions but was reporting only a small fraction of the massive distribution of common stocks then occurring. Not all sales were registered and that was additional cause to believe that the true number of secondary distributions was even higher than the expanded figures I had compiled. "Sometimes the holder of a large block is not under legal restriction to register the sale. Such holders would include, among others, mutual funds, pension funds, endowment funds. The sales are effected on short notice, hence the name 'spot secondaries.' "[2] Mutual funds, pension funds, and endowment funds could move out of the market without having to register with the SEC, their selling intentions *completely hidden* from the current blind buyer of stocks.

The public was so caught up in the rising stock prices that they didn't realize what was being done to them. It became increasingly obvious what was happening, but the public still didn't catch on that they were being had right at the top. For instance, American Motors had risen from $3 a share the

[1]Gordon Thomas and Max Morgan-Witts, *The Day the Bubble Burst* (New York: Penguin Books, 1980), p. 179.
[2]Richard Teweles and Edward S. Bradley, *The Stock Market* (4th ed.; New York: John Wiley & Sons, 1982), p. 258.

previous fall and was selling at $11 a share when the company announced that it was issuing an additional 75 million shares. That was a tremendous quantity of new stock and it, of course, signaled the top of the run for the stock. It was soon to collapse. That was the game then going on.

I I

While Wall Street continued to preach the sermon of profit, extolling the virtues of the assured great bull market, one that was expected to be rolling through most of the decade of the 1980s, words being used by the press were sounding a loud warning. Articles describing the market were using words such as "hot," "stampede," "rebirth," and "new." Such words do not crop up early in a market rise but become common at the top. Their use in June 1983, together with the massive evidence elsewhere, lent further authority to my market warnings. If an editor had dug back into the past, he would have discovered a similar array of equally euphoric writings in 1929.

I was contending that volume was running far ahead of normal measurements. In support of my thesis that this high volume was *borrowing from the future* and thus shortening the cycle, I was intrigued by a statement Martin Pring had made in his excellent work on technical analysis: "Volume reflects the intensity of changes in investor attitudes. For example, if stock prices advance on low volume, the enthusiasm implied from the price rise is not nearly as strong as that present when a price rise is accompanied by very high volume."[3] The volume measurement thus far in 1983 proved that investor sentiment was making a more *intense* transition from bear to bull than would be expected in a normal cycle. I estimated that volume was running three times the normal pace, and if my conclusion was to prove accurate, *then the normal duration of the cycle would be shortened by approximately two-thirds.*

It was already apparent that the bull market was no longer technically genuine, inasmuch as the maximum number of new individual stock price highs had been recorded the month before, but June brought the clinching technical proof that the brief bull market had spent the bulk of its upside momentum. The important advance/decline line peaked on June 16.[4] In so doing, it recorded one of the most telling of the 1929 parallels:

[3]Martin Pring, *Technical Analysis Explained* (New York: McGraw-Hill, 1980), p. 9.
[4]One of the most important measurements used in technical analysis. Every day the number of advancing and declining stocks is given. The net differential is plotted each day, and that constitutes the advance/decline line.

Technical
The Advance/Decline Line Tops Out

In December 1928, the reconstructed New York Stock Exchange advance/decline line peaked out *eight months* ahead of the Dow Jones Industrial Average. On June 16, 1983, the New York Stock Exchange advance/decline line peaked out *five and a half months* ahead of the Dow Jones Industrial Average.

Market volatility continued to increase. Splits in Procter & Gamble, American Express, and General Electric had lowered the divisor to 1.248. That meant that any move of 1¼ points in one of the thirty stocks making up the Dow was equivalent to a 1-point change in the average itself. Back in 1957 the divisor was over 4.500; thus the volatility of the Dow had since then quadrupled. Nobody was paying much attention to this increasing volatility factor, but the day was to come in the developing bear market when this factor would contribute 50- to 60-point daily swings in the Dow. In a bull market this adds weight to the upswing. In a bear market it adds weight to the downswing. With a new bear market just getting under way, the lowered divisor was deemed to be bearish.

III

I stood virtually alone as I viewed the events and markets of 1983 as constituting a financial bubble of speculation, a type of mania that had repeated itself at the most critical market turning points. In order to demonstrate that market truths never die, I had underscored some of the more salient points of the English panics of the nineteenth century to show that all the common denominators that precede all panics and crashes were in evidence in June 1983.

The first of those salient points was that *what everybody thinks, is worthless.* That is the crowd factor, and it ran as a common thread through all critical peaks and ensuing panics. Checking out the advisory services at this time, I saw that I was the only bear around, predicting the start of the new bear market in 1983, a date considered far too soon by everyone else. That meant that I was standing alone against the informed opinion of all other advisers. Being a student of history, I felt totally comfortable in that position because my evidence was historically and technically 100 percent sound, and I knew that *the maximum rewards in life go to those who are alone at the critical turning points.* Thus, being in the barest minority of opinion was not scary. It was actually a bed of confidence as I watched the best-documented mass distribution of common stocks in history taking place. Robert Stovall at this time stated that the market always does what it has to do in order to make most people wrong. It was doing exactly that, precisely when he made the statement. Everybody was relying on a normal cycle, and internally it was blowing up in their faces in June 1983. In ironic contrast, some analysts were so bullish that they were stuttering in their wild forecasts of how high the Dow was headed. At the great turning points, majority opinion was worthless, and in June 1983 everybody was wearing rose-colored glasses.

Another recurring truth of the English panics was the *overproduction of the things they had to sell,* whether it be commodities or stocks. Corporations in 1983 were seeking to produce more than the usual quantity of common stocks with a view to dumping them into the hands of a greedy and unsuspecting public. The psychology was absolutely identical. It didn't matter whether it was a glut of goods or a glut of stocks. Whatever the case, there was always a glut of something on the market that brought it down. The bigger the glut, the more severe the decline. The 1983 glut was record-breaking.

I couldn't make enough references to the 1983 glut of new issues. On June 5, the *Miami Herald* ran a feature article titled "New Issues Rushing to Market." In it the figures gave further statistical evidence of the size of the speculative bubble. The dollar volume of roughly $3.8 billion exceeded anything seen in the past decade, and that figure was based on the first five months of 1983 as compared with figures for past annual totals. The Dun & Bradstreet figures wouldn't leave my mind—11 percent vanish, 41 percent go bankrupt, 25 percent remain unprofitable, 20 percent are barely profitable, and only 2.4 percent prove to be worthwhile holdings.

The opening paragraph in the *Miami Herald* piece was as follows:

> Electronic Financial Systems, Inc., was considerably more than a gleam in an entrepreneur's eye when it offered some of its stocks to the public last month. But the Miami company *had no operating history, no profits and no paying customers.* For a year it had been getting ready for action. When the 600,000 shares came out at $7.00 each, the demand was almost double the supply. They were snapped up quickly and, by the end of their first day on the public trading market, were selling at a premium—a dollar or so higher than the offering price. Another new issue had been launched successfully, a situation that is occurring with growing frequency as American business takes advantage of a receptive market to sell shares to the public.

A year later the stock had fallen to under $3 a share. But there was no way to stop the buying; no words of warning got through. The public were determined to snatch the shares between 7 and 8. They could only be taught by their own experience. They had to prove once again that the Dun & Bradstreet figures were right, that most new issues end up as worthless junk.

The English panics had demonstrated the *principle of encapsulement,* that at a peak everything was speeding up, borrowing from the future. Certainly this speculation in June 1983 was putting the cap on the bull market bottle. In the English panic of 1825, it was stated that the commitments entered into by Great Britain were on an astonishing scale—a scale more suitable to the end than to the beginning of the nineteenth century, *and certainly more fitly representing the investments of twenty years than of two.*

In keeping with the overproduction of things, the brief 1982–83 rise also produced the largest number of new stock market advisory services, another key 1929 parallel.

PARALLEL 31

Historic
Too Many Market Letters

According to the Securities and Exchange Commission, over 500 new investment advisers registered in 1983, the highest number in SEC history. If one checks the records of the SEC, one will find that peaks in new registrations are always followed by major bear markets. It went hand in hand with the matching incentive that drove so many to become stockbrokers in the 1982–83 period. The reasoning was that one could make money either directly in the marketplace or indirectly by selling stock market advice to others. As at the peak of all bull markets, too many cooks were in the kitchen and too many cooks spoiled the broth. There was a plethora of new market letters back in 1929, and shortly thereafter most of them went out of business.

PARALLEL 32

Market
Parabolic Rise in Low-Priced Stocks

At the peak of the general blindness, the low-priced stocks were going off the top of the charts. *Barron's Financial Weekly* was about to change its low-priced stock index and for obvious reasons. The stocks in the current index were no longer low-priced. It was the fourth change since the index was started in April 1938. Such parabolic rises in that index were always followed by bear markets, and the biggest rise to date had occurred in the 1982–83 period. This served as an index of speculative fever. And in terminating the upswing with an index change, it served the same bearish notice that splitting a stock would do. What made the evidence all the more compelling was that low-priced stocks, new highs, and the advance/decline line had all peaked in December 1928 also. The parallel was clear: the countdown was starting that would lead up to the predicted panic and crash.

Volume was running very high, but that in itself was not bearish. What made it bearish was the fact that it was occurring against the background of the boom in low-priced stocks, the new issue mania, the record number of stock splits, and the highest number of secondary offerings in ten years, a figure soon to rise to all-time record levels. The year 1983 was already well on the way to a new all-time record in the volume of trading, which was also true for the American Stock Exchange and the over-the-counter market. Not only was the volume running at record highs, but the previous records weren't even close. Volume through June 3 on the New York Stock Exchange was 9,-378,840,189 shares; the corresponding figures for 1982 stood at 5,557,020,000 shares. History would record the same type of *volume parabolic* as occurred in 1929.

And just at the most sensitive of times, along came Uncle Sam, who was about to drop *the greatest bundle of paper ever dropped on the American public,* the codicil of Reagan supply-side economics.

History teaches us that before a major stock market smash a collection of events occurs so as to provide an excuse for heavy selling. Market warnings were occurring *prior* to those events, and thus one didn't have to wait for the events themselves.

IV

PARALLEL 33

Market
Pension Funds Loading Up on Stocks

The amount of money invested by the pension funds in 1982–83 broke all records. Traditionally, pension funds tend to split their investments evenly between debt instruments and equities. However, by early 1983 they were weighting their stock portfolios to the tune of 65 percent of their entire portfolios. This love affair with the stock market resembled previous love affairs that went on the rocks.

On June 12, *The New York Times* ran a piece by Fred Bleakley titled "Pension Funds Loading Up on Stocks." The more conservative pension funds were the last of the wildly bullish species, and when they loaded up on stocks, then one knew that the bull market days were numbered. A particularly intriguing final pair of paragraphs in the Bleakley piece raised some interesting questions:

> When stocks are booming, of course, it hurts portfolio performance to hold cash investments that produce a low rate of return. And the fear that stocks may again take off, in fact, may be keeping many fund managers from acting on their belief that a market correction is overdue.
>
> The chairman of a multi-billion-dollar money management fund, who asked not to be named, said he was faced with just such a dilemma. He is convinced the market has already seen its highs for this year. But his fund managers, he said, say that the clients are bullish. "God forbid," the fund managers tell their boss, "if the market continues going up and we are not in it. Whereas, if the market goes down and we are heavily committed to stocks, we'll be like everyone else."

That very dilemma was adequately discussed by Richard Crowell:

> A recent development in the pension area *makes going against the trend particularly difficult.* Many large pension funds are hiring several money managers to competitively manage their investments. Usually these investment managers are selected because of their particular success in such investment areas as managing bond portfolios or picking hot stocks. Under this arrangement several different firms simultaneously handle stock market investments for a particular pension fund. Each handles a segment of the total portfolio, and the one who does the best (often measured over a very short time span, say three or six months) receives additional funds to manage. Additional funds mean higher fees. This competitive environment with very short-term awards and penalties makes going against the stock market trend particularly difficult.
>
> Suppose some bright investment managers feel that the current market is too speculative, detect a coming peak and want to sell. They start selling while competitors remain fully invested and are telling the client that fully invested is the only place to be. Since the bright money managers would have to be very lucky to pick the exact market peak, the chances are good that they are starting to sell a little early, while the market is still advancing. Because they are selling and are partially in cash, they start to underperform both the advancing market and the competitors. And all the competitors, no doubt, are telling clients that it is crazy to sell when such great profits can be made. Is this any way to get additional funds to invest? Or is it a good way to lose a valuable client? The end result once again is that it is easier not to sell. Ride it out with everyone else.[5]

So the large pension funds became *entrapped* right at the top, and due to their overwhelming size, lacked the flexibility of the individual, who could at least sidestep the catastrophes with greater agility. Crowell called attention to R. W. McNeel's book *Beating the Stock Market,* published in 1927. "McNeel

[5]Richard A. Crowell, *Stock Market Strategy* (New York: McGraw-Hill, 1977), p. 109.

attributed investors' failure to sell during speculative binges to weaknesses inherent in human nature. He mentions instinctive fear, the tendency to do as the crowd does, the inability to think for oneself against the overwhelming trend of others. These factors tend to make all men panic together as the market falls in the face of worsening economic news. And we all take comfort in the fact that we are all losing money."

Ironically, for all his market sagacity, R. W. McNeel was completely blinded in 1929 by those same weaknesses of human nature. "Only two days before the panic, the Boston News Bureau quoted R. W. McNeel, Director of McNeel's Financial Service, as suspecting 'that some pretty intelligent people are now buying stocks. Unless we are to have a panic—which no one seriously believes—stocks have hit bottom.' "[6] The intelligent people that McNeel talked about were about to be wiped out. And note here once again for the record *that nobody saw the panic coming outside of the barest minority.*

Here is another reference to what I have called the "wineglass" principle: steady selling bringing a market down, with the final fear being the fear of selling at a loss. Then that gives way and everybody sells at once, thus the panic. During the decline, the large funds, both mutual funds and pension funds, while caught up in the competition among fund managers, also do little or nothing until it is too late.

This was all handwriting on the wall in June 1983. The opportunity to sell out at the top had fully arrived, but very few seized it. In fact, Drexel Burnham Lambert ran a full-page ad in *The Wall Street Journal* with the question: "Are You Afraid You've Missed the Market?" This underscored the very psychology that *entrapped the 1929 crowd.*

In June 1983, the *fear of missing out* was a powerful force. Instead of *selling everything,* as the market was telling them to do, most people preferred to listen to the brokers, Wall Street pundits, economists, and politicians, much to their later regret. This psychological trap, so well documented for June 1983, was an exact parallel with 1929. In order not to miss the rises, the majority inherited the declines.

Public participation in the stock market at this time was so nearly total that it had instantly reminded me of George Lindsay's statement, mentioned earlier, which virtually made it certain that the true top in the market was being recorded. Lindsay had observed that when it could be shown that the public was coming into the market, then 63 to 75 percent of the entire up move had already taken place. The documented evidence clearly showed that as early as November 1982 the public was starting to come into the market in a big way. That meant that the spring of 1983 would be the top—and it was.

[6]Frederick Lewis Allen, *Only Yesterday* (New York: Perennial Library, Harper & Row, 1964), p. 269.

V

In light of the heavy evidence of new highs and the peaking of the advance/ decline line, it became immaterial from then on out when people sold out, *as long as they did it in 1983.*

PARALLEL 34

Market
Selling at Any Time in 1983
Was the Correct Thing to Do

In terms of technical comparison, June 1983 equated with December 1928. Both dates saw *the true end to the bull market.* The advance/decline line and new highs had peaked by those months. Therefore, selling stocks at any time in 1983 proved to be the right thing to do, just as selling out any time between January and August 1929 proved to be the right thing to do.

Knowing that anything the Dow did from this point on would be nothing more than a *solitary walk,* I was not concerned whether there were two or three more flings in the wings. It didn't change the scenario one iota. I pleaded with my subscribers to treat this market from this point on with the assumption that *it was 1929 revisited.*

During a stock market high, Wall Street morality typically sinks to new lows. The Texas Instruments debacle at this time pointed up *erratic price action* which underscored a *growing instability* in the general market. It served as a warning that shouldn't have gone unheeded. Here 72 percent of the stock was owned by the institutions and the lesson was clear: When the majority of a company's capitalization is in institutional hands, *it offers no net of safety.* On the contrary, such concentrated ownership *increases downside vulnerability when air pockets occur. That air pocket wiped out almost a third of the entire market value of the company in two days.* If Texas Instruments had been a Dow industrial stock, it alone would have pushed the Dow Jones Industrial Average 40 points lower in two days. If all the Dow stocks had acted in similar fashion, the Dow Jones Industrial Average would have dropped to zero in two days, theoretically falling 1,200 points. The 50-point drop in Texas Instruments stock came in response to the expectation of the company's losing $100 million in the second quarter. The result was a market loss of well over ten times that amount. It would have been better if all the owners of the 23.6 million common shares volunteered to take a $4-per-share loss to offset the $100 million company loss. Instead, the market whacked them for a

$50-a-share loss. That was a nervous market. It implied that no stock with heavy institutional holdings was safe in that market.

According to the *Report of Special Study of Security Markets, Securities and Exchange Commission*, Part IV, page 566, a corporate head is required to report all company changes that may affect the stock of his company to the New York Stock Exchange within ten days. Yet neither the Exchange nor the specialists reported that valuable information to the public. The public has been given to understand that a prime function of the stock specialist is to provide and maintain an *orderly* market. Texas Instruments dropped over 50 points in two days, and that was supposed to be an orderly market. It was disorderly for everyone else, but *very orderly* for the specialist's bank account as he walked heavily later to his bank. It created a new type of fear. *It implied that nobody would ever want to buy a stock again for fear of what the specialist might do to ruin the investor the next day.*

It was later revealed that company officials, capitalizing on inside information, were heavy buyers of put options before the news was announced in *The Wall Street Journal*. The specialists took the stock up on light volume upon receiving the advance word of the trouble ahead and then heavily shorted it in preparation for the *Journal* announcement.

Margin debt continued to soar, up for the eighth straight month by the end of May, topping $16 billion for a new record. I saw margin debt as the opposite of the short interest. Short sales eventually have to be covered or bought in. Margin debt eventually has to be paid by the selling of stocks. Thus, while margin debt was rising, it appeared to be bullish but actually *it was building up eventual selling pressure*. That was dramatically demonstrated in 1929 when broker loans rose rapidly to $8 billion. The bubble then burst and the entire process reversed, the loans rapidly being liquidated as margin accounts were liquidated in the crash. So, while it could be argued at this time that the growth of margin debt was bullish as long as it was expanding, so it could also be seen that it would add tremendously to selling pressure when the downturn commenced.

Peaks in the number of secondary offerings occurred in 1959, 1961, 1965, 1969, and 1972. By June 1983 the peak overshadowed all the previous ones and only half the year had gone by. In just one week in June, *Barron's* showed a rise of 17 in the number of secondary offerings, a fantastic number, considering that *Market Logic* had called attention earlier to the 7 secondaries for the week ending March 25 as being the highest number in ten years.

––––––––––

Market
Record Insider Selling

The year 1983 witnessed the most pernicious, continuing, concentrated insider selling in the history of the New York Stock Exchange. An insider is a corporate officer who buys or sells shares in the company he works for. Such transactions are reported to the SEC and reported upon. But by the time one reads the SEC report, it is usually too late to capitalize immediately on the information. As in secondary distributions, somebody wanted out. The heavy insider selling in 1983 was the very antithesis of the popular cover story as told by the economists and the Wall Street pundits.

V I

The Wall Street Journal on June 22 provided the latest Securities and Exchange Commission report on the record number of security offerings.

> Corporate securities offerings surged to a record $40 billion in the first four months of this year. The jump in public offerings coincides with the continuation of the "bull market" that has boosted stock prices and investor demand for new stock issues. The previous record for securities offerings was set in the first four months of 1981, when $20.8 billion in corporate securities were sold, an SEC official said. In the like period last year, before the start of the market boom, $17.5 billion in securities were publicly sold.
>
> The agency said the average size of each securities issue in the first four months of this year was $40.1 million, or 35% greater than the year before. Of the total offerings, 48% were for common or preferred stock, and the remainder for debt securities. The year earlier, equity offerings in the recent period were financial and manufacturing concerns, according to the SEC.

There it was, $10 billion of new paper being thrust upon the marketplace every month. But the most significant fact of all was right there for people who remembered previous bear markets. The previous record for security offerings was set in the first four months of 1981. I had been widely criticized for telling people to sell everything on January 6, 1981, 20 points short of the Dow peak, which occurred in April of that year. It was a bear market. Now here we were in June 1983 with a new all-time record in security offerings, and my advice to sell everything was again being ridiculed. To me, the very fact that I was again being ridiculed confirmed the validity of the advice.

The overissuance of securities was the overriding factor that brought the market down in 1929, and that was the dominant factor bringing on the beginning of a new bear market in 1983.

On June 15, I appeared on *Good Morning America* with David Hartman. I told him this was the time to get out of all stocks, because I saw a 400-point decline coming within the next six months. My forecast, based on the massive amount of bearish evidence I had already compiled, was not borne out right away, and when the decline did occur it was not as extreme as I had believed. But the timing of the forecast was perfect: the advance/decline line peaked the very next day.

Things were looking so good for the brokerage industry on the brief 1982–83 upswing that they all committed the cardinal error that they always commit at the peak of every bull market. They all overhired. This constituted another of the most important of the 1929 parallels:

PARALLEL 36

Market
Record Hiring of Brokers

By June 1983 it was apparent that the brief but meteoric rise coming off of the August 1982 bottom had produced *the widest spread hiring of new stockbrokers in the history of Wall Street.* Nothing could have opened the jar of honey faster than what was widely hailed as the most important bull market in history. The flies seemingly came out of nowhere, attracted to the tantalizing smell of easy money. While corporations glutted the public appetite for stocks, the brokers performed the task of feeding the public the stock produced. According to the National Association of Stock Dealers (NASD), 48,000 new applicants took the broker-dealer examination in the 1982–83 period, a record number. Most of these were hired, and then they spread out to the sharply expanded network of regional brokerage offices throughout the country. The expansion of the brokerage industry is always greatest at the end of a bull market. The previous period of heavy broker hiring was in the spring of 1981, right at the peak of that bull market. All such heavy hiring periods, *without exception,* have been followed by bear markets. The record clearly showed that Wall Street hires at the top and fires at the bottom.

The parallel with 1929 was exact. The great bull market then produced the smell of easy money and Wall Street was more than eager to serve the record number of new shareholders with an expanded number of regional offices equipped with the latest high-speed tickers, even providing special boardrooms for the women. The S.S. *Berengaria* provided a modern brokerage service for its passengers so that they could place their orders while at sea. Nothing was overlooked. Wall Street had made it to the front pages across the country, and

for the first time the message was getting across clearly that the stock market was everybody's business, a theme to be capitalized on by Merrill Lynch years later—"Bullish on America." It required many new brokers, called customer's men in those days, to service the 3 million stockholders. In 1983 there was a record 42 million stockholders, and, of course, that also required a record hiring of new stockbrokers to service them. The bubble analogy was ominously clear: If 3 million shareholders collapsed the market in 1929, what would happen when 42 million shareholders all wanted to get out of the market at the same time?

The collapse of the brokerage house stocks coming off the 1983 highs served as the clearest possible warning of major trouble to come. So while the industry couldn't hire new brokers fast enough in the spring of 1983, the pink slips were going out in great numbers in 1984.

Merrill Lynch gave much lip service to the bull market, but its actions were more eloquent. It declared a 2–1 split on its own stock and also offered 2 million shares of new stock to the public. At the time of the split announcement, Merrill stock stood at 110, two points shy of the peak.

VII

Paul Volcker's term as Chairman of the Federal Reserve Board would be drawing to a close in August. There was much speculation about whether he would be replaced. Volcker was now very popular with Wall Streeters since they saw him as the man who was at the helm when interest rates were coming down in 1982 and 1983, fueling the spectacular but short bull market. They wanted him kept on. Since President Reagan seemed to have every intention of running for reelection in 1984, it would have been politically stupid to replace Volcker with a new man. By reappointing Paul Volcker, if anything went wrong now, and something was going to go wrong, then Volcker would get it in the neck and not Reagan.

As it turned out, Paul Volcker was chosen by the president to stay on, and the announcement was made on June 18. It took place on a weekend and Wall Street braced for a huge rise the following Monday. Instead, the market fell. The reappointment of the Fed Chairman produced another 1929 parallel:

PARALLEL 37

Historic
Mellon and Volcker Stay On

Back in 1929 Andrew Mellon was the Secretary of the Treasury in the Hoover administration. He, too, was very popular with Wall Street. By late 1929 rumors were flying that Mellon was going to resign. Quelling that speculation,

Mellon announced on October 9 that he would remain with the Hoover administration until 1933. Wall Street loved it, but it was all part of a sucker rally, and the Mellon rally proved to be no more effective in stemming the tide of the new bear market than did Volcker's reappointment. *Both events turned out to be market sell signals.*

<hr>

PARALLEL 38
Historic
Andrew Mellon and Donald Regan

Andrew Mellon's many optimistic statements regarding the stock market and the economy are a matter of public record. The historical parallel with Treasury Secretary Donald Regan is of importance in two respects: their optimistic statements and examples of official references to the stock market. Donald Regan, former head of Merrill Lynch, the world's largest brokerage firm, was brought into the Reagan administration as Secretary of the Treasury. Nobody in that administration was more bullish on the economy and the stock market than Regan. His loyalty to his boss was intense and unwavering. Right or wrong, never was a Regan criticism of Reagan recorded. If Reagan was a supply-sider, then Regan became a supply-sider.

At the very height of the early 1983 runaway speculation, Secretary Regan pumped air into the financial bubble with statements that were foolishly euphoric. Nothing would line voters up faster at the polls in 1984 than stratospheric new highs in the Dow. With a Merrill Lynch background, it came naturally to Regan to be a super bull. And could there be anything more combustible than being Secretary of the Treasury with a Wall Street background at the peak of what seemed to most people to be the greatest bull rise in history?

Not at 776 in the Dow in August 1982 did Regan make his most optimistic public stock market forecast, but at the 1,248 level on June 16, when the Dow was 472 points higher. The *New York Daily News* on June 17 ran the following piece:

> Treasury Secretary Donald Regan said the stock market, which reached all-time highs this week, "will remain on high ground" for at least 18 months.
>
> The former chairman of the Merrill Lynch stock brokerage company made his prediction yesterday after the Dow Jones Industrial Average rose to yet another peak.
>
> Stocks are "a lot better buy . . . than we've had in two decades," Regan said.
>
> Regan said the economy will be "looking good for the next four quarters, and probably beyond."

So, right on the very day the advance/decline line peaked out, Regan put his foot in his mouth and predicted that the stock market was the best buy in twenty years! That was five and a half months before the Dow peaked the following November.

On March 14, 1929, President Herbert Hoover talked optimistically about the stock market and that was five and a half months before the Dow peaked out.

Of course, Donald Regan wasn't alone. More and more "new era" quotations were showing up in *The Wall Street Journal.* On June 23, one observer was quoted as follows: "This is basically a continuation of the irrepressible bull market. We're in *a new era of investor confidence* which will be helped by good second quarter earnings reports and even better reports for the third quarter."

The market wasn't listening. The bull market died in June 1983.

PART TWO

ILLUSION

5

Dead Chicken

[JULY 1983]

I

Cut the head of a rattlesnake off and it can still curl around your arm, even though it is dead. Cut the head of a chicken off and it will still run around for a while. Cut the head of a bull market off and, like the chicken, it will still make movements for a while. But then a bull market, also like the dead chicken, will suddenly collapse. It has to collapse, for the very simple reason that it is dead. When a bull market passes, a bear market is born. There is no final death in the market. A bull market simply reincarnates to a bear market and life goes on. In order to survive, one has to reincarnate with the market from bull to bear. The short bull market of 1982–83 had been dying for several months, and the technical verdict pronounced it officially dead by June 1983. Unlike what happens in a normal bull market, all three phases of the typical upswing were quickly traversed, and the true market top was recorded by the number of new highs in May and the advance/decline line in June, far sooner than most people thought possible. The Wall Street euphoria had blinded the public to the massive stock distribution that had been going on around them, and they weren't conscious at all that now the general euphoria was making the subtle change to illusion. Since very few people had the remotest notion that a bear market was possible, the shock would prove to be much greater.

At all times there is a cover story that the majority subscribes to. The cover story at this time was the general expectation that after current irregularities had run their course the bull market would resume, fueled mainly by corporate earnings. Nobody cared to assign much importance to any kind of correction, and analysts were using descriptive terms ranging from "interlude" to "mini-correction." For a while the whole Street was talking about a 10 percent correction, but that thinking went out the window when the Dow Jones Industrial Average had managed a new high in mid-June. Ironically, that was when the lightning struck, catching the Street at the very fullest extent of the bullish enthusiasm. But nobody expected a bear market at this time.

The general lack of concern was well attested to by the volume. The decline in prices from the June peak also saw a matching decline in the trading volume. It was rather amusing to listen to the television market commentators tell the public that the market was going down on light volume, the implication being that this was a bullish characteristic. They couldn't have been more wrong. There is a three-step process involved in investing. The first step is the buying. The second step is the holding. The third step is the selling. Rarely does an investor buy a stock and then turn right around and sell it. One would hold it, awaiting a profit. If there is no profit, it continues to be held because it goes against the grain of human nature to take a loss. Visualize the market scales which balance supply and demand. If there is a steady supply of stock coming on the market and the number of buyers diminishes, then supply overtakes demand and prices come down. The smaller number of buyers (earlier buyers now holding stocks at a loss) cuts the volume of trading, and thus volume shrinks as prices decline. While the bull market had been strong, there had been a plethora of buyers and prices rose. But now that the true market had topped out, a plethora of holders existed. They had bought while prices were rising, but now had become holders not willing to sell and take a loss. The market declines very easily with an absence of buyers, and thus light-volume market declines had to be deemed bearish.

At the beginning of the bear market, the implications for the future included the following scenario: Holders of stock, no longer seeing their profits rise but watching them shrink with losses mounting, become restless. These holders then eventually become desperate sellers, and when that ultimately becomes a plethora of sellers with no buyers, a crash ensues. The market was now set on that course and there was to be no turning back.

The silly season was about to end as the market moved into July, and I determined that the pinnacle of the junk market was reached when it was announced that a company called Indian Bingo planned to offer 5 million shares of new stock at $1 a share. The concept was very simple. One simply handed over $5 million to two consultants and their families who had no qualifications other than that they were smart enough to know that the public had reached the maximum point of gullibility when it came to buying stocks that would later be consigned to the ash can. Fund raising had no peer when it came to floating a new stock issue. One simply registered with the SEC, ordered up a batch of brand-new stock certificates, and dumped it all on the public via the services of an underwriter. There didn't have to be a thing behind the stock other than the idea of the promoter that people might find the shares attractive and take them off his hands. Indian Bingo was the latest entry in the junk parade.

The Wall Street Journal ran the Indian Bingo story on July 1: "Indian Bingo says in a preliminary registration statement filed with the Securities and Exchange Commission that it wants to get into the business of operating bingo games on Indian reservations. But Indian Bingo points out that the company would be a 'high risk' investment. Among the reasons: the company is a month old, such bingo games may be held illegal, third-party studies of such activities haven't been made, the company doesn't yet have any source of income and the underwriter hasn't any experience as a securities dealer." The Journal story also stated that "one of the main consultants had served time for conspiracy and mail fraud. Both had also received civil sanctions from the SEC for allegedly fraudulent activities, according to federal court records and SEC documents." The sad commentary about it all was that the public would buy the stock, push it to a premium, and then wait and wait and wait, looking for the greater fool to pass it off to. But, as in all such cases, the public would discover that they themselves were the greater fools.

The printing presses were humming, disgorging the greatest tonnage of new stock and bond offerings on record. It was announced in early July that corporate debt and equity offerings added up to almost $50 billion through the first five months of the year. Assuming, as I did, that the pace of offerings speeded up in June, I estimated a six-month total of offerings to be in the neighborhood of $65 billion. Interestingly enough, that equaled the total outflow from the money market funds since the assets of those funds had peaked at $232 billion the year before. Obviously only a portion of that outflow went back into the stock market. The point was that corporations were issuing paper faster than it could be comfortably absorbed, underscoring the law of all markets that supply rises to meet price but is always overdone, thus glutting the market with too much supply which then must ultimately topple prices.

Stock splits were rife, the powers-that-be striving to make the merchandise look as cheap as possible. Then the very ultimate took place. The American Stock Exchange split its Market Value Index 2–1. If a split is bearish, which it is, what in the world did splitting an entire market index imply? It was the deathblow to the American Stock Exchange. They said that it was done to facilitate trading in lower-priced Amex market index options. It was the big sucker play which should have been seen by everybody for what it was. It marked the very peak of the American Stock Exchange price upswing. It was the first time that an entire market index split 2–1. Nobody should have missed the implications of that move.

Simultaneously, Barron's changed its low-priced stock index for the first time since 1960. Barron's changed the index because there were no longer any low-priced stocks. That was the fourth change in the index since April 1938.

I immediately deemed that to be very bearish because *Barron's* had changed the low-priced stock index at or near bull market peaks.

It was also rumored that the Kansas City Value Line contract was going to be split five for one to facilitate trading on a lower-priced scale, letting in a greater number of players by reducing the standard contract from $6,000 to $1,200. The theory was simple. If they made cheaper chips available, more people would play the game. Many people took the bait, and later bitterly regretted being sucked into the market right at the top when they realized that they had been made the bag holders.

But to make the trap more nearly perfect, the news was all good. Over the previous weeks, the public had been bombarded by probably more bullish news than had been seen in the previous two-week period. June 18 saw the reappointment of Paul Volcker. On June 22, *The Wall Street Journal* announced that the economy was expanding faster than generally expected. On June 24, the Commerce Department stated that it expected spending on housing to rise 31.5 percent in 1983. On June 27, it was announced that machine-tool orders in May rose 28 percent over the 1982 level. On June 28, President Reagan at his eighteenth press conference stated that the economy was sparkling. On June 30, it was announced that the leading economic indicators rose again for the eleventh straight month. Single-family home sales rose 4.3 percent in May, the highest level in three years. The help-wanted-ad index rose 7 points in May, the biggest gain in three years. On July 1, the third-round tax cut of 10 percent went into effect. The stock market went down in the face of all that news, dropping in the weeks ending June 24 and July 1.

The media were full of stories telling the public how bullish the tax cut would be. It was supposed to put $30 billion back into the economy and be of great benefit to the stock market. Nobody told the people that the cut would average about $2 a week in the pocket of the average citizen, about the price of two extra beers or two packs of cigarettes or eight games of Ms. Pacman. Yet the way the media told the story, one would have thought everybody was about to be flush with cash. And while the media were talking about this $30 billion windfall, the Wilshire 5000 Equity Index was reflecting a drop of much more than $30 billion in stock values in but a handful of days! In other words, the tax cut was of no economic benefit to anybody. As fast as it was received it was gone.

Despite that string of bullish news items, the stock market began to shuffle to the slow beat of another drummer. Low-keyed by the media was a looming trade deficit that was already projected to rise to $70 billion by the end of 1983, and the budgetary deficits were worsening. The stock market was paying far more attention to these things than to what the media were passing out for public consumption.

The public were beginning to get confused by seeing the market go down in the face of all the good news, and a number of conflicting statements began to show up. Typical of such statements are the following: *The New York Times* on July 2 had this comment on the bond page: "Bad News for the Stock Market. Mr. Hale, saying that the bond market tanked in response to the new money supply figures, added that he expects the figures to be received as bad news for the stock market." Then, in the same edition, Philip H. Wiggins started his stock market column off as follows: "The stock market ended its week-long roller coaster ride slightly ahead yesterday, but signs persisted that it is poised for stronger gains after the Independence Day weekend."

Wall Street optimism would not cool off. On the contrary, the *Wall Street Week* TV panel, which on July 1 consisted of Dr. Martin Zweig, Bernadette Bartels, Monte Gordon, and Peter Calhoun, predicted that the Dow in 1983 would surpass the 1,300 level, a striking example of the unanimity of bullish opinion always seen at major stock market peaks. The stage was gradually but very certainly being set to ensnare the majority in what would turn out to be one of the most celebrated bull traps of the century.

Meanwhile, the exit door was violently revolving as a new and very astute generation of entrepreneurs were piggybacking their way to wealth, using the paper chase of the corporate new offerings to unload their holdings in a record-breaking string of uncounted secondary stock distributions. Already my count of these secondary offerings was up to 334 just since January, while *Barron's* was reporting only 127. There was no doubt, even then, that 1983 was the all-time record high year for secondary stock offerings, more than sufficient reason to be 100 percent bearish on the stock market, which, of course, I was.

II

In the summer of 1982 there had been an excess of cash and cash equivalents that flowed into the stock market. The public had been coming in since November 1982. A vast majority was rather fully invested, awaiting a higher market, totally unmindful of the risks that had arisen by virtue of the 472-point advance that had taken place by mid-June. Meanwhile, the ten-month period which had culminated with the Dow at 1,248 in June saw the greatest outpouring of paper ever created by the corporations in financial history. The great demand for stocks fathered the supply which would soon engulf the market. The lessons of history were very clear. The corporations would overdo it. The dictates of human nature weren't about to reverse and see the corporations feeling sorry for the public and warning them of their greed and the high risks that then existed. They weren't about to turn off the spigot. They had a good thing going and they were going to print all the stock certificates that the traffic would bear. They had a legal right to do this, and they were exercising it to the very limit. It was the next-best thing to printing money. They figured that if people wanted stocks that badly, why should they, the corporations, be the ones to spoil their fun? So, as always, it was *caveat emptor,* let the buyer beware. The corporations were setting the public up to hold the bag in the coming bear market.

And yet, while that tremendous speculative bubble had been building to enormous proportions, an undertow of selling pressure was developing, spelling the end of the brief 1982–83 bull market. Even at that time, long before an additional massive pile of evidence was to surface, the record number of secondary offerings and the most concentrated and persistent insider selling in history were attesting to the disturbing fact that all the good news was being taken advantage of by some very astute sellers. What did all this mean? It simply meant that the most knowledgeable people in the business knew that this was not a normal bull market and that they had to race for the exits just as fast as people would take the stock off their hands.

Robert Stovall appeared on *Moneyline* on July 19 and said that he didn't see anything like 1,100 on the Dow. He then said that the market always makes the majority look foolish. It was a prophetic statement, because that is exactly what the market was going to do. He acknowledged the fact that the market had been slanting downward for the past eleven weeks, but he was not the slightest bit aware that that slant was the forerunner to the severe bear market that lay ahead.

The next day the Dow Jones exploded 30 points higher, the rally attributed to Paul Volcker's remarks pertaining to raising the money supply targets. The rally proved to be a hook but it produced further euphoria. The guest that night on *Moneyline* was Carolyn Cole of Paine Webber. She was long-term bullish, seeing the Dow at 1,340–1,350 for 1983 and as high as 1,700 for 1984, with a minimum upside 1984 target of 1,450–1,500. She saw the stock market as being an interest-rate-driven market. Obviously she had bought the 1983 cover story hook, line, and sinker.

III

Nobody at this time could believe that the 1982–83 rise was going to turn out to be one of the shortest bull markets on record. Virtually everybody, with very few exceptions, viewed the rise as being the *first leg* of a powerful long-term bull market. From the technical point of view, the ten-month rise in the Dow couldn't have possibly been the first leg of a bull market. Major stock distribution to the extent recorded would never occur in the first leg of a bull market. It would require an entire bull market to record that much distribution and, of course, that was the case. The bull market was over.

At this time nobody knew to what degree "off-track betting" was distorting the picture. The whole spectrum of option trading meant that billions of dollars were being wagered on the stock market without a penny of it moving through the New York or American stock exchanges. The losses that were to ensue from this "off-track" area were not included with those recorded by the Wilshire Equity Index, which measures the dollar value of 5,000 stocks.

Lower interest rates had not helped the budgetary deficit problem and had failed also to help the U.S. balance of trade. Higher rates would exacerbate both problems. Consulting my notebooks, I felt strongly that what I was seeing in the market was pretty much what Jesse Livermore saw in early 1929. Throughout late 1982 and the first half of 1983, the double sensations of the stock market—unprecedented volume and soaring prices—had been front-page news. That was the most definitive of the 1929 parallels. Now the killer of all bull markets began to stir—interest rates. I saw the same dilemma facing the federal authorities that Livermore saw in 1929: If they raised the interest rate, it could seriously handicap the economic recovery, but if they didn't, the recovery could later generate inflation. A rise in rates would not please the Reagan administration, which was facing an election year, but my gut instincts told me that Paul Volcker would not play footsie with the administration. Thus the stage was being set for a major impasse in 1984. I was seeing the same technical situation that had confronted Livermore in 1929, the subsurface decline not yet being adequately reflected by the popular Dow Jones Industrial Average. The world situation was becoming "uneasy," but the general public was going about its business totally unaware of the chess stalemate that could only be resolved by a bust.

Everything in the marketplace by this time was almost diametrically opposite to August 1982. I carefully reviewed the evidence and again stressed my five principal areas of concern: new issues, low-priced stocks, stock splits, secondary offerings, and insider selling. By July 25 a particularly significant article by Ann M. Morrison, "Boom Time for Equity Mutual Funds," appeared in *Fortune*. Most interesting was the chart that accompanied the article. It stretched across two pages and showed the flow of dollars into and out of equity mutual funds from 1965 to date. Compared to what happened in the 1982–83 period, the rest of the chart looked virtually flat. The article stated: "The money pouring into equity mutual funds, which invest in common stocks, dwarfs the previous surge in 1968–69. Throughout the Seventies, when stocks in general performed listlessly most of the time, investors drained more money out of these funds than was coming in. April's record $1.8 billion in net sales was boosted by investors rushing in to beat the deadline for setting up 1982 individual retirement accounts." The chart indicated that the resurgence of interest in equity mutual funds constituted a true parabolic rise, and for those who had forgotten, the mutual fund surge of 1968–69 led into a severe bear market in stocks. It was one more significant piece of evidence pointing toward the predicted 1983 bear market then underway.

PARALLEL 39

Market
Formation of New Mutual Funds

The 1982–83 period was no different from that of 1929 in the formation of new mutual funds. Back in 1929 there were over 500 investment trusts, most of them formed during or near the end of the bull market. Prudential-Bache started a new mutual fund on June 13, 1983, based on analysts' choices. A month later it was down 5 percent compared to a 2.3 percent drop in the Dow Jones Industrial Average. That firm was reported at the time as saying that there was only a 10 percent chance that the bull market was over. They had it backwards. If they had said that there was only a 10 percent chance that the bull market was still alive, they would have been much closer to the truth.

By late July the Reagan administration made it official that the recession had ended. Interestingly enough, my buy signal of April 21, 1980, which had sent the Dow soaring over 30 points the next day, coincided with the Carter administration's announcing that an economic recession was official. Obviously, if a genuine buy signal can accompany an officially recognized recession, then a genuine sell signal can accompany an officially recognized end of a recession.

With the anniversary of the August 1982 bottom coming up in a few days, there was much speculation that the market would again explode into that magical second leg of the great bull market. All predictions now were for the Dow to close out the year above 1,300.

The first decline coming off a top was not going to have much effect on speculative sentiment, which was as strong as ever, as reflected by the publication of the June figures for margin debt, a new record at $17.9 billion. It was also, accelerating rapidly.

The biggest unknown was the shadow market where ersatz stock was created. One could participate in the stock market via options with no statistical impact on the New York Stock Exchange or one could create an ersatz portfolio of stocks by participating in index options. The growth of the option market was masking the full extent of the size of the speculative bubble.

IV

Having completed an enormous top formation, the market gave every signal that it was readying for a straight-down smash. All the early warnings had been flashing after the internal top of late April, and by the time the external top was seen on June 16, there was no technical justification for holding any stocks. The market had shifted from a bull market to a bear market right in the face of the extreme Wall Street optimism. The Wilshire 5000 Equity Index had shown a drop of $56 billion in stock values following the brief 30-point Volcker rally and the Wilshire highs were not to be seen again for a long time. But the media continued to describe the stock market in terms of wine and roses.

The optimists based their rosy forecasts primarily on expected higher corporate earnings. Nobody could fault their evidence, but, on the other hand, neither could a historian escape seeing the great parallel with 1929, when similar fundamental evidence of corporate well-being masked the great trouble that was soon to befall all markets.

PARALLEL 40

Historical
Great Expectations for Corporate Earnings

I used the 1973 market peak to expose the major cover story that was certain to entrap the majority in the 1983–84 period. The big cover story on Wall Street as the year 1973 was starting was the outlook for rising corporate earnings. It was not a question whether the forecasts on earnings were correct or not. Corporate earnings did rise sharply in 1973 and 1974, but apparently it had all been *discounted*, because in 1973 and 1974 stocks were in the grip of a severe bear market. The cornerstone of the 1983 bullish scenario was corporate earnings. The bulls explained the first leg of the bull market as based on the economic recovery. They were banking on the second leg to be based on rising corporate earnings. The choice was clear: either one could rely on the bullish earnings forecasts and get caught up in the developing bear market or one could accept the warning of market history and step aside. The majority chose to follow earnings, and, as in 1973 and 1929, it was a bad choice.

In the first week of January 1973, the *Barron's* roundtable made its forecasts for the year: all the members looked for 1,200 on the Dow for 1973. They were right about the 1,200 level, but it took ten years to get there. Instead of going to 1,200, the Dow collapsed from 1,051 to 577. A January 1973 *Barron's* article stated that 1,200 on the Dow was a modest expectation for the 1973 market. All agreed that the outlook for business was good and that rising interest rates did not pose a threat to the recovery. *Barron's* said that price/earnings ratios would follow corporate profits. They looked for a 10 to 15 percent rise in profits, and they agreed that 1973 would be a good year for the market. One member of the panel thought the Dow would climb to between 1,100 and 1,200 and then fall back to the current level of around 1,000. Another saw a catch-up phase for second-tier stocks selling at moderate price/earnings ratios.

That was an exact fit with the general scenario of late July 1983. Just about everybody and his brother were looking for the Dow to close out the year well above the 1,300 level. Nobody was worried about a rise in interest rates, because an election year loomed ahead and that suggested to most people lower interest rates. All agreed that rising corporate earnings would be the driving force to take the Dow over 1,300. They felt that all pullbacks would be modest, and they all thought that stocks then coming down would have to play catch-up later with a rising Dow. But nobody thought at that time to read the *Barron's* roundtable account of January 1973 and learn a valuable lesson, least of all its brilliant editor, Robert Bleiberg, who was a roaring bull in June when we shared the podium in Montreal.

The Wall Street Journal quotes at this time reflected the January 1973 sentiment: "The market has been consolidating the past few sessions," commented Chester Pado, vice president of technical analysis at G. Tsai & Co., Los Angeles. "The fact that selling pressure didn't build up and that volume tended to contract when the market was retreating indicates it will head higher again soon. We look for the summer rally to carry the industrial average to the 1,300 level or higher."

Henry T. Blackstock of Blackstock & Co., Jacksonville, Florida, asserted that "we don't look for interest rates to rise much further, although they may stay near current levels through the third quarter, and we now believe that this moderate rise in rates will do little to slow the growth rate of the business recovery."

Then the quotes of July 27, when the Dow was poised to make new highs:

"Investors became aggressive buyers as many earnings reports exceeded analysts' expectations," observed Jacques S. Theriot, senior vice president at Smith Barney Harris Upham. "The absence of any negative news on the interest rate front coupled with new highs for GM and IBM forced sideliners to commit funds."

"The gross national product has been expanding at a much greater rate than had been expected, and this means that the earnings numbers of many individual companies are going to be better than has been expected," asserted William J. Landes, president of W. J. Landes & Co., Milwaukee. "And even though interest rates have blipped up, we expect them to stay at current levels or decline."

Peter Glanville, head of research at Dain Bosworth, Minneapolis, contended that the market was "responding to favorable earnings progress." Asserting that "earnings will be the key over the coming year," he said, "the current market has demonstrated underlying strength unlike anything seen in recent history."

Since early May, the bull market experienced a "pause" or "intermission," said Robert E. Walsh, first vice president at Rotan Mosle, Houston. This period allowed "various industry group and individual issues to regroup and

consolidate the substantial price increases which have been achieved since August 1982," he added, observing that "similar sideways resting periods" had occurred in last November and December.

The July 27 break did little to stem the continued bullishness of the Street. The next day in the *Journal* the bullish quotes continued:

Ernest Rudnet, managing director of block trading at L. F. Rothschild Unterberg Towbin, agreed that the "IBM report was just an excuse for selling the technology issues which had been in a weak technical position for the last few weeks." As for the general market, he said that "people became discouraged when the industrial average wasn't able to hold its new highs." However, he added, "we're still in a bull market, and after this correction has been completed we expect the technology issues to lead the market to new high ground."

And on the same day, John Brush of Columbine Capital Services, Colorado Springs, stated, "As soon as the really good corporate profit numbers are chalked up we'll see the next leg of the bull market. Over the next six months, long-term interest rates should be flat, and short-term rates will rise a little."

There was absolutely no statistical comparison that would show the July 1983 period as being similar to the previous November and December of 1982. One only had to riffle through any chart book and view the extreme deterioration that had been taking place while the Dow Jones Industrial Average was mesmerizing the public. There, one would have seen the increasing number of stocks starting to move under their long-term trendlines. Technology stocks could not lead the market to new high ground because their break in the summer of 1983 had broken their technical backbones, something that wouldn't happen in a continuing bull market in a stock group that most thought would lead a second bull market leg. The market seldom accommodates the majority, and the overwhelming majority were all long-term bullish.

The majority were all relying on normal measurements and did not realize that their assured "long-term" bull market had already died in the spring of 1983.

One of the outstanding characteristics which showed the bull cycle to be of relatively short duration was the early influx of the public. *The Wellington Letter*[1] in its July issue referred to that phenomenon, pointing out that stock purchases by individuals in the market bottoms of 1970, 1974, and 1978 ranged from a negative $3.5 to $8.9 billion but was a staggering positive reading of $33.9 billion in August 1982. Additional evidence of the extraordinary public interest in the market was shown in terms of equity mutual fund sales. *The Wellington Letter* pointed out that in the market bottoms of 1966,

[1]Bert Dohmen-Ramirez, *The Wellington Letter* (newsletter), Honolulu, Hawaii, 1983.

1970, 1974, and 1980, mutual fund sales ranged from $128.8 million to $394.5 million, but in August 1982 swelled to $1.66 billion!

The initial warning of major trouble ahead had been the breakdown of the price structure of the technology stocks. The same thing had happened in 1929 to the super growth industries of that time—the radio and movie stocks.

6

Last of
the Summer Heat

[AUGUST 1983]

I

By early August the Dow had declined 64 points since the morning of July 27 in the sharpest break thus far since the rise started in August 1982. According to the Wilshire 5000 Equity Index, $91 billion in stock values had been wiped out. Ironically, the Reagan tax cut was going to pump $35 billion back into the economy, but almost three times that amount had gone up in smoke on Wall Street.

Everything on the downside was passed off as a correction. The chorus went like this: *We see interest rates declining and corporate earnings rising. We think the Dow has solid support at 1,180 but might temporarily drop to 1,150; however, thereafter we see the Dow between 1,300 and 1,400 by the end of the year.* Day after day Wall Street pundits appeared on the nightly TV and their words were parroted by the media commentators.

By this time brokers were getting many calls from worried speculators who couldn't understand why their stocks were going down. The concern was mostly stemming from larger-than-normal declines in the over-the-counter market and stocks listed on the American Stock Exchange. Broker recommendations at this time were switching from buy to hold. I could never understand the sense of such advice. If a stock isn't rated a buy, why hold it? Wall Street, convinced that the stock market was in the longest and strongest of bull markets, was quick to pass off the declines in the more speculative stocks as a non-event, believing that as long as the Dow Jones Industrial Average was in a bull trend everything would have to follow.

The collapse in these speculative markets was my best proof of what was to follow. All new issue booms had been followed by severe market downturns, the market glutted with worthless paper. The same conclusions were applicable to the over-the-counter market. Nobody could accurately gauge the amount of money being lost there. It had to be tremendous. While the Wilshire 5000 Equity Index is, of course, comprehensive, the over-the-counter market deals with over 25,000 stocks. Those stocks were being hurt badly, and what was the advice the public were getting at that time from stockbrokers? HOLD. If the Dow Jones Industrial Average had done what the over-the-counter market had done in the first week of August, it would have dropped over 100 points. I was critical at this time of the worth of the NASDAQ Composite Index. Convinced that it was not giving a true reflection of the damage then taking place, I compiled a list of outstanding decliners, proving that what was going on was comparable to the worst of the percentage declines at the bottom of the 1929 crash. In studying the figures below, keep in mind that this was in August 1983, three months prior to the peaking of the Dow Jones Industrial Average.

Stock	High	Low	Last	% Decline
Adac Labs	27.38	9.75	13.00	52
Altos	39.00	12.50	13.75	64
Amarxanh	6.38	.75	2.13	66
Apollo C	50.50	25.75	36.25	28
Apple Com	63.25	12.00	34.88	44
Bliss	40.75	6.00	22.00	45
Brw Tom	14.63	4.88	8.38	42
C Cor	35.75	14.75	16.50	54
Carolin	20.75	7.00	11.38	45
Cobe Labs	31.75	10.25	20.00	37
Coir Tie	28.00	13.88	16.13	42
ComAm	15.25	6.38	6.63	56
Compop	23.25	9.13	11.50	50
CmpDv	21.25	6.88	7.50	64
Cmputn	37.75	13.25	13.75	63
Cmsrve	20.25	10.00	11.00	45
Diasonc	29.75	15.00	15.25	48
Diglog	27.50	9.25	14.25	48
ElModl	25.00	11.50	12.00	52
Fortn S	22.50	8.38	9.38	58
Graph Sc	28.88	7.88	16.75	42
Hithdy	54.25	13.75	25.75	49
Lama T	29.00	12.38	16.25	44
McRae O	16.63	9.00	9.63	42
NtDatC	19.75	3.50	5.25	73
Nuke B s	28.00	15.13	16.75	40

Stock	High	Low	Last	% Decline
Nucl Ph	18.63	9.75	9.75	47
OCG Tc	15.38	3.75	9.25	39
Pizza Tm	28.00	14.25	14.50	47
Ramtek	26.25	11.50	16.00	37
Reeves s	28.63	13.50	14.00	51
Sykes	16.63	5.75	8.33	49
TceCom	28.00	12.25	17.50	37
Telvid	40.50	18.00	21.00	48
Texon	13.00	3.63	5.13	60
TwatEx	6.38	1.50	3.50	45
Triad Sys	27.25	9.50	16.25	40
Vector G	15.25	4.38	5.75	62
Veta	13.75	2.75	4.75	65

I stressed the point then that stocks don't break like that in a continuing bull market. They do break like that, however, in a bear market.

The General Motors Bellwether Theory contributed at this time to confusing people as to what was really going on in the stock market. On April 25, 1983, the stock had provided an all-clear signal ahead by failing to make a new low for four months. A sell signal based on General Motors could not occur any earlier than August 25. But all during these periods between fresh GM signals, the market had topped out and was definitely on the way down in terms of most stocks. This was but one of many things that served to mislead the public at such a critical time. It served to keep most of the public bullish when they should have been selling all their stocks. It pointed up a market truism that should always be followed. Never, ever, swing on one branch. If that branch breaks, those who hang from it become total losers. Those who relied on General Motors to tell them where the market was headed overlooked much more important indicators, such as the Greed Index,[1] the high/low indicator, and the advance/decline line, which all clearly predicted the end of the bull market, a new and severe bear market, and an ensuing panic and crash.

Ironically, Robert H. Stovall, the chief spokesman for the GM Bellwether Theory, headlined his column in the June 15 *Financial World:* "All Clear from GM." The Greed Index had already peaked on June 16. But Stovall's GM signal said to buy at the very worst of times, and he, like everybody else, went down with his signal.

---

[1]The Greed Index was developed by Lee Idleman. Consisting of ten factors, graded 1–10, it measures certain statistics and the confidence—or lack of it—of a cross section of pros who move the market: financial institutions, money managers, and corporate financiers. When their confidence gets really high, so does the greed factor, the stock market, and the index. That is the time to sell. A reading above 60 is a sell signal. The Greed Index was at 69 in March 1983, when the stock market's major troubles really began.

The bulls were looking for an extension of life after death. They loved to talk about rotating strength in the market when it was actually rotating weakness. First one group would top out, then another, then still another. Rotating strength would never have gone from top to top, but from bottom to bottom. When I had given the stern warning in March to Flee for Your Life and had been greeted by total disbelief, there had been well over 300 big board stocks making new highs at that time. Only on two subsequent occasions had the number of new highs touched higher levels than in March: briefly in early May and one more time in mid-June. A review of any chart book revealed an astonishingly high number of big name stocks that had peaked out in March, and subsequent moves showed that all rotation of interest went from weakness to weakness. Delta Air Lines was an excellent example of a big name stock peaking out ahead of the Dow at exactly the time when the Street was totally blinded by its love affair with the airlines in March 1983. The stock was at 51 in March and by early August was down to 30⅛. My market letter headlines in the spring of 1983 were very similar to those of the spring of 1981. The same type of internal weakness was expanding rapidly while the Dow, as late as June 1981, was still trying to act like a bull market. But, as history proved, that market was a dead chicken and had seen its internal top several months before, history proving the validity of my January 7, 1981, sell-everything signal that rocked the world.

My critics at this time were contending that the stock market could not go into a new bear market in 1983 so soon after the bear market of 1981–82 because that went against the grain of the standard four-year market cycle. That is what upset all the cycles people. They were all counting on a normal cycle, and right from the outset, the 1982–83 rise was abnormal in all respects, no different from what took place in the 1928–29 period. These were not normal times. Here the market was sitting on the very pinnacle of financial history and Wall Street, always seeking to feather its own nest, was not going to warn the public about something coming that they could not see.

Newton Zinder made a good observation in the August 4 *Wall Street Journal*, noting that the previous four sessions had seen more than 1,100 declining stocks each day, the first time that had occurred in two years. What he didn't say, however, was that two years earlier the market was bearish, in the early stages of the 1981–82 decline.

By this time, the Wilshire 5000 Equity Index was recording a loss of $109 billion. Still nobody was breathing a word about the bear market. A continuing bull market could not compensate for the degree of damage already seen in the more speculative stocks.

II

Every week I consistently advised my followers to sell all stocks. People did not take the decline to the August 1983 low seriously, still mesmerized by the bullish sermon of long-term advances lying ahead. Whatever rallies were to transpire this month were seen to be final opportunities to clean house before the major smash that all the major technical indicators were pointing toward.

With the Dow at 1,183, Joseph Barthel, director of technical strategy at Butcher & Singer, stated: "Stock prices are close to being at the lowest levels we'll likely see over the next two years."

Terry Diamond of Steiner Diamond, Chicago, said: "Speculation was getting out of hand and, painful as it may be, the correction that's taking place is healthy and necessary if the bull market is to continue. The percentage declines in the smaller-capitalization companies have been significant. If the fundamentals are intact we would start dipping into our dry powder for investment in this sector."

Meanwhile, interest rates were moving up. The yield on three-year Treasury notes had leaped to 11.43 percent, up sharply since the 9.48 percent yield on the May 3 auction. The yield on the thirty-year bond rose to the highest level seen in a year and a half. A bank in Texas raised the prime rate to 11 percent. When queried about the rise in rates, Larry Speakes said that the administration thinks they are just "short-term." What else could he say? After all, lower rates were promised at Williamsburg.

The Dow continued to plummet, coming to a stop at 1,163.06 on August 8. For the developing scenario to continue, it was not necessary that a market crash take place this early. With the market decline coming to a halt on August 8, however, subsequent advances failed to offset the definitive major bearish pattern of the high/low indicator and the advance/decline line which had been put in place in May and June. Regardless of the market's hitting a low now in August 1983, at this stage the high/low indicator was telling a tremendous story. On March 3, as many as 337 stocks were making twelve-month highs. Subsequently, the figure exceeded the 300 level two more times —once on May 6 at 388 and for the last time on June 16 at 306. The lowest number of new highs during that March–June period was 58, recorded on June 1. I looked upon the three peaks above the 300 level as forming a "head and shoulders" pattern, and I designated the 58 figure as the neckline of that formation. That neckline was broken on June 28 when the number of new highs had shrunk to 44. That was the clear sign that the highs and lows were soon to cross, one of the principal characteristics of the developing bear market.

Having the high/low indicator and advance/decline line highs of May–June 1983 carved in stone, I was able to correlate those highs with those of December 1928, and thus my 1929 scenario was keyed to the timing of those two important indicators. Thus the failure of the market to crash on the June–August 1983 slide did not change the relevance of the 1929 scenario. There were market breaks in 1929 prior to the crash, notably that of May 1929.

In May 1929, there was a price break that carried the Dow Jones Industrial Average down to the low of the year on May 27, at 293.42. What followed

next was the famous blowoff rally carrying the Dow to the September 3 peak
of 381.17. The popular conception of that rally was that the market as a whole
ran wild on the upside. Nothing could be further from the truth. To set the
record straight, I refer to an article that appeared on the front page of *The
Wall Street Journal* on July 20, 1929. The headline read as follows: "Stock
Recovery Seen as Limited. Few Selling Higher Than Before May Break.
Selectivity Stabilizes Market. Many Issues Sell Lower." The text of the article
read as follows:

> Measured by all standard indices, the stock market is now in new territory,
> apparently having fully recovered from the spring decline. As a practical matter,
> considering the stock market as a whole, however, comparatively few stocks have
> recovered fully and almost an equal number are currently selling lower than on
> May 27 when the Dow Jones averages reached the year's lowest levels.
>
> On July 17 the market, as measured by the Dow Jones averages, was at
> practically the highest level ever reached. The railroad average was 177.52, only
> 0.55 points below the high of July 15 and 30.34 points above the May 27 low.
> The industrial average was 345.63, only 0.92 points below the year's high regis-
> tered July 8 and 52.21 points above the May 27 low.
>
> A comparison of prices of common stocks July 17 and May 27 shows that out
> of 522 stocks which sold on both days, only 114 are selling higher currently than
> the highest point they had reached prior to the May break. In other words, only
> 22% of these 522 stocks have fully recovered from the spring setback. Even more
> surprising, perhaps, is the fact that 113 stocks out of the 522 currently are selling
> at lower levels than on May 27. There remain, therefore, 295 common stocks that
> have recovered only partly from the May reaction and of these the recovery of
> 85 has been insignificant, for they are selling currently only fractionally higher
> than on May 27.
>
> These figures would appear to indicate that the stock market is now highly
> selective. A study of the 114 stocks that are selling higher now than they had sold
> prior to the break bears out the supposition. It shows that broad advances have
> occurred in only five groups of stocks: rails, utility, foods, chemicals and steels;
> and that the other advances have been widely scattered among individual compa-
> nies in many industries.

▬▬▬▬

PARALLEL 41
Market
Dow Embarks on Solitary Walk

In August 1983, the Dow bottomed after the first major reaction coming off
the true May–June highs. It was at this point that the march to still higher
Dow highs was to begin, a run for the roses similar to the May–September

1929 rally. The bulk of all stocks failed to follow the Dow, however, thus matching the identical "solitary walk" in 1929 that preceded the great crash.

This was one of the most striking of the 1929 parallels, the steady loss of upside momentum—one stock after another topping out while the Dow industrials gave the surface impression of continued strength. The great selectivity of the 1929 market just a month prior to the top was aptly shown by the fact that on July 30, 1929, seven stocks made new highs and 32 made new lows, the crossing of the high/low indicator in what was popularly described as a runaway market just a few weeks before the greatest crash in history.

This was the identical evidence that so disturbed Jesse Livermore, Joe Kennedy, and Roger Babson. The market was not keeping pace with the popular averages. The identical evidence in 1983 was equally overwhelming. I now had the parallel evidence of the May 1929 break with the June–August 1983 downturn. It was an important precursor of the major trouble to occur further down the road. Now the market was about to provide an illusion of strength, the final run-up with strength mainly confined to a handful of blue chip stocks.

Having such precise evidence, I could confidently, week after week, tell my followers to sell all stocks. I saw the sucker rallies ahead as occurring so as to distribute a vast amount of stock, and thus warned my readers in my August 1983 market letters to recognize all such coming rallies for what they were— sucker rallies.

III

Going into late August, it was important to review the big picture. The Dow Jones Industrial Average had risen 472 points in the short but violent bull market of 1982–83, cresting in June 1983 at 1,248.30. Thereafter, a reaction set in which had dropped the average to 1,163.04 by August 8. Wall Street proclaimed that 85-point drop as a *correction* in an ongoing major bull market. My letters, with overwhelming evidence, had shown that decline as the start of a bear market.

PARALLEL 42

Psychological
Bear Market Met with Disbelief

At the start of all bear markets, they are greeted with mass disbelief. Some would begin to believe in the bear market when the Dow moved under the 1,100 level, but nobody was believing it after the upturn from the August low of 1,163.04. Such beliefs in lower stock prices were remote at this time because the Dow was crossing the 1,200 level again on the August rally. The public, with their visions of higher Dow levels ahead, had based their belief on the illusion of hope. There is a strong tendency in bear markets for the Dow to mount a rally sixty days after the top. I saw such rallies as continuing opportunities to clean house before the major smash that was coming.

Psychologically, the late August heat was not surprising. The anniversary of the famous August 1982 bottom had occurred earlier in the month. In keeping with that anniversary, I had thought it fitting to return to Minneapolis, where I had been at the time of the August 1982 upturn. There I made my fifty-first speech since March 6, documenting step by step the approach of the predicted start of the severe bear market in 1983. Since people love anniversaries, it was fitting and proper that there be an anniversary rally of sorts in the market. What was seen was close to a carbon copy of July 26. It was only the Dow industrials celebrating the anniversary. There were only moderate rallies in the over-the-counter market and the American Stock Exchange and the transports were sadly lagging.

The TV commentators were ecstatically reporting the move back above the Dow 1,200 level. Listening to them and the bulk of all stock market analysts, one would have thought that the widely advertised bull market was one year old. Nothing, of course, was further from the truth. The bull market had died on June 16, and thus while August 12 was being celebrated as the one-year anniversary of the bull market, the bull market had not celebrated a one-year anniversary. It had lasted only a brief seven to ten months. As I pointed out at the time, can you imagine then telling a holder of Delta Air Lines, Texas Instruments, Tandy, or Apple Computer that the bull market was a year old?

What was happening in the stock market in 1983 was exactly what happened in 1929. The bulk of the market was no longer following the leaders, and that is exactly what Roger Babson based his famous warning on, which was given on September 5, 1929, two days after the exact Dow peak. *But Babson wasn't bearish enough.* He was warning of an 80-point decline, which would have been a 25 percent drop in the Dow. Instead, the crash took the Dow from 381.17 to 198.69 and ultimately to 41.22. That was a 90 percent wipeout! *The Wall Street Journal* laughed at Babson's prophecy, citing his previous miscalls, but the Dow never recovered from where it was when he gave that final warning. The fact that the stock market in 1929 was no longer following the Dow was documented by the fact that the maximum number of new highs was seen in January 1929, and by the time the Dow peaked in September that year, there were barely more highs than lows, a carbon copy of what was happening in the 1983 stock market.

Just as Wall Street thought the 1929 bull market would spill over into 1930, 1983 bulls thought that the bull market was still alive and would spill over into 1984; just as Wall Street thought that rising corporate earnings would guarantee the continuation of the bull market into 1930, so did Wall Street bet on corporate earnings as the guarantor of new bull market highs to come; just as Wall Street thought that the very large short interest in September 1929 was a precursor of a higher market to come, so did Wall Street think that the current high short interest was a guarantor of higher markets to come; just as Wall Street thought in September 1929 that the decline off the highs was a correction in an ongoing bull market, so did Wall Street see every drop after June 1983 as a correction in an ongoing bull market.

The public at this time were being bombarded with a plethora of new market letters, and the record would show that in the next one to two years most of them would go under. And, as I have said, *this was one of the most certain of the 1929 parallels.* Some of them went to outlandish lengths to entice the public to subscribe. One of them was offering 100 shares of stock in a publicly owned company free with a year's subscription to the letter. A two-year subscription would give the subscriber 300 shares of free stock. The prospective subscriber was then told that, in October 1982, Basis, Inc., was recommended at one cent a share. Five months later it could have been sold for nine cents a share, an 800 percent profit. In April 1983, Du Pont Instruments Corp. was recommended at one cent a share. By May it hit fourteen cents, a 1,300 percent profit in one month. Those were the claims designed to entrap the prospective new subscriber. Obviously, the free stock promised was a penny stock. The publisher of the stock market letter would give $1 worth of stock in return for a $70 subscription or $3 worth of stock for a $115 subscription. The reader of the literature was then told: "The underlying favorable trend will carry the Dow Industrial Average to the 2,000 level— according to the Value Line Investment Survey." I was certain that that quoted phrase had been well used by the new crop of penny stock newsletters to sell their wares. While Indian Bingo had seemed to be the ultimate in new issues, this seemed to be the ultimate in the 1983 generation of new market letters. It demonstrated a flagrant disregard for the welfare of the subscriber and was simply a get-rich-quick scheme for the benefit of the newsletter promoter. It was the typical newsletter that would quickly disappear in the developing severe bear market.

IV

The August upturn brought with it a whole new generation of bullish forecasts. Bob Nurock was a guest on *Moneyline* on August 17 and saw 1,400 for the Dow by the end of the year. On August 29 Standard & Poor announced that the market would turn in a month and go up 30 percent in 1984. That would mean a Dow of 1,552 in 1984, one of the more ridiculous of the forecasts. On *Moneyline* on August 29, Charles Comer, caught up in the fallacious "second leg" school of thought, equated the market with the 1975–76 period.

━━━━━━━━

PARALLEL 43
Market
Parabolic Rise in Margin Debt

Margin debt expanded substantially in the late 1920s, and it was the liquidation of that debt which contributed to the severity of the crash and the ensuing great bear market. Traditionally, rising margin debt was supposed to be a bullish sign. It obviously reflected the willingness on the part of an increasing number of people to open margin accounts, a sign of confidence. But all movements tend to go to extremes, as they did in 1929, and rising margin debt *after* the market had technically proven the bull market was over in 1983 was an important precursor to the trouble that was to follow. The more rapid the rate of climb in margin debt, the more likely the rise was entering a terminal stage. By August 1983, the rise could already be seen to be a parabolic curve. The debt in round numbers had grown from $10 billion in August 1982 to over $18 billion a year later. The implications for the stock market were ominous. The bigger the bubble grew, the louder the burst would be. Already standing at the highest level in financial history, the historic parallel was crystal clear. As brokers' loans in 1929 exceeded an unheard-of $8 billion, the crash that followed halved that debt in only nine weeks. In other words, such excessive debt correlates with the degree of severity of the liquidation that follows it when the stock market crashes.

A bear market wreaks havoc on the potential for capital gains, and when that realization sinks in, the liquidating trend commences. Margin debt has flattened or declined within three months of all but one of every market peak since 1932. Unless the stock market, by some unseen miracle, got a new lease on life, I contended, the bull market ended on June 16.

The bearish potential of rising margin debt was made clearer when it was compared with what was normally considered the bullish potential of a rising short interest. All stocks sold short must eventually be bought back or covered; thus the potential buying is normally deemed to be bullish. In a comparison very few people ever take into consideration, all stocks bought on margin must eventually be liquidated, and thus rising margin debt is potentially a source of supply, posing eventual selling pressure. The greater the debt, the greater becomes the ultimate selling pressure.

The parabolic rise in margin debt by August 1983 correlated with the explosive rise in the number of new issues, a veritable paper blizzard which sat on the market like a dead weight. Many of the issues were marginable, and thus all new issues markets were accompanied by big increases in margin debt. But this time, all records were broken. As in 1929, the brief explosive rise of 1982–83 was unprecedented in recent times and could only draw a parallel with the frantic Dow upswing of 1928–29. Margin debt kept pace with that great upward climax. Weak arguments to the contrary would not hold water. One such argument was that never in history had a violent seven- to ten-month bull market been snuffed out in such a brief period of time. But if they had seen that rise as the parabolic blowoff to a nine-year cycle and the culmination of the 54-year Kondratieff Wave, they could have argued just as forcefully as to why it took so long to blow itself out.

Psychologically, people make promises to themselves during bear markets that they forget to keep in bull markets. They see their stocks dropping sharply in a bear market and they promise themselves that if such and such a stock ever gets back to such and such a price, they will get out. The odds are that by the time the stock does get back to their get-out level, the market is then bullish. They forget their promise to themselves and continue to hold on, seeing themselves once again holding at a loss. They then make the old promises to themselves and the cycle repeats. These people I describe as "bag holders." In the movie *The End,* you will recall, Burt Reynolds was trying to commit suicide. He swam out too far and then changed his mind about killing himself. He then began promising God that if he could just get back to shore he would do this and that and anything required of him. As he got close to shore, the memory of the promises began to vanish; when he made it to safety, he was down to only one or two token promises. That is what happened in 1983. People saw their stocks return to levels where they had bought them near the top of the previous bull market in 1981. Forgetting their earlier promises, they continued to hold those stocks well past the 1983 spring peak and a few months later woke up to the sorry fact that once again they had played the role of bag holder.

What happened to MCI, Digital Switch, Convergent Technologies, Apple Computer, and many more issues by this time was not shocking at all. It was normal for a developing bear market. All the shocks were hitting the bulls and not the bears. A bear market shakes complacency and keeps shaking it until there is no complacency left. It had only been a month since *The Wall Street Journal* was quoting a raft of bullish comments. There one read that the summer rally would carry the Dow to 1,300. There one read that the current market was demonstrating underlying strength unlike anything else seen in history. There one read that the market since May had experienced a "pause" or "intermission." Such definitions could not be accepted if you ran your eye down the high, low, and last figures on the over-the-counter stocks. Those stocks were the wave of the future. Those stocks constituted the bloodstream of corporate America, and what people were looking at by late August 1983 in that area was something akin to pernicious anemia. It was certainly not a case of bullish rotation any more than the same sickness in 1929 was a case of bullish rotation. The Dow Jones Industrial Average was not yet reflecting what was going on by this time in most stocks, but it would, and to that there was no exception in financial history.

Corporations did more than their part in helping to create bag holders. Their favorite device was the debt-equity swap. Debt-equity swaps in 1983 were common. In late August, International Harvester's debt-restructuring plan proposed conversion of $600 million of debt to equity. In such cases, the shareholder bears the ultimate burden and the market is not kind when rewarding such stupidity. As the public had assumed the burden of supporting an intolerably large increase in equity creation, the wide acceptance of all that questionable paper occurred virtually at the end of the bull market. And while the blind masses clutched at all that paper at the worst of times, the smart money ran for the exits as quickly as possible, that exodus so well documented by the largest number of secondary stock offerings in history. By this time, that number had climbed to an unprecedented total of 443 during the first eight months of 1983.

PARALLEL 44

Psychological
Advertised Bragging about Past Performance

In 1929, after stocks began to break down, there was evidence here and there of advisory services running ads proclaiming their good past performance right in the midst of the price breakdown. A flagrant example of this was seen in the August 29 *Wall Street Journal*. Fidelity Select Portfolios ran an ad claiming that their technology portfolio had risen 157 percent in the past year. At the time the ad was run, technology stocks were getting killed.

Hope, however, was slow to die. Virtually everybody saw the June–August 1983 downturn as a correction in an ongoing bull market. It was no different in 1929. The market downturn in September 1929 was received with the complacent opinion that the bulls would take charge later in the year. Here was another parallel:

PARALLEL 45

Psychological
Bulls to Resume Charge Later This Year

A headline in the August 29 *Wall Street Journal* on the market page was: "Some Managers Expect the Bulls to Resume Charge Later This Year." That headline might have provided mild encouragement to the bullish contingent, but to a market student steeped in financial history, it simply marked one more of the dozens and dozens of parallels with similar statements made in 1929 just prior to the great crash.

The "Broad Street Gossip" column in *The Wall Street Journal* of September 27, 1929, printed the following comment: "The consensus is that after the current period of adjustment is over, stocks will again rebound and make new highs. They have done so every time since the major bull market began. This, of course, will depend largely on the course of business. If mills and factories continue active through the last quarter of the year and there is a revival in certain lines that are not doing so well, a continuation of the major bull market will be in order. At least, *everything points that way"* (emphasis added).

In the same column in the September 24, 1929, *Journal* appeared the following paragraph: "Basic conditions, so far as business is concerned, are as sound as ever. Some lines of industry are tapering a little. However, in most cases, this is seasonal. *A revival is looked for in the last quarter.* But the falling off in certain lines of business has been offset to a large extent by gains in other lines. The consensus among traders is that *it is still a major bull market* and that prices of the selected issues *will work higher in the last quarter"* (emphasis added).

Meanwhile, returning to *The Wall Street Journal* of August 29, 1983, Kenneth S. Rolland of the Chemical Bank is quoted: "Even if interest rates stay near current levels, investors' confidence still will grow *because of an expected increase in earnings and in their quality"* (emphasis added).

Now for the 1929 parallel. The *correct* expectation of higher third and fourth quarter earnings in 1929 sucked more people into the continued holding of stocks at the top than any other single factor. Here is what one's grandfather was reading in *The Wall Street Journal's* "Broad Street Gossip" column on September 17, 1929: "The stock market will continue under the influence of brokers' loans, *but the actual trend will be governed by earnings of the various lines of industry.* No stock is going off much on increased earnings. Profits of many corporations this year have shown increases of 20% to 75% or more over last year. If earnings next year are to show substantial increases over 1929, market reactions are about all one can expect" (emphasis added).

In the "Abreast of the Market" column in *The Wall Street Journal* of September 24, 1929, the following paragraph appeared: "While many conservative observers are of the opinion that nothing more than irregularity can be looked for during the remainder of the current month because of the uncertainty created by the market recently, it is felt in many quarters that October is likely to be a month of considerable market activity. Factors which could induce a resumption of interest on a large scale *include prospects of remarkably favorable earnings to be reported in the third quarter,* and possible split-ups in various stocks. Another influence might be investment trust funds available for the purchase of standard stocks at favorable prices" (emphasis added).

It had been clear for some time that the consensus in the summer of 1983 was saying that *we were in a continuing major bull market and that prices would resume the upward course sometime in the fall of the year.* That was also the consensus in 1929 just prior to the crash.

On September 18, 1929, the following observation was made in the "Broad Street Gossip" column in *The Wall Street Journal:* "There may be a secondary reaction. This is anyone's guess, *but the traders who have had years of experience in the Street say it is still a major bull market.* Transactions involving billions are scheduled to go through during the next twelve months and everyone knows these cannot be successfully concluded when stocks are declining and the public is in a pessimistic frame of mind" (emphasis added).

Then there was the statement on the front page of *The Wall Street Journal* on September 20, 1929: *"Price movements in the main body of stocks displayed the characteristics of a major bull market"* (emphasis added).

It was this easy and complacent assumption in 1983 that we were still in a bull market that so clearly harked back to the same dangerous assumptions that were made in 1929, as late as a week before the actual crash.

Victor Hillery's column in the August 29 *Journal* started out with a misleading phrase. He said, "The year-long bull market . . ." The bull market did *not* last a year. In terms of the Dow Jones Industrial Average, it lasted ten months, but in terms of *most* stocks it was closer to only seven months.

PARALLEL 46

Psychological
All Reactions Were "Healthy"

Also in the August 29 *Journal,* James D. Hardesty of Mercantile Safe Deposit of Baltimore said: "The market's pullback this summer is 'healthy' because it toned down the level of speculative fascination with high technology and other issues."

Another pullback in market history was termed "healthy." On September 28, 1929, the "Broad Street Gossip" column in the *Journal* stated: "There has been no panicky selling and the market is free of demoralization. The Street terms it *the type of healthy reaction* from which there is always a substantial recovery. Whether or not stocks have bottomed, no one can say, but the consensus is that many good stocks bought at current prices will return substantial profits in the long run" (emphasis added).

It can be seen here that the worst of all market fetishes that entrap the majority is corporate earnings. That factor, more than any other, is what catches people off guard at a major market top. Since earnings are a lagging indicator, they are still going up after a bull market has changed to a bear market. Since most people follow earnings, they are completely blind to the major change of trend. They are following a useless will-o'-the-wisp.

On October 24, 1929, *The Wall Street Journal* carried an interview with the famous economist Irving Fisher of Yale University. That was five days before the fateful crash. In that interview, Fisher presented the ridiculous notion that the higher stocks go, the less likely they will be sold because of the high income-tax payments on the profits. He concluded that the higher stocks go, the more likely they are to go still higher. Here are the actual words of the Yale University economist:

> A holder of Allied Chemical and Dye stock told me that he acquired it at 35 and now would like to sell it at over 300 but avoids doing so because he would be soaked in his income tax if he shifted the investment in something else. This means that the stocks which advance the most will not be sold, or sold the most reluctantly, or only on a still greater advance. That is, the more they advance, the more they tend to advance still further.

This comes under the heading of "ridiculous theories," but it had credibility at the time because it came from an academic authority.

The reasons given for an extension of the 1982–83 bull market were just as ridiculous, but instead of being beamed to 3 million shareholders as in 1929, the 1983 message was aimed at 42 million shareholders.

V

<hr>

PARALLEL 47

Market
Raising of Dividend Payments

Another factor in 1929 that severely hooked the bulls was the assured outlook for higher dividend and interest payments slated for the latter months of that year. Here are some further choice quotes from the *Journal:*

September 19, 1929: "October is one of the biggest months of the year from the viewpoint of dividend and interest payments. Thus it is safe to say that October 1929 will break all past records in this respect. Therefore, so say the bulls, there will be good buying of securities from money paid out in October to share- and bondholders."

October 4: "October dividends and interest now being paid to holders may run in excess of $750,000,000, the largest in history, of course. Payments in November and December will also be record-breaking. There will be disbursed $1,000,000,000 or more in January, to say nothing of bonuses and other end-of-the-year payments. *A large part of this money will be available for investment and help to support securities popular with the investment classes"* [emphasis added].

It was difficult for most people in 1983 to envisage a severe bear market because they were looking at the identical things that entrapped the majority in 1929. The economic recovery appeared to be on such a "sound" footing. Who would have had the audacity to suggest that the bull market would be over in a mere ten months? But I stressed this strongly in the blowoff letter of April 23, 1983, underscoring the point that the entire upswing since August 1982 was *an ending to the great cycle and not the beginning of one.*

7

The Emperor
Wore No Clothes

[SEPTEMBER 1983]

I

The summer decline in 1983 did not produce widespread heavy selling because most people thought the bull market was being threatened in no serious way. Volume was running at substandard levels. The media, impressed by the lack of concerted selling pressure, repeatedly misinterpreted the light volume as being very bullish. The correct reason for the lighter volume on the summer slide was the fact that an increasing number of holders were becoming locked in to the higher prices of May and June and were now holding their stocks at losses. They didn't have the degree of buying power that they had earlier in the spring when stocks were topping out. If one had purchased a stock at 50 and it was now down to 33, the buying power for the next turn was seriously impaired. The market would not and could not go up with the force of several months earlier. This was an increasingly bearish omen for the market.

Kicking the new month off, Lee Idleman was the guest on *Moneyline*. He did a good job of sketching in the popular cover story, the story that was to ensnare the majority as the market prepared to go diametrically opposite to what that popular cover story portrayed. He saw nothing of importance on the downside, expecting the Dow to stay in its high range. He looked for a strong economy and said that the summer decline had slowed greed. He was referring to his Greed Index, which had peaked in March 1983, but there was no reference to when it had peaked. He thought it was better to be in stocks than in bonds and he stated that corporate profits would be higher in 1984. He especially liked cyclical stocks, energy, and basic metals. That was pretty much the popular view, and it was a hard one to knock because what they were leaning on was solid. The only problem was that it had very little to do with the stock market. Yes, corporate earnings were slated to rise, the economy was getting stronger, and everybody knew 1984 was a presidential election year. It would have been difficult not to be bullish. However, the market was not properly responding to these things. Memories were short. Sure, corporate earnings were rising and would also rise in 1984, but they had risen sharply in 1973 and 1974, and that period was the worst since 1929. Most people were following the economy and that was their major error. People don't buy and sell the economy, they buy and sell stocks, and the majority of stocks were no longer following the economy. As for the 1984 election year, that was to go hand in hand with probably the greatest of all bull traps.

Probably at no other point in financial history had so many believed that the bull market was good for another twelve to eighteen months. Ironically, this belief had extended well past the time when technical analysis had attended the funeral and quietly ushered in a new bear market which promised to be the most severe in fifty-four years. I had expected only very few people to take me seriously because it was human nature to shy away from advice that was so out of step with the pack.

The arguments against my thesis came thick and fast. Since I had such clear documentation that the market was in the first phase of the new bear market, it was fun knocking down the expected bull arguments. As fast as they could be contrived, they could be demolished with counterarguments based on the history of 1929. *Argument number one:* This market cannot go down importantly because there is a very high short interest. That argument was easy to handle. The short interest was at a record high in September 1929, a month before the crash. *Argument number two:* The market cannot go down importantly because there was a period of high corporate earnings ahead. That one was equally easy to knock down. The majority opinion after the Dow peaked in early September 1929 was looking for higher corporate earnings to turn the market around in the fourth quarter. *Argument number three:* Most market letters are bearish. In September and October 1929, 75 percent of all the market letters were bearish. *Argument number four:* There is a vast amount of money sitting on the sidelines awaiting investment. That argument has been used at the outset of virtually every bear market in history. In 1929 it was used extensively, the favorite argument then being the $2 billion that was to be paid out in increased dividends and interest payments between October 1929 and January 1930. That was a great deal of money in those days, inasmuch as the annual income in 1929 was $90 billion. *Argument number five:* The Dow cannot go down importantly because the blue chips are being used as a haven of safety. After the general list tops out, attention is always riveted on the blue chips, a handful of leaders, their temporary strength masking the developing bear market until it is too late. The new issue market and low-grade stocks take the lumps first and then money is increasingly concentrated in the blue chip stocks, exactly what happened in 1929.

The most popular bullish argument was that the market could not go down importantly in an election year. It was a foregone conclusion that President Reagan would run for reelection in 1984. To say that that was proof positive that the market could not go down importantly made as much sense as saying that the market could not go down in 1931 and 1932 because President Hoover intended to run for reelection in 1932. But the stock market at this time was telling a story of major trouble ahead, and the only stock market authority is the stock market itself.

From the very outset, I had to make a key assumption. If that assumption was wrong, then my entire crash thesis was wrong. That assumption was simply that this was *not* a normal cycle. Nothing happened thereafter even remotely to threaten that assumption. Right from the August 1982 upturn something was wrong. One could simplify and say that any market upturn that makes the front page of *Time* magazine was heading for trouble, but of course there was much more to it than that. Virtually everything went into a parabolic curve, setting all-time records—new issues, low-priced stocks, stock splits, money flowing into mutual and pension funds, the hiring of new brokers, the number of market letters, the number of secondary stock offerings, the degree of insider selling, the rise of margin debt, the low mutual fund liquidity, mergers and acquisitions, and the number of new money managers. The most pronounced parabolas were in price and volume, and thus there was a solid foundation supporting my initial assumption. The brief 1982–83 rise had to be an ending rather than a beginning. Kondratieff was coming full circle.

Since most people were expecting a normal cycle, they were ill prepared for the series of upsetting market moves and events that were to predominate in the months ahead. In terms of my "wineglass" principle, rising bearish sentiment would eventually break the wineglass as it had done in 1929. At this time, it was the most misunderstood area of market analysis. If this had been a normal market cycle, then the normal parameters of sentiment would have provided reliable buy and sell signals. Too many bulls would constitute a sell signal and too many bears would constitute a buy signal. But if the wineglass was to be broken, then the point would have to be reached where the market looked radically oversold and an overwhelming number of bears were in evidence, such a condition occurring just prior to the crash. Since absolutely nobody was looking for a crash, nobody expected all those checks and balances to go out the window.

When the Dow peaked on September 3, 1929, one of the outstanding characteristics of the decline that followed was how quickly the Street turned bearish. It was reported that 75 percent of all market letters were bearish. The brokerage houses of the day were constantly telling their clients to lighten up on all rallies and to do buying only on a scale-down. If one had adopted normal measurements, with that degree of sentiment one would have been a raving bull all the way down into the crash. In other words, sentiment indicators only work in a normal market. The market in 1983 was not a normal market. In time, market sentiment was going to turn very bearish and it would not help the market one bit. It is axiomatic that the market cannot crash until most people are bearish, when most people want to sell at the same time. Ironically, all the bears in 1929 were *short-term* bears. Nobody saw the crash coming. Even Roger Babson, who had predicted a smash from Dow 381 to 300, had nothing in mind comparable to what actually did happen—the crash to Dow 198 that year and the ultimate debacle to Dow 41 by July 1932. In 1983, the most bearish signal the market could render was already on the technical drawing board, but it was not to be triggered until 1984. That signal is sounded when the market turns a deaf ear to what would normally be considered bullish sentiment signals, the market continuing to go down in the face of the mounting bearishness.

Another key 1929 parallel was in the making at this time, but it was not to surface until 1984. It could be presented only *after* the crash. That parallel, then only a potential, was that *nobody was bearish enough.* By September 1983, the most bearish forecasts saw nothing under 1,100 in the Dow. The majority was married to the concept that 1982 had ushered in the longest and strongest of all bull markets. They were completely blind to the important broadening top formation then in evidence. They paid no heed to all those areas which had shown parabolic rises, the peaking in such areas having always been followed by bear markets. They were all looking for that great "second leg" to their bull market, completely ignoring the overwhelming evidence that their bull market had died and had already given them three completed legs by the spring of 1983.

The post-Labor Day advance was seen to be the most blatantly false show of strength since the transitory Volcker rally in July. The bulk of the general list had failed to follow the leaders and the specialists were setting themselves up again for a killing.

It was at this time that I addressed a crowd of over a thousand at the Royal York in Toronto, reiterating every point of the developing bear market. The die was cast. There was no turning back.

II

The Dow Jones Industrial Average hit an intraday high of 1,262.80 on September 12, and that was the precise moment when the Emperor was caught naked. If you owned a home computer and had the software correctly programmed to follow the stock market, then that computer would have flashed red and told you to sell everything immediately. September 12 was the classic example of the *solitary walk*—namely, that the Dow wandered off course into dangerous airspace and it became obvious that it was going to be shot down.

The Dow walked alone, totally unaccompanied by the rest of the market. Not one single indicator confirmed the September opening upsurge. One could have pictured a military leader named General Dow. General Dow attempted to lead his troops through the stock market Maginot Line, and just when he thought he was ready to go for the big kill, he shouted orders to his troops to advance, and then, turning around, he made the shocking discovery that his troops had totally deserted him. He stood alone facing the enemy, naked and without support. Naturally the enemy shot him on sight. Thus, the 30-point reversal on high volume was the only possible conclusion that could follow such a serious military faux pas. Every attempt to better the Dow 1,248.30 level had been turned back and this latest attempt, which had appeared to be the most serious threat to the bears, had reversed with great authority, verging on a rout.

I had called attention to the fact that Wall Street hires at the top and fires at the bottom. I had referred to the heavy hiring of brokers in the spring of 1981 and saw it then in that cycle as an important precursor to the 1981–82 bear market. Now it was time to refer to it again. In the September 5, 1983, issue of *Barron's* it was stated that the National Association of Securities Dealers reported that more than 4,000 persons took the broker-dealer exam in the previous month, a record number. That boosted the 1983 total to more than 24,000, breaking the annual record of 23,509 set in 1982. That made a total of almost 48,000 brokers hired since the 1982 bottom. As in the spring of 1981, there was solid proof that we had seen the top in this market.

By this time, the charts of all the brokerage house stocks were in severe downtrends. The reason for their bear market trends was simple. Volume had peaked months ago, and that was the characteristic early warning of all bear markets. Volume precedes price. The brokerage house stocks were clearly indicating tough times ahead for the brokerage industry over the next six to eighteen months. As business fell off, their expenses rose and they were to pay the price for their blindness and greed at the spring 1983 peak.

In July I had been very excited over the implications of the 2–1 split in the American Stock Exchange Market Value Index. Inasmuch as any split is a form of distribution, I had treated it as an extremely bearish signal. The split had been effective as of July 5, just short of the 500 level, putting the next index just under 250. Despite the early September euphoria stemming from the turn following the August low, the new Amex index had come back only to 235, pitifully short of the July peak. Many said, "But give it a chance. It may come back to a new high soon." Such a bullish hope was quickly destroyed by a look at the other Amex statistics. For instance, when the 2–1 split in the Amex Market Value Index was announced, the Amex high/low indicator had completely collapsed, and by August the number of new lows was exceeding the number of new highs for the first time since August 1982. Upside/downside volume had already peaked at the end of May 1983 and had accelerated on the downside following the 2–1 split in the index. More important, the Amex advance/decline line had peaked by the third week of June and it, too, had plummeted following the 2–1 split announcement. Significantly, the Amex advance/decline line was by this time back to the January 1983 levels, when the adjusted level of the index had stood at 175. That clearly implied an early break in the index below the thirty-week moving average, which then stood at the 218 level. Most revealing of all, if one had examined the long-term chart of the Amex index, he would have discovered that a major nine-year cycle was ending with the 1983 blowoff, the end of a perfect parabolic rise. That was also a picture of the stock market in the decade of the 1920s, that same cycle having matured in 1929. All in all, as previously cited, the 2–1 split in the Amex index on July 5 was the technical kiss of death. It was the last nail in the coffin of the Amex bull market, which had suffered an untimely and inconvenient early demise.

There were growing concerns that one could feel and sense among the overcrowded bullish fraternity. John Templeton was a guest on *Wall Street Week*. He was concerned about the new issues market and told Louis Rukeyser that he never advised buying them. He was also concerned about the fact that never had he seen a new issue boom this *early* in the cycle. That had been one of the cornerstones of my contention that the bull market was ending in the spring of 1983. Mr. Templeton also said that his mutual funds were seeking most of their investments now outside of the United States. Reading between the lines, one could see that John Templeton was having growing concerns over the U.S. stock market.

Many were continuing to grind out the standard forecast, which went something like this: The Dow would close out the year somewhere between 1,300 and 1,400, and 1984 would be a year of smooth sailing because it was a presidential election year. No trouble was to be expected until *after* November 1984. But even the most astute were beginning to get some second thoughts. The closest scenario to mine was that of Donald J. Hoppe.[1] He was looking for a crash in 1984. In August, Hoppe's market letter stated the following:

> There is an old Wall Street proverb that the stock market does whatever is necessary to deceive the great majority of speculators. We just had a classic example of this when the Dow Jones Industrial Average gave not one but two false buy signals in July, just before plunging almost 100 points in two weeks. In past issues of the *Donald J. Hoppe Analysis* I have used the Kondratieff cycle, Elliott waves and various other cycles, individually and in combination, to project a final supercycle top for the New York Stock Exchange in 1984. Now this could still work out as originally projected, but I'm beginning to get a little concerned about the popularity of this view. I have talked to a number of other analysts who

[1]*Donald J. Hoppe Analysis*, August 1983, Crystal Lake, Ill.

employ cycle projections and cycle theories, and they ALL agree that the final top will not come before 1984, and that New York stock prices will be much higher when it does come. The only disagreement is whether the top will come in 1984, 1985, 1986 or even 1987. With the possible exception of Joe Granville (who is now largely ignored by the Wall Street crowd that once thought him to be infallible) there is hardly anyone who thinks that a primary top in the New York stock market could actually occur in 1983. *Yet there is a considerable amount of evidence, technical, cyclical and fundamental, that this could indeed be the case"* [emphasis added].

The primary function of an attorney is to gather evidence and to present that evidence in such an effective manner that he wins the jury over to his desired verdict. At this time, I felt very much like such a prosecuting attorney. My evidence was so overwhelming and so damning to the stock market that I was certain of getting my verdict of guilty, and that the defendant, the stock market, would be put away for life, and even if it tried to get by on brief shows of good behavior, there would be no parole.

Bullishness was difficult to put down. My voice was lost in a storm of public conviction. Everybody was convinced that the Emperor still had his clothes on and that a huge second leg to the bull market would be well underway by the fourth quarter. I quickly countered with two excellent quotes from *The Wall Street Journal:*

September 12, 1929:

As autumn approaches, Wall Streeters are beginning to show signs of Christmas good cheer. A consensus is building that something big and good will happen in the stock market—whether immediately or after some moderate price correction a few weeks or months ahead. Dreams of a stock market killing are spinning in the heads of margin clerks and moguls alike.

September 23, 1929:

The Street will soon begin talking about big end-of-the-year bonuses, hundreds of millions of end-of-the-year dividend and interest money seeking investment, things that some of the big wealthy corporations propose to put in the stocking of their shareholders, etc. *It certainly looks like the most prosperous Christmas in the history of Wall Street* [emphasis added].

III

By late September, there was increasing illusion, confusion, and deception. The illusion was one of strength. The confusion was seen in the indicator mix. The deception was one of bullish entrapment. Years ago, Gerald Loeb said that when most people think that they have the key to the market, then the market changes the lock. Every market top in history is accompanied by illusion, confusion, and deception. The new closing Dow high of 1,249.19 recorded on September 20 was a technical freak, and not only did not change the bearish scenario one iota but enhanced it. Outside of a .04 confirmation by the Dow Jones Utility Average, not a single indicator confirmed the new Dow high. That was the situation I had observed on January 6, 1981, which had prompted that famous sell-everything signal. When the general market stops following the Dow, then the Dow is sooner or later forced to follow the market. Radio and TV commentators rarely take the time or trouble to make a distinction. The Dow makes a new closing high and they give the public the impression that the market made a new all-time high. That is illusion, confusion, and deception. In this case, did they tell the public that only two stocks in the Dow Jones Industrial Average made new twelve-month highs? Those two stocks were American Brands and General Foods. The fetish with the Dow, as always, was magnified far beyond its importance. It was no different in 1929. Back then, the Dow made an all-time high closing of 381.17 on September 3 and it was no more reflective of the market than was this September 20, 1983, high. When Roger Babson had given his final warning on September 5, 1929, he had based that signal mainly on the fact that out of the then 1,200 listed stocks, 614 of them had declined in value since the first of the year. Anybody then could have computed the high/low indicator, and it was telling the same story in 1929 that it was telling in 1983.

The market was following all the laws of physics, and one of the primary truths, which is virtually a law, is that in order for a market advance to be genuine, it must demonstrate *a constantly expanding number of stocks making new highs.* New highs stopped expanding in the spring of 1983, and thus *no rise after May 1983 was technically genuine.* Not only had the expansion ceased, but the contraction since May had been severe. The previous Dow closing high of 1,248.30 on June 16 saw 306 big board stocks making new twelve-month highs. The higher Dow reading of 1,249.19 on September 20 saw only 76 new highs. To further underscore the total falseness of the higher September closing, the number of new highs on September 19 was also 76, and on what the commentators described as an explosive rise, September 20 *saw an unchanged number of new highs.* The earlier September 12 rise in the Dow had seen 90 new highs, and that was the day the Dow intraday high hit 1,262.80. That was simply one more of the numerous non-confirmations on September 20, the intraday high that day being well short of the mark at 1,257.01. Other non-confirmations occurred in the Dow Jones Transportation Average, the New York Stock Exchange Composite Average, the Standard & Poor 500, the American Stock Exchange Market Value Index, the NASDAQ average, the advance/decline line, the high/low indicator, the Net Field Trend Indicator, the Climax Indicator, and the Wilshire, among others.

Donald Hoppe was not alone in having some second thoughts, citing the possibility and increasing probability of the abortion of the normal bull market cycle, the new bear market to start in 1983 rather than much later, which practically everyone else thought. Now somebody else was coming on the scene, somebody of great repute. I have the greatest respect for Ian Notley of Dominion Securities Ames, of Toronto. I think Notley is the greatest living authority on stock market cycles. We first met at the Market Technicians fourth annual meeting, which was held in the Poconos in Pennsylvania in May 1977, where I gave the keynote address.

Speaking about the long-term trend, Notley said: "Theoretically, the bull phase of a normal four-year cycle would persist through May 1984. *The extraordinary nature of the present cycle indicates that long-term bull phase maturity could well be reached starting in the third quarter 1983*" (emphasis added). That was a refreshing departure from the majority thinking that was so closely welded to the classical four- to four-and-a-half-year cycle. For months I had recognized the current rise as being a technical rarity, very definitely an ending rather than a beginning. Notley greatly reinforced my bearishness and complete conviction that the developing bear market would also contain a panic and a crash. More from Notley: "Long-term-cycle bottom phase registered in August 1982 during a record-breaking buying climax to the upside. *The extraordinary nature of the entry into the bull phase caused early cycle maturity within a period of 11 months!* Added to this is the fact that many major corporations present in the D.J.I. Index commenced their bull phases in the September 1981–March 1982 period and were already well developed when the August 1982 bottom registered for the general market. This trend *crosscurrent* enhances the likelihood of our Market Possibility Two arising. *Market Possibility Two would cause the cycle to stumble and would give us a long-term-cycle bottom in the fourth quarter of 1984.* This would greatly differ from the recognized classical model for the 1982–86 cycle where the idealised peak for the 1982–84 bull phase would naturally fall during the May–July 1984 period, with the next idealised bottom (cycle trough) occurring in June 1986" (emphasis added).

The market ran upstairs so rapidly in 1982–83 that it became winded far earlier than it would have if it had walked upstairs during a normal market cycle. Have you ever seen anyone get stronger after running upstairs a mile a minute, three steps at a time? Of course not. Do it fast enough and one will collapse with fatigue. Also, a stock market does not go up 473 points to build a base. The market goes down to build bases. The market goes up to build tops, the roof of the house. In order for thirty men (thirty Dow stocks) to climb to the top of a mountain, all thirty have to keep going and not drop dead from fatigue. Are the thirty Dow Jones industrial stocks climbing together today? No. Using the Net Field Trend Indicator as the best single technical measure of strength and weakness for the thirty individual Dow stocks, we see that nineteen of them peaked at the end of April. By the June 16 Dow high, only ten remained at the peak, and by September 20, widely heralded by the TV commentators as a day of strength, only five remained at the peak. It is tiring going up, and the steeper the climb and the shorter the time to complete the hike, the more rapidly the climbers tire and start to fall down the mountainside. Thus the normal cycle was stumbling, aborted by sheer fatigue.

But what was everybody hearing? The great cover story with a few embellishments added: The Dow will close out this year somewhere between 1,300 and 1,400 and go to much higher levels in 1984 and 1985. President Reagan will be reelected in November 1984, and the stock market cannot go down importantly before that date. Economic recovery will continue, interest rates will come down, and corporate earnings will be sharply higher. That was the cover story, but it only encouraged one to buy stocks at the worst of times, the function of all Wall Street cover stories. Somebody has to own the stocks all the way down, and everybody was a candidate.

I stated again at this time that if the bull market was going to be as good as the Wall Street pundits and economists said it was going to be, why was there a record number of secondary offerings and the most pernicious and concentrated insider selling in history? At the very least, if there was to be no crash or panic selling, the current evidence overwhelmingly pointed to a bear market, with or without a crash. But a student of history could not escape the mounting number of 1929 parallels. Whether the government would decide at some future time to reflate was a subject I would save for later discussion.

While many stocks were going down at this time, Wall Street, never saying sell, always had to keep bullish hopes alive. An ad appeared in the September 19 *Wall Street Journal* that caught my attention. It was headed: "Market Correction? 8 Stocks to Stay Ahead, Even If the Market Doesn't." In a bear market, 90 percent of all stocks go down. Until recently, one could not place a bet on the market. An old saying used to be that one couldn't buy the market but could buy individual stocks. But this was all changing. Now one could bet on the direction of the market. Even if the advertiser was looking only for a market correction, why bet on eight stocks when one could have placed one bet on the market? More and more I noted the term "selectivity" showing up when market experts were being interviewed. That word would always appear when the market was getting into trouble. Fewer stocks were making new highs, and thus one had to be selective if one wished to continue to be a buyer. But it certainly made more sense to get off the sinking ship rather than search for some of the ship's timbers to keep one afloat.

Some advisory services by this time did not like the brokerage house stocks, but were still bullish on the market. I had considered the best market bellwether stock to be Merrill Lynch. It was already pointing to severe market weather ahead. One could not be bearish on the brokerage house stocks and bullish on the market *because the brokerage house stocks were forecasting a bear market by their actions.* I had warned of that in June when Merrill Lynch sold an additional 2 million shares of stock and warned again when the figures came in on excessive hiring of new stockbrokers. Still ignoring such warnings, Merrill Lynch was contracting for additional floor space at this late date, oblivious to the collapse that lay ahead, a collapse their very own stock was warning of.

The new Dow highs this month prompted me to remind my followers that such new highs did not change the major scenario one iota since all new highs were totally unconfirmed by the important high/low indicator and advance/decline line. Such highs I called naked highs, the Emperor being caught without any clothes. The great broadening formation stretching back to March threatened something tremendous to come on the downside and the die was cast for the market regardless of what the Dow did over the near term.

PART THREE

THE GATHERING STORM

8

Malfunction Junction

[OCTOBER 1983]

I

Events were now speeding up, casting some ominous shadows. On October 1, banks were deregulated and could pay any interest rate they chose on certificates of deposit. Since banks dealt in money rather than the sale of airline tickets, a rate war meant that banks would compete for deposits by offering the highest interest rates possible, whereas airlines, when faced with deregulation, were forced to cut their rates. I could see billions upon billions of dollars soon to flee the stock market as interest rates, which had already bottomed, were on the way up. The deregulation of the banks came at a most sensitive time for the stock market, a time when most technical market indicators were flashing the identical message to get out. If enough people had acted on that message, then the financial panic would have been imminent. But people are slow to act. While the stock market had been flashing warnings persistently since the spring of 1983, most people were still hanging on to their stocks, fully oblivious of the seriousness of those warnings.

Nobody was going to take the suggestion of a possible panic seriously. The common characteristic preceding all panics and crashes was that *nobody saw them coming.* In 1929 the Dow Jones Industrial Average peaked on September 3 at 381.17. Here is what was said on the front page of the September 4 *Wall Street Journal:*

> Wall Street entered the autumn financial season in a definitely *optimistic frame of mind.* With railroad traffic showing steady gains, and production in the major branches of industry continuing at a high rate, the *earnings prospects* of the

principal corporations with shares listed on the Stock Exchange were looked upon as *extremely promising* [emphasis added].

The very next month saw the greatest panic and crash in financial history, and the Dow did not return to the 1929 high for twenty-four years. Nobody could say that the market dropped without warning. As in 1983, the market back then had been giving strong technical warnings for eight months prior to the peak and ensuing crash.

During the recession, while the banks were regulated, we saw a number of bank failures. I reported that I saw the handwriting on the wall, and it said that bank deregulation would culminate in a greater degree of malpractices and the ultimate number of bank failures would sharply increase over a period of time. I felt that if Congress voted to bypass the U.S. contribution to the International Monetary Fund, then the banks themselves would strive to bail out their bad loans with taxpayer monies. I saw deregulation as preceding a rising problem period in which many banks would go under. The big picture was getting progressively clearer. One could make a case that Paul Volcker's desire to do away with the bank reserve requirements could lead to a free-for-all that would see the public the loser. One way or another, inflationary money would be destroyed and a stock market crash would do the job. The Federal Deposit Insurance Corporation was to be severely tested in the months ahead.

The brokerage house stocks were clearly pointing the way to the trouble ahead. They were under heavy pressure at this time, along with the airlines, the selling especially significant in American Express, E. F. Hutton, and Merrill Lynch. Again, I repeated, one could not be bearish on the brokerage house stocks and bullish on the market and be right about the market, inasmuch as the brokerage group was the best single bellwether for the general market. As the bull market had transformed into the early stages of a bear market, I could see a number of things surfacing which provided the rationale as to why the brokerage house stocks had peaked and were now definitely on the way down. At this time, Merrill Lynch was hit by the default of a Panama firm and a lawsuit stemming from the Baldwin-United fiasco. At the same time, a $1 million bank embezzlement was reported. More and more, increasing troubles were surfacing in the news, but it was still seen to be only the tip of the iceberg.

There is a serious tendency to feature things in the news *after it is too late as far as the stock market is concerned.* In May, *Business Week* had published the most effective of all sell signals, featuring on their cover "The Rebirth of Equities," subheadlined "The Rally Launches a New Age for Stocks." The article was released at the peak in the high/low indicator, *precisely when everybody should have sold every stock he owned.* That article was the very *kiss of death for the stock market.* However, they never learn. The cover of the October 3 issue of *Business Week* contained its prediction that *the price of IBM stock was about to collapse.* Of course, it didn't say that, but the cover of the magazine forecast the end of the line for IBM by featuring an article titled "Personal Computers and the Winner Is IBM." In a horse race, a winner implies that all the other horses were losers. It also implies that *the race is over.* What do you do when you have a winner at a horse track? You get out of your seat and go to the cashier's window. That is what was about to happen to IBM. The *Business Week* article was followed soon thereafter by IBM peaking out at 134¼ at the end of its broadening top formation. Sure, IBM won the race and those who bet on it were streaming to the cashier's windows and selling their stock. Whereas 1929 had a superstar stock called Radio, 1983 had IBM. If one had examined a number of previous major market tops, it would have been discovered that, in most cases, it was the key stock most people got hooked on at the top.

PARALLEL 48
Technical
Record High Short Interest

The favorite bull argument at this time was the record high short interest. Short interest was at a peak in September 1929 and it had absolutely no bullish significance whatsoever. Why? The bull market was ending, and when a bull market is in the late stages of maturity, there are a large number of stock splits and new issues. *When a stock splits, the short interest automatically is increased, even though not one additional share of stock is sold short.* One can go short on a new issue. If that stock becomes listed on the big board, then the big board *inherits* the already existing short interest in that stock; so there again, *the short interest can rise without one additional share of stock being sold short.* Now, applying the analysis to the 1983 market, the latest figures for September showed a record 168,682,123 shares sold short with a short interest ratio of 2.23. The short interest ratio is simply the ratio of the monthly short interest to the average daily volume for that month. In this case, the short interest was running over twice the average daily volume. Anything over the 2.00 level is normally considered very bullish. However, a true rise in the short interest ratio would stem from a fixed monthly trading volume. Since May, however, there had been a steady drop in monthly trading volume for four consecutive months, and that mathematically created a dramatic rise in the short interest ratio, something that was misleading all the bulls. If trading had remained at the May levels, then the current short interest ratio would have been a more moderate 1.73 reading. The year 1983 had seen an extraordinary rise in the number of stock splits. If one had scanned the big board listings, one would have noted that there were 255 stocks which were either splits within the past twelve months or new issues. By matching those stocks with the stocks listed in the monthly short interest report, one would have seen that 91 of those issues were included, and *the combined built-in adjustment had radically expanded the short interest total with not necessarily one additional share of stock sold short.* Now one can see why there had to be a clear correlation between a bulge in stock splits, a bulge in new issues, and a bulge in the short interest. It logically followed that if a record number of stock splits and a record number of new issues were always followed by a severe bear market, *so then did record high short interest also have to be followed by a severe bear market.* My analysis was diametrically opposite to that of Wall Street.

One could have pondered the following examples: The short interest in American Express topped out at 1,222,714 shares in May 1983. The stock price peaked in June slightly above the May levels. Thereafter, the short interest dropped rapidly, falling to 405,885 shares in August. But then the stock split 3–2 in late August, and the short interest rose to 598,996 shares in September. But the 3–2 split automatically put the short interest at 608,827 shares for the new stock, and thus while the September short interest report gave the impression that there was a genuine *rise* of 193,111 shares, one can see that it was an actual *decrease* of 9,831 shares! In order to appreciate the degree that stock splits distort the short interest, consider Merrill Lynch. The short interest stood at 2,620,244 shares in May, and it appeared that the short interest had moved higher in July when the figure hit 3,078,681 shares. Nothing was further from the truth. The stock had split 2–1 in late June, and that had contributed most of the rise from the June level of 1,330,529 shares to the July total of 3,078,681 shares. The sharp drop in the September figures to 1,629,494 was equal to only 814,398 shares in terms of the large 2,620,244-share May short interest. One could see how a large short interest at the end of a bull market serves as an important hook, designed to mislead the bulls.

It was not wise to look at one side of the equation and not the other. Everybody talked about the large short interest but never mentioned *the much larger long interest.* The long interest was simply the combined stock holdings of everybody less the short interest. In comparison, the short interest was minuscule. With the additional paper printed and heaped upon the market in the past year, it was safe to say that the long interest was the largest in the history of the market. In a bear market, only the longs suffer, and thus the collective damage to the shorts in the brief 1982–83 bull market was insignificant when stacked up against the potential damage of this record number of longs in this bear market. Thus, with a record number of longs, *the bear market would collectively produce the highest combined dollar losses in history.*

No technical indicator in 1983 misled technicians more than the record high short interest. It was constantly cited as the cornerstone of all technical arguments for a higher market. Those misled technicians were counting on a normal bull market coming off the August 1982 bottom and were totally unaware of where that market stood in history, a replica of 1929. After the May–June 1983 internal market highs were well documented, the short interest and the short interest ratio continued to rise, and it was in the period *after* June 1983 that the record high in the short interest and the otherwise bullishly high short interest ratio served to lead most technicians astray.

The thrust of my counterargument aimed at these misled bulls destroyed the technical myth surrounding the misplaced bullishness based on their short interest misinterpretation. First of all, I had the advantage of knowing about the hundreds of other 1929 parallels, and thus I knew that the short interest and the short interest ratio were magnificent camouflage serving to deceive the majority at the top. But I did not require that additional knowledge, for the short interest itself could be shown to be totally misleading. First of all, the record high short interest was a *natural corollary* of the 1983 record high trading volume. Inasmuch as a parabolic rise in trading volume denoted terminal market action, *so then did the record high short interest also have to coincide with terminal market action.* Also, inasmuch as 1983 was a record year for stock splitting, a good proportion of the short interest had to contain meaningless data, puffed up artificially. If a stock splits 2–1, the short interest in that stock automatically doubles without adding a single new share on the short side. If a stock splits 10–1, then the short interest automatically rises tenfold. But I also drew attention to the surprising fact that a good proportion of the entire short interest was concentrated in a handful of stocks that had recorded the sharpest 1983 price declines! John "Bet a Million" Gates, one of the legendary market plungers of the 1920s, was known to have said, "Take a stock down 10 points and the short interest will rise. Take it down another 10 points and the short interest will double." What he was observing was the fact that people don't short on a rising market. They short on a declining market. And the conclusion was startlingly clear: The true 1983 market was a *declining* market. The confused bulls, while harping on the size of the record high short interest, failed to look at the other side of the coin. Nobody was talking about the record high in the long interest. If there had been any technical strength in the high short interest, it had to be seriously offset by the technical weakness of a record high short interest. One who had gone short eventually had to buy. One who had gone long eventually had to sell. And the weight of all that paper in unstable hands represented a dangerous sword of Damocles.

Most people never go short on a stock, and thus I had to assume that most shorting was done by market professionals and a tiny minority of other informed people. That is generally considered to be the "sophisticated" money, or "smart" money—implying that the general public is unsophisticated or not wise. In a proven bear market, the general public can be said to be long and dumb while the informed player is short and smart. What happened caught most people long and dumb.

A high short interest can never be assumed to be bullish, inasmuch as it reflects an expectation of a declining market on the part of those who are short. A panic and crash is impossible until a point is reached where most people are bearish on the stock market at the same time. *That implies that one must see a large short interest prior to a panic and crash.* That is what was taking place in 1983 prior to the 1984 slide. The final and most damning proof that the 1983 record high short interest represented a supreme technical trap was the 1929 parallel itself.

Numerous references were made in *The Wall Street Journal* in September and October 1929 to the very high short interest which then existed. I cite the following references: September 16, 1929, "Abreast of the Market"; September 18, 1929, "Abreast of the Market"; September 26, 1929, "Broad Street Gossip"; and October 9, 1929, "Abreast of the Market." All the conditions explaining the high short interest were the same in 1983 as they were back in 1929. In 1929 there was record trading volume, the high short interest being a natural corollary. In 1929 there were many stock splits. In 1929 the highest long interest was seen. In 1929 half the stocks were already bearish, and, finally, history proved the shorts to be right.

One now had to give some hard thought to percentages and probabilities. Even if the Dow did go to the 1,300 level, it meant that 96 percent of the rise in the Dow was over in early October. In terms of most stocks, however, the bull market had ended the previous spring.

As the Dow gave a key sell signal on October 10 at 1,284.65, much was said in the financial press at this time regarding the Dow Jones Utility Average. It closed at 140.08 on October 6, the highest closing since November 29, 1968. That fact was well publicized in *The Wall Street Journal.* But what it didn't tell the public was that *four days after November 29, 1968,* a major bear market had started, not to reach its bottom until the end of May 1970! Thus it was in keeping with the big picture that the utility average should be peaking at this time. As at all key market tops, Wall Street was exulting in the strength in the average *at the very worst of times.*

In the fall of 1983 I was giving many speeches, among them one before the first annual Futures Symposium in Chicago, where I was also taped for the Financial News Network *Moneytalk* show. Before about 700 at the Palmer House, I enumerated ten areas of phenomena which had always been followed by a major bear market without exception. Once again I was met with disbelief. I could feel their thoughts: Here was the man who missed the 1982 bottom. What in the world could he tell us today of any importance? Here we were in a proven bear market and I doubted if there was anyone in the room who believed me. *The Wall Street Journal* called me at this time, fascinated by the fact that I had sent out a short-term buy signal on October 3 at Dow 1,231.30 and a sell signal on October 10 at Dow 1,284.65. Here was a change of pace they weren't used to. I had introduced a trading barometer at this time, based on on-balance volume, which was to dispel the myth that I was *always* a bear. From here on out, all short-term buy signals were going to be reported as well as the sell signals, something that was to propel me back to the number one spot in the *Hulbert Financial Digest.* [1]

Since most people were mesmerized by the Dow Jones Industrial Average, using that average interchangeably with the market, they did not see the internal cancer which was steadily eating away at the market's vital organs. They saw the rising Dow as the rosy sign of continuing health, never suspecting that what they were actually seeing was the flush of fever. In the great mountain climb that started in August 1982, many climbers got tired as the calendar switched to 1983. One by one the weaker ones collapsed, but General IBM, the champion climber, pleaded with his blue-shirted followers to plod on toward the summit. Time was running out and only a handful of the blue chip climbers had enough strength left to struggle to the peak with the General. On the ground, the media, with their cameras trained on the little band, could only now and then get a glimpse of the blue-shirted crew, and they reported immediately to the world that all the climbers were well and continuing their climb. But later, they had to report to the world that most of the climbers had quit the race early and were not to be heard from again. Then the word came. It was electrifying. General IBM had made it to the peak, and with him were his two most trusted companions—General Motors and his aide Woolworth. The race was over, and the three of them sat there for a few moments, inhaling the rarefied air and congratulating themselves on the fact that they, the three of them, were the only survivors in the great climb. They broke out a bottle and glasses and toasted themselves, and then, in their fever of exultation, they tripped over each other and fell to their death. The great climb was over and there were no survivors. The bear market of 1983 had become official.

On October 10, the media announced to the world that the Dow Jones Industrial Average had climbed to the highest closing level in history, closing that day at 1,284.65. But they also implied that the market was at a new high, and that was, of course, totally wrong. There are thirty stocks in the Dow Jones Industrial Average, and on October 10 only General Motors, IBM, and Woolworth made new one-year highs. On that day, despite a final gain of 12½ points in the Dow average, the number of stocks making new twelve-month highs contracted sharply from 135 to 75, a most dramatic illustration of a fatal loss of upside momentum.

[1] Best known stock market letter rating service, 409 First Street S.E., Washington, D.C.

The flat-top pattern in the Dow had demanded another set of new highs in October, and thus, having given a buy signal on October 3 at 1,231.30, I had to make it very clear that the predicted rise had to be treated as the final power play in the bull market, the final run for the roses. I stressed that the rise was only good for a few days, just long enough for the trading barometer to go from buy to sell. The figures as of October 7 made it virtually certain that the sell signal would be forthcoming on the tenth. Knowing this, I sent out the signal to my telephone subscribers the night of the ninth.

While it is always nice to be able to pinpoint moves in the market, I could not stress enough the vital importance of the big picture at this time. If a train is coming down the track, it is not important when a person jumps off the track, just as long as he jumps before the train hits him. Thus, moving too soon in a market will not hurt. In this case it was to save millions of financial lives. Most stocks had been coming down since June, and thus those who jumped off the track prior to that time had not been hurt by the dramatic declines which had occurred since. History showed that even if one had sold out in January of that fateful year 1929, he was a winner, even though the Dow made that final run to the September 3 top. In October 1983 I felt confident that that type of financial history was repeating itself. Already the evidence and market performance documented the 1983 bear market many months before Wall Street was even to whisper about such a possibility. There was no way of getting out of the calendar year without a full-fledged, proven bear market underway.

One had only to run his eye down the highs and lows on the over-the-counter market to see that investors were being destroyed. My S indicator was taking its toll (S standing for stock splits). Now a growing number of the split stocks were showing the worst declines. Wall Street had done its work well in the mass distribution of stocks at the top.

Yet the media had been keeping score by following the average price of thirty blue chip stocks. I then borrowed a phrase from William Jennings Bryan: "I refuse to be crucified upon a cross of thirty stocks."

One had to go with the odds. Wall Street analysts were telling their clients that the market was getting more selective, that it would be increasingly difficult to pick winners. What they were actually saying was that most stocks would not be going up, and therefore it would be more difficult to find rising stocks. In other words, they were saying that the advance/decline line was more likely to trend downward, and that was true. Since it was true, why didn't they recommend playing the odds and bet on the 90 percent of the stocks that were going to go down? Ninety percent of all stocks go down in a bear market and the proof was overwhelming that the 1983 bear market was developing right on schedule. The previous bull market, the shortest one in history, had used up all its legs. All those who were looking for a second leg to that dead market were doomed to disappointment.

II

The number of secondary offerings was continuing to soar, and it was at this time that *Market Logic*[1] gave me full credit for discovering that *Barron's* had been inadequately reporting the number of secondary offerings, documenting that my greatly expanded record-high number was absolutely correct. One by one the pieces were falling into place that showed this period to be one of fast-developing storm clouds. Much to my amazement, *Market Logic* persisted in its bullish posture despite the highest number of secondary stock offerings in history. It was going 100 percent contrary to its own book.

Alice in Wonderland discovered that at the most important moment, everything went *backward*. Life became a *hall of mirrors*. I had told my subscribers for many months that *computers* and *off-track betting* would destroy this market. There were now millions of computers in the homes of America and many of these were programmed to the stock market. When traditional indicators said buy, they bought. But these were not traditional times, and at the most critical market times, the traditional indicators *malfunction*. Knowing that the majority had to be hooked at the top, the specialists performed like virtuosos at this top. They made sure that the New York Stock Exchange Composite Average *confirmed* the Dow high. They made sure that the Dow Jones transports *confirmed* the recent Dow high. They made sure the Standard & Poor 500 *confirmed* the recent Dow high. They made sure that General Motors and IBM also confirmed the recent Dow industrial high. Then I surmised that the specialists made one clever move which fooled all the followers of the traditional indicators. They knew that if they shorted heavily, it would show up in the Specialist Short Sales indicator as being bearish. They also knew that if there were more buyers of calls than of puts, that also would be classed as bearish. I theorized that they had to create a façade of bullishness, and yet, at the same time, capitalize on the coming crash. I guessed that instead of going heavily short, which would look bearish, *they had hit upon the idea of buying put options*. In one brilliant stroke, they *artificially* created *two bullish-looking* indicators. By *buying put options*, they made the Specialist Short Sales indicator look bullish, and they simultaneously made the put/call ratio look bullish. They would achieve their purpose. In this way they would make many Wall Street advisers eventually look foolish in their misplaced bullishness based on *false* bullish indications of the Specialist Short Sales indicator and the put/call ratio.[2]

This brilliant gambit was a fascinating modern-day application of reverse-thinking strategy. Not only that, but the specialists would have reaped a

---

[1] *Market Logic*, 3471 North Federal Highway, Fort Lauderdale, Fla. 33306.
[2] A call option is simply a bet on the long side and a put option is a bet on the downside, not affecting the actual ownership of securities.

tremendously higher profit by buying the put options than by shorting the stocks. At that time some of the put options in the stocks that dropped sharply were selling at $\frac{1}{16}$ of a dollar. The profits could have been *astronomical.* It was a theoretical masterstroke. I say "theoretical" because there was no hard evidence that that is what actually happened. But it was the only logical way to explain why the Specialist Short Sales indicator and the put/call ratio were giving out false bullish signals. I felt that there had to be a rationale to explain the increasing number of malfunctioning indicators.

I was quickly reminded of the words of Henry N. Southworth, who had reviewed my works in the British journal *The Chartist* back in 1977. He had noted the repeating tendency for major indicators to *malfunction* at key market turning points. At such times, I always turned to those indicators which, mathematically, are the most difficult to manipulate. Over and over, I had always returned to the advance/decline line. The specialists did not have enough money or credit to manipulate that indicator. They did not have enough money or credit to manipulate the on-balance volume of a majority of stocks. They could only play games with the Dow 30, which, of course, made the media their handmaidens. But even that game had become outworn and could no longer fully disguise the growing cancer of the general market. I surmised that the specialists had discovered the back door of *off-track betting* to cover their footprints and thereby had set up some of the best minds in the business to become prize suckers. They had created *false* technical *confirmations* which would go down in history as the *great sucker hooks of 1983,* absolutely no different from similar hooks used back in 1929 to bait the suckers at the top. The specialists are human beings, not immune to fear and greed, and I saw no earthly reason why they couldn't buy put options, either directly or indirectly through their families and friends, to achieve their purposes.

Corporate earnings were most commonly given as the reason for a continuation of the bull market. I had explained at great length in my 1976 book[3] that corporate earnings do not provide an adequate guide to what the market is going to do. Regardless of what a company earns, what is important is whether those earnings are going to be undervalued or overvalued by the market, and that is a function of supply and demand, not a function of fundamental analysis. Page 105 of *A New Strategy* contains an Arthur Merrill chart which shows the rise and fall of corporate earnings. Contrary to popular thinking, the great turning points from bear to bull markets occur when corporate earnings are falling, and the great turns from bull to bear markets occur when corporate earnings are rising. The Merrill chart shows the transition from the 1972 peak into the 1973 bear market at a time of rising earnings.

---

[3]Joseph E. Granville, *A New Strategy of Daily Stock Market Timing for Maximum Profit* (Englewood Cliffs, N.J.: Prentice-Hall, 1976).

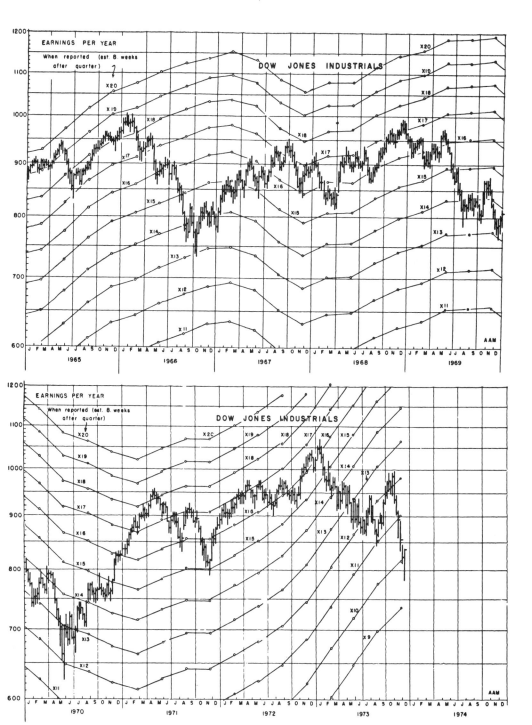

Chart Courtesy of Arthur A. Merrill, Technical Trends, Chappaqua, New York

In the Trendline chart book[4] the companies having *the most rapid earnings growth* were marked with a large triangle. A study of those charts reveals that these not only were the stocks that had come down considerably from the lofty prices of the previous spring, but also were those showing the *most severe* price declines. By October 1983, only a small handful of these stocks had resisted the major declining trend. This again illustrated why the lure of corporate earnings was so completely diluted in the developing bear market and yet, at the same time, was used as the largest of all the hooks to bring buyers back into the market at the very worst of times. The Merrill chart allowed me to discount completely what Wall Street was saying about corporate profits. The identical arguments were being given in September 1929 for the continuation of the great bull market.

At this time, institutional cash was very low, and it was to prove to be a restraining influence on any future rallies, the Dow already hitting the roof of the great broadening top formation. Another restraining influence was the evidence that money was starting to flow back into the money market funds, responding to the inching up of interest rates. Most technical changes at this time in the marketplace were pointing toward increasing weakness. The important advance/decline line had broken under the October 3 level, indicating a lack of support at the Dow 1,231.30 level. The high/low indicator showed the significant crossing, new lows now outnumbering new highs, the big lie given to any retained strength in the Dow 30. Dow attempts to rally were pitifully inadequate.

I continued to send out the clarion call to sell all stocks. The market was still under the influence of the major October 10 sell signal. The Street was in an increasingly nervous state, the latest single stock casualty at this time being Digital Equipment. More stocks were to follow this pattern, and I saw many additional signs suggesting an approaching panic. On balance, money was leaving the stock market. Some of the stock breaks were demonstrating how rapidly a stock could lose half its value in a matter of days, certainly not a characteristic of a continuing bull market.

III

There was nothing holding the market up except the blue chips, and that statement could have been made in the summer of 1929. The last fling in that fateful year was completely concentrated in about forty blue chip stocks. The rest of the market had already embarked upon the great down cycle, while for a few short months the blue chips had given the surface impression that the bears were wrong. The general market put the lie to the Dow Jones Industrial

[4]Trendline Daily Action Stock Charts, a division of Standard & Poor's Corporation, 25 Broadway, New York, N.Y. 10004.

Average as it again put the lie to the Dow in 1983. Any short-term buy signals were therefore not compatible with the big picture, for they simply depicted the probabilities of perhaps one more desperate power drive in the Dow to complete more adequately the massive broadening top formation. But to say that the stock market was not extremely dangerous was to ignore a dozen or so massive warnings which historically, without exception, had been followed by major bear markets. To be more concise, the bull market was over for most stocks, and it only remained for the final topping out in the Dow to become a proven fact, whether it was to be at 1,284 or slightly higher. In either case, the risks of new buying far outweighed any rewards, and I assumed that my followers were out of the market, only the traders playing the ins and outs of the market's final upside convulsions. In such a dangerous market, only astute traders had the agility to trim sail on very short notice.

The short interest took another quantum leap in October, soaring to an all-time record high of 182,886,740 shares. Most analysts again rejoiced, thinking this to be bullish. With great patience, I again explained that this indicator was flashing extremely bearish signals. Contrary to popular belief, the high short interest was not bullish; it was a natural reflection of the growing weakness in the general market and was therefore paradoxically bearish. My source was irrefutable, that source being history. The short interest had been very high in September 1929, and it would have been fatal to ignore that great 1929 parallel. It was, at that time, simply indicative of the panic that followed. History showed that the short sellers in September and October 1929 were right, and I took this opportunity to demonstrate that the short sellers in late 1983 were also going to be proved right, any short-term rallies notwithstanding. I took the thirty-two big board stocks having a short interest of a million shares or more and proved that these stocks, comprising 37 percent of the entire short interest, *showed the sharpest price declines!*

Stock	Short Interest	% Decline
American General	4,372,744	− 7
American Medical	1,145,309	−27
American Motors	1,054,562	−30
Baldwin-United	3,555,872	−94
Chrysler Pfd.	2,140,984	− 1
Chrysler Wts.	1,010,214	−27
Church's Fried Chicken	1,012,052	−24
Coleco	2,106,349	−59
Diamond Shamrock	4,486,618	− 9
Eastern Airlines	1,154,010	−49
Exxon	2,186,288	− 3
Financial Corp. of America	1,828,780	−23

Stock	Short Interest	% Decline
Ford Motor	1,283,825	− 5
Goodyear	2,152,905	−18
Great Western Fin.	1,098,995	−23
Gulf United	1,106,367	− 3
Hercules	1,350,077	−14
IBM	1,294,307	− 5
International Harvester	1,726,238	− 1
Mattel	1,301,310	−77
Merrill Lynch	1,884,736	−47
North Telecon.	1,154,217	−14
Pan American	12,927,148	−12
Prime Computer	2,494,105	−51
P.S. Colorado	1,683,252	− 5
Sony	1,123,162	−13
Southmark	1,161,915	− 8
Storage Tech.	1,208,483	−46
Teradyne	1,438,564	−20
U.S. Steel	2,130,927	− 7
Wal-Mart	1,587,690	−12
Western Air	1,065,984	−40

The table shows that all the stocks with the largest short interest were underwater as of October 21. That meant that the short sellers were right. The average decline for the thirty-two stocks was 24.2 percent. Back in 1929, as in 1983, trading volume was at an all-time high, and so was the number of stock splits, and thus the short interest also had to go to record levels, proving John Gates right: the size of the short interest reflected the extent of the subsurface decline in the market. That was well highlighted in the table by stocks such as Baldwin-United, Coleco, Eastern Airlines, Mattel, Merrill Lynch, Prime Computer, Storage Technology, and Western Airlines. Right there was a good chunk of the short interest in stocks that had collapsed. In other words, the shorts were right.

Yet there were many market letter writers who exulted in the twenty-five-year high in the short interest, forgetting the much higher short interest ratio in August 1931, which proved to be extremely bearish. Those same writers called attention to what looked like a bullish put/call ratio, but hey were making the same mistake as in their short interest analysis. It naturally followed that if the shorts were going to be right, the buyers of put options were also going to be right, and in both cases, the bullish label on those two indicators had no meaning. I stated at this time that if the market was going to collapse in the near future, then it was certain that bearish sentiment had to increase, the short interest must rise, and there would be more buyers of puts than calls. That is what those indicators were reflecting.

While all the pieces were steadily falling into place, documenting the authenticity of my 1929 thesis, I nevertheless had to make a judgment call at this time. A judgment call on the market is the most difficult type to make because it implies that there are crosscurrents among a number of indicators, involving a crossroad whereby the market could jump sharply either way. With the indicator scales that affected the short-term outlook so precariously in balance, I wanted to lock in some profits. The call was made on October 24 and I chose to go with a short-term buy signal. It was not an easy decision to make, inasmuch as the A-Dis Trading Barometer was still under the influence of the sell signal of October 10. But I had to demonstrate once again to my readers that I would never blindly swing on one branch. The short-term trading barometer the previous January had given a sell signal, only to see the Dow rise another 100 points, and thus this judgment call was made in keeping with a large number of other technical considerations. There was no one magic key that would always unlock the market's secrets.

The case I presented simply implied that *the Dow would not go importantly lower without another blue chip rally occurring first.* One had to reflect on the events of the recent days. If one was a betting person and knew about the rise in the money supply and the terrible tragedy in Beirut prior to the October 24 market and had to bet everything then on the direction of the Dow Jones Industrial Average, which way would he have bet? It was assumed that most people would have wagered that the Dow would close lower that day. But it didn't. It actually went up, making a 100 percent reversal from the morning lows. Here we saw the largest number of military casualties since Vietnam, and the Dow closed up. I was impressed. The next day the U.S. Marines landed in Grenada. The Dow closed up. Again I was impressed. The next day the Dow had a 9-point setback, which seemed largely short-lived. It looked like some support was developing in the Dow, and though the buy signal of October 24 proved to be a bit premature, it was justified on the following counts:

1. Highly positive Climax Indicator readings against the background of events in Beirut and Grenada; refusal, thus far, of the CLX to break the −5 level of October 11.
2. Continuing new highs in the Cumulative Climax Indicator.
3. Continued strength in General Motors.
4. Other key indicator stocks such as Merrill Lynch and American Express reaching support.
5. Indicated support in the 1,225–1,235 area as signified by upside reversals from low Dow intraday readings.
6. Proximity to major rising trendlines in a number of indicators as well as short-term oversold condition.

Then, on October 27, the Dow was in another obvious tailspin, but once again met support well above the 1,231 level, closing above 1,240. If the specialists were ready to crack the market wide open, they would never have had a better excuse to do so that week, using the war as the cover story. I had all investors out of the market, and only the traders were playing the short-term swings. It looked like there had to be one final run in the Dow coming up.

My advice at the time hewed to the big picture: sell all stocks. The general market looked pretty washed out, while the last haven of strength remained in a handful of blue chip stocks. While another run in the Dow looked probable, no buying was recommended. If one had not already cleaned house, he had another opportunity here to sell into strength. The bull market was over for most stocks and would soon prove to be over for the Dow stocks as well, the last bastion of strength.

9

Up the Down Staircase

[NOVEMBER 1983]

I

The market was about to be rescued from the abyss. The stakes were extremely high. If the market crashed now, it would spoil Christmas. There had to be a last-minute rescue; and to be frank, if I hadn't had the A-Dis Trading Barometer at this time, I would have joined the bearish portfolio managers and said that all last-minute rescues were impossible. Christmas might have been celebrated by a rally from a much lower Dow level, but the early November readings were calling for another upward pop, the blue chips doing their thing against the background of an already proven bear market in the general list.

Wall Street always has perfect 20/20 vision in hindsight. I was so alone in my bearishness at the exact top in the spring of 1983 that by June 1983 Bob Gross of *The Professional Investor*[1] showed that I was 50 percent of the bearish opinion on the primary trend, listing the *Insider Indicator* as the only other bearish service in the country. The *Insider Indicator* was later to turn bullish, basing its market calls on insider activities. It was in June that I had talked about the stench of the sardines and was being bashed about in the media. Since that time, the guts of the market had fallen out. I was interested at this time in the comment by Bob Farrell of Merrill Lynch in *The Wall Street Journal* of November 2, 1983: "The retreat from the June highs in aggressive growth and technology [issues] has been one of the severest in many years. The NASDAQ Industrials are down 20.5% in four months, *which is the worst relative performance for this index in a similar time period in 10 years*"

---

[1]Robert T. Gross, ed., *The Professional Investor*, Lynatrace, Inc., P.O. Box 2144, Pompano Beach, Fla. 33061.

(emphasis added). Yet the majority held to the thesis that this was a young bull market, simply awaiting the second leg. But the treatment that Bob Farrell described was not the treatment one would get in a continuing bull market. In fact, the ten years Farrell mentioned covered the bear markets of 1973–74, 1977, and 1981–82.

To keep your job in Wall Street, you are not allowed to be out-and-out bearish. You are allowed a modicum of caution, but woe be it to anybody who remotely suggested a Wall Street crash. I remained alone in that contention, unfettered by Wall Street brokerage house restrictions that had tended to hamper my free expression back in my E. F. Hutton days. The guts of the market had been spilling out since the spring of 1983, and the average market player was beginning to hurt. Wall Street forgot to tell such players that the game is played *both* ways.

At this point, I was not misinterpreting rising bearishness as being bullish for the market. I saw one more rise coming for the Dow, but I certainly didn't see it as the second leg to a bull market.

I was intrigued by the fact that every time the Climax Indicator was in a position to drop to a −20 reading or lower, programmed support showed up. Everyone knew my basic theories so well that money managers could program their buying to such times, foiling the millions of amateur technicians who by this time had bought stock market software for their home computers. That was typically the case on November 1, the market going from plunge to recovery. However, there was a growing problem. This time, the big boys were running out of money. Mutual fund cash had just reached a five-year low. They couldn't spread the jam over the thirty Dow Jones stocks, but had to spark rallies by concentrating in the few, hoping that it would inspire buying in the many. Their short-term inspirations centered on IBM, General Motors, Merck, and Minnesota Mining, in the hope that the game could be extended. They banked on stock splits for a new lease on life.

Emotions were dominating the trading at this time. The Dow had dropped over 18 points on October 28 to 1,223.48. On that day, the A-Dis Trading Barometer had flashed a buy signal on the close, an event anticipated a few days before in my market letter of October 29, which had gone to press just prior to the October 28 slide. I could stand pat because the trading barometer was giving uncannily accurate signals. Short sales were being covered prior to this last run in the blue chips. I underscored to my subscribers that this short-term flexibility was no significant change in the big picture. The short-term barometer was, of course, for the short-term traders, and I was gratified by the volume of letters coming in from brokers attesting that at last we had something of great practical value for the short-term trader.

At this time, I was getting many questions on gold and silver. I had been bearish on both since January 21, 1980, when I told everyone in the world to get out of gold at $875 an ounce and silver at $40 an ounce. The continued loss of value in those two assets had increasingly threatened other assets. The Arab nations, for example, seeing the loss in their gold assets, got to a point where they had to liquidate other assets, and thus the drop in the price of gold also related to the stock market. The same reasoning applied to the price of silver. According to Frederick Lewis Allen, the collapse in the world price of silver was a strong contributing factor in the world depression of the early 1930s.[2] Gold was coming down because of the trend toward deflation, and deflation threatened ultimate economic depression. No definitive trend on the upside in gold was going to take place until the price moved well above the $420 level, and at this time, that was a very remote occurrence, overhead supply at $400 looking formidable. I told my people never to try to get their money back in the medium they lost it in. That is the human nature trap *that turns traders into long-term investors.* Silver was in more dismal shape, any significant upside change requiring a move back to the $12 level. Both the gold and silver charts showed the probabilities much greater that the prices of both would move back to their June 1982 lows of $300 for gold and $4 for silver. Nevertheless, I knew that a stock market crash could change those projections. I was already committed to a tour of South Africa in February 1984, to give speeches in Durban, Johannesburg, and Cape Town, and I was sure that their desperate interest in gold would coincide with a buy signal by the time I got there.

I fielded many questions as to why I had put so much stress on the current 1982–83 cycle as being more of an ending than a beginning in the long-term sense. My conclusion was heavily weighted by my interpretation of the long Kondratieff Wave (average length, 54 years) and the Juglar cycle of nine years. I maintained that the 1982–83 rise was the blowoff phase of the nine-year cycle which had begun at the 1974 low. To illustrate the nine-year bull market, as well as the parabolic 1982–83 rise which was ending that cycle, I reprinted *Market Logic*'s chart of their New York Stock Exchange Total Return Index, as well as their description of it. It spoke for itself. There was the evidence of the nine-year cycle, the nine-year bull market which, according to the 1982–83 upward slope, was at the end of the line, with probably one more blue chip rally ahead.

[2]Frederick Lewis Allen, *Only Yesterday* (New York: Perennial Library, Harper & Row, 1964).

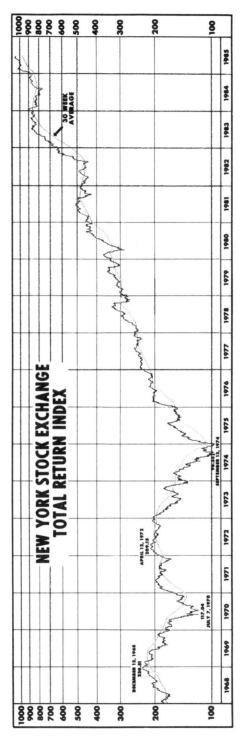

Market Logic's NYSE Total Return Index

It was reported at this time that the money market fund assets had increased for the fifth consecutive week, further proof that there was a decided rise in the number of people getting nervous about the stock market. Ironically, while *The Wall Street Journal* reported the increased bearishness among portfolio managers, and while columnists such as Dan Dorfman (who had excoriated me as recently as early October) were telling their listeners how bad this market had been since June, *the signals were coming in loud and clear that the blue chips had another run coming.*

II

In order for the Dow Jones Industrial Average to make its final top, the public had to be enticed back into the stock market, the first order of business being this November rally. The second order of business, in time for Christmas, might have been some additional splits in some of the Dow industrial stocks. I felt that such splits would set the stage in 1984 for the anticipated 50-point swings on the downside due to the increased volatility stemming from a still lower Dow divisor. *Those swings were reserved for the great down trip which would follow the ultimate Dow peak which I was predicting would be made on this run.* I felt that what we could be seeing was the sixty-day rally that fools the majority, and thus I envisaged the Dow holding up pretty much through December. The rally had caught most analysts with their pants down, most of them short-term bearish, looking for more correction. A more important top was coming, the end of the line for the Dow, but it spelled out doom thereafter.

The language of the market was coming through loud and clear, and the message was undeniably that there had to be another important and final upward explosion in the Dow. It was not the news at this time that I was considering, but the market's response to that news. The tragedy in Beirut was announced on Sunday, October 23. The Dow was bombed on October 24, but closed *up* 0.10. That was impressive. On October 28, the bulletin was flashed about the incident in Grenada concerning the Russian Embassy. The market tanked, but at the close, the A-Dis Trading Barometer flashed a buy signal. That was impressive. The Capitol in Washington was bombed on November 8 and the Dow closed *up* 0.10. That was impressive. On November 9, *The Wall Street Journal* printed a full-page ad stating that 1983 equaled 1929. The Dow closed *up* almost 18 points. That was impressive. In fact, the publication of that ad almost *guaranteed* that the Dow was going to be taken up again. Even the bearish comments on the inside back page of the *Journal* indicated that the Dow was being prepared once again for a rise.

Newton Zinder of E. F. Hutton said that the stock market continued to be hostage to the bond market. Frank A. Russo of Autranet said that the entire week was likely to be uneventful. Peter Furniss of Lehman Brothers Kuhn

Loeb said that current psychology was one of taking profits in defensive stocks and that such action was expected to continue for the next few weeks until the tax-loss selling had been completed. David H. Allen of Interstate Securities in Charlotte, North Carolina, didn't expect any important rally prior to year end. He said that since secondary stocks had declined about 15 percent since June, he wouldn't be surprised to see the blue chips and defensive stocks also give up some of their gains. And Stan Weinstein of the *Professional Tape Reader* stated that while we might be only a few weeks from the next intermediate bottom, it could be a very dangerous few weeks. So what did the market do in the face of all that caution? It went up.

Then it happened, as predictably as the sun will rise tomorrow morning. *The Wall Street Journal* ran a front-page story on November 10 telling how bad the market had been in 1983, documenting everything I had identified since the previous spring. That was the fallacy of financial reporting. They tell you that the barn is empty rather than give you the chance to save the horses before the thieves arrive. I had warned for months that the horses would be stolen while they were still in the barn. Now they were gone. I urged my readers to review that article carefully and to dwell on each point, realizing that they could have done something about it at the time it was occurring. At last, the surface revelation of the dirty laundry simply signaled the current upswing and *return to quality.* The psychology was plain. The castles they had built in the air the previous spring had now vanished, just like the mirage in the famous Merrill Lynch ads. The sadder but wiser neophyte then said to himself: No more speculation for me. From now on, I buy quality only. Could one imagine how many young husbands had to take the heat from their wives and vice versa for blowing the family nest egg? So the riot act had been read to them. Get out of this market if you can't stick to quality and proven stocks. So at last the stage was set for the last act—an *all-quality show.*

As all proven rallies show, the market cannot hear bad news. Nothing bothers it. It was announced on November 10 that a U.S. plane clashed with a Syrian jet. A weak market wouldn't have stood up under a piece of news like that. It would have collapsed as it had on the afternoon of October 28, when the incident involving the Russian Embassy was announced. Instead, the Dow broke out above the down channel that had been effective since the October 10 high of 1,284. Not only did it break out convincingly on the upside, but it had the authority of volume as well as the momentum of continued follow-through. Technicians were especially interested in following the Dow Transportation Average, because any closing above the 600 level would prove to be extremely exciting, the breakout above a flat-top formation, normally projecting sharply higher. All the ingredients were coming together here, underscoring the great validity of the A-Dis Trading Barometer.

While the Dow was positioned to make the big final run, the rest of the market had a very important technical function to perform. Most of those stocks outside the quality circle would be attempting to come back up to their trendlines, and when the Dow made the final top, most stocks would then be set to collapse. The psychology was simple and very effective. When I did ABC *Nightline* with Ted Koppel the previous March, Delta Air Lines was topping out at 51. My message on the show was to Flee for Your Life and, of course, I was met with disbelief. Delta bounced off the trendline in May and made a final failing stab at the March high. It then came down and broke under the trendline in June and then rallied back to the declining trendline in July. That return to a falling trendline was *the technical kiss of death.* What was reflected was the *changing psychology of traders.* Those who did not sell Delta stock between 45 and 50 told themselves that if the stock ever got back to 45, they would move out fast. They did so on schedule in July, and the stock plummeted to 29. Now the psychology was at work again. The stock rallied from a maximum distance below the trendline and currently was working back toward the declining trendline. Translating that action to the broad, general market, one could begin to see what was going on at the tail end of the November rally in progress. While the Dow Jones Industrial Average was expected to make at least one more new high, *most stocks simultaneously would be simply coming back up and touching their declining trendlines and touching the fatal third rail.* What had happened to Delta Air Lines stock in July would shortly be happening to the entire market, including the darlings of Wall Street—the blue chips. That was the technical background to the November rally, making for crash action thereafter.

Gold shares were not responding normally to the events in Lebanon and Grenada. The events there brought no strength into bullion or the shares. Seeing the developing pieces for a stock market crash, I asked myself whether a buy signal in gold would be compatible with a stock market crash. Again I turned to history. What was the one group of stocks people should have been in in 1929? The answer: gold stocks. On September 3, 1929, Homestake Mining closed at 80. That was the stock to buy that day. Throughout the worst economic debacle and depression in financial history, Homestake rose all the way to 550 by 1935. Then came the technical kiss of death. The stock was split 10–1. And as I had preached all through 1983, *the record number of stock splits that year signaled the end of the bull market.* So there was a buy signal in gold which proved to be compatible with a stock market crash. Gold was being used as a haven of safety. I felt that it could happen again. Don Wolanchuk and I contrived a Gold Barometer based on the same technical principles as the A-Dis Trading Barometer. I knew I had to be in South Africa in February 1984 and had to come up with the best advice on gold. Gold was not going to do well against a background of rising interest rates, but in 1929 the turn in the gold shares had more than adequately predicted the collapse in interest rates which went along with the stock market crash. So, from this point forward, I was closely watching gold and silver, and by the end of the month started reporting the short-term swings based on the new Gold Barometer.

One of the many myths about 1929 is that everything was red-hot that year, culminating in a profitable pinnacle not to be matched in the Dow until almost twenty-five years later. Nothing could be further from the truth. The year 1929 was a mirror image of 1983. Most stocks had reached their bull market highs six to eight months prior to the top in the Dow. For example, on September 3, 1929, the very peak day in that great bull market, there were 54 stocks making new highs for the year and 19 making new lows. Like the advance/decline line, the high/low indicator had peaked by December 1928, just as in the current market the advance/decline line had peaked in June and the high/low indicator had peaked in May. The technical similarities were scary.

Money market fund assets had increased for the sixth consecutive week, and this time the increase was much greater than it had been in more than a year. That was properly construed as money leaving the market on balance, and it supported the overwhelming evidence that the primary trend had changed, although this was yet to be seen in terms of the Dow Jones Industrial Average.

The technical background of the market at this time was almost exactly what it had been in October–November 1972. Most stocks had topped out and there was one more run left in the Dow Jones Industrial Average. A near-term signal on the A-Dis Trading Barometer was expected shortly to precede the final Dow top.

III

The great sell signal by the A-Dis Trading Barometer was forthcoming on November 14. Since most such signals always come a few days prior to the actual Dow high or low, I would go with this and let the chips fall where they may. The barometer rose to a bearish +4.33 as the Dow closed about 40 points above the November 7 low. The advice was very specific. My subscribers knew that at this time I was playing the market very close to the vest. The bull market was over for most stocks, and this was simply a maneuver to be in position for the end of the game.

Sir William Rees-Mogg, writing in the *London Washington Report,* applied probability to nine significant breaks in trend, ranging from nuclear war, hyperinflation, the price of gold, all the way to a Democratic victory in 1984, giving the odds based on cyclical research. Conspicuously absent was a stock market crash and the odds in favor of its happening. I liked his example of how to read the probability of an event's occurring. He referred to major earthquakes and used San Francisco as his example. If San Francisco has a major earthquake every fifty years, then the odds in any single year are 50–1 against its happening. But as the fiftieth year is approached, the odds against that San Francisco earthquake drop rapidly. And by the fiftieth year, the odds are in the vicinity of *virtual certainty*. In applying the probabilities to a major stock market crash, of primary concern is the 54-year Kondratieff Wave. Adding those years to 1929 gives the year 1983. The odds against a stock market crash had been dropping dramatically as 1983 was approached, and by this time the odds were getting close to the point where such a momentous event was increasingly imminent!

Quoting no less an authority than Donald Hoppe: "The peak for the New York stock market and the end of one of the greatest speculative eras in history is very close." Hoppe said that we had to be prepared for a New York stock market liquidation and an imminent and unexpected collapse in commodity prices. He thought this was due to begin no later than April 1984. Hoppe's scenario was beautifully documented, and the only thing I disagreed with was its timing. I thought that advertising a date of April 1984 would bring on the event sooner. Hoppe made a prediction that has haunted me since. He said that the top of this supercycle would come when it was *least expected*. He also said that the top would pass *unnoticed* when it did occur.

While I could see some more froth in the Dow, there was more than enough evidence to support a crash thesis, with or without a new Dow high. I had carefully documented ten areas of concern this year, showing that each area had always been followed by a bear market. *But the year 1983 had seen all ten areas being activated simultaneously, and thus, at the very least, a severe bear market was imminent.*

I turned to no less an authority than Milton Friedman. Dr. Friedman, a Nobel Prize-winning economist, thought that the U.S. economic recovery could end a full year before it was generally expected to—in the first quarter of 1984. Regardless of economics, I had stated that the market would soon start discounting that, and that meant that the market was sitting on a powder keg.

I was on a short-term sell signal at this time, and I could not get out of my head the fact that *every crash in history started with a short-term sell signal.* This sell signal dated back to November 14 at Dow 1,254.07. One of these short-term signals was going to be seen in retrospect as the *big* one, and thus no sell signal could be treated lightly.

On November 16 I knew exactly where the market was in relation to 1929. I turned to page 4 of *The Wall Street Journal* that day and I knew I was looking at another great 1929 parallel:

Psychological
Big Deals Hide Major Stock Distribution

"After more than 22 months of planning, the biggest financial transaction in corporate history is about to begin." That was the opening line in the *Journal* story about the AT&T breakup. While the spin-off of all the Bell operating companies had to be completed by February 24, 1984, the company had set January 1, 1984, as the target date. It was unthinkable that a stock market crash could take place before these giant transactions were completed. Such news immediately dominated the financial media and it drove into the background any sensible vision which might otherwise have seen through the smoke screen. It muddied up the waters of daily trading, the heavy volume in the Bell companies distorting the normal volume patterns, thus disguising to a degree what was going on elsewhere.

The same type of thing had happened in 1929, temporarily diverting attention from the fast-growing internal market weakness. Here is a paragraph from the "Broad Street Gossip" column in *The Wall Street Journal* of September 18, 1929:

> There may be a secondary reaction. This is anyone's guess, *but the traders who have had years of experience in the Street say it is still a major bull market. Transactions involving billions are scheduled to go through during the next twelve months* and everyone knows these cannot be successfully concluded when stocks are declining and the public is in a pessimistic frame of mind [emphasis added].

Then two days later, on September 20, 1929, the following from the same *Journal* column appeared:

> The news of the day has been big financially and promises to get bigger. We read one day of the formation of a $100,000,000 investment trust and the next day rumors have it that a $1,000,000,000 investment trust is in the course of formation. Newspaper headlines during the last day or two said that a great oil merger was in the making and that a large steel merger was under way with prospects of another very big consolidation in the same line. Loree is planning a merger of 17 eastern railroads and there is to be an alliance of some sort between General Motors and Radio. There has been talk of bank mergers, chemical company mergers, gas mergers, power mergers, aviation mergers, food company and asbestos-gypsum mergers. All of which involves billions of dollars. *While things like this are going on one could hardly expect a bear market.* It will be to the advantage of the so-called big interests to keep the public in a cheerful frame

of mind until all these big transactions are concluded successfully. At least this is the opinion of the Street [emphasis added].

There was great confusion in the Street at this time regarding the primary trend of the market. I related this confusion to that of 1929, and to demonstrate my point, I had indexed every key word used in *The Wall Street Journal* in 1929 just prior to the great crash. From that, indicators could be derived. For instance, I constructed a Confusion Index. Every time the word "confusion" appeared in the *Wall Street Journal* market column on the inside back page, I scored a point for the index. For instance, in the November 17 *Journal*, Robert Kahan of Montgomery Securities in San Francisco was quoted as saying, "There is a great amount of *confusion* in the institutional community." Now the CI stood at +1. Then, a few lines later, Francine Bovich of Citicorp Investment Management was quoted as saying, "Investors are generally *confused* about the direction of interest rates and the valuation of fixed-income investment." That scored another point, bringing the CI reading to +2. *Confusion accompanies all major changes of market direction.* There was a time in 1929 when the legendary Jesse Livermore was "confused." It occurred just before, during, and after the great September 1929 market top. For the history buffs, I came across the word "confusion" nineteen times in the September 1929 editions of *The Wall Street Journal.* A CI reading of +19 was very high, and thus confusion was a necessary ingredient in this major peak.

The market could not crash until it could be proven that the indicators were breaking down badly. Bob Gross of *The Professional Investor* said that there was serious deterioration in the indicators. In his November 4 letter he said: "Worse yet, the deterioration is as bad in the long-term indexes as it is in the intermediate ones. At this rate of decline, if it were to continue, we would be negative (that is, bear market-type numbers) within a month. But we also think this entire bull market will have a much shorter life than is generally projected for it."

They were all still hanging on to a bull market definition as they had done in 1929, long after the market in general had peaked. The market's true message at this time was very definite and I interpreted it to mean that all my original views would be fulfilled:

1. Economic recovery to be aborted;
2. Short bull market with all three phases abbreviated and concentrated in a number of months, rather than years;
3. Completely untraditional election-year market;
4. 1982–83 blowoff market ending nine-year cycle;
5. Completion of the Kondratieff long wave stretching back to 1929;
6. Stock market crash; and
7. Deflation-depression.

One by one, all the bulls who had been relying on a traditional 1982–85 bull market would have to succumb to market reality. The first to top out in a bull market is the junk. A look at the over-the-counter stocks and the American Stock Exchange market showed the return to the junkyard at this time, right where most of those issues belonged in the first place. No bull market ever survived a crash in the over-the-counter stocks and the Amex stocks.

At this time, the American Stock Exchange advance/decline line was back down to the low levels of late August 1982, almost a full round trip. Hardly a day went by without some big-name stock biting the dust, and the Dow Jones Industrial Average provided the cover so that one wouldn't notice that the big money was leaving the market. In December 1982, the maximum number of stocks were above their 200-day trendlines, and by November 1983, almost half of them were under their trendlines. It had been almost six months since the big board advance/decline line had been in gear with the Dow. Since it had recently made a low on November 8, breaking under the August low, I felt that the next break in that key indicator would put a fatal strain on the Dow. Even with this final Dow run-up, the advance/decline line was too near the November 8 low level to dismiss easily the near-term implications of the severe technical consequences following a break under that level. Against this very weak technical background, the widespread complacency was ominous.

At this late date, six months after the 1983 general peak, Bob Gross was listing only three market letters as being long-term bearish. That meant that since June, the true technical top, only one new bear on the primary trend was picked up. That was scary.

I expected market sentiment to swing much more to the bearish side in the next few weeks. There would be no one event accounting for increased bearishness, but if my other assumptions were going to be correct, the market sentiment in 1984 had to swing toward a bearish extreme to produce the situation in which almost everyone wanted to get out of the market at the same time. This would come in steps and would be in evidence in early 1984 as I had predicted.

On November 22 another sell signal of *compelling importance* was flashed, this occurring right in the midst of the giant telephone stock distribution. Again I stated that the distribution presented a smoke screen behind which the specialists could effect big block distributions of stock. The breakup of AT&T was a major stock distribution and in its implications was no different from any other large stock split. Any split against the very weak technical background then existing had to be very bearish, but this, the largest such stock distribution in financial history, could be devastating.

Then on November 29, market history was made—and nobody knew it. The Dow Jones Industrial Average recorded its bull market peak, and rolled over and died with no pain, a merciful death. The peak had come and gone. Another 1929 parallel had been recorded:

PARALLEL 50

Market
Dow Final Peak Comes and Goes Unnoticed

On September 3, 1929, the Dow Jones Industrial Average peaked at 381.17, never to see that level again for almost twenty-five years. It came and went, nobody thinking for a moment that day that the great bull market, as far as the Dow was concerned, had quietly died. The next day *The Wall Street Journal* described the market action: "Wall Street entered the autumn financial season in a definitely optimistic frame of mind. With railroad traffic showing steady gains, and production in the major branches of industry continuing at a high rate, the earnings prospects of the principal corporations with shares listed on the Stock Exchange were looked upon as extremely promising."

The gathering storm was soon to gain momentum.

10

The Coming
Stock Market Bum

[DECEMBER 1983]

I

I noticed the quiet passing of the November 29 Dow. I saw it as such a perfect top that I headlined the December 3 market letter "Classic Top." The bull market had ended for most stocks several months before, and had probably ended, in my opinion, for the blue chip Dow Jones Industrial Average in the past week when a massive 120-million share reversal at an intraday high of 1,296.95 occurred on November 30.

The very same thing that had bothered Jesse Livermore in 1929 had been concerning me for months. Livermore briefed his staff in June 1929 and ordered a different sort of market analysis. They compared the current stock prices on the New York Stock Exchange with those of earlier in the year and discovered significant losses in some of the most prominent stocks traded. They discovered that most stocks were under their January highs. Then they made an additional discovery that greatly influenced Livermore's operations several weeks prior to the great crash. They discovered that on the Curb Exchange—among the so-called unlisted securities—the losses were truly staggering. In May alone the paper value of 240 stocks shrank $3 billion, a fact verified by *The New York Times*. According to Thomas and Morgan-Witts: "More significantly, one of Livermore's sources had made available to him in advance the contents of a survey by the Midland Bank of Cleveland. It had studied the behavior of 1,002 stocks listed on the New York Exchange. More than 60 percent, 614 shares, were lower now than they had been in January; only 338 stocks had shown any real and sustained advance during the past six months."[1]

---

[1]Gordon Thomas and Max Morgan-Witts, *The Day the Bubble Burst* (New York: Penguin Books, 1980), p. 191.

Obviously Roger Babson had done the same research in 1929 that Livermore had, for it was the large discrepancy between the general market and the Dow that had bothered them both. *It was the identical thing that I saw in 1983 which had to precede a stock market crash.* The pattern in 1983 was ominously similar to that of 1929. Out of over 2,000 stocks listed on the New York Stock Exchange, a mere handful, fewer than 100 issues, were registering new highs late in the year when the Dow Jones Industrial Average was telling the false story that the bull market was continuing without a blemish. And, as in 1929, the losses in the more speculative issues of the over-the-counter market and the American Stock Exchange were equally staggering, losses ranging as high as 75 percent and in some cases (Baldwin-United) even more.

And, as in 1929, the Cassandras of the day were discredited by the financial press. But as history ultimately proved, their warnings were well founded. It took a great deal of will power in 1929 not to get sucked back into the whirlpool of speculation then blinding the masses to the big picture. Joseph Kennedy had gotten out of the market completely by December 1928, which proved to be the true internal market top. As he later related, he was sorely tempted to come back in 1929, but a shoeshine boy changed all that. He was sitting outside the Exchange one day having his shoes shined by his favorite bootblack. The time was September 1929. He was getting much free advice on the market. The shoeshine boy was telling Kennedy that the place to be was in oil and rails. That did it for Kennedy. He said to himself that day that he wouldn't touch the market with a 50,000-foot pole.

The most reliable parallel technical indicators which had homed in on the developing trouble in 1929 were the high/low indicator and the advance/decline line. Both of them had peaked in December 1928, and both of them had given the best evidence that the Dow Jones Industrial Average in 1929 had embarked on the "solitary walk." In the current market, the high/low indicator peaked on May 6, with 388 stocks that day making new twelve-month highs. The advance/decline line had peaked on June 16. The Dow had risen to 1,248.30 on June 16, the last day in the 1982–83 brief bull market when market breadth was in gear with the Dow. The rise to a new high in the Dow on November 29 saw the advance/decline line far below the June levels. On the same day as that final Dow peak, the number of stocks making new twelve-month highs was down to a mere 73. In other words, the Dow Jones Industrial Average, five and a half months after the internal June top, *had tacked on a mere 39 points,* and the individual losses recorded while the Dow was adding those 39 points were, in many cases, simply staggering. In achieving that 39-point gain in the Dow, *the cost was simply too high.*

Profits are only paper profits until stocks are sold. Since human nature in the marketplace has a herdlike instinct, most speculators moved into the most popular areas, and the siren song of the 1982–83 advance was technology— more specifically, video games and home computers. While brokers put many millions of eager buyers into those stocks, they failed the acid test of getting their clients out at the top. They had also pushed their clients into airlines, brokerage house stocks, and anything else they thought would balloon their commissions, but again were, in the main, negligent in getting their clients out at the top. As millions of investors and speculators saw the value of their portfolios going in the opposite direction of their broker's advice, many changed brokers, which they should have done months earlier, and, of course, that fed the already plagued industry.

A lot of water had gone over the dam since the euphoria in the brokerage industry a year before. Memory of the huge year-end bonuses paid at that time had completely faded. Following a wave of the most widespread hiring of new stockbrokers, the brokerage industry found itself surfeited with brokers. Not only were too many brokers hired, but the palmy days of months before had led to the renting of too much additional floor space, the industry always making its biggest expansion moves at the top of the market. The same thing had occurred in 1929—too many brokers, too many branch offices, too many investment trusts, too many market letter writers, too much market volume, too many speculators, too much insider manipulation, too many stock splits, too many secondary offerings, etc. Back in that fateful year, the Chicago Stock Exchange's volume was seventeen times greater than it had been ten years earlier. During the same period, the annual volume on the St. Louis Exchange had grown from 80,000 to 1 million. The Los Angeles Curb Exchange had been founded in 1928. In the first year of trading, it had handled 18 million shares. Everybody seemed to be buying and selling, running to and fro in a frantic attempt to enrich themselves.

The situation was identical in 1983. The financial supermarkets catered to the largest number of investors and speculators on record. The combined exposure to mutual funds, pension funds, options, and futures dwarfed any-thing seen in the past. But what of the future? Part of the answer was readily seen in terms of the Merrill Lynch chart. Since Merrill Lynch stock peaked in July, the 2–1 split coincided with the top and the stock made a sharp decline from 56 to slightly under 30 by this time, the vicinity where shorts had been previously covered in October. But the rally since then had been weak and was simply building the extremely bearish right shoulder of a massive head-and-shoulders formation which would ultimately take the stock a lot lower. I had not dismissed the notion at this time that the stock could drop to as low as 9 in the developing bear market. The implications for the general market were thus frightfully clear. Not only was the brokerage industry headed for severe trouble, but so was the stock market. One went hand in hand with the other; this is why Merrill Lynch was considered a premier bellwether stock. If the chart of Merrill Lynch was sick, then the health of the entire market was in serious jeopardy.

The fuel that had driven the brief, but powerful, 1982–83 rise was running out. In keeping with the overall pattern of excess that had signaled the end of that brief rise, another 1929 parallel was recorded:

Technical
Mutual Fund Liquidity Drops to Five-Year Low

Reflecting the tremendous mutual fund resurgence in 1983, the funds overin-
vested in common stocks, they too believing the cover story that nothing could
go wrong before the 1984 presidential election. They had such a love affair
with the market that they let their cash reserves get too low, in fact the lowest
in five years. Such illiquidity has been a precursor of bear markets. A serious
downturn would catch them in a highly vulnerable position.

The 1929 parallel can be drawn with the comparative illiquidity of the
investment trusts. Partially explaining the illiquidity of 1929 was an insidious
method of stock distribution. Having much unsalable stock, some promoters
would set up an investment trust, sell shares in it, pocket the cash, and put
questionable securities in the trust. Such a practice always made sure there was
plenty of stock to be held but very little cash in the trust, the cash having gone
into the pockets of the promoters. When the great break came in the market,
there was no market for much of the stock in these trust portfolios and
investment trust shares took a terrible beating. Most of those trusts were no
longer around soon after.

By December 1983 nobody seemed to be overly concerned or aware of what
lay around the corner in 1984. The government kept reporting that more and
more people were making money, and that was yet another 1929 parallel.

Historical
New Highs in Personal Income

Despite the 1981–82 economic recession, personal income was soaring to new
highs.

On September 19, 1929, it was stated in *The Wall Street Journal*'s "Broad
Street Gossip" column that "the public appetite for securities is large because
the income of the people is larger than ever before in history."

I was now monitoring the great telephone distribution carefully, seeing it
being used by the powers-that-be as a smoke screen deflecting attention away
from the massive stock distribution going on elsewhere, notably in IBM and
General Motors. The breakup in AT&T was no different in any way from a
7–1 split, and certainly I had pounded the theme all year about the bearish
implications of the record number of splits. *The Wall Street Journal* was

running a little box so readers could readily see what the seven dwarfs were quoted at. Merrill Lynch had set up the Humpty Dumpty fund embracing the AT&T spin-offs so as to clarify some of the confusion and also to promote confidence. After all, some people had held AT&T stock for two or three generations, and seeing it breaking up was a trifle upsetting, to say the least. Memories were short. Many investors had already been stung by buying Baldwin-United annuities through Merrill Lynch, but that was all forgotten as Merrill pushed its Humpty Dumpty package. Like all Humpty Dumptys, this one would succumb to the great fall. It was a great time to market the package because, having been burned in the collapse of the speculative euphoria the previous spring, people were all "quality" conscious.

But it didn't stop there. The virus of a developing severe bear market and probable stock market crash would spread until it affected everything, and with the world growing smaller every day, the virus would be expected to spread to foreign stock exchanges in 1984. Sixty-five percent of all stocks are American securities, and thus my conclusions for the American market would have a shattering effect the world over. As the Hatry affair in England had a reinforcing effect on the September 1929 downturn, I expected that there would be several financial scandals in this developing down cycle which would reinforce the downturn. Such a scandal was brewing at this time in West Germany, where it was discovered that a cabinet member was taking bribes.

For my thesis of a coming stock market crash to be validated, there had to be a *series of stock market breaks* preceding the crash. There was a break after November 30, but I felt at this time that the first order of business was to assess the market's ability to recover. If that ability was found wanting, then it would bring out more stock and the declining process would be reinforced. During such times, the market increasingly turns a deaf ear on bullish news and is increasingly receptive to bearish news. One could sense the repeated attempts to rally the troops behind IBM, but this ploy was beginning to run out of steam. I felt that historians might draw a parallel here with the bankers' pool in 1929, a strategy that was designed to keep the market up long enough for the insiders to get out.

II

The feature article in the December 5 issue of *Barron's* was titled "The Coming Stock Market Boom," by my good friend Richard Russell. The article immediately drew from me a full-scale rebuttal. My contention was that if one cast his vote for the Russell position, he was going to lose a great deal of money in the months ahead.

First of all, I contended that Russell's entire position was based on *a false assumption*—that the primary trend was still bullish. If I was correct, then all of Russell's arguments could be *reversed.* Taking the article's key statements one by one, I started with the statement that "a bull market climbs a wall of worry." That in itself was true, *if the primary trend was still bullish.* But my rebuttal was based on the opposite of Russell's thesis—*that the primary trend had turned bearish.* If I was correct in that assumption, it followed that one could say that *a bear market falls on a wall of confidence.* In other words, the market tends to turn a deaf ear to bullish news and becomes increasingly sensitive to bearish news. As the true technical peak of the stock market prior to the 1929 crash occurred in December 1928, the time when the advance/decline line and the high/low indicator peaked, so then was the true technical peak of the 1982–83 bull market recorded in the spring of 1983, new highs peaking on May 6 and the advance/decline line peaking on June 16. While buyers of stocks in 1929 were ultimately crucified on a cross of thirty Dow Jones industrial stocks, they had already taken a bath in the general market for several months prior to the crash itself. Likewise, in 1983 a sickness had enveloped the general market which was thoroughly documented by the performance of a vast number of over-the-counter stocks and Amex issues as well as many big board stocks since the spring of 1983; thus the general market had not been rising on a wall of worry, but had, more accurately, *been declining in the face of a bullish consensus regarding 1984,* a presidential election year and a year predicted by the economists to show a further economic expansion. Many stock buyers in 1983 had already regretted their entrance into a bull market that had been steadily blowing up in their faces, and recent strength in the Dow 30 had done little to bolster their weak portfolios.

Noting the weakness in the advance/decline line since June, Russell's bullish argument contended that it was not important, because the Dow Jones Industrial Average and the Dow Jones Transportation Average had failed to confirm the weakness in the advance/decline line, such a confirmation requiring a drop in the industrials below the August 1983 low of 1,163 and a drop by the transports below the October low of 560. But, to use Russell's own argument underscoring the importance of non-confirmations, *he completely ignored all the upside non-confirmations,* which, at this late date, had far more meaning than downside non-confirmations, technical phenomena which were increasingly likely to be aborted in the coming market collapse.

It was out of character for Russell now to put more faith in the Dow Jones Industrial Average than in the time-honored advance/decline line, which, in his earlier writings, he had always championed over the Dow. Now he said: "Moreover, if this were a bear market which topped out in mid-June, then it would be almost unprecedented to see the major averages at or near their bull market highs six months later." There were many examples to prove that statement false. I presented three: The advance/decline line topped out in December 1928, a major warning of trouble ahead for 1929. Six months later, the Dow industrials were scoring new highs in June 1929.

A few months later, the Dow peaked, and then a month later, the market crashed, a prelude to the most severe bear market in history. The advance/ decline line gave early warning to the severe 1973–74 bear market by scoring a secondary peak in March 1972. Six months later, the Dow Jones Industrial Average was making new bull market highs. The Dow peaked a little more than three months later, and the 1973–74 severe bear market became a historical fact. The advance/decline line peaked in September 1980, and six months later, the Dow was scoring new bull market highs in March 1981. However, a month later, the Dow peaked, and the sharp downturn of 1981–82 followed. Russell used to preach the doctrine that *whenever the Dow is moving out of gear with the advance/decline line* that is incontrovertible technical proof that *something is wrong.* I threw it back to him that something was terribly wrong technically with the 1982–83 bull market.

Russell emphasized the point that when the bull is in command, the averages and the majority of stocks will head to new highs. But we must deal now with the facts. The fact of the matter was that the majority of stocks had seen their highs the previous spring. That was not opinion. That was fact. As for the averages, the Standard & Poor 500 topped out in October, the New York Stock Exchange Composite topped out in October, but the Amex Market Value Index topped out in July and the OTC Composite Average topped out in June. That is what should have concerned Russell, because there was the best technical proof that the bull was not in command. But, more important, I called attention to the advance/decline line in those other markets. The OTC advance/decline line had topped out in June and had since made a horrendous drop back to February 1983 levels. The Amex advance/ decline line also had topped out in June and had since retraced all of the 1983 advance. These things do not happen in bull markets. They were the time-proven early warnings of developing severe bear markets.

Russell wrote that major tops are accompanied by high volume and high excitement, by hot tips and juicy rumors. Those characteristics were thoroughly documented the previous spring by the new issue mania, articles appearing in *The New York Times* on April 24 titled "Financial Futures: A Hot New Act" and "The Stampede to Equity Mutual Funds"; the April 30 *Financial World* cover story, "New Issues Stampede"; the May 9 cover story in *Business Week,* "The Rebirth of Equities"; the May 30 cover story in *Fortune,* "The New New Issues Market." Such writing showed the bull market burning itself out by June 1983, and all new highs in the Dow Jones Industrial Average since that time were all technically *non-confirmed* new highs, the Dow dangerously out of step with reality. Russell also stated that the final top would see a general consensus that the market would head higher for at least another year or so. That *was* the general consensus, most analysts married to the concept of the classical bull market cycle, not expecting the bull market to end until late 1984 or early 1985. But the majority of technical indicators said, without a doubt, that the true internal peak of the bull market was recorded in June 1983, as reliable an early warning as the true internal peak of December 1928 preceding the crash of 1929.

Then Russell talked about the high short interest and the high readings in the short interest ratio. That was an easy argument to knock down. Analysis of the November 1983 short interest report showed that the short interest in 81 stocks accounted for 51.5 percent of the entire short interest, and all of those stocks were under their 1983 highs, with drops in price mostly in the double-digit percentage declines. That meant that the shorts were right! The record shows that people do not short on a rising market, but increase their short selling on a declining market. The record-high short interest therefore showed that most stocks were declining, not advancing. That was proved by the advance/decline line and the high/low indicator. Over a quarter of those 81 stocks accounting for the largest short interest positions had shown stock splits in 1983; this meant that almost 10 percent of the entire short interest was due entirely to stock splitting, not reflecting one additional short sale. A high short interest is also a natural reflection of high market volume. Russell did not say that the short interest was at record highs in September 1929, a month before the greatest stock market crash in history. He also stated that the high short interest was a reflection of increasing bearish sentiment. But he did not remind the *Barron's* readers that a stock market panic and crash is impossible unless bearish sentiment increases to a point where everybody wants to get out at the same time. In September 1929, 75 percent of all market letters were bearish, but they were all short-term bears. However, every sharp decline in history starts with a short-term sell signal. Wall Street then, like Wall Street at this time, was long-term bullish. Then they talked correction, but they talked it so well and so convincingly that everybody tried to get out at the same time (either by choice or by the forced selling of unmet margin calls) and were crushed between the pages of market history.

In the Russell article, the reader was told that the Dow Jones Utility Average struck the highest level on October 31 since late 1968. But what the reader was not told was that the late 1968 high in the utility average was followed shortly thereafter by the severe bear market of 1968–70, a bear market that began in the seasonally strong month of December.

I then went on to list examples of major phenomena that occurred in 1983, phenomena that had always been followed by bear markets without exception. So I had thrown down the gauntlet. Was it to be boom or bum? Being a historian as well as a stock market technician, I was certain that Russell's "Coming Stock Market Boom" would soon translate into a *stock market bum* and that Russell would be forced to reverse his thinking.

As I was rebutting the Russell piece, the A-Dis Trading Barometer came up with another buy signal. Hastening to explain to my readers, I underscored the term "short-term" in reference to all the trading signals, especially the buy signals. However, important price swings all begin with short-term signals, and thus they had to be recognized, regardless of any preconceived notions regarding the primary trend. The important thing was to nail down profits on every signaled change of direction. Recognizing that a perfect broadening top formation could take the Dow as high as 1,310, I could not readily dismiss the potential importance of that December buy signal.

III

As I was writing the December 17 weekly letter, the market had reached a critical point from which it had to rally or it would cave in completely. In other words, the market was about to state in its own unique language whether the crash was to take place then and there or would be postponed until 1984. It would convey that message in a number of ways. First of all, it was essential that the Dow not move under the November lows. Secondly, it was essential that the advance/decline line not break under the November 8 low. If that level was decisively broken, then it would be very difficult for the Dow to go back above the high of November 29, when the Dow had closed at 1,287.20. The bear market would then be out in the open and a great decline would follow. On the other hand, if those technical landmark levels could hold, then there would be one more scene in the unfolding drama. The critical do-or-die day was December 15, the day the lead article was being written for the December 17 letter.

However, in the face of the Street bearishness over the recent Henry Kaufman statement concerning the course of interest rates, we had a number of interesting December parallels that suggested the possibility that the bulls would be sent home with hope still in their hearts. Of course, we knew that this was the month of the traditional year-end rally, but aside from that, I recalled a number of past Decembers when early in the month it looked as if the market was falling apart, only to lead into a rally which peaked in January–February the following year.

The market hated uncertainty, but once the feared events materialized and were clearly seen, the market often reversed direction, at least for a while. In December 1965, the Fed raised the discount rate and the market fell and then rallied into the following February. In December 1972, the Dow stood at over 1,036 but dropped sharply to the 1,000 level, only to rally to 1,051 the following month. In December 1980, Henry Kaufman predicted sharply higher interest rates, with a prime going to 24 percent. The Dow had peaked on November 20, 1980, at the 1,000 level and dropped sharply to 911.60 by December 15. On December 16 the prime rate was raised to 21 percent. Did that hurt the stock market? No, the market had bottomed out the day before the announcement. And on the day of the announcement, the Dow closed *up* over 6 points and then continued to climb to a new high, to over 1,004 on January 6. In December 1982, the Dow had dropped sharply to 990, only to turn around dramatically. The big picture at this time was totally different, but the December syndrome could not be quickly dismissed. There was usually one more scene to be played out by the bulls *even though the three-act play was a tragedy.*

The story of the possible rebound from those critical levels was well told in the on-balance volume figures. A crash had to be preceded by a technical situation in which a maximum number of field trends[2] could be lost on a protracted decline. That was not the situation at this time. The market was at an intermediate bottom in mid-December with an increasing probability of starting a sharp rally that could drive the Dow to levels above 1,300. The Dow was seen at this time to have one final go for the top. The most certain proof that there was one rally left was the proliferation of higher down designations among the thirty Dow Jones industrial stocks. Such a short-term rally, however, had the potential to put the Dow in a position to lose more field trends than at any other time in my memory. In either case, it was clear that any rally was going to put the market in an extremely vulnerable position.

Gold was going straight down because of crisis news—in keeping with my late November Gold Barometer sell signal. The crisis news was helping the dollar and hurting gold. I stated at the time that until it could be demonstrated that people would rather hold gold than dollars, the dollar would get stronger and gold weaker. Higher interest rates were hurting gold and I saw any move under $375 for spot gold as a signal for lower prices. With my South African trip coming up in a few weeks, I was hoping that I would at least be on a short-term gold buy signal by the time I got there.

While the short-term upswing might look attractive to some, I underscored the great risks. I pleaded with my readers to sell into all strength as it developed over the near term and told them that the percentage gains would be minimal on that predicted short-term rally. It was emphasized as the *last chance* to move out of the market before major trouble ensued. The next sell signal had to be extremely important.

I V

It came on December 23 after the close. *I treated it as the most important sell signal I had ever issued.* I told my readers that it was no ordinary sell signal, but that it constituted a major signal aimed at all market participants and virtually affecting everybody. The last holdout had been the Dow stocks themselves, and at this time an overwhelming assortment of technical

---

[2]The Net Field Indicator, an invention of the author, was featured in *Granville's New Strategy of Daily Stock Market Timing for Maximum Profit.* It measures how many of the 30 Dow Jones industrial stocks are in positive or negative volume trends.

indicators had converged to say that such a sell signal could very well be followed by a severe market collapse, an election year notwithstanding.

As it turned out, the December 17 market letter was written on the very day of the December 15 market bottom at Dow 1,236.79, and the A-Dis Trading Barometer was still operating on the December 9 buy signal, the door left open for some degree of rally from that level. The sell signal then recorded was accompanied by the expected relatively lower levels among the Dow industrial stocks. Thus the technical stage was set for a severe drop, even if the Dow went a bit higher for a few days. A higher Dow would simply have driven the A-Dis Trading Barometer into a still deeper sell area. So regardless of whatever action the Dow was going to take in the days ahead, the barometer had put a final cap on the last rally of the year, and the bear market was then about to come fully out in the open.

I was so positive that this was the big one, the most important sell signal in my life, that I recommended going short on all thirty Dow stocks, using no stops! I added to the list of short sales such stocks as E. F. Hutton, Holiday Inns, Honeywell, Hewlett-Packard, Household International, Merrill Lynch, Mellon National Corp., and Metromedia. The small rally off the Dow 200-day trendline was seen as the weakest response to date, and thus the Dow was finally set to plunge importantly below that trendline for the first time in the overall cycle. Again I pleaded with everyone to sell everything and told them that it wasn't going to be pleasant being on the wrong side of this call.

The market follows all the laws of physics, and none of those laws had been repealed. Throw a ball up into the air. A momentum is created that drives the ball higher. Then momentum loses force, but the ball is still going up. Then the ball stops going up and drops to the ground. Before the ball fell to the ground, the upward momentum had dropped to zero. In the marketplace, we follow momentum and not the ball. The ball in this case is the stock market. We can say with conviction that the stock market will go higher as long as it can be shown that there is an upward momentum behind it. But what could one say about the stock market in late December 1983, when it could be clearly demonstrated that the stock market had been losing upside momentum since the previous spring? The market had to come down just as certainly as God makes little green apples.

The descent is always in steps. First of all, the speculative stocks peak out and the flow of money thereafter is always toward safety, ultimately concentrated in the blue chip stocks and then out of the market completely. This is why the Dow 30 are always the last to peak out. But most people look at the Dow and tend to forget the entire market. They lost sight of the fact that the market contracted a form of terminal cancer in the spring of 1983. After all, if a market is to stay healthy, an increasing number of stocks have to be making new highs. But since fewer and fewer stocks had been making new highs since the spring of 1983, I had to conclude that from that time on it was no longer a healthy bull market. A healthy bull market does not see more stocks making new lows than stocks making new highs, and the technical situation at this time had worsened to the point where this was happening every day. A healthy bull market must see a record of more stocks advancing than declining. But that had not been the case since the previous June. There was an ever-widening divergence between the advance/decline line and the Dow Jones Industrial Average, and either the advance/decline line had to turn around and better the June highs or the Dow would get caught up in the suction that had been affecting most stocks for months.

None of the stock market averages was making new highs. The OTC Composite Average had topped out in June. The Amex Market Value Index had topped out in July. The Standard & Poor 500 Stock Index and the New York Stock Exchange Composite Index had topped out in October, and, as I stated at the time, the Dow Jones Industrial Average had peaked in late November. When no averages whatsoever are making new highs, then an additional burden of proof is placed on those who proclaim a strong and continuing bull market. And strength in the Dow alone was not enough. There was strength in the Dow in the summer of 1929, but it could be easily proved that the bull market was dying by December 1928, the month the advance/decline line and stocks making new highs had peaked. Strength in 1929 was restricted to a handful of forty or fifty blue chip stocks, and the situation by late 1983 was absolutely no different. One could not expect the laws of physics to be repealed. Every nook and cranny of the market showed that deadly loss of upside momentum. One could see it in the Dow Jones Transportation Average and one could see it in the Dow Jones Utility Average. Just as the loss of upside momentum predicted by the laws of physics meant that the ball had to come down, the same loss of upside momentum told me, without a shadow of a doubt, that this stock market must and would come down.

But the big question, as always, was when? It was like the doctor who knew his patient was dying with terminal cancer but could not predict the precise day when the patient would die; nevertheless, he knew the patient was dying.

There were important clues, however. One clue was the rapid breakdown in the Net Field Trend Indicator. Such a breakdown had to be preceded by a proliferation of Dow stocks losing volume strength, thus positioning the Net Field Trend Indicator to fall. As I stated in late December, such a proliferation of lower ups was being recorded. That was the precise function of the December rally—to put the Dow in a position to collapse technically. It was really immaterial whether the Dow made a new high or not on such a rally. In any case, when the move was over, the collapse would follow. While I had my short-term traders long on the December rally, something suddenly happened that showed that we had run out of time. The A-Dis Trading Barometer had produced an emphatic sell signal on December 23, and it was clear that any further rise in the Dow would simply drive the barometer into still deeper bearish territory. It was the last and best opportunity to sell into strength. The stage was now set for an extended decline.

Another clue that indicated that the bear market would soon be fully out in the open was seen in the overall performance of the market since the Dow last touched the trendline in mid-December. All previous dips to the trendline had been followed by sharp and extended rallies. This time, however, the Amex and the OTC market went dead, the advance/decline line on the big board broke under the November 8 low to set new lows since June, and the futures markets failed to keep pace with the Dow. This told me that the next important move in the market would be the breaking of the Dow trendline, which then stood at 1,230, but rather than signaling some kind of bottom soon thereafter, the break would be sharp and extended and the advance/decline line would fail to recover from it for the balance of the developing bear market. A bear market is more quickly validated by an early break under the trendline soon after the Dow made the final high. That then would turn the trendline down, and all the bear market rallies would simply see the Dow attempting to get back to that declining trendline. That was currently the case with the Amex Market Value Index. The trendline for that market had been broken in October and that was soon followed by a sharp decline. Since then, the line had flattened out and the November rally was nothing more than a rally in a bear market, the index attempting to come up and touch the declining trendline. I then stated that the Dow was about to duplicate what the Amex had been doing since July.

Still another clue to the increasingly obvious bear market was seen in the price of gold. Many construed gold to be in a bull market along with the stock market, ever since both had bottomed in the summer of 1982. The argument then was that the stock market would get three traditional upward legs and so would the gold market. By late 1983 there were still those who were looking for a big second leg to the bull market in stocks in 1984 and were also looking for a second leg to the gold bull market. Neither event, of course, was going to occur because both bull markets had died in 1983. Stocks had peaked in the spring of 1983 and gold peaked at over $500 in February 1983. Like the bulk of the stock market that soon followed suit, gold broke its trendline, and all rallies thereafter simply hugged the trendline all the way down, proving technically that gold had been in a bear market since February 1983. As long as that trendline was declining, with the price of gold failing to move importantly above that line, the bear market in gold would continue. Naturally, now having the Gold Barometer, I expected periodic short-term buy signals for gold, but until it was proved otherwise, I needed only short-term implications for my readers until the trendline was bettered. I had contended that the break in gold early in 1983 was simply a forerunner of the expected major break in stocks.

The market never wastes time making totally meaningless moves. It comes to do a job, and when the job is done, it doesn't linger around. It rapidly goes on to other things. Although I had seen some validity in a scenario that could have taken the Dow to over 1,300 on the December rally, I had also seen that the point of the rally would produce a dangerous number of lower up designations in the Dow stock on-balance volume figures, thus positioning the Dow to collapse. But when I saw the same objective accomplished on a substandard rally cut short by the A-Dis Trading Barometer sell signal, the market had done what it came to do. There was no longer any point in wasting time trying to vault the 1,300 level. Obviously, then, the sell signal coming at this highly critical time could not be treated lightly. It had to be a sell signal of major import affecting all market participants, regardless of whether they were investors or traders.

PART FOUR

THE STORM BREAKS

11

Raising the Guillotine

[JANUARY 1984]

I

Picture the Dow industrial trendline as being the neck of the market. For almost a year, that neck was very tough and impenetrable. The Dow Jones Industrial Average managed to stay very comfortably above that trendline and did not come down to touch it until August 1983. It touched it again in November and still again in December. Thus, something had been happening since the previous August that did not occur during the first year of rise. Prior to each of those three tests on the trendline, the Dow Jones Industrial Average had scored important rally highs. I then gave the analogy that before the neck of the market could be severed, the guillotine had to be raised, and thus the December–January rally was serving that purpose. The Dow rally peak in June preceded the assault on the trendline in November. The Dow rally peak in January 1984 was *suspect* because not only were the assaults on the trendline becoming *more frequent*, but the distance between the trendline and each rally high was *shortening*. The June spread was 140 points. The October spread was 75 points. The November spread was 70 points. If the Dow failed to better the November 29 high, it would be the first time that the next assault on the trendline would occur from a declining top. That would be a dramatic shift of pattern, and it would strongly suggest that at long last the powerful neck of the Dow would be subjected to the guillotine.

As I was describing this in the opening days of January, the Dow enjoyed the sharpest one-day rise since November 29, vaulting over 16 points to 1,269.05 on heavy volume. That was on January 4. The rise was accomplished on the heaviest volume since November 29, and thus one could not construe a higher Dow based on simply a volume explosion, since an increasing tendency had been shown relating high volume to price peaks. Being aware of the volatility of new year markets, I felt that there was too much risk of possibly getting stopped out on the latest barometer sell signal, and thus I took a calculated risk *and advised using no stops on the latest short positions taken.* That action was predicated on the assumption that this was the final run in the blue chips, *and even an end run to over the 1,300 level would not reduce the risks of what I expected to follow that run.* Even if the Dow had run to 1,300 and peaked out, it would have meant that 96 percent of the bull run in the Dow was over at the 1,269 level. The point I was trying to make was that *I didn't want to see my followers buying into the last 4 percent of the bull move in the Dow.*

Reinvestment demand in January is generally a normal year-to-year occurrence, and thus the January 4 run-up could not be deemed a total surprise. It would have been deemed more welcome had it occurred against the background of a barometer buy signal, but occurring on the heels of a sell signal simply implied that the top was imminent. While the barometer signals, by their very construction, tended to occur a trifle early, they nevertheless signaled all developing moves. The December 23 sell signal, seen to be the most important, was expected to precede a near-term top. Unless the rally in progress could abort the very high number of lower up designations among half of the Dow industrial stocks, the Net Field Trend Indicator would be set to plunge to bear market levels in the January–February period. A failure to return to the high Net Field Trend Indicator levels of late November, when the NFI had stood at +15, would be deemed to be a major technical failure and would be the type of thing that had preceded major downturns.

Cyclically, the market was coming into a time which had proved increasingly vulnerable to the four-year cycle. The peaks of 1972, 1976, and 1980 were all followed by bear markets, and now that 1984 had finally arrived, the cycle was again about to be activated. But having proved the *abnormalities* of the *shortened* bull cycle of 1982–83, the bear market had arrived *far earlier* than anyone expected. Normal cyclical analysis was failing miserably since normal parameters would not fit an abnormal market.

Going into the new year, money was being *wantonly* committed to the stock market. It was very important to note, however, that *for the first time in at least ten years, mutual funds investing in common stocks in 1983 failed to outperform the overall stock market.* That was highly significant, because 1983 saw a record $13.4 billion in new money poured into the stock mutual funds. The conclusion was clear. In the very early part of 1983, it was all clear sailing, but ever since the spring of 1983, *an increasing number of mutual fund holders were becoming locked in with mounting losses.* The decline in most stocks since May 6, 1983, explained why the funds could not outperform the market. But blindly believing that the bull market was still alive, the mutual fund managers stupidly shoveled the new money into the market as fast as it was coming in; this was reflected in the huge parabolic curve signifying termination. The amount invested in 1983 was over 300 percent more than in the previous record year, and its investment at the very worst of times, just prior to the great bear market, meant that such funds weren't likely to be replaced to fuel another upswing. It was the final blowoff. Most of the money had been wrongfully invested right at the top, a stinging indictment of most of the money managers.

January was always an important month because of the January Indicator. The popular notion was that as January went, so did the entire year. Most people would not wait for the statistics of the entire month, but would pounce on the findings of the first three trading days and the first five trading days. Instead of merely looking at the opening days of January and basing a forecast on that limited evidence, I always break up the January Indicator into five parts, and the latter two are the all-important ones. First of all, I look at the first three trading days in January. That is the first step of the January Indicator. The second step comprises the first five trading days of the month. Those readings are then compared with the Dow in the middle of the month and the end of the month. That comprises steps three and four of the indicator. The fifth step is to check whether the December Dow low has been violated. That is a very important point—whether it is done in January or later in the year. The most bullish conclusion would occur when all five parts give positive readings.

On January 5 all hell broke loose—on the upside! The Dow soared for the second day, this time rising 13.19 points to 1,282.24 on all-time record volume of 160 million shares. The Dow closed just 4.96 points short of the November 29 bull market peak reading. My office in Kansas City was deluged with worry calls from subscribers who were short across the board with no stops. *They were calmly told that this was a bull trap and to maintain their short positions.* It was not an easy time because when the Dow is soaring it is almost impossible to convince someone that the market is about to fall apart. But the evidence of a major bull trap was certain. Not only was the A-Dis Trading Barometer reconfirming the current sell signal, but the Climax Indicator soared to a +23 reading, the most certain evidence one could have that the market was at the end of the line. At the most, another day on the upside might be eked out, but the non-confirmations would be glaring.

This was a time that tried men's souls, a time of great confusion. Jesse Livermore spoke of the times when it was very difficult to make a rational decision, and his first instincts always proved to be the best ones. At such times, his first gut instinct was *to do nothing until the smoke had cleared away a bit, so that he could make unpressured decisions.* All market tops are designed to make one feel like a sap if he dared to buck the herd. Whenever it looks like the height of folly to sell or go short, then that is usually the time to act. Livermore was always conscious of which way the herd was going, and when it looked like a *stampede,* then he made his carefully chosen moves in the *opposite* direction.

I knew exactly what Jesse would have done under these circumstances. It was a tremendous opportunity to be short across the board.

II

Livermore's "herd" was knocking the doors down to buy stocks. Here was the greatest of the 1929 parallels staring me in the face!

Psychological
Optimism at the Top

Early January euphoria had done its work well. It converted virtually all of Wall Street into a tidal wave of super-optimism. The biggest names on Wall Street were totally "hooked" and their words in *The Wall Street Journal* forever inscribed them in the annals of losers. Wall Street analysts had all fallen for the big cover story—hook, line, and sinker—and were about to be responsible for decimating the public's capital.

Watch the great transformation as *The Wall Street Journal* chronicled those fateful days:

January 3, 1984—Dow 1,258.64

SOME MANAGERS LOOK FOR NEW FUEL TO POWER ANY
FRESH SUSTAINED RISE

Transportation stocks were in the spotlight in an otherwise lackluster market that closed out the year mixed on Friday.

Investment officers generally agree that the bull market, which began in August 1982, has completed the first phase of its climb. But some are less certain on whether the elements are present yet to fuel another extensive upswing.

"We expect the bull market to continue, but until it gets some new ammunition we think its upside potential will be limited," says Wayne A. Stork, executive vice president of Delaware Investment Advisers, Philadelphia.

Before the market can take off on another big move, he thinks at least one of two things must occur: "Interest rates will have to fall about 1½ percentage points, and investors will have to gain confidence that the economic recovery will extend beyond 1984."

However, Mr. Stork emphasizes that "we're not in the camp of those who expect long-term interest rates to move up, and *we also think the current market holds very little risk*" [emphasis added].

Delaware Investment Advisers, which guides assets of $6 billion, *currently is maintaining cash reserves of just 2% to 3%* [emphasis added].

"We expect the market to show an upward bias during 1984's first half, but also to experience an extension of the stock rotation that characterized the past six months," asserts Robert C. Gray, Jr., senior vice president and chief investment officer at Liberty National Bank & Trust, Louisville [emphasis added].

January 4, 1984—Dow 1,252.74

INDUSTRIALS START YEAR BY DECLINING 5.90 POINTS IN RELATIVELY SLOW DAY

The stock market stepped timidly into the new year and finished slightly lower in relatively slow trading activity. Telephone issues rang the bell and some of the drug issues also rose. But the retail, oil, chemical and some technology stocks retreated.

"The reluctance to commit funds to the equity market seems to have spilled over into the new year," observed Michael T. Murray, vice president of Loomis Sayles, Chicago. "In spite of this caution a number of obstacles, such as fear of tighter money, high inflation and difficult earnings comparisons, have crumbled."

Mr. Murray added that he believes *"the ingredients for an above-average stock market performance in 1984 seem to be in place"* [emphasis added].

"I expect a strong market to get started in the next several weeks," asserted Stephen Leeb, vice president of Money Growth Institute, Jersey City, N.J. On the fundamental side, he said, "the economy has definitely slowed without stalling and commodity prices are down, which will give the Federal Reserve room to ease credit policy."

He also mentioned positive technical factors, *including "near-record short interest figures but with a near-record low" on short-selling by specialists* [emphasis added].

January 5, 1984—Dow 1,269.05

BROAD RALLY PUSHES INDUSTRIALS UP BY 16.31 TO 1,269.05 IN BUSY TRADING

The "year-end rally" came with a flourish yesterday. The Dow Jones Industrial Average jumped 16.31 points on the heaviest volume in more than a month. The upswing was helped by a strong bond market and also by the flow of reinvestment funds that normally come into the market at this time each year. Volume was nearly 113 million shares.

"Interest rates are expected to decline and the economy couldn't be doing much better," asserted L. Crandall Hays, vice president of Robert W. Baird, Milwaukee. "We are now going into a period when the December-quarter earnings will be reported, and that should make good reading." He added that money deposited in individual retirement accounts was among the funds coming into yesterday's market.

"It was encouraging that the breadth of the advance was the best we've seen in a long time," said Ralph Acampora, vice president and technical analyst at Kidder Peabody. He noted that the lead that the Big Board gainers held over the losers yesterday was the widest since November 29. He looks for the market to move higher over the near term.

Harry W. Laubscher, analyst at Paine Webber, contended that "the strength should continue over the next several weeks, led by the big-name blue chips and heavy capital goods stocks." *He thinks the industrial average will climb to about the 1,350 level* [emphasis added].

James Finucane, analyst at Illinois Co., Chicago, *expects the market to reach the 1,340 level in February but then top out.* He said that currently "too many investors can't make new purchases before first selling something." He contended that money generally has been moving into the market for about 16 months, since August 1982, after about a 17-month period when money was moving out of the market [emphasis added].

January 6, 1984—Dow 1,281.24

BROAD RALLY CONTINUES AS VOLUME RISES TO RECORD 160 MILLION SHARES

The stock market rally surged ahead on a broad front yesterday as volume soared to a record of nearly 160 million shares and the Dow Jones Industrial Average neared a record.

Analysts again attributed the gains to the movement of reinvestment funds that traditionally come into the market at this time each year and to a growing belief that interest rates will edge lower over the next few months.

"Pension fund contributions are flowing in at a rapid pace," asserted Robert Stovall, investment strategist at Dean Witter Reynolds, Inc. "Institutions had been waiting for a signal to move into the market, and the improved outlook on interest rates and the easing of tensions in the Middle East this week helped persuade them to act."

"The continued rise (yesterday) on increased volume proved that Wednesday's rally wasn't a one-day wonder, and the market now shouldn't have any trouble reaching a new record," commented Newton D. Zinder, senior vice president at E. F. Hutton & Co.

"As the new year started, some people had been waiting to see whether there would be further profit-taking before placing new buy orders," said Eldon A. Grimm, senior vice president at Birr Wilson & Co. He also noted that "the rally's leadership has been good, starting with the Telephone issues on Tuesday."

"What's impressive about this rally is that it has broadened out as it continued," asserted Chester Pado, technical analyst at G. Tsai & Co., Los Angeles. "A year-end rally had a great deal of difficulty getting started because a broad segment of the market had been taking a beating for several months." He added that "if this broadening advance can continue, it will eliminate fears of a substantial vulnerability on the next pullback."

Turning in the January 7 market letter on the morning of January 6, this was all I had to go by, but it was more than enough. It more than matched the optimism recorded in September 1929.

The blowoff record volume of January 5 strongly suggested to me that things would be very different by the end of the month. Checking out all the advisory hot lines at this time showed that just about everybody had jumped on the bandwagon on this one. It was so nearly unanimous that it smacked of the lemmings all rushing toward their destruction.

The burst of Wall Street optimism in early January 1984 was seldom exceeded in market history. As shown by *The Wall Street Journal*'s puffy quotations, leading analysts were putting themselves on record, covering the full range of bullish expectations: interest rates were expected to decline, the economy couldn't be doing better, fourth quarter earnings will make good reading, IRA money coming into the market, breadth of the advance the best seen in a long time, higher market expected, pension fund contributions flowing in at a rapid pace, institutions coming back in, easing of tensions in the Middle East, market should make new records, and the leadership is excellent (*The Wall Street Journal*, January 5–6, 1984).

Now look at the *identical optimism* expressed in the September 4, 1929, *Journal*, written at the very peak of the great Dow rise:

> Wall Street entered the autumn financial season in a definitely optimistic frame of mind. With railroad traffic showing steady gains, and production in the major branches of industry continuing at a high rate, the earnings prospects of the principal corporations with shares listed on the Stock Exchange were looked upon as extremely promising.

Can one imagine a worse-timed statement than this? Talk about things that always look the best right at the top! When it was written, the Dow had just closed at 381.17, *a level that wouldn't be seen again for twenty-five years!*

In 1983 and 1984, warnings, both technical and vocal, were drowned out in an ear-deafening chorus of "expert" announcements by business, political, and economic prophets. *The Wall Street Journal* had carried the comments of the fundamentally bullish with their predictions of Dow 1,400, 1,500, and even 2,000 and higher, their thinking ensnared by a continuing economic recovery. Everybody was bullish, all the way up to the President of the United States. The record-high numbers in the Dow Jones Industrial Average mesmerized all the economists to a man. The ascending Dow neatly disguised from most the growing internal trouble and, it is safe to say, few saw the fatal handwriting on the wall.

As 1984 opened, the bullish chorus grew to a crescendo, the big Wall Street houses looking for stratospheric levels to occur in the Dow in the weeks ahead. They still couldn't recognize the terminal disease that had set in the previous spring. Immediately following this barrage of optimism, the first in a series of powerful stock market breaks occurred, bringing the great bear market of 1983–84 out into the open.

It was absolutely no different in 1929. The bull chorus back then embraced the biggest names in business and politics, as well as the hallowed greats in the world of academics, the latter featuring Professor Irving Fisher of Yale University. Against that background, no wonder nobody could hear the warnings from the few. Back then, warnings from the White House and the Federal Reserve Board were totally ignored by Wall Street.

III

I felt that the time had now arrived for the compression that had been building up all through the 1982–83 rise to be released in a deluge of selling. Up until this time, the Dow Jones Industrial Average had never recorded the normal one-third to two-thirds retracements so common to a normal bull market. That produced a great compression that sooner or later had to be relieved.

PARALLEL 54

Technical Compression

This growing strain was dangerous, and the predicted major decline in 1984 was the natural resolution of such a bearish chart pattern. That compression was even more acute in the more speculative areas of the over-the-counter market and the American Stock Exchange, such compression giving way to the early declines in the spring of 1983. The time frame was seven to nine months. The final run in the 1928–29 market also recorded no normal one-third to two-thirds retracements, building up a similar dangerous compression. The speculative areas were the first to give way under that strain, finally hitting the blue chips seven to nine months after the internal peaks.

By January 1984, the maximum strain was hitting the blue chips, then about to give way. Alan Abelson typified the confused thinking at this time, and in the January 2 issue of *Barron's*, unwittingly mouthed another 1929 parallel:

PARALLEL 55

Psychological Overreliance on the Federal Reserve

Abelson said: "And, more than anything, it's because we have such faith in the Federal Reserve to do the right thing that we're convinced interest rates will be lower and stock prices higher in 1984." I sensed a parallel statement here remindful of what E. H. H. Simmons said a month before the greatest crash in history. Simmons, the president of the New York Stock Exchange in 1929, gave a major speech in September of that fateful year a few days after the Dow peak, stating that the days of panics and crashes were over, citing as his main reasons that the United States was a creditor nation and that we had that great business stabilizer known as the Federal Reserve. Special attention was on the Fed in 1984 to do the "right thing" since it was a presidential election year, and according to Abelson and all the other people who were to be so utterly wrong in 1984, the "right thing" meant that the Fed was going to play footsie with the administration.

IV

Here I shall use a football analogy to describe the tremendous upthrust in early January and the quick destruction that followed. The Dow made a first down on January 4, closing at 1,269.05. Ten points were needed for another first down. On January 5, the Dow closed at 1,282.24, thereby making another first down. But then trouble began to appear. On January 6, it was second down and five to go, but the Dow closed short of the mark at 1,286.64, missing a first down by a yard. Going into January 9, it was third down and inches to go. Once again, the Dow failed to better the late November high of 1,287.20, closing at 1,286.22. Now it was still inches to go on January 10, and the bull coach on the fourth down that day decided to go for it. For a very short while, it looked like a successful play, because they got the ball to the Dow 1,291 line for an easy first down, but then the bulls were thrown for a bad loss of seven yards at 1,278.48. The bulls thereby lost possession of the ball. For four high-volume sessions, all the bulls needed to do was to push the Dow over the 1,287.20 level for a touchdown, but the formidable line of the bears held solid and the bulls lost possession. The bulls needed that touchdown desperately, because they knew the clock was running out and the score was 14–6 in favor of the bears. With the bears now in a position to run the clock out, it would not matter even if the bulls had made a touchdown with a new closing Dow high, because then the score would have been 14–13 in favor of the bears, with no time left on the clock.

If that much power could not take the Dow to a new high, then obviously something was very wrong. The all-time high volume of the opening week of January attracted a great many people. All they could think of was the volume explosion of August 1982 and believed that the second leg of the bull market was at hand. The difference, however, was as vivid as night and day. August 1982 was coming off a bottom whereas January 1984 was coming off a top. It was as simple as that. While the bears were caught in August 1982 (this writer among them), January 1984 presented a classic bull trap.

Very little is said about bull traps in stock market literature and most people are not aware of the characteristics of such traps. Jiler's description of bull traps has never been bettered: "Prices break out of the range into new high ground and then suddenly decline through the lows (support levels) of the previous trading range, leaving the 'bulls' stranded with losses. The more significant Traps feature a splurge of volume: the more volume in the Trap, the more bulls have been caught."[1] The description exactly fit what happened in the fateful early days of January 1984. As I applied that description to the action at the time, it was immaterial whether the Dow closed at a new high or not. On an intraday basis, the Dow did temporarily break out into new high ground, thus fulfilling Jiler's requirement of a genuine bull trap. Jiler talked of the rather quick move down below the support levels and that neatly tied in with the January Indicator.

Dangerous misinformation had been propagated about the January Indicator. It had been oversimplified to give the impression that all one had to do was to look at the first five trading days in January. If the Dow rose on balance during that brief period, then it was supposed to forecast an up year. It was totally misleading. January 1973, a month that was to start the worst bear market since 1929, offered a good example of how to read the January Indicator correctly. In the first five trading days of that month, the Dow showed a net gain of 27.84 points. That was supposed to forecast a good year for the stock market in 1973. However, the Dow recorded the bull market high three sessions later at Dow 1,051.70, and promptly began the great two-year slide. By January 15, the Dow had closed at the low of the new year at 1,025.59. By the end of the month, the Dow had closed at 999.02, thus breaking under the December 1972 low of 1,000. That was a true technical forecast of what lay ahead. Ever since then, I have broken the January Indicator down into five steps.

V

———

PARALLEL 56

Psychological
Nobody Is Anxious to Sell Any Stocks

Another key 1929 parallel was spotted in the January 10 *Wall Street Journal.*

January 10, 1984—Dow 1,286.22

TRANSPORTATION INDEX SETS RECORD BUT INDUSTRIALS
EASE BY 0.42 POINT

The stock market finished slightly lower after failing to push its rally into a fourth session. Trading continued heavy, totaling more than 107 million shares.

[1]William L. Jiler, *How Charts Can Help You in the Stock Market* (New York: Commodity Research Publications Corp., 1962), p. 149.

"The market was just backing off a little before making a run to a new high and through the 1,300 level," commented James C. Andrews, first vice president of institutional trading at Janney Montgomery Scott, Philadelphia. *"No one was really anxious to sell any stocks,"* added Mr. Andrews [emphasis added].

"Institutions apparently have no excuse to sell stocks," contended Peter Furniss, first vice president of Lehman Brothers Kuhn Loeb [emphasis added]."

The *reluctance-to-sell* theme was also expressed in *Journal* columns of January 20 and January 24:

Eldon A. Grimm, senior vice president at Birr Wilson & Co. said, "The institutions weren't chasing much stock *but at the same time there wasn't any rush to get out"* [emphasis added].

Alfred W. Harris, Jr., senior vice president at Josephthal & Co., St. Louis, said, "The market is awaiting something to send it higher and I think the catalyst will be lower interest rates." He added that the market appears to be in a "period of profit-taking *but there's no rush to get out"* [emphasis added].

The parallel with 1929 was quite precise. Coming off the September 1929 top, we find the parallel in the September 18, 1929, *Wall Street Journal* in the "Broad Street Gossip" column: "From the recent action of the market, one could conclude *that the public is not in a selling mood.* The same can be said of the so-called large interests. If the latter had not been in favor of a strong market, it would not have enjoyed the pronounced rally since the discount rate was raised" (emphasis added).

There it was, five weeks away from the worst crash in history, and the public was not in a selling mood, and would regret that mood for the rest of their lives. The parallel warning was there in January 1984, and once again millions of investors would live to regret that expensive mood.

───────

PARALLEL 57

Psychological
People Are Back to Buying Good Investment Values

The January 10 *Journal* pointed out that "with tax selling and other year-end considerations out of the way, William A. Goldstein, president of Selected Special Shares, Chicago, said, 'People are back to buying stocks that represent good investment values.' He also maintained that 'stocks which lead during the next 30 days probably will be the leaders for the rest of the year.' "

Goldstein's statement was a perfect prediction, but he didn't know it at the time. The market started the first of the major 1984 downswings right at that time, and the stocks that led the market down were the very ones that continued to lead the market down for the year. After people got their hands burned in the speculative euphoria of 1983, they would naturally tend to adopt a more *conservative* market attitude, and, ironically, while they reached for the high-quality blue chip stocks they did so at the very worst of times—right at the top!

PARALLEL 58

Market
Liquidation of Large Blocks on Enthusiasm

The blowoff volume record on the New York Stock Exchange occurred on January 5, volume soaring to 160 million shares. Subsequent market action proved, beyond the shadow of a doubt, that this was big block distribution taking advantage of the public enthusiasm. Some big interests were heading for the hills.

The September 24, 1929, *Journal* carried the following in the "Abreast of the Market" column:

> Whenever the market has reacted there has been talk of "good selling," meaning, of course, that important holders of stocks are liquidating. Usually such a supply does not come on the market during reactions. The important interests with large blocks of stock generally liquidate when the market is having one of its spectacular spurts during periods of great enthusiasm. However, as there is really no precedent for the current market situation, many in the financial district at this moment are decidedly puzzled regarding the outlook for the immediate future and sources of selling therefore will be watched closely.

While bullishness on the early January run-up was rampant, the first decline of any size coming off the January 6 top revealed *a quick sensitivity to unease,* a characteristic noted on the September 1929 declines. The January 6 top did not immediately reveal itself as such until the decline of January 10, which saw a reversal from an all-time Dow record high that could not be sustained.

The January 11 *Journal* reported the reversal in a straightforward manner, there being no hint as yet that something was fatally wrong:

> Oils were a bright spot, but the general stock market ended moderately lower after again failing to hold early gains. Trading continued heavy with volume of nearly 110 million shares.
>
> The Dow Jones Industrial Average, which was up a net 33.48 points in the previous four sessions, climbed 5.24 points in yesterday's first half hour, putting

it above its closing high of 1,287.20 set last November 29. But the gain slowly faded and the index finished at 1,278.48, off 7.74 points. The transportation and utility indicators also closed lower.

PARALLEL 59

Psychological
The Market Is "Consolidating"

The first decline following a wave of bullishness that sends the Dow to a new high introduces a word serving to defend the bullish attitude. At the same time, however, it correlates with the first hints of "unsteadiness." That word is "consolidation." The January 11 *Journal* account saw the word introduced to describe the first of a series of very important market declines:

> "The market was *consolidating* after its recent gains, but its failure to follow through after the industrial and transportation averages reached new highs during the morning was moderately disappointing," commented Fred W. Lange of Lange Financial Services. "This action diminished the prospect that we'll see a runaway market during January."
>
> Also disappointing, Mr. Lange added, has been "the recent sluggish performance of International Business Machines which stems from the recent news that IBM is going to have competition in the computer field from American Telephone."
>
> "Perhaps the market is taking a necessary breather before lunging toward new high territory," contended Frank A. Russo, senior vice president at Autranet. Yesterday's *consolidation*, which he thinks probably will continue over the short term, "should be viewed as bullish," he maintained.

Declines disturb market sentiment. If there was any subsurface weakness not apparent on the previous rise, only a few declines are required to dredge up that weakness quickly and cause a decided shift in sentiment. But the first reported reactions are that such declines are "healthy" consolidations that technically strengthen the general list. They are called needed corrections from a previously overbought condition. The famous "Babson break" in 1929 occurred on September 5, two days after the Dow peak. On the day of the break, *The Wall Street Journal* had stated that *technical conditions in the general list had been strengthened by corrective selling the day before the break.* So the reaction to the start of the decline was the usual ho-hum response, accepting it as "normal," "healthy," and "needed," as well as "expected." The deeper decline the day after, however, set in motion the same forces that were set in motion in January 1984. The further the Dow drops from the high point, the more likely it is that people will increasingly sell into any new strength, and thus the decline becomes self-perpetuating until that move is overdone.

V I

The January 10 reversal to the downside, while viewed by analysts as a bullish consolidation, nevertheless introduced a division in viewpoints that was increasingly to widen as the decline deepened. This "double" view showed up in the *Journal* on January 11:

> However, Kenneth S. Hackel, president of Systematic Financial Management, Fort Lee, New Jersey, asserted that "with long-term double-A industrial bonds currently yielding 12.8%, the relative attraction of investing in stocks has diminished quite a bit over the past quarter."

Then, in sharp contrast:

> Robert Walsh, senior vice president at Rotan Mosle, Houston, views the market as "in the early stages of the second phase of the bull market." He expects the industrial average at some point during 1984 to reach the 1,480–1,530 level. He notes that the market reached bull market peaks during three of the past four presidential election years.

The bulls were completely hooked on the election year syndrome.

PARALLEL 60

Market
Blue Chips Topped Out Last

If people had watched the entire stock market with the same rapt attention they gave to the blue chip stocks, they would have seen the great 1983 early warnings that reliably pointed to all approaching bear markets. In every bull market, the blue chip stocks are the last to top out, and thus with most people watching them and not their own stocks, the bull market usually ends with losses in the majority of stocks. For this reason, it was very important to track the progress of the over-the-counter stocks and the American Stock Exchange issues. In the aborted 1982–83 brief rise, most stocks had peaked by June 1983, but Wall Street pundits and the media kept shouting bull market because the Dow Jones Industrial Average consisting of thirty blue chip stocks kept rising. By the time the Dow peaked in late November 1983, most people were sporting losses ranging as high as 50 to 70 percent in the OTC and Amex issues.

The same key warnings were there in September 1929. Most stocks had been in a bear market since the end of 1928, but the small handful of blue chip stocks kept trending higher until September 1929.

PARALLEL 61

Psychological
The Fed Will Ease Money and Prevent a Collapse

In the January 12 *Journal,* Bruce Bradley said that the Federal Reserve would adopt a policy of credit ease in 1984. Many of the wildest of the bullish predictions were based on such a belief. Most analysts and economists were to be proven dead wrong on the stock market in January because of that belief. The most widespread popular notion was that a decline in interest rates would put the stock market into the second leg of what they all believed was still a bull market. They were certain that, since 1984 was an election year, the Federal Reserve would opt in favor of lower rates so as to prevent any serious slippage in the stock market.

Coming off the market top, Bradley's belief in an easier credit policy had overlooked the certain problems of the budget deficits as well as the growing likelihood of a banking crisis. Then, a few days later, the *Journal* on January 18 ran the following:

> "The market is coming out of six months of consolidation and its target on the industrial average will be 1,500," asserted Richard E. Minshall, president of Capital Advisors, Inc., Tulsa, Oklahoma. The sustained climb that he expects during the first half of this year "will be fueled primarily by a 1 to 1½ percentage point drop in interest rates and by good earnings reports."

The mistaken idea that the Federal Reserve Board had the power to prevent a collapse was an exact parallel with the same dangerous thought in 1929. In the *Journal* of October 8, 1929, the *Harvard Business Review* was extensively quoted: "Moreover, should the speculative recession induce a business curtailment beyond that probably rendered necessary by the great activity of the past nine months, *we have no doubt that the reserve system, which has ample resources, will ease money and thereby moderate such curtailment. Under these circumstances, prolonged liquidation in stocks appears unlikely"* (emphasis added).

Historical
All the Trouble Is in the Market Itself

Most people missed the opportunity to get out of the stock market in January 1984 because most people follow fundamentals, and all the fundamentals looked good. It therefore follows that *all the trouble had to be in the market itself.* Going into 1984, the economy was strong, expectations for higher corporate earnings were running very high, there was low inflation, and economists and Wall Street analysts were all bullish. The majority opinion was that there would be some slowing in the economy which would bring down interest rates and put the stock market in the second leg of what most thought was still a continuing bull market. What went wrong? The answer was very simple. It was the stock market. As in 1929, the market topped out several months before the peak in the Dow Jones Industrial Average, peaking in May–June 1983. Thereafter, a bear market was underway and it caught the entire fundamental school with their pants down.

This is one of the most telling of the 1929 parallels. In the October 28, 1929, *Journal* the following appeared in the "Broad Street Gossip" column: "The recent break was *due to the position of the market itself.* It came when money was 5%, with a plethora of funds available, purposes, normal inventories, corporations flush with surplus money, sound industrial conditions and so on" (emphasis added).

That characteristic had been present for some time. The *Journal* on September 23, 1929, had stated it as follows: "However, *the stock market temporarily had little thought for conditions outside of itself, and technical influences continued dominant in the early dealings.* Attempts to attribute Friday's break to the troubles in London and the further increase in brokers' loans were recognized as pretexts for a condition which resulted from an overbought situation in the general list" (emphasis added).

Market
Fundamental Strength and Technical Weakness
Go Hand in Hand

Never was there a better example of the total uselessness of fundamental analysis than just prior to the great 1984 stock market decline. In January 1984 fundamental strength was outstanding and Wall Street made sure that the public was well aware of that strength. Comments pertaining to the fundamental strength were given in the *Journal* day after day in January 1984, and this hurt millions of investors who had to learn the hard way that fundamental analysis is not the way to go.

At the same time that the fundamental strength was present, the technical position of the market was extremely weak. Such a dichotomy has preceded all the worst types of stock market declines.

The 1929 parallel is quite specific. *The Wall Street Journal* of October 21, 1929, ran the following paragraph:

> Sydney Loeb, of E. F. Hutton & Co., apparently does not believe that the leading industrials have yet sold ex-public imagination. He says, "As far as second-grade and low-grade issues are concerned, the disposition to hold these stocks and add to them is dangerous to a degree. We continue to feel that stocks should not be measured by yield, but by a combination of financial policy, management, earnings, financial strength, prospects and rate of growth. The great fundamental strength in the market is the outright attractiveness of issues such as U.S. Steel, American Can, American Telephone, National Biscuit, Eastman Kodak, Bethlehem Steel, U.S. Industrial Alcohol, Air Reduction, Commercial Solvents, and all the good rails. The great technical weakness in the market is the fact that the public is still long a tremendous amount of stock and that if large-scale liquidation ever began, it would mean an eight-million-share day of steady selling that would bring prices down more sharply than ever in the recent few reactions."

PARALLEL 64

Historical
Favorable Earnings and Dividends

Market fundamentalists were totally hooked on earnings and dividends prior to the crash and it was from that area that most of the dangerously useless information was broadcast by Wall Street to a seriously misled public.

Dividends in 1983 and 1984 were thought to be a stock prop and it turned out to be one of the great hooks of the bear market. *Investment Quality Trends* of La Jolla, California, was quoted in *USA Today* as stating that 224, or 64 percent, of the 350 blue chip companies it follows increased their dividends in 1983. In an improved economy, it expected even more blue chips to share the wealth. "Higher dividends (historically) support higher stock prices," *I.Q. Trends* said. Obviously, they were to be dead wrong. It might have been true in a normal bull market, but not in a 1929-type market about to collapse.

PARALLEL 65

Historical
End of a Major Merger Cycle

Typical of all bull markets that were ending, there had been a rapid step-up in the number of corporate mergers and acquisitions. As this cycle was maturing, it tended to deflect attention from the growing market deterioration elsewhere. The year 1983 saw a nine-year cycle in mergers and acquisitions coming to an end.

After it was too late, *The Wall Street Journal* editorialized on the subject of mergers and stock prices on November 9, 1929:

> Among the offhand judgments upon the effects to be expected from the stock market collapse which have been so freely given in the news columns of late has been the sweeping dictum that the chapter of mergers is closed, not to be reopened for an incalculable time. This could in any case be little more than a personal opinion, containing just the germ of truth needed to make it misleading.
>
> There are mergers and mergers. The sort of combinations, of which there may have been a few, prompted chiefly by the desire to whip up a group of uninformed speculators to a higher pitch of excitement, or to support a market against "wise" selling, is quite certainly off for an indefinite period. But there are reasons why a generally lower level of security prices is favorable to the unification of manufacturing or distributing units based on definitely realizable economies and efficiencies. Not a few illusions concerning the value of this or that corporation as part of a combination have been dispelled since the ides of October; the real reasons for bringing it in, if they ever existed, are as sound as they were.
>
> In a typically bull market there is an atmosphere that works against cold scrutiny of values and it sometimes affects the executive of a great corporation only less than the small market follower. More than that, the ease or apparent ease with which new securities can be floated exerts a still stronger influence toward a generosity in the making of merger terms not always justified by the end in view. Such a state of mind has not improbably played its part even in some fairly recent purchases of railroad stocks in contemplation of eventual unification, though in a field so strictly regulated by public authority it is particularly inappropriate.
>
> If the market decline means fewer mergers hereafter, though that is not yet a certainty, it must also mean better and stronger combinations, in the making of which exaggerated idea of value and of obtainable economies will have little weight. There will be less disposition to arrange terms according to imaginable developments of the next five years, and more to consider how the proposed combination will justify itself this year and next.

But the public was blinded in 1983 and 1984 to the implications of the merger trend, and the media simply made the situation far worse by ogling the takeover game as a source of something to talk about with absolutely no regard for the number of people who were going to get hurt.

VII

The strong economy going into 1984 and the large recurring budgetary deficits were beginning to get interest rates up to disturbing levels. But the bulls didn't seem to mind any such impediment. In the January 13 *Journal*, the Dow at 1,279.31, Don Kimsey, senior market analyst at Dean Witter Reynolds, viewed the market performance as a continuation of "a normal consolidation considering its recent advance." He was encouraged by "the significant increase in the number of stocks that participated in the market's rally last week." He said, too, that "the recent fairly nice performance of the financial sector issues *suggests that investors aren't overly concerned about a rise in interest rates*" (emphasis added).

Such a lack of concern over the rising interest rates pointed up simply another 1929 parallel.

━━━━━━

PARALLEL 66

Psychological
Investors Not Overly Concerned
about a Rise in Interest Rates

The ability of the market to move ahead despite stiffer interest rates was a characteristic that had caused a dangerous complacency in 1929 prior to the break. After the Dow turned down in September 1929, however, investors increasingly began to get more nervous. Complacency over the higher rates was replaced by growing concern.

The September 11, 1929, *Journal* made reference to this:

> All evidence recently has pointed to increased nervousness on the part of the longs. *Whereas in the past the market has moved ahead even while money was firm and brokers' loans were rising sharply,* it is now noted that there is what appears to be frightened liquidation at the first sign of any unfavorable development [emphasis added].

The January 1984 downturn not only caught all the bulls completely off guard, but they were extremely slow to respond to the developing decline, viewing months of what they thought to be good "consolidation" as merely a refreshing pause in a long-term uptrend.

"After the needed pause that refreshes following the market's dramatic rise from August 1982 to mid-1983, it appears ready to break out of the doldrums and make an assault on the 1,400 level," contended John Groome, senior vice president at U.S. Trust. He said that there was a confluence of favorable news, including rising earnings, and "expectations of dividend increases, a sanguine outlook for inflation and anticipation of at least a modest dip in interest rates" (January 13 *Journal*).

PARALLEL 67

Psychological
A Pullback Would Be "Healthy"

There were a growing number of bears going into 1984, but the whirlwind rise early in January transformed most of them back into raging bulls. Those who were bearish, however, were practically all "short-term" bears, simply looking for a correction in an ongoing bull market.

Reference to the "short-term" bears was made in the September 26, 1929, *Journal:*

> Market sentiment is very much mixed again. You will find, however, that bulls are still in the majority. *There are plenty of bears but many of them are temporary bears. They believe the market will do little on the bull side until there is some contraction in the brokers' loan item* [emphasis added].

In other words, they all thought the developing decline was "healthy."

The "Broad Street Gossip" column in the September 28, 1929, *Journal* after the initial declines coming off the September top said: *"The Street terms it the type of healthy reaction from which there is always a substantial recovery"* (emphasis added). On September 30 the *Journal* said: "This house-cleaning had a *salutary* effect on technical conditions within the market" (emphasis added). A month later the market crashed.

PARALLEL 68

Technical
Up in the Morning, Down in the Afternoon

The January trading pattern turned very weak technically coming off the earlier high. The Dow would rise in the morning and fall in the afternoon. Anyone listening to the TV market commentators in the morning got a rich diet of bullishness, only to be sorely disappointed on the close. On January 12 the Dow was up over 7 points in the morning, bringing it back above the 1,284 level. Myron Kandel, announcing for Cable News Network, called the rise "a nifty little rally." However, like all the other rally attempts for some weeks to come, it fizzled out.

Failing rally attempts were the key characteristics of the September–October 1929 trading program. Back then they also had "nifty little morning rallies" and dreadful closes.

Not everybody was totally blind to the problems that lay ahead. The *Journal* of January 16:

"If last year's second half was a difficult period for the stock market, this year is going to be even more trying," contended Josiah J. Willard III, senior vice president and research director of Financial Programs, Denver. He regarded the current equity market as "fully valued unless interest rates come down."

He emphasized that picking the right stocks would be paramount in 1984. "It will be a year of fundamental analysis and you can put away your chart books" used in technical analysis, he maintained. Investors will be looking for "predictability and visibility of earnings," he said.

William B. Astrop, chairman of Astrop Advisory, Atlanta, expected the Dow Jones Industrial Average to rise above 1,300 later in the year. But he also contended that investors would find the market "much more difficult" in 1984 because its forward momentum peaked in mid-1983 and since then it had been decelerating. "The widely held perception that 1985 will represent a significant slowdown in the economy will tend to put a damper on the overall market in 1984," he argued.

PARALLEL 69

Psychological
Increase of Bearishness

Negativism crept into the *Journal* quotes on January 17.

"People have become a little discouraged because the market didn't follow through on the big moves early this year," commented Leslie M. Pollack, chairman of Shearson Management, Inc. "But I expect the market to move higher because some interest rates are easing and there's a very low level of speculation in the market."

Ira Ross, vice president of Dean Witter Reynolds InterCapital, contended that the market is consolidating and that he expects it to resume its rally later this month or early next month. He is encouraged by the *recent increase in bearishness* among investment advisers because he sees "cash building up and setting the stage for a good upside move" [emphasis added].

The very fact that *it could be noted so soon coming off the January highs* attested to the fact that most people were getting concerned over months of a declining market, regardless of the Dow. If the general market had been strong right up to January 1984, *then a decline* of only 19 points in the Dow could not possibly have produced an increase in bearishness so soon. I interpreted this quite bearishly, seeing an immediate parallel with 1929.

The increase in bearishness was a key characteristic of the 1929 slide. Coming down from the September 3, 1929, top, *The Wall Street Journal* called attention to the increase in bearishness on September 26:

> *Bearishness was increased* by another flurry in call money, which carried the demand rate to 10% from the renewal charge of 8%. Steel common was under special pressure, breaking to new low ground on the reaction on pessimism induced by the weekly trade reviews which reported that producers in many instances were shading prices to induce buying [emphasis added].

PARALLEL 70

Psychological
Groundwork Being Laid for a New Upward Movement

"Encouraged by the recent increase in bearishness among investment advisors, some analysts saw 'cash building up and setting the stage for a good upside move'" (January 17, 1984, *Journal*).

In the *Journal* of September 23, 1929, in the "Abreast of the Market" column, it was stated that "it is the general feeling that the groundwork is being laid for a new upward movement." That was again expressed in the September 27 *Journal:* "The consensus is that after the current period of adjustment is over, stocks will again rebound and make new highs."

Sounds familiar.

Coming off the January highs in the Dow, the media kept saying that the market was flirting with all-time highs. Of course, that hadn't been a true statement since June 1983. Only the Dow had been flirting with new highs, and it was common to see the media make the mistake of referring to the Dow 30 as the market. The futures charts were far more revealing, particularly the Standard & Poor 500 and the New York Stock Exchange Composite. For instance, if one could have looked at the March 1984 contract of the NYSE

Composite, he would have seen the very disturbing pattern of declining tops. The major top was in June 1983. The first declining top was in July 1983. The next was in October 1983, then November 1983, and then January 1984. The sharpest drop in the tops occurred between October 1983 and January 1984. The identical pattern was seen in the Standard & Poor futures contract of March 1984 as well as in the Kansas City Value Line futures contract of March 1984. That smacked of a *major internal non-confirmation of the early January 1984 strength.* All important momentum studies revealed the same disturbing pattern.

Major trouble lay ahead. One was not required to know the shape or form of that trouble. The market simply said with full authority that there was trouble ahead, and the few wise ones made their move. Ordinarily, such trouble always is flashed in the stock market first. Trouble to occur in an *election* year, however, implied that *the degree of stock market disappointment would be that much greater,* and that is why I had consistently drawn attention to the fact that all the important market phenomena in 1983 constituted the fullest extent of an exponential curve—the parabolic rise. It meant that when the nets were thrown out to gather in the market losers in the developing bear market, *they would be bulging with the largest possible catch.* There are few accidents in cyclical history. And it was no accident that 42.36 million Americans owned stock in 1984 and that 51.5 percent of the shareholders were female. But the important fact here was that there had been an increase of 10 million shareholders just since 1981 and therein lay another key 1929 parallel:

PARALLEL 71

Historical
Terminal Rate of Growth in Number of Shareholders

Everything went to excess in 1929. The enormous percentage growth in the number of shareholders between 1927 and 1929 went hand in hand with the bubble of speculation and the record increase in the volume of trading. When the flames of speculative excess burn brightly, enticing a new generation of suckers with their eyes on quick profits, the fire is soon to burn low, ending in the ashes of a collapse, driving millions out of the market, not to return for many years.

VIII

By mid-January the Street was still holding to the ridiculous bull scenario and thus was looking for market weakness to offer a new buying opportunity. They saw such an opportunity on January 17. The Dow was down early in the day but managed to close up after it was announced that IBM would declare earnings the next day.

One could sense frustration developing among the bulls and some of the developing problems were aired, but the consensus remained on the bullish side.

As reported in the January 18 *Journal:*

"In spite of some recent favorable economic news, the market acted unusually sluggish," observed Jacques S. Theriot, senior vice president at Smith Barney Harris Upham & Co. "Institutional investors were buying stock but not as aggressively as earlier this year." He added that some people were waiting for International Business Machines' earnings report, which some people expect today.

William Dudley, partner in sales and trading at Montgomery Securities, San Francisco, saw the market as continuing "in a consolidation phase." He said it had been "frustrating" watching the several failed rallies in recent sessions before yesterday's late upturn. But he also noted *that each time weakness appeared, buyers came into the market* [emphasis added].

"The market is coming out of *six months of consolidation and its target on the industrial average will be 1,500,"* asserted Richard E. Minshall, president of Capital Advisors, Inc., Tulsa, Oklahoma. The sustained climb that he expects during the first half of this year "will be fueled primarily by a 1 to 1½ percentage point *drop in interest rates* and by *good earning reports"* [emphasis added].

Charles LaLoggia, publisher of the *Special Situation Report,* Rochester, New York, contended that "if interest rates don't come down there's a danger that the economic recovery will be aborted during 1984." He said that "most businesses, especially small businesses, can't pay interest rates on loans of 13% to 16% in an environment of 3% inflation."

PARALLEL 72

Psychological Weakness Brings in Buyers

This is an illusion that is common among frustrated bulls. To rationalize their mistaken judgment at the top, *they think they see buyers coming into the market every time weakness appears.* Of course, it is a figment of their imagination and a product of their desire to see buyers appear so as to support their erroneous thesis. As the record was soon to show, if there were buyers on weakness, *they were outnumbered by sellers.*

Coming off the great 1929 peak, *The Wall Street Journal* on September 7 said: "A good part of the selling in Thursday's late trading represented panicky liquidation by commission house traders. Investment trusts and powerful groups sponsoring representative issues *took advantage of the break to increase their holdings.* This passing of stocks from weak to strong hand was reflected in sharp recoveries in the early dealing" (emphasis added).

The September 17 *Journal:*

> Sentiment is somewhat improved. While it is maintained that there might be some further correction in the market, many believe that the purging process of the past ten days has done much to improve the technical position, and *these observers are advising the purchase of the good stocks on any further reaction which might come during the middle of this week* [emphasis added].

The September 19 *Journal:*

> Somewhat more cheerful market opinions were heard around the Street. It was pointed out that *stocks had indicated ability to attract buying when they became reactionary* and as a result *a number of observers were advocating the purchase of leading shares on any setback in the near future* [emphasis added].

The market, marching downhill to a different drummer, couldn't hear the bullish chorus that saw every dip as a buying opportunity. The next parallel to show up came on schedule. The bulls, seriously misled on what they saw as downside buying opportunities, were equally quick to see the market as being "oversold" as early as January 19.

PARALLEL 73

Psychological
The Market Is Oversold

The January 19, 1984, *Wall Street Journal* quotes, with the Dow only down 17 points off the earlier peak, reflected an adamant position among the analysts, stonewalling their way through what was to prove to be a hopeless situation. For example:

> David Bianchi, vice president of equity trading at First Boston Corp., attributed part of the early weakness in IBM stocks "to selling on the expected earnings news." He contended that the overall market is *"in an oversold condition,"* and he looks for a substantial rally to start soon. "The market's breadth has been improving recently and fourth-quarter earnings results are generally coming in on target," he said [emphasis added].

On September 25, 1929, with the Dow down less than 19 points from the earlier peak, *The Wall Street Journal* stated: "Signs of a temporarily *oversold condition* were shown in the early dealings and rallying tendencies developed in the principal trading issues" (emphasis added).

The pattern of thinking (or lack of thinking) was following the same dangerous pattern seen in 1929: (1) the peak—Wall Street bullish, (2) general reluctance to sell stocks, (3) attraction to good "investment values," (4) optimism tied to earnings and the economy, (5) important subsurface selling, (6) market consolidating, (7) blue chips peaking out, (8) temporary disregard of rising interest rates, (9) all pullbacks seen to be "healthy," (10) up in the morning, down in the afternoon, (11) increase of bearishness, (12) groundwork being laid for a new upward movement, (13) weakness expected to bring in buyers, and (14) the market seen to be oversold.

Any student of history could have predicted the next market symptom: Nervousness.

PARALLEL 74

Psychological
Investors Are Nervous

By January 23 the Dow had dropped to 1,244.45, still only 42 points under the earlier January high, but contrasts were beginning to show up which were later to prove extremely embarrassing to Wall Street, something that would never be apologized for. The earlier enthusiasm wasn't panning out. Words such as "nervous" and "frustrated" showed up in *The Wall Street Journal,* just as they had in 1929 when the decline was just beginning to get a trifle out of hand. Another word beginning to show up was "worry." The January 24 *Journal* said it well:

> Analysts noted investor *worry* about what effect a slowing economy would have on corporate profits (emphasis added).
>
> "Investors are nervous about the apparent slowing in the economy with the attendant negative effect on profits," commented John Groome, senior vice president at U.S. Trust Co. He added that investors are *frustrated* by the market's "meandering rotational" action and "its failure to follow through after the initial burst of activity early this year," and also by the continuing high interest rates [emphasis added].

Three weeks off the September 1929 high, the key word "nervous" showed up in *The Wall Street Journal.* September 27: "Stocks better despite spasmodic selling. While the trading community was still in a decidedly *nervous state* stocks generally gave a better account of themselves yesterday" (emphasis added).

PARALLEL 75
Market
Stocks Decline on Higher Earnings

A key pattern change was increasingly evident. The market had apparently discounted higher corporate earnings. That characteristic was especially evident as IBM turned in record earnings for the fourth quarter. The January 23 *Journal* told the story well:

> International Business Machines, a stock many market watchers consider a bellwether for the health of the overall market, on Wednesday reported a 24% earnings gain for the fourth quarter, at the high end of analysts' expectations.
> That was the good news.
> The bad news is that IBM shares, already off about 10% from their high before the announcement, fell a few points further Thursday and Friday.
> The reaction to IBM's rosy profit picture may serve as an important signal about the market's future direction. While some experts think expected big gains in corporate profits during the current quarter could move stock prices higher, *there is a fear gnawing at the confidence of many investment managers that stock prices already discount the best possible news* [emphasis added].
> "Most economists are looking for first quarter earnings to be 40% to 50% higher than the depressed year-ago quarter," says Michael C. Aronstein, senior investment strategist for Merrill Lynch Pierce Fenner & Smith, Inc. "It strikes us that such an increase is the minimum necessary to justify stock prices where they are today."

Very few thought that stocks could go off very much on increased earnings. In 1984 people had the identical idea about earnings as they did in 1929.

On September 17 in that fateful year, the following appeared in the "Broad Street Gossip" column in the *Journal:*

> The stock market will continue under the influence of brokers' loans, *but the actual trend will be governed by earnings of the various lines of industry.* No stock is going off much on increased earnings. Profits of many corporations this year have shown increases of 20% to 75% or more over last year [emphasis added].

IX

PARALLEL 76

Market
Most Market Advisers Turn Bearish Far Too Late

Over the next several days the market was to take several hard jolts which were to knock the wind out of the sails of Wall Street complacency. The break below the December 15 low of 1,236.79 on January 25 tore a gaping hole in the fabric of the bullish thesis and was enough to lead some to switch to the bear side. Others would wait to see if the Dow held above the November 7 low at the 1,214.84 Dow level. That wait took only a week. Bearish sentiment in this short period of time took a quantum leap.

The late January slide had conviction, and the analysts who switched to the bear side at this time were to look back proudly many months later and advertise the fact that they had turned bearish near the market peak. Of course, they had actually missed calling seven to nine months of the bear market, as had those analysts in 1929 who turned bearish in the September–October period of that year. No participant in the over-the-counter market or the Amex was about to award a medal to somebody turning bearish in late January 1984. The correct time to have sold all stocks was in the spring of 1983.

The Wall Street Journal on October 21, 1929, belatedly admitted to a ten-month-old bear market. The "Broad Street Gossip" column stated: "We also know that it has actually been a bear market since the first of the year as the average price of all stocks traded in on the Exchange is lower by something like ten points."

PARALLEL 77

Market
Many Selling Out to Be on the Sidelines

Whenever people think that the market is simply treading water, that many are sitting on the sidelines or marking time, that is always when the excitement is about to begin. Such a lackluster day was January 24, the Dow slipping by a paltry 1.57 points, closing at 1,242.88.

The January 25 *Journal* quotes reflected a general boredom:

"The market continued to trade in *a narrow range* as people looked for some news development to give it direction," asserted Ernest Rudnet, partner in charge of block trading at L. F. Rothschild Unterberg Towbin. "Most of my accounts were *sitting on the sidelines* trying to decide what to do." He added that the market needs a decline in interest rates to send it up again [emphasis added].

Fred Dietrich, vice president of Dickinson Co., Chicago, expects the market "to continue *marking time* until investors hear the State of the Union message and learn whether President Reagan will run for a second term." The State of the Union address is scheduled for this evening and President Reagan is expected to announce Sunday whether he will seek another term [emphasis added].

The 1,235–1,240 area of the industrial average is regarded by some analysts "as a technical support level," asserted Jerry Hinkle, manager of trading at Sanford C. Bernstein & Co. He pointed out that the market "bounced off" that level yesterday and he expects the market to move up from that level.

The function of a bear market is to break all "popular" support levels. Mr. Hinkle's support was immediately destroyed that very day.

On September 21, 1929, the *Journal* stated: "Many operators were selling out with the idea of *sticking to the side lines for a while,* and their offerings started a decline in recent trading favorites" (emphasis added).

PARALLEL 78

Psychological
Susceptible to Rumors

An impaired technical position makes the market a sitting duck for rumors. It was documented that investors were already "nervous." Regardless of the validity of a rumor, the market acts first and thinks later. The sharp January 25 decline to Dow 1,231.89 was due to a circulated rumor that President Reagan intended not to seek a second term. The White House had quickly denied the rumor, but the rumor seemed to help explain why the market went down. People love logical explanations. But it was more difficult to explain why the market dropped again on January 26 after the rumor had been denied.

The Wall Street Journal on January 27 quoted Newton D. Zinder of E. F. Hutton:

"The market was trying to stabilize, but after the market's reaction to the Reagan rumor on Wednesday traders don't want to get aggressive until they get the official word that the president will run for another term." The White House on Wednesday quickly denied the rumor, and noted that Mr. Reagan will announce his plans Sunday night.

Sunday came and went, President Reagan announcing that he would run for a second term. *The market collapsed the next day.* The lesson in all that was that rumors haven't anything to do with the true course of the stock market.

Likewise, some *three weeks* off the September 1929 high, the market was in a seriously impaired position, completely open to wild rumors. The September 25 *Journal* in the "Abreast of the Market" column stated:

> Many wild rumors were circulated during the late afternoon. One report was that "something was hanging over the market," but no details were mentioned. Another rumor was that a bearish announcement would come after the usual monthly meeting of directors of the U.S. Steel Corp. Naturally, with so much confusion existing, the reports had an effect on the market.

Later on, there were many rumors that Andrew Mellon would resign as Secretary of the Treasury. He denied that rumor on October 9, 1929, stating that he would remain in the Hoover administration until 1933. Following that denial, the market turned down and kept going down, culminating in the great crash of 1929.

PARALLEL 79

Psychological
They All Fell for the Sentiment Indicators

Not aware of what lay ahead, the Street was brainwashed to believe that increasing bearish sentiment could be interpreted to be bullish.

The January 27 *Journal* carried quotes to that effect:

> "The market's outlook will remain clouded until we see a definite improvement in the industrial average and the breadth figures," contended John Brooks, first vice president at Robinson-Humphrey/American Express, Atlanta. "The recent string of strong openings and weak closings has worried a lot of the short-term traders." However, he added, *"the investor sentiment indicators are strong and could quickly flip the market to the upside"* [emphasis added].

Back in 1929, after the initial downward jolts of September, rising bearish sentiment was misinterpreted as being bullish.

In the October 1 *Journal* appeared the following in the "Broad Street Gossip" column:

> "Reading the market letters of forecasters," commented Old Timer, "I find that 75% of them are bearish. They cannot see anything but lower prices,

although stocks have had a very pronounced drop, some of them 30 to 70 points. Most of these same forecasters were telling how much higher the market was going when stocks were at peak prices and optimism filled the air.

"Now, why is it that everyone seems to get bearish when stocks have had a bad break and bullish when stocks have had a big rise? Why wouldn't it be logical for us all to buy when things are low and sell when things are high? But it isn't human nature for us to be bearish at the top and bullish at the bottom. Pessimism prevails when the market is breaking and optimism prevails when new tops are being reached. It is hard for the average trader to sell when things look rosy and hard for him to buy when things are gloomy, although if this policy was adhered to there would be fewer margin calls.

"As matters now stand, with Steel off nearly 40 points from its high of the year, General Electric 44¾ points, General Motors 24⅞, Chrysler 79⅛, Texas Gulf 17¾, Allied Chemical 39¾, and Kennecott 22⅞, it is strange that a majority advise the sale of stocks. They may be right, although this will not shake my theory that it is the better policy to keep away from the selling side after a break such as we have had, just as it is a good policy to keep away from the buying side after the market has had a big bulge."

The bearish sentiment proved to be a reliable forerunner of the crash that was soon to follow.

X

The year 1984 had started out exactly as had the year 1973—a year of high hopes followed by the worst bear market since 1929. Michael Hayes wrote an excellent description of the January 1973 stock market top, which was seen by this writer as an exact fit with the January 1984 top:

Commonly, after a sustained period of rising prices and improving economic conditions, a degree of unrealistic speculation will become evident. Inspired by good and improving earnings reports, some analysts begin to issue stock recommendations based on earnings growth projected many years into a "new economic era" of the future. Rationality often gives way to greed as the "greater fool" strategy characterizes the speculative demand for secondary issues. As the typical stock approaches its speculative peak, the more conservative investors who still hold the high-quality group are much demeaned for failing to "get with the action."

As with all manias, from tulips to gold, something eventually happens to break the speculative fever. Prices of the secondary issues, which had been propelled upward on a wave of promise that is now suddenly unfulfilled, may begin to drop rapidly. Meanwhile, slower but more assured earnings and dividend increases keep the Dow moving upward toward its final peak. As prices break in the lower-quality issues, some investors rush for the safer havens of the investment-grade securities which are approaching their peak.

"Not a Bear among Them" is the general consensus of the investment experts
as the Dow makes its final peak. The speculative sector and the typical stock are
usually well below their peak levels and have fallen into a pronounced bearish
formation as the final peak is made in the popular indexes. To the top, the Dow
has been supported by optimistic forecasts of future business conditions and by
institutional accumulation of investment-grade favorites. This divergence of price
behavior between the high-quality sector and the typical stock has happened so
frequently in past cycles that it has forecasting implications: When the Dow is
still bullish after an extended rise while the typical stock is distinctly bearish, the
direction is usually resolved in favor of the bear.

Eventually, when professional forecasters begin attaching numbers like 1,400
to their predictions, something happens and the Dow begins to break. Perhaps
profit-taking, perhaps a political or economic mishap, or perhaps dumping by
those wise enough to recognize fantasy. Usually, the reason for the break in the
Dow is not obvious at the time. Only after a serious rally attempt has failed and
a few months have passed will the deteriorating business conditions become
evident. Usually, the institutions will support the high-quality sector, being buyers
on early bear market declines and keeping the Dow from falling too far. Of
course, the lowered expectations for the earnings and dividends of the marginal
companies and the typical stock will continue to plummet with the last greater
fool holding a bag of losers.[2]

"Not a Bear among Them" was the January 1973 *Barron's* characterization
of its annual panel of investment experts. They were all looking for 1,200 in
the Dow for 1973. Probably the most thrilling of the early 1973 market
forecasts was the one by James Dines, who was looking for 1,500 in the Dow
by Easter. He soon retracted that forecast. The Hayes book was published in
1977, and even back then he regarded Dow predictions of 1,400 as fantasy
predictions at a typical major market top. In a footnote he stated: "Whether
1,400 or 2,000, the forecasters invariably attach big numbers to their predictions made at market peaks and small ones to their forecasts made at market
troughs." I saw at this time close similarities with the 1973 top. The Hayes
description fit the 1983–84 market to a T. I noted the heady Dow predictions
made right at the top. Martin Zweig was featured in the January 16 issue of
Barron's with a forecast of Dow 1,450 to occur before the end of the first 1984
quarter.

Of course, with the technical position of the market so very weak in early
January 1984, it was glaringly obvious that Dr. Zweig had not made a technical
market forecast, but, rather, a forecast based on fundamentals, which, of
course, was worthless. In the *Barron's* interview, Zweig said that he did not
look at charts. He said that what he looks at is earnings, and since stocks
decline while earnings are still rising, Dr. Zweig was looking at a lagging

[2]Michael Hayes, *The Dow Jones–Irwin Guide to Stock Market Cycles* (Homewood, Ill.: Dow
Jones–Irwin, 1977), pp. 97–98.

indicator. No technician could possibly predict that the Dow would rise to 1,450 before April 1, but one who followed earnings could. Those who followed earnings in 1984 were doomed to failure.

Noting the proliferation of 1929 parallels as the January 1984 market traced out its bearish course, I headlined the January 28 market letter: "On the Edge of Panic." In the closing days of the month, three additional parallels were clicked off. The momentum was unstoppable.

PARALLEL 80

Psychological
Wall Street Unanimous That
the Bull Market Is Not Over

The Wall Street Journal stated on January 30: *"Wall Street is nearly unanimous in the conviction that the record-breaking market surge that began in August 1982 isn't over yet"* (emphasis added).

The September 18, 1929, *Journal* in the "Broad Street Gossip" column said: "There may be a secondary reaction. This is anyone's guess, *but the traders who have had years of experience in the Street say it is still a major bull market"* (emphasis added).

The September 20, 1929, *Journal* stated: "Before the late unsettlement developed, *price movements in the main body of stocks displayed the characteristics of a major bull market"* (emphasis added).

On the same day in the "Broad Street Gossip" column: *"While things like this are going on one could hardly expect a bear market.* It will be to the advantage of the so-called big interests to keep the public in a cheerful frame of mind until all these big transactions are concluded successfully. At least this is the opinion of the Street" (emphasis added).

On September 21, 1929, the *Journal*'s "Broad Street Gossip" column stated: *"You hear that the bull market will run well into next year. This, notwithstanding mounting brokers' loans and continued high money rates"* (emphasis added).

On September 24, 1929, the *Journal*'s "Broad Street Gossip" column stated: *"The consensus among traders is that it is still a major bull market and that prices of the selected issues will work higher in the last quarter"* (emphasis added).

On September 27, 1929, the *Journal*'s "Broad Street Gossip" column stated: *"The consensus is that after the current period of adjustment is over, stocks will again rebound and make new highs"* (emphasis added).

Psychological
Short-Term Opinion Sharply Divided

On January 30, 1984, *The Wall Street Journal* said: "We'll get back to the bull market in stocks, folks, but first a time out for total confusion. . . . Analysts, money managers and investors are sharply divided about whether the market will go up, down or sideways over the next several months. . . . One thing there's no doubt about is that the once ebullient market is in a stall."

On the September 1929 slide, the drop stupefied the bulls and brought many bears out into the open, and thus *divided market sentiment*, producing a confused mix similar to that reported in the January 20, 1984, *Wall Street Journal.*

The *Journal* of September 13, 1929, stated: "Sentiment is still mixed."

The September 25 *Journal* in the "Abreast of the Market" column stated: *"Sentiment was confused with most observers inclined to be cautious and reduce long holdings on any rebound in the general list"* (emphasis added).

Psychological
Confusion

The market hates confusion. The January 30 *Wall Street Journal* headlined the inside back page market column: "Investors Are Divided on Direction of Stocks in Next Several Months." The optimists saw Dow 1,500 ahead and the pessimists saw Dow 1,100 ahead. The *Journal* summed up the degree of confusion beautifully. Even a psychiatrist couldn't have unraveled the knot as it existed at the end of January. (In the following quotes, emphasis has been added.)

Richard I. Sichel, vice president of New Jersey National Bank in Trenton, believes that the market "might pull back a little more in the immediate future, but it appears ready for an upturn, and February could be a good month."

Consistent with this outlook, New Jersey National has 90% of its $400 million in trust funds invested in stocks and bonds and just 10% in cash. But that's an indication of an obstacle to a renewed rise in stock prices, according to some analysts.

Their theory is simple enough: Rallies occur when investors have cash to buy stocks. At the market's bottom in early August 1982, institutional investors were flush with cash, according to several surveys at the time. Furthermore, interest rates were falling and many big institutions were reaping big profits on their bond holdings, which they plowed into stocks.

Today, the situation is reversed. Recent surveys find that institutions' cash reserves have dwindled to the lowest level in years. Therefore, some market analysts assert, there isn't enough cash left to stoke the fires—and there won't be until a wave of stock selling can replenish the institutions' coffers.

There are other reasons why the stock market is in confusion. Many professional money managers are finding the market increasingly difficult to navigate, in large part because the economy has changed sharply in the past two to three years.

Investment professionals, used to making decisions based on assumptions of high inflation, have been forced to come to grips with disinflation. U.S. business continues to lose out to foreign competitors that enjoy lower labor costs and, in the past two years, cheaper currencies. Once based on smokestack industries, the U.S. economy increasingly is undergirded by technology, information and other services.

"This is a different world than most money managers are used to," says John B. Ryan, a partner in New York-based KR Capital Advisors, Inc. "It's a new game with which most of us are unfamiliar. We're kind of awkward explorers in a new world."

So, he says, money managers "are calling into question all the old givens and are more willing to question even the smallest disappointments." As a result, he says, the market has become more volatile. Once sacrosanct stocks such as utilities and insurance issues, which investment professionals used to buy and forget, have started jumping wildly, like obscure high-tech stocks.

Investors' *confusion* can be partly blamed on the army of securities analysts who follow thousands of companies.

They have been too optimistic. Convinced early last year that the economy was primed for explosive growth, analysts were forecasting record profit gains and urging clients to buy stocks based on estimates for three or four years ahead.

What followed, through 1983 and into this year, has been a steady erosion of profit forecasts—about 1% to 1.5% a month, according to Zacks Investment Research, a Chicago-based firm that tracks earnings estimates on several thousand companies.

In mid-October [1983], for instance, Zacks found analysts predicting average profit-per-share growth for 1984 over 1983 of 32% for the companies included in the Standard and Poor's Corporation index of 500 stocks. The latest reading is 30.3%, and forecast changes "still are running negative," says Benjamin Zacks, president.

It isn't that corporate profits are shrinking, says Mr. Zacks. "The analysts just start out way too optimistic, possibly because they are pushing stocks or have investment banking relationships with their companies," he says. As a result, as each quarter's earnings come in, they drop their forecasts and come closer and closer to reality.

Individual investors shouldn't think they're alone *in their confusion.* Here is the market appraisal of William K. Hamer, vice president and portfolio manager of Texas American Bank, Fort Worth, which manages trust assets of $3.6 billion:

"A lot of people on the equity side of the market are waiting for something dramatic to happen in interest rates, but I don't think we'll see such a dramatic development.

"The equity guys are looking for a lead from the bond market, but it has been relatively flat for the past few weeks.

"We're not doing much of anything. We're sitting on a bunch of cash reserves —about 20%—and trying to be patient. I don't want to throw it at the market, but I also don't want to be out of it."

There you see what weather people would call a "front." The hot air of the market and the cold air had met, and without the correct technical analysis, one would have been totally lost.

Thus, January 1984 ended on a note of total confusion, when in actuality the market had hammered out a message as clear and succinct as a Western Union emergency telegram in ten words or less. The Dow closed out the month at 1,220.58, over 66 points under the January 6 pinnacle of euphoria. Much more was to come.

12

Over the Edge

[FEBRUARY 1984]

I

If there were any lingering doubts concerning the seriousness of the January slide, these were largely dispelled on February 1 as the Dow broke under the November 7 closing low of 1,214.84 to settle at 1,212.31. After a confused pause on February 2, the Dow plummeted on February 3 to close at 1,197.03 in the worst break thus far in 1984, dropping 16.85 points and eclipsing the 14.66-point break of January 23. That was immediately followed by sharp breaks on February 6 and 8, of 22.72 and 24.19 points, respectively. The Dow chart began to look like Niagara Falls.

Just prior to this latest slide, I had sent out an emergency bulletin on February 1 announcing a mechanical buy signal based on the A-Dis Trading Barometer. I doubted the validity of the signal but, nevertheless, felt obliged to report it. My heart wasn't in it, and I said as much in the bulletin: "Nobody knows how valid this signal is, but we have to go with the traditional indicators *until the market proves that something untraditional is going on.* Our emotions sense the proximity of panic, but our head tells us—not yet, not yet . . ." I stated that *a closing below 1,205 on this run could be very, very serious* and call for *reversing all the stock positions.*

The signal aborted, as I suspected. Here was the acid test of the *malfunctioning* of short-term indicators, the market failing to rally from normal oversold parameters. I quickly recalled Henry N. Southworth, who had noted the tendency of many indicators to malfunction at key market turning points. Of course, the normal things were going to malfunction. This was not a normal market. This was a severe bear market and, despite later "sucker" rallies which on the surface sought to discredit my major thesis, I knew the 1983 high was secure, not to be challenged during this entire coming cycle.

Thinking that the new month would bring better tidings after the January slide, *Barron's* said, "Thank heavens for February." Of course, there was a reason for that undying optimism. The employees of *The Wall Street Journal* and *Barron's* are not allowed to go short on a stock, and thus there is a definite built-in bullish bias in everything written by the *Barron's* staff.

PARALLEL 83

Psychological
A Technical Correction of Overbought Market

The February 1 *Journal* revealed a common human failing. Nobody likes to admit his market mistakes, and thus all countermoves in their early stage are downgraded in importance by those who did not see them developing in the first place. Thus, inasmuch as most people found themselves wildly bullish in the early days of January and did not see the bull trap they were ensnared in, *they naturally downgraded the importance of the slide that followed.* They were quick to label the January downswing as *a technical correction of an overbought market.* Most people tend to accept the market opinions they read in the *Journal* without bothering to check the record of those who state the opinions. In this case, if one was talking about the market correcting from an overbought condition, an astute market detective would first determine if that quoted person had described the market as being overbought at the top. Those who did see the market as being seriously overbought in early January also saw the seriousness of the decline that followed. Those who missed the top (and that was the majority) sought to rationalize their mistake and call the January slide a natural technical correction.

The Wall Street Journal, February 1:

> "The market is in a corrective phase which may have further to go," contended William A. Goldstein, president of Selected Special Shares, Chicago. *"Before this correction the market had become overbought* in the strongest sustained advance (since August 1982) of the past 20 years." The catalyst for the correction, he added, is that "although earnings are coming in at favorable levels, some are now below analysts' expectations and are causing disappointments" [emphasis added].

Goldstein had been optimistic in the January 10 *Journal,* but most people had forgotten that.

We find the parallel in the *Journal* of September 26, 1929:

It is generally thought the market has now reacted to a point where there should be some sign of resistance to any further selling after the forced liquidation has been exhausted. *Many still contend the recent reaction has been a technical affair to correct an overbought position* and to bring over-exploited stocks to more reasonable levels. If this view is correct it is likely that, with a so-called secondary reaction completed, the market will be in a position to move forward again [emphasis added].

While I couldn't prove it, I felt that it was likely that the specialists started the rumor on January 25 that President Reagan would choose not to run for reelection. Ironically, I had stated at the time that if President Reagan could have seen what was likely to happen in the financial markets in 1984 and 1985, he would have chosen not to run for reelection. Obviously, he did not see what was coming. What had been accomplished carried a very high price tag with it, and, there being no free lunch, the bills came due in 1984 and beyond, and they ran awfully high. The probability was extremely high that President Reagan would rue the day that he decided to run for reelection. As with Gene Tunney, history would show that he would have been better off if he had quit while he was ahead.

While President Reagan was throwing his hat in the ring for another four years, big things were happening in the stock market. The Dow had broken under the important 200-day trendline and the move was confirmed by an equally significant break by the Dow Jones Transportation Average below its trendline, both moves occurring on heavy volume. Those twin downside breakthroughs completely knocked out all the January bulls.

As the Dow turned down from the November 1983 and January 1984 highs, pessimism began to mount and I found myself surrounded by a number of new bears, those who had been following the popular Dow rather than the general market. I knew the cycle wouldn't end until at some future time virtually everybody was bearish and I would have an opportunity of again standing alone —the only bull. To turn everybody bearish would require a crash. At this time, though, there were still far too many bulls around, and thus there could be no important market bottoms of long-term proportions. As the market was now skirting the edge of panic, about to go over that edge, it was interesting to watch the rapidly changing market sentiment. The farce of the Dow façade was being seriously called to account following the great bull trap of early January. The market guillotine had a lot of work to do, and it was quick to chop off the heads of all the market analysts who had jumped on the bull bandwagon in early January.

Most stocks were now going down *regardless of earnings.* Earnings had nothing to do with market timing. Anyone who followed earnings in the 1984 market was going to end up a lemon. *Wall Street Journal* quotes in January had sought to explain the market downturn by citing *fears of an economic slowdown.* As the slide was set to accelerate in February, *Journal* quotes attributed the continuing downturn to *fears that the economy was too strong.* No wonder the average investor was *confused.* The argument was that a slowing economy, while good for interest rates, would hurt corporate earnings. On the other hand, too strong an economy would raise interest rates. Either bottom line would be bad for the stock market.

PARALLEL 84

Market
No Lasting Overall Pattern

Going into February, Wall Street was cast in a cloud of confusion. Stocks had gone up and down completely out of step with the economic news, and since most people follow the economic news, they were very confused. There was no lasting pattern on which they could base their decisions. Stocks were up in the morning, down in the afternoon, and then there were sudden gains, occurring just often enough to keep the dying hopes of the bulls barely alive.

This was one of the most interesting of the 1929 parallels. A few weeks prior to the great crash, the legendary Jesse Livermore entered a similar period of confusion.

> Yet, despite his success, he was still unable to discover *any lasting overall pattern.* One day the market was up; the next, often for no apparent reason, it plunged. Then, just as quickly, it climbed again.
>
> In a note on his pad Livermore scrawled: "For the professional, the most dangerous time of all is when the market see-saws under the influence of unknown forces. It is no place for an amateur."
>
> Another market observer at the time counseled those who had "cleared out" to stay out; the market was becoming increasingly difficult to fathom, even for dedicated professionals.[1]

On February 3, it became crystal clear that the stock market might have reached that magic and stunning moment in its rendezvous with destiny. Everything snapped, and now came a rather general rush for the exits. In keeping with the parabolic market rise of the past year, the gambling instinct was well reflected in a parabolic rise in margin debt, more than doubling since August 1982 and now standing at an all-time high of just under $23 billion. It paralleled the identical curve of brokers' loans in the 1920s which had peaked in September 1929. The severe drop in the Dow in the opening weeks of 1984 increased the probability that margin debt was peaking (see Parallel

[1]Gordon Thomas and Max Morgan-Witts, *The Day the Bubble Burst* (New York: Penguin Books, 1980), pp. 297, 302.

43). Later on, however, this important indicator was to become clouded by the combining of bond margin debt, simply seen as another example of the muddying of the waters at a very critical time.

The misguided bulls attributed the downturn to emotions, implying that there were no sound reasons for the decline.

> In the selling this month, "there has been a lot of *emotional liquidation,* especially in the growth stocks and those that have done well in the past few years," observed Leslie M. Pollack, chairman of Shearson Management, Inc. "Investors are now overdoing it on the downside just as they earlier had overdone it on the upside. They are overlooking the recent good news, especially lower inflation figures and the fact that President Reagan will run for another term" [emphasis added]. [February 1 *Journal.*]

As the slide worsened, the bulls insisted in calling the downswing a correction, or adjustment. Their thoughts remained tied to the bull market of 1982–83, which had died months before.

PARALLEL 85

Psychological
Market Going Through Period of Adjustment

> "We've had a correction in the secondary issues in recent months and now we're seeing a correction in the blue chips," asserted Fred W. Lange of Lange Financial Services. "The market is in the process of testing its early November lows of 1,200 to 1,210 in the industrial average." [February 2 *Journal.*]
> "The market has been going through *a period of adjustment.* Evidently many stocks were selling too high and when stocks are selling too high one can always look for a reaction" [emphasis added]. [September 27, 1929, *Journal,* "Broad Street Gossip" column.]

The slide prompted rumors of foreign selling:

PARALLEL 86

Market
Foreign Investors Pulling Out of U.S. Stock Market

> There is rising speculation that foreign investors are pulling out of the U.S. market and moving their funds back home. [February 6 *Journal.*]

There was another reference to this later in the month, on February 17:

> "One reason for the market's recent weakness is that the value of the dollar is peaking, which is prompting some selling of U.S. stocks by foreigners." This comment was made by Robert Walsh, senior vice president and research director at Rotan Mosle of Houston.

While such foreign selling based on a peaking of the U.S. dollar was premature, it was a reason that would crop up later when the dollar had actually peaked.

Despite whether the reason was valid or not as a contribution to the January–February market slide, it was interesting to note that the initial statement was made *one month* after the Dow Jones Industrial Average had recorded the 1984 peak of 1,286.64 on January 6.

The Wall Street Journal on October 2, 1929, *one month* after the September 3 peak in the Dow at 381.17, reported: "Renewal of the decline was set in motion by important liquidation from abroad."

By February 7 the Dow had dropped sharply to the 1,180.49 level. But there were still far too many bulls who wouldn't believe that a major bear market was fully underway. The February 8 *Journal* carried the following: "However, James Finucane, technical analyst at Illinois Co., Chicago, thinks the current retreat is near a bottom and he expects the industrial average to start up this month and reach 1,400 by June or July."

On that very day, the Dow recorded *the worst break of the year.*

PARALLEL 87

Market
Worst Break of the Year

Matching similar 1929 patterns, the year's worst market break thus far in 1984 was that of February 8, the Dow breaking that day by 24.19 points. The break occurred *roughly a month after the January 6 high* and brought the Dow down to 1,156.30.

October 3, 1929, saw the worst market break of the year thus far, the Dow breaking that day by 14.55 points, bringing the Dow down to 329.95. That break occurred exactly a month after the September 3 high.

II

After all important market breaks (and there is no exception to this), *The Wall Street Journal* always quotes someone who thinks that stocks appear attractive.

PARALLEL 88

Psychological
Stocks Are Beginning to Look Attractive

Harry Laubscher of Smith Barney Harris Upham was quoted in *The Wall Street Journal* of February 10 as saying that institutions with low cash reserves had been selling stocks so they would have funds to buy bonds that they considered more attractive. *"But stocks now have come down to a level where they appear more attractive"* (emphasis added).

On October 8, 1929, the *Journal* in the "Broad Street Gossip" column stated:

> *There are a number of stocks that are beginning to look attractive.* This refers in particular to stocks of companies that will be able to report record-breaking earnings in the current year. Some of these stocks have either reached new lows for the year or are selling close to the lows [emphasis added].

Stocks were considered "attractive" all the way down from the 1929 peak. On September 30, 1929, the *Journal* had stated:

> During the last few days the selling has become more urgent, and many brokers reported that public liquidation was beginning to appear. Industrials used in the Dow Jones average have broken practically 40 points from the September 3 high, *and levels have been reached that make the leading stocks again attractive to investment purchasers.* On Friday's decline, the buying was described as considerably better than the selling, an indication which caused shrewd students of speculation to look for a substantial rally in the near future [emphasis added].

But it was not to be. In keeping with the big picture, the technical damage on the January–February slide had been *so nearly fatal* that it held all later rallies within the downward channel until the nadir was recorded. It was too early in the developing massive bear market to expect any significant recoveries. There was far too much stock overhanging the market. The market had been building up to this historic turn since the previous June, just as the 1929 collapse had been foreshadowed by the peaking of most stocks by December 1928.

As the slide worsened, it exerted great pressure on a large number of impaired margin accounts, a situation that could easily have gotten out of hand just as the steady stream of margin calls in September 1929 had, more than any other factor, undermined the market.

PARALLEL 89
Market
Margin Calls Going Out

"Stocks were whipsawed throughout the day, reflecting the continued investor concern over the economic and international outlook," asserted Jacques S. Theriot, senior vice president at Smith Barney Harris Upham. Another negative, he added, was *the continued heavy selling triggered by margin calls*, or requests by brokers to their clients for more cash or securities when the client's equity in a margin account falls below a minimum standard [emphasis added]. [*The Wall Street Journal*, February 10.]

Many additional references were made to the pressure of a growing number of margin calls throughout the month as the market continued to collapse.

The 1929 experience clearly showed the effect of a growing number of margin calls:

Many marginal accounts were impaired by this break, and necessitous liquidation during the morning started resumption of the downward movement. [*Journal*, September 26, 1929.]

Further declines took place in active stocks throughout the list, reflecting necessitous liquidation of marginal accounts impaired by the recent break. [*Journal*, September 30, 1929.]

Trading yesterday was largely devoted to the adjustment of marginal accounts impaired by the recent convulsive declines in the main body of stocks. Commission houses sent out the biggest number of margin calls after Thursday's close that had been found necessary this year, and forced liquidation came into the market in huge volume during the morning. [*Journal*, October 5, 1929.]

Yesterday's market was in many respects the most extraordinary in the history of the Stock Exchange. With margins drastically impaired by the convulsive declines in Wednesday's late dealings, wholesale liquidation of accounts proved necessary. [*Journal*, October 25, 1929.]

In early 1984, few foresaw the coming margin account impairment, but I could see an inevitable trend underway which would ultimately bring the market to its knees. The later general rush to get out of the market would result in massive stock liquidation and suggested the following series of events: As volume would later build to 200-million-share days, there would be a mechanical breakdown and the New York Stock Exchange would close. Such a closing would produce massive fear, and upon reopening, there would be huge downside price gaps created by the specialists who would not want to see orderly markets. They make more money on *disorderly* markets. Being fearful that the Exchange might again close, the general rush to get out would then reach a new frenzy. That would bring about another Exchange closing for perhaps a longer period of time. The openings and closings of the Exchange, accompanied by massive margin debt liquidation and downside price gaps, would constitute a full-fledged panic, as was so clearly indicated by historical parallels. Confidence would be destroyed. As bull markets climb a wall of worry, the great bear market now in force was crumbling on a wall of confidence. That confidence would later give way to naked fear. It was to follow a blueprint of what had all happened before under similar circumstances. After all, history is simply a history of people, and that means that history is a record of human nature. Since human nature never changes, history would therefore predict history.

In keeping with the general immorality of Wall Street, the Exchange would never close on a rally. But the Exchange had a record of closing during panics. It would always discriminate in favor of buyers and against sellers. One of the reasons for the 1929 crash, as outlined by the president of the Stock Exchange at that time, was *the overwhelming willingness to buy and the overwhelming unwillingness to sell.* Now all that would be painfully *reversed.* I could not allow investors to be in this market, in view of what I had seen developing the previous spring.

PARALLEL 90

Historical
News Developments Have All Been Bullish

Most people could not understand how the stock market could ignore good news and go down. *The Wall Street Journal* on February 21 stated:

> When the stock market behaves contrary to current economic indicators, traders like to call it "perverse." If that definition applies, last week was the height of depravity. The week featured day after day of roaring economic news. Personal income, retail sales, industrial production, plant utilization, housing starts, and factory shipments all posted gains—some of them by amounts well in excess of expectations. Yet the Dow Jones Industrial Average fell in four out of five sessions, closing its sixth consecutive declining week with an 11.84-point drop.

All the news was excellent in early October 1929 just before the crash. In the *Journal* of October 12, the "Broad Street Gossip" column carried the following:

In the way of news developments, bulls have had much the best of it over the last week or so, and this, perhaps, is the main reason why the market has been able to score such a quick comeback. A week ago you heard all over the Street pessimistic forecasts as to the future of the market. You read in a number of newspapers comments to the effect that we were in a major bear market. Stocks are now 10, 20, and 30 points above where they were a week ago and optimism again prevails. One reason for this optimism was the ability of business to keep its head above water when many stocks were declining to new low levels of the year. The bullish news breaks have been the real foundation under the rise.

The February market was proving to be a shocker to most people inasmuch as they had been brainwashed for so long. The media were equally perplexed.

PARALLEL 91

Historical
Many in the Financial District Are Puzzled

On February 3, Lou Dobbs of Cable News Network's *Moneyline* was confused as to why the market could decline in the face of all the good news. A market that goes down in the face of good news is bearish and illustrates the point that one should follow the market and *not* the news. Back in 1929, the financial community was equally puzzled to see the market decline in the face of what they thought to be good news.

The important interests with large blocks of stock generally liquidate when the market is having one of its spectacular spurts during periods of great enthusiasm. However, as there is really no precedent for the current market situation, many in the financial district at this moment are decidedly puzzled regarding the outlook for the immediate future and sources of selling therefore will be watched closely. [*The Wall Street Journal*, September 24, 1929, "Abreast of the Market" column.]

However, at the moment most interests admitted that they were puzzled and declined to make a prediction regarding the immediate future. [*Journal*, October 26, 1929, "Abreast of the Market" column.]

The initial thrust of the February decline prompted a call from Financial News Network on February 6 for an interview. The interview was as follows:

The last time we talked with you was on January 11 when the Dow had stood at 1,277. I stated at that time that the market was headed sharply lower, and by late January, I had announced that we were on the edge of panic. Now I say we are *over the edge*, the bear market of 1983–84 now coming fully out into the open. Unfortunately, most people are not aware of the cycle of major panics and crashes occurring roughly 54 years apart. Wall Street knows this, but they won't tell you. So we have to be prepared for *abnormal declines* in the stock market. Merrill Lynch is down over 50 percent, and that would never happen in a continuing bull market, and thus that key bellwether stock is clearly telling you that the bull market is over and we are in a major and severe bear market. That doesn't mean that we won't see very sharp advances from time to time, but none of them, in my opinion, will reverse the bear market primary trend. Anyone reading my 1976 book will know that we are in the first phase of a new bear market.

Ray Dalio, an economist, told Bruce Paige on the same day that he didn't see anything below Dow 1,150 *because that would mean a recession was signaled.* By February 20 the Dow had dropped to 1,148.87 and Dalio's prediction became parked in the back of my head for later use.

PARALLEL 92
Market
Increase of Mutual Fund Redemptions

The February 13 *Journal* carried the following quote:

> "We raised some cash and increased our diversification a few weeks ago but now we want to sit back for a while and watch what develops," comments Arnold J. Midwood, senior vice president of Crocker Investment Management, San Francisco.
>
> He thinks the market could retreat an additional 5% to 7%. From this year's high of 1,286.64 reached on January 6 the Dow Jones Industrial Average dropped 133.90 points, or 10.41%, to 1,152.74 on February 9 before rebounding a bit Friday. "If it would come down hard, the sooner we could get the correction over with," asserts Mr. Midwood.
>
> The "main thing" he'll be watching is "whether institutional cash reserves build up." He notes that these reserves fell to an exceptionally low level this year and he suggests that one reason for the decline was *an increase in redemptions of equity mutual funds* [emphasis added].

The "Abreast of the Market" column in the *Journal* of September 24, 1929:

> There is a growing belief that investment trusts have been reducing their long positions during favorable opportunities. This does not mean necessarily that

interests directing such organizations are bearish, but is considered to be due to the desire to have realized profits to report at the end of the current year.

The Street was so nervous by mid-February that the bulls jumped on the first sizable advance to state their case. On February 14 the Dow shot up 13.71 points to close at 1,163.84. The *Journal* carried the following quote on February 15:

> "We were very encouraged that the market could bounce back as rapidly as it did yesterday after the rumors about President Reagan's health were denied," said R. Jerry Falkner, first vice president of Johnson, Space, Smith & Co., Atlanta. He also contended that *"the current market is very close to offering the best opportunities of the past 10 years"* [emphasis added].

PARALLEL 93
Market
Light-Volume Declines

Among the most misunderstood precursors of a very weak market are the light-volume declines. The media have brainwashed the public into thinking that a decline on light volume is bullish because there was no selling pressure. There is nothing more bearish than light-volume declines in a proven bear market. Inasmuch as most people *buy* stocks rather than sell stocks, the public is never anxious to sell stocks at a market top. Also, being human, they don't like to take a loss. Thus, when the market tops out and starts down in a new bear market, those who bought at the top *hold* their stocks. Buying a stock contributes to market volume. Selling a stock contributes to market volume. *Holding* a stock contributes nothing to market volume. People never go from buying stocks to selling stocks. There is always that middle step known as holding. Therefore, when one sees a trend going from high volume to low volume while the market is declining, it simply reflects the fact that *most people are locked in with stock paper losses.* They are mostly holding those losing stocks, and thus this *cuts the volume of trading.* Bear market declines are thus mostly low-volume declines. High volume comes later when the public panics.

III

On February 3, when the Dow had just broken the 1,200 level, Louis Rukeyser told his millions of viewers on *Wall Street Week* that the huge short interest was bullish because all those shorts had to cover at some time in the future. What he didn't tell them was that every coin has two sides. While the market did show the largest short interest in history, *it also showed the largest long interest in history.* A good portion of that record long interest consisted of *margined* accounts. Thus, while all short sellers eventually had to buy (cover), all long margined accounts eventually had to sell. If a large short interest was deemed by most to be potentially bullish, so then was a large long interest which was margined deemed to be potentially bearish. Since the long interest so vastly outweighed the short interest, my concerns were rightfully directed toward the bearish potentialities.

One would have thought that Rukeyser would have been impressed by the fact that the true general market had been declining for months in the face of record short interest figures. Furthermore, his famous father, Merryle S. Rukeyser, financial columnist and lecturer, who was often mentioned in the 1929 *Wall Street Journals,* could not have failed to notice that the great crash of 1929 followed a record high short interest in the market.

I had demonstrated my *roulette principle* in the Sun City casino in South Africa. When I placed a chip on the color red and a red number came up on the wheel, the croupier paid me. When I placed a chip on the color black and a black number came up on the wheel, the croupier paid me. How then could I conclude that red was good and black was bad? Yet in the marketplace most people think up is good and down is bad, and Wall Street *encourages* them to think that way.

Winners have long memories and losers have short memories. The headline in *The Wall Street Journal* on February 21 was: "Surging Earnings. Firm's Profits Soared 64% in Fourth Quarter from Weak '82 Period." Most people thought that was good news. They couldn't have been more wrong! They had completely forgotten that corporate earnings had the sharpest two-year rise in 1973 and 1974 during the worst stock market decline since 1929! I had contended for almost twenty-seven years that corporate earnings was the very worst indicator that one could look at. Timing is everything, and the market had already totally discounted those earnings improvements many months before.

In this seventh week of decline, the bear market locomotive was smashing everything in sight, demoralizing sentiment, causing all normal market measurements to malfunction, and creating deficits far greater than the budgetary deficits that everyone was talking about but doing little or nothing to reduce. According to the Wilshire 5000 Equity Index, over $230 billion in stock values had been wiped out since the spring of 1983. I told the South African people that Wall Street was one huge casino and was a form of organized grand larceny. Those who had stated that the stock market was having a correction in an ongoing bull market were suffering from market amnesia, and their untenable position was a cruel joke.

IV

PARALLEL 94

Market
The Fraudulent Complete Reversal

One of the outstanding characteristics pertaining to the first leg of a major bear market is the wide bullish acclaim given the first rally of any substance, no matter how brief. The bulls get so carried away that they want to believe that it is a *complete reversal.*

I appeared again on *Crossfire,* the Cable News Network show originating in Washington, featuring Tom Braden and Pat Buchanan. The date of the appearance had been set for February 24, arranged before I had left for South Africa earlier in the month. The Dow had closed at 1,134.63 the previous day, making an upside reversal. Having been on a plane most of the day, I didn't learn until minutes before the show that the Dow had jumped over 30 points that day, the sharpest one-day rise since the Volcker reappointment rally of July 20, 1983. The technical evidence showed that all rallies were bear market rallies, having limited lives. I explained on the show to Braden and Buchanan that if you drop a dead body from the top of the Empire State Building it will bounce. The 1984 market was dead. It had died in 1983.

There was a growing consensus, however, that the market had made a major turn for the better, some beliving it to be a *complete reversal.* The way *The Wall Street Journal* described it on February 27, one would have thought that it was the real thing:

> Favorable news on the Federal budget deficit and on the recent money supply figures helped fuel the Dow Jones Industrial Average's 30.47-point spurt Friday. Its gain was the sharpest since a jump of 30.74 points last July 20. In a vigorous stock market turnabout Friday, the Dow Jones Industrial Average catapulted 30.47 points for its biggest one-day gain in seven months. Volume rose to more than 102 million shares.

Five weeks later, the Dow was making new bear market lows.

Extreme optimism in a proven bear market is always suspect. Here is what was seen in *The Wall Street Journal* of October 7, 1929:

> Stocks recovered sharply for the better in the week-end session. Confidence regarding the immediate position of the market was greatly strengthened by the various recoveries which took place in Steel, American Can, Westinghouse and other leaders in the last minutes of Friday's session. This development was interpreted to mean that a good part of the forced liquidation had been cleaned up, and that prices in the principal trading stocks had reached levels which made them attractive to important buying.

That was the final rally prior to the great 1929 crash. They got very bullish on that turn. In fact, the "Broad Street Gossip" column in the October 7, 1929, *Journal* said: "The market underwent *a complete reversal* with substantial gains in all stocks" (emphasis added).

On the same night that I was appearing on *Crossfire*, Louis Rukeyser was being interviewed by Ted Koppel on ABC's *Nightline*. The conversation went as follows:

> *Koppel:* All right, Lou, old friend, PBS doesn't pay you vast sums of money so that we're going to let you get away without some kind of a prediction. What is going to happen to the market over the next few weeks and months then?
>
> *Rukeyser:* Well, I think the best answer to that was given by J. P. Morgan. He said the market will fluctuate. I suspect that maybe it hasn't had its final washout at this point, that there's still the final throwing of all prudence to the wind, and total despair hasn't quite set in; and then the moment comes when everybody says it's the end for the stock market, the bull market is over, we are now heading straight to the Great Depression—and I think we're not too far from that moment now—then you'll see this market go up again, and the great bull market will resume.

The statement by Louis Rukeyser spelled out another 1929 parallel:

PARALLEL 95

Psychological
New Highs to Follow End of Current Adjustment

One of the most exact of the 1929 parallels was the general consensus that the decline was simply an adjustment that would be followed by new highs in the Dow. All the way down in the first several weeks of the January–February slide, Wall Street was nearly unanimous in the conviction that the record-breaking market surge that began in August 1982 wasn't over yet. Louis Rukeyser simply repeated that same sentiment.

> It is generally thought the market now has reacted to a point where there should be some sign of resistance to any further selling after the forced liquidation has been exhausted. Many still contend the recent reaction has been a technical affair to correct an over-bought position and to bring over-exploited stocks to more reasonable levels. If this view is correct it is likely that, with a so-called secondary reaction completed, the market will be in a position to move forward again. [*The Wall Street Journal*, September 26, 1929, "Abreast of the Market" column.]

The consensus is that after the current period of adjustment is over, stocks will again rebound and make new highs. [*Journal*, September 27, 1929, "Broad Street Gossip" column.]

What Wall Street thought was a secondary reaction, adjustment, or correction in a bull market was simply the advance rumblings of major troubles to come.

13

Sucker Rally

[MARCH 1984]

I

The opportunity to buy stocks at bargain prices does not come very often, about once every five years, according to one economist. Last Thursday was the big bargain day, but few were able to take advantage of it as the dips and rallies were too fast to enable one to buy at much lower prices than now prevail. But there are many stocks that are still selling at bargain prices. They may go a little lower, but in the long run they will sell higher. They are cheap from the viewpoint of earnings as well as yield. The problem is to select the right stocks.

One could have read that in any current *Wall Street Journal*, because it echoed the current Wall Street majority opinion. But that paragraph appeared in *The Wall Street Journal* on the morning of October 29, 1929, the very day of the greatest Wall Street crash in history!

Here are some paragraphs taken from *The Wall Street Journal* which illustrate the extreme swing in sentiment from early September 1929 to late October 1929:

The *Journal*, September 11, 1929:

One of the outstanding features of the current financial situation is the ability of large investment trusts and holding companies to attract new capital. The public seems to be willing to assign millions to various organizations for the purpose of buying securities which it would not buy for its own account because of what it apparently regards as high prices. Trusts managed by interests who have built up widespread reputations for financial acumen are among the most popular, and invariably their offerings have been tremendously oversubscribed. The average individual believes that the trusts have proven their ability to accumulate equities in the past, offer a sounder basis for the handling of his funds than his own meagre knowledge of financial values and prospects.

Many financial observers also believe that this attitude lends a sounder basis than has ever existed before. It concentrates large sums in the hands of experts who finance their purchases conservatively or buy outright for permanent investment. Such securities cannot be dislodged with every temporary shift in speculative currents, as in the case of margined securities in the hands of weak holders with insufficient knowledge to hold selected stocks.

Now contrast that quotation with the following one from the *Journal* of October 29, 1929:

> Investment trusts were unusually popular only a short time ago, whereas today outsiders are keeping away from these stocks entirely. It is felt that the enthusiasm which existed was shattered by the action of some of these stocks and the fact that many investment trust issues which are not listed could not be disposed of when holders needed funds badly.
>
> There are reports that investment trusts were among the largest sellers of stocks about a week ago and the supply from this source had much to do with starting the decline which resulted in the disastrous break about the middle of last week. It will probably be some time before the public has confidence again in the investment trust issues.

Yet, despite that swing in sentiment, the 1929 decline was at that point merely the tip of the iceberg.

The bulls were so discouraged at missing the 1929 top that they were pretty certain that the drop from the Dow high of 381.17 to 325.17 by October 4, 1929, put the market in a *super-oversold* condition. The *Journal*, October 5, 1929:

> The market can be oversold just as easily as it can be overbought. Many stocks were probably too high and they declined from 20 to 100 points or more. Some of them are now probably too low and are due for substantial comebacks when the market turns. The available supply of money for investment purposes is as large as it ever was. From reports concerning the hundreds of millions of money the investment trusts are lending on call we judge the latter, in time, will become active on the buying side of the market.
>
> Investment trusts are not formed to lend money, but to invest money. They will buy when they think certain stocks have reached attractive levels. Payrolls of the country have reached record proportions. So have earnings of corporations. Dividend and interest payments are larger than they have been at any time in history. Don't get too bearish on the shares of the well-managed, growing companies. *Wise traders do not sell stocks after a decline running from 20 to 100 points or more* [emphasis added].

That sounded just like March 1984. No two cycles are ever exactly alike, but human nature never changes. The majority was beholden to what seemed obvious to most: rising corporate earnings, the reelection of the president, sustained economic strength, etc. But the January–February downturn was as definite a warning as the downturn of January–February 1973. And the upturns were as transitory as those in earlier bear markets, born of hope but lacking in staying power. As in all severe bear markets, the initial downturn caught most people by surprise. Since they didn't expect it, they did not sell on the way down. At this time, there were literally tons of stock waiting to get out on the next rally, and that was why the first rally was quickly doomed to failure.

I had constantly referred to the *immorality* of the Street throughout the peaking 1983 market. The actions did not match what the public was led to believe. Merrill Lynch saw trouble ahead when they split their stock 2–1 in June 1983, and the 55 percent decline in the value of the stock by March 1984 had proved that their unreported fears had been well founded. American Motors had brought out an additional 75 million shares of common stock when the shares had been selling at $11 the previous June. Now those shares were down to $5.75. I had reported these things at the time they were occurring, but nary a warning ever came from the Street or the companies involved.

Interpreting actions rather than words, I had made a prediction eight months earlier that was then being fulfilled. In my June 25, 1983, market letter, the following paragraph appeared:

> Ronald Reagan, our President, *sees possible trouble ahead.* Since it is a foregone conclusion that our President has every intention of running for reelection in 1984, it would have been politically stupid to replace Paul Volcker with a new man. If anything went wrong, as it is going to happen, such a new man would have meant that Reagan would get it in the neck in 1984. But, by reappointing Paul Volcker, if anything went wrong now, and something is going to go wrong, then Volcker will get it in the neck and not Reagan. That is just good politics; and, of course, as we all know, politics is a dirty business.

Now that idea, eight months later, was creeping into the press. On the front page of the business section of *The Washington Post* on February 24 appeared an article headlined: "White House Seen Setting Up Volcker." Here is a quote: "If something does go wrong and the economy dips before the election, then the finger of blame can be pointed at Fed Chairman Paul A. Volcker, the official noted."

Politics was heating up. Rising interest rates were arousing the ire of the White House, but President Reagan's troubles were more importantly reserved for 1985 and beyond, long after the current economic boom had ended.

PARALLEL 96

Historical
We Are Richer Than Ever Before

In the economic recovery of 1982–84, personal income reached new all-time highs. There was a new national sense of well-being providing no hint of the great changes to come.

Likewise, in 1929 new levels of record prosperity were reached, and as late as October 4, 1929, *The Wall Street Journal* in the "Broad Street Gossip" column stated: "We are richer than ever before, with more surplus cash for investment purposes than ever before. The foundation for a prosperous 1930 is even stronger than it was a year ago, when we were concerned as to whether 1929 would be a good year or a bad year." Three weeks later the market crashed.

II

The February 22 market bottom at Dow 1,134.21 and the violent upturns of February 24 and 27, which sent the Dow almost 46 points higher, prematurely encouraged the Street. *The Wall Street Journal*, March 1:

> James C. Andrews, first vice president at Janney Montgomery Scott, Philadelphia, contended that the vigorous rally last Friday "broke the back of the downside move." He also called encouraging yesterday's news that the U.S. composite index of leading economic indicators rose 1.1% in January.

Peter Eliades was quick to say that the market had seen the lows for the year. James Dines called for an explosive rally to Dow 1,230.

PARALLEL 97

Psychological
It's Too Late to Be Bearish

During the first leg of a serious bear market the market invariably drops far enough to produce a conclusion among the casual observers that *it is too late to be bearish*.

On October 12, 1929, in *The Wall Street Journal* a comment was made in the "Broad Street Gossip" column that fully expressed the sentiment that it was too late to be bearish: "The market can be oversold just as easily as it can be overbought. *When you are unable to find one lone bull you can depend upon it that the market is due for a rally*" (emphasis added).

All the usual arguments were trotted out as to why March was the time to buy stocks. Arther Laffer on March 13 said to buy stocks because the economy looked outstanding well into next year and beyond. Peter Eliades stated that there was no way the Dow could close under 1,115. Later in the month Lee Idleman was quoted as saying that this was a *once-in-a-lifetime opportunity to accumulate stocks and that one should not be left out.* He also said he was looking for the Dow to go to 3,000 in this decade. Nine months earlier, Donald Regan, the Secretary of the Treasury, thought that *stocks were the best buy in two decades.*

PARALLEL 98

Market
Trouble in the Utilities

By this time the utility segment of the market was in deep trouble. Most people had forgotten how enthusiastic *The Wall Street Journal* had been the previous fall. On October 7, 1983, it was reported that the Dow Jones Utility Average had closed on October 6 at 140.08, the highest closing in that average since November 29, 1968. What they did not tell their readers was that four calendar days later, after the November 29, 1968, reading, the vicious 1969–70 bear market started. I had revealed that important fact in a bulletin dated October 10, 1983, and pointed out that such strength in the utility average was in keeping with the end of the bull market.

Was it any different in 1929? No, it was exactly the same. The peak of the market in 1929, in terms of the Dow Jones Industrial Average, occurred on September 3, 1929. The September 4 *Wall Street Journal* market comment was headlined "Utilities Lead." The comment is worth repeating:

> Wall Street entered the autumn financial season in a definitely *optimistic frame of mind.* With railroad traffic showing steady gains, and production in the major branches of industry continuing at a high rate, the *earnings prospects* of the principal corporations with shares listed on the Stock Exchange were looked upon as *extremely promising* [emphasis added].

Note the key words in the *Journal* piece: "optimistic" and "promising" with the accent on "earnings." Buyers of utility stocks are primarily interested in earnings and yield. They were ill prepared for what came after September 1929, just as utility stock buyers were ill prepared for what followed the peak levels of October 1983. Back in 1929, Samuel Insull's utility empire fell apart, and utility stocks got smashed like everything else in the market, with the sole exception of the gold stocks. By March 1984 the awful facts were emerging pertaining to the frightfully high costs of converting to nuclear power. Whatever the reason, the market itself pointed the way first to the emerging fundamental problems. Therefore, why follow fundamentals? Well, I don't, and that is my very point. *The market is the finest substitute for fundamentals ever conceived.* Earnings are the very worst of all things to follow in the market. If one had followed earnings in 1929, one would have been wiped out in the great crash. Earnings were excellent in 1929, and the market was terrible. Follow the market, not earnings. Dividends? These are the biggest of all hooks in the market. The corporations were raising dividends across the board in 1929, trying to shore up the market. What good is a $1 boost in dividends if the price of the stock drops 10 to 15 points? All one was getting was a partial return of capital, and one was taxed on that as income. But that is a lesson that most people refuse to learn.

PARALLEL 99
Market
Misplaced Emphasis on the Oils

In the oil group the parallels with 1929 were also exact. I could not forget that the final sucker rally before the 1929 crash was led by the oils. Such rallies are generally the sharpest. Thereafter, the oils fell back with the general market. In March 1984 the oils collapsed following an upswing based on merger mania. Losers had very short memories. Bullish sentiment dies rapidly in major bear markets.

Here is what *The Wall Street Journal* said about Cities Service on October 8, 1929, three weeks before the great crash:

> Cities Service touched record high ground during the morning, on a continuation of the heavy buying that kept the stock above 60 through the break of last week. Announcement of rights to stockholders is anticipated this week and is believed to account for many of the new commitments in the issue. Company has a long record of paying cash and stock dividends, enhanced by the rights that are issued from time to time. In line with previous offerings, many expect that the new rights will offer holders the privilege of buying one new share around $40 for every ten shares now held.

Now contrast that paragraph with the following one that appeared in *The Wall Street Journal* on October 30, 1929:

> The battle in Cities Service continued to rage with the sponsors making fair progress in their terrific effort to keep the stock from collapsing altogether. The

incessant bombardment from short sellers and from frightened traders seeking to dispose of their holdings at any price cut into the market to some extent, but offerings around 22 and 23, the prevailing price during the morning, were taken in blocks of four and five thousand shares with impressive regularity. In the first hour of trading, 619,000 shares of this stock changed hands.

That is how fast sentiment had changed on one of the key oil stocks of the day. At the top they were all fighting each other to snatch the stock at 60, and just three weeks later there was the terrific effort to keep it from collapsing, the stock having dropped from 60 to 22. Note in the first quote that holders were given the "privilege" of buying new shares at $40 for every ten shares held. Three weeks later, after it was too late, they realized that it wasn't a privilege, it was a penalty.

While the oils were rallying in early October 1929, a key line was given in the "Broad Street Gossip" column in the October 8, 1929, *Wall Street Journal:* "The view of one large house is that the recent break makes a firm foundation for a big bull market in the last quarter of the year." That is exactly what people were hearing when the Dow jumped sharply from the February, 1984, low of 1,134.

Part and parcel of the big picture, mergers and acquisitions reached a nine-year peak, and the huge sums involved were to create problems later on. Many previous corporate marriages had foundered on the rocks, the peak of the merger craze usually occurring at important market tops. At this time, SoCal wanted Gulf, and apparently had it for $13 billion. The details didn't interest me, but the timing of this and other takeovers did. I saw the days of the huge mergers quickly coming to an end because nothing would kill them off faster than an extended decline in the stock market.

The remaining market bulls were notably those who had missed the January top and sought to rationalize their position with their ever-recurring story of a correction in an ongoing bull market, it being simply a matter of time before the second leg would start.

PARALLEL 100

Psychological
Dow Won't Fall under Book Value

Stephen Leeb of Money Growth Institute, Jersey City, New Jersey, was quoted in *The Wall Street Journal* of March 8 as saying: "It's unlikely that the industrial average will fall much below the 1,100 level because that's the estimated book value in 1984 of the Dow Jones Industrial Average's components." He repeated this assertion a month later in the *Journal* of April 11, stating: "The market's downside risk is limited. The current estimated 1984 book value of the Dow Jones Industrial Average's 30 components is $1,080 to $1,100 and during the past 60 years it has always paid to buy the industrial average's stocks when they traded below book value."

Here is the parallel reference in 1929 to book value: In the October 28, 1929, *Wall Street Journal*, it was reported that "moneyed people were picking up issues which they considered attractive as to earnings and book value." In the October 29, 1929, *Journal*, Baar, Cohen & Co. made the following comment: "There is no question but that the market got completely out of hand last Thursday and again on Monday, and there is no question but that a preponderance of stocks are now quoted many, many points below even a conservative market valuation. We believe the time is not far distant when we will look back upon these prices as a golden opportunity to buy something for less than its true worth."

PARALLEL 101

Market
First Mention of Bear Market

When a bull market turns into a bear market, it is interesting to note when the bear market is first mentioned in *The Wall Street Journal*. The final peak in the Dow occurred on November 29, 1983, at 1,287.20. It wasn't until the Dow failed to make a new closing high in January 1984 that the famous blue chip average was in major technical trouble. But the term "bear market" did not show up in the *Journal* until March 9, 1984:

> "We see small chance of any loosening of credit policy by the Fed over the next month or two," asserted Ned Babbitt, president of Avatar, which manages $460 million, and last month increased the cash reserves in its equity portfolios to 85% from 20%. He added that *"there's a 50/50 chance we may be in a bear market"* [emphasis added].

When that statement was made, the Dow stood at 1,147.09, down 10.8 percent from the peak.

Back in 1929 the term "bear market" was first seen in the September 30, 1929, *Journal*: *"We are now beginning to hear queries as to whether this is the start of a bear market"* (emphasis added). When that quote, from Baar, Cohen & Co., appeared in the regular market column, the Dow stood at 347.17, down 8.9 percent from the peak.

These comparisons demonstrate the fetish of following the Dow as the "market" rather than the entire market. Any competent market technician could have seen that 1929 was in a bear market *many months before the Dow had peaked on September 3 of that year.* The high/low indicator and the advance/decline line had peaked in December 1928, over eight months ahead of the Dow. Likewise, those important indicators had peaked in the spring of 1983, many months before the late November 1983 peak in the Dow. Market letter writers who had proclaimed that they had called the top in January 1984 *had not called the top at all.* Most stocks were showing very sharp declines by the time those Johnny-come-latelies were beginning to turn bearish in the early months of 1984. The true call to sell everything had arrived in the spring of 1983 at precisely the time when nobody was listening. Whenever the Dow would rise, one encountered the term "bull market" over and over. But when the Dow would drop, nobody was saying "bear market."

III

A number of people were on record that the great decade of the 1980s would see the Dow Jones Industrial Average soar to 3,000. Among them were Thomas Blamer and Richard Shulman, who published a book entitled *Dow 3000.* [1] Reading the book, however, one discovers that the authors carefully hedged their forecast, leaving several escape hatches. They stated their forecast could be upset by nuclear war, nationalization of Dow companies, a depression, or a complete shutoff of OPEC oil. While they thought such occurrences were possible, they didn't believe they would take place in the 1980s. John Templeton was equally optimistic, actually going Blamer and Shulman one better. He saw the Dow rising to 2,800–3,150 by 1988. Robert Prechter, who writes the *Elliott Wave Theorist,* was on record that the decade would see the Dow 2,000 level.

Perhaps these super-optimists saw the 1980s as duplicating the 1920s, interpreting the 1982 bottom as equivalent to that of 1921. I countered such a notion at this time by stating that the 1982–83 rise was not a beginning, but an ending similar to that of 1928–29.

Astute market technicians had become aware that the advance/decline line on the American Stock Exchange had by this time given back more than the entire 1982–83 advance. In the 1981 bear market, that indicator had given back the entire 1980 advance, and thus there was no doubt that the 1983–84 bear market was serious and would get a great deal worse.

Nobody was talking about the vast number of margin calls going out. There were reasons why the subject seldom came up. First of all, exact figures were difficult to come by, brokerage firms being reluctant to make such announcements because that simply advertised that their customers were losing money.

[1] Thomas Blamer and Richard Shulman, *Dow 3000* (New York: Harper's Magazine Press, 1982).

Secondly, customers did not like to report that they were getting margin calls, because that called attention to their errors. But a study of any current chart book would reveal that most traders were getting margin calls. Most of those calls were not being met because the accounts had become seriously impaired. This progressively added to the selling pressure, a pressure that restricted all rallies to rallies in a bear market.

The bulls still didn't give up on their story that this was a correction in an ongoing bull market. But the technical facts at this time delivered a severe jolt to the bullish hopes: (1) a new low in the Amex advance/decline line below the August 1982 bottom; (2) a break in Merrill Lynch commensurate with all other bear market first-phase movements; (3) a certain failure of General Motors to make a new high within four months; (4) a virtual low-volume decline to new lows, which was absolutely the worst type of technical performance, negating the widely hoped-for selling climax; (5) most stocks below their 200-day trendlines, with the trendlines themselves rolling over; (6) January–February pattern worse than the start of the 1973–74 bear market; (7) corrections in a "bull" market lasting abnormally long; and (8) too much price damage for the correction to be deemed normal.

The "correction in a bull market" story had no more substance to it than did the similar story in 1929:

PARALLEL 102

Psychological
Correction in an Ongoing Bull Market

The January 1984 market downturn caught so many bulls at the top that they had to rationalize the downturn as simply *a correction in an ongoing bull market*. The downtrend started with the word "consolidation," as used in the *Journal* market columns of January 11, 13, 17, and 18. By January 19, the downtrend was called a "little correction." That turned into a "major correction" by January 26. The "correction in an ongoing bull market" theme was played in the *Journal* market columns of February 1, 2, 8, 13, 22, as well as March 7. In that two-month period, nobody thought that the "correction" was the first leg of a serious and extended bear market.

It was no different in 1929. Coming off the September 3 top at Dow 381.17, the decline on September 4 was called "the first technical correction of importance." The famous Babson break occurred on September 5. By September 10 the *Journal* talked of "further correction." On September 11 the *Journal* stated that the process of correction was still incomplete. An interchangeable word used at that time was "readjustment," and by September 12 it was generally felt that the downward readjustment had not yet been completed. By September 17 the *Journal* alluded to some further correction. By September 18 the *Journal* reported that many observers thought the correction had completed itself and was starting a substantial upturn. By September 23 the *Journal* carried comments that the correction had gone a long way toward improving the technical condition. By September 24 the reported consensus was that it was still a bull market. The term "corrective period" was still used as late as September 26 in the *Journal.* By September 27 it was still called "a period of adjustment." Thereafter, the word "correction" didn't show up again. By September 28 it was seen that *the market had suffered a severe break.* Even at that point, however, it was looked upon as a *healthy reaction* from which there is always a substantial recovery. The parallel with 1984 was exact.

Misreading the growing bearish sentiment, a hard core of bulls persisted in their belief that the brief 1982–83 rise would be resurrected. Although beginning to postpone their hopes for new highs to later in the year, they were convinced that the bulk of the correction was over, that the worst had passed. A few key technicians were turning more bullish on the market. One of these was John A. Mendelson of Dean Witter Reynolds, who turned bullish on stocks and bonds for the "intermediate term" of six to nine months. At the same time, however, an increasing number of market letter writers were turning bearish, as their correct reading of the technical picture was forcing them to do. It was a confusing period for the public, not knowing which side had the true message.

Adding greatly to the confusion was the evidence that the stock market was demonstrating that it liked neither a slowing economy nor an improving economy. Early in the year, market declines were attributed to fears of a slowing economy. By mid-February, however, the pattern changed. Declines were then explained in terms of fears of a growing economy.

The last time that type of confusion existed was in 1929. It meant only one thing. Money was fleeing the stock market back in 1929 because it was no longer a safe or profitable place to be. History showed that the trouble began in the stock market and later on spread to the economy. Back then, all who had based their decisions on what the economy was doing were doomed to be wiped out. They had failed to heed the message of the market itself. They were foolishly looking at the great expectations regarding corporate earnings and dividends and listening to their president extol the virtues of a prosperous economy. It was no different in 1984.

Few of the day's money managers remembered 1929, much less studied the mounting number of parallels. They could no longer decide whether they were for an expanding economy or a contracting economy. The market had totally negated their fundamental training. These very people were guiding many, many billions of dollars of the public's money. Now, if they were confused and didn't know what to do, that destroyed public confidence in the intelligence of their decisions, and it was that real and growing lack of confidence that the primary trend of the stock market was all about. The record was clear that it was these very money managers who had fallen in love with the market in the spring of 1983 at the very worst of times. This was now well-established fact. Pension funds were 65 percent invested in equities at that time, the highest imbalance in the history of their portfolios. These people managed the public's money. With 75 percent of all trading dominated by the institutions, it was becoming increasingly evident who would have to bear the brunt of the major losses in the bear market. At one time the institutions were considered to be the "smart money," competing with a less-informed public. That is no longer true. Today, the institutions almost precisely represent the public, and that observation was also made in 1929, when the institutions took the bath with the public because they had become interchangeable.

I V

I had stressed how dividends can mislead investors. They had lulled the public to sleep in 1929.

Investment Quality Trends of La Jolla, California, reported that in 1983, 224, or 64 percent, of the 350 blue chip companies it follows increased dividends. In an improved economy, *IQT* expected even more blue chips to share the wealth: "Higher dividends [historically] support higher stock prices." Did those 1983 dividend increases support a higher stock market in 1984? No. The market topped out in the spring of 1983, and by 1984 $200 billion in stock values had been wiped out. But, more important, there was the 1929 parallel to consider. (See Parallel 64.) The biggest dividend boosts in history up to that time took place in 1929. In that fateful year Wall Street had been banking on over $2 billion in fourth-quarter boosts to push the market higher, and the market crashed right in the face of those bullish dividend expectations.

Despite the unending chorus of this being a correction in an ongoing bull market, nobody seemed to be bothered by the fact that corrections in bull markets had never lasted this long. This one had been going on for the better part of a year, and that, as I had reported, was proof enough that the market was very definitely in a bear phase. Waiting for the Dow to exceed a decline of 15 percent in order to claim a bear market seemed to be foolish. My calculations told me that the coming decline in the Dow in the months ahead would exceed all current projections. No major long-term bottom could even begin to come into sight until everyone *knew* that this was a bear market. As long as people talked about a correction in an ongoing bull market, the market would fail to accommodate them. There were too many impaired accounts from which to launch anything more than bear market rallies.

Stan Weinstein of the *Professional Tape Reader* at this time called it a *junior* bear market. Since when does a girl get slightly pregnant? The market is either in a bull market or in a bear market. There are no junior bear markets. One cannot have it both ways. The market forces one to choose one way or the other. There are no markets that are non-bull or non-bear. This gradation of language was interesting, and implied a number of 1929 parallels. In 1929, the decline was progressively described as a pause, normal profit taking, a brief consolidation, a consolidation, a normal pullback in a continuing bullish trend, a normal correction, a correction, the continuing correction, a normal secondary, the secondary, a severe secondary, and, finally, a crash. As late as October 21, 1929, William Peter Hamilton, in his famous "Turn in the Tide" editorial in *Barron's*, described the market action at that time as *a severe secondary.* A week later came the great crash!

One of the best methods to determine if a market rally had no lasting foundation was to identify which analysts who were very bullish about the rally were the identical people who had missed the January 1984 top. In September 1929, the analysts who were so quick to proclaim the return of the bull on the brief early October 1929 rally missed all signals of the crash. It is just pure and predictable psychology. With their analysts having totally missed the top, and making ridiculous forecasts in early 1984 of Dow 1,450 by April 1, clients were hopelessly locked into huge losses. Human psychology demanded that they be bullish, borne on the wings of hope. They craved to be bailed out, and the market knew this. The market would not reward losers. This was a bear market, and thus the losers were the bulls and the winners were the bears.

I had previously called attention to the *reverse head-and-shoulders pattern* which had deceived most technicians in August 1981. The identical pattern had showed up in 1984 coming off the February low. It had excited all those who had missed the January top. They read into that pattern a chance to be bailed out. So, like those who foolishly thought a high short interest ratio was bullish in 1983, they promoted that reverse head-and-shoulders story for all it was worth. Ironically, on the day the neckline was penetrated, I received a confirming signal from my trading barometer that the rally was over.

About this time *USA Today* reported the growing woes of mutual fund managers as they suffered the collective headache of *net redemptions.* Net redemptions, like secondary stock offerings and insider selling, mean simply that *someone wants out.* Net redemptions were rising rapidly at this time, and that meant that more money was going out than was coming in, and with low cash positions, more shares had to be sold. It was part of the overall trend in which money was on balance leaving the market. I saw the proof of this not only in the lower stock prices but also in the increasing shift of funds out of the market and back into the money market funds that now, with rising interest rates, were increasingly popular. Margin calls continued heavy. With all this evidence that money was leaving the stock market, no further proof was necessary to identify correctly the bearish primary trend.

Justin Mamis appeared on *Money Line,* the Cable News Network program, on March 23. He told Myron Kandel that we were in a bear market. Kandel responded by asking, "If this is a bear market, what stocks can we buy?" That was a typical media response. Having spent most of my working life in this business, I have never had anyone come up to me and ask me what stocks they should sell.

PARALLEL 103

Psychological
Street Fooled by Bearish Sentiment, Thinking It Bullish

Ira Ross, vice president of Dean Witter Reynolds InterCapital, stated in *The Wall Street Journal* on January 17, 1984, that he was encouraged by the recent increase of bearishness among investment advisers because he saw "cash building up and setting the stage for a good upside move." Leslie M. Pollack, the chairman of Shearson Management, Inc., drew attention to emotional liquidation in his comments in the February 1 *Journal.* He stated that "investors are now overdoing it on the downside just as they earlier had overdone it on the upside." (There was no mention of how bullish Mr. Pollack had been in his January 17 *Journal* comment.) Terry Diamond, partner of Steiner Diamond, Chicago, was quoted in the *Journal* on March 8 as stating that psychology had turned negative and that it was too late to be bearish.

It was clear that during the first three months of 1984 the growing increase in bearishness was generally interpreted as increasingly bullish. In a normal market that would have been a valid reason for increasingly turning toward the bull side. However, with the stock market crash being but a few months away, the increased bearishness was leading toward the inevitable crushing of the wineglass, the simultaneous dumping of stocks regardless of fundamentals. The year 1984 was no more a normal market than was 1929. Normal yardsticks went out the window. An increase in bearish sentiment could not be seen to be technically constructive. It would turn out to be as totally destructive as the abnormality of the year predicted it would be. Without the 1929 parallel, most people would misread the growing negative sentiment, only to be caught up in the later selling vortex.

The Dow peaked on September 3, 1929, at 381.17. Bearish sentiment was *almost nonexistent at the market peak.* By September 23, with the Dow down to 359.00, *The Wall Street Journal* began to call attention to bearish sentiment. The further the Dow dropped, the more numerous the comments became. Here are those comments:

Date	Dow Closing the Day Before	Wall Street Journal Comment
9/24	359.00	There are many bears in the financial district. . . . Many observers are advising clients to remain on the sidelines for the time being. . . . Commission houses were sellers on balance . . . many outsiders have been liquidating recently.
9/26	352.57	Bearishness was increased by another flurry in call money. . . . There are plenty of bears but many of them are temporary bears.
9/28	344.87	Sentiment among professionals and traders is still quite bearish.
9/30	347.17	. . . Public liquidation was beginning to appear. . . . We find the Street just as bearish now as it was bullish two weeks ago. . . . We are beginning to hear queries as to whether this is the start of a bear market. . . . Sentiment generally continues bearish. . . . It is pointed out that sentiment has been so upset that it will take considerable time to get outsiders back into the market on the long side with any degree of enthusiasm.
10/1	343.45	I find that 75% of them [market letters] are bearish. They cannot see anything but lower prices. . . . Now, why is it that everyone seems to get bearish when stocks have had a bad break? . . . It is strange that a majority advise the sale of stocks. . . . Don't forget to buy a few stocks when 75% of the trading element is bearish.
10/4	329.95	Sentiment, of course, is bearish.
10/17	336.13	Sentiment of the Street was about as bearish as it was in the preceding break, with "business depression" the main argument of the bears. . . . Sentiment has naturally been affected by the latest decline and it is difficult to find a bull in the financial district.

Date	Dow Closing the Day Before	Wall Street Journal Comment
10/18	341.86	Over the last few weeks the bears have enjoyed the most profitable period experienced in a long time. In their efforts to put stocks down, they have been helped by pessimistic prognostications from market forecasters who have a big following.
10/21	323.87	The Street is about as bearish as it has been at any time this year. . . . When you are unable to find one lone bull you can depend upon it that the market is due for a rally. . . . Sentiment continued pessimistic.
10/24	305.85	The air has been saturated with pessimism for the last two weeks, but things will change. They always do.
10/25	299.47	STOCK MARKET IN COMPLETE PANIC.

In other words, the bears were right.

PARALLEL 104

Psychological
Stocks Are Cheap—Bargain Prices

After an extended market decline that proves to be only the preliminary swing in a far more extended decline, one will invariably see statements about how cheap stocks are and how they are sitting on the bargain shelf. Peter Furniss of Lehman Brothers Kuhn Loeb, who was wildly bullish on the stock market in early January, was quoted in *The Wall Street Journal* of March 30 as saying: "Individual Retirement Account money will be coming into the market in April, and *stocks are cheap*" (emphasis added).

On October 5, 1929, *The Wall Street Journal* said that "the downward movement was assuming an unreasonable character, and this thought encouraged substantial buying by people who step into the market when *bargains* are available" (emphasis added).

On October 22, 1929, *The Wall Street Journal* quoted Jackson Brothers, Boesel & Co. extensively. They had called the decline up until that time, which was exceptional, to say the least. However, *they turned bullish about a week before the great crash*. They made that great mistake by basing their bullishness on the *economy*. Here is what the *Journal* said:

After taking a bearish stand on the market for the last six weeks, Jackson Brothers, Boesel & Co. now feel that recent distress selling has gone a long way in correcting the technical position of the general list and has created exceptional opportunities to acquire sound first-class stocks at *bargain prices.* "As there is nothing in the business situation to warrant further liquidation," the firm declares, "we consider a substantial recovery from current levels a strong probability. We hesitate at this juncture to predict a definite reversal of the downtrend, but there is strong evidence that *the size of the short interest alone* is becoming untenable. In addition to the expected banking support, it would be logical for *bargain hunters* to make their appearance" [emphasis added].

As the stock market continued to move inexorably closer to its rendezvous with destiny, stocks then seen to be on the bargain shelf would, in retrospect, be seen as overpriced merchandise.

Seeing the U.S. stock market fall in 1984 and foreign stock markets rise, those who did not see the U.S. market as the leading indicator for all stock markets made the serious error of being attracted to foreign stocks at the worst of times. The March 19 *Journal* ran the following:

Patrick Kildoyle, who manages the First Investors International Fund, believes that the Democrats will block any deficit solution this year, preferring to keep the problem alive as a campaign issue. He says he's optimistic about some sectors of the U.S. market, *but has switched more of the money in the mutual funds he manages to foreign markets lately.* First Investors International, the leading mutual fund in the U.S. this year, outside of those that invest in gold, has gained 11.1%. It has about 80% exposure to foreign stock markets [emphasis added].

So, while the January bulls thought that March was telling them that the worst was over, the bear market was simply flexing its muscles for much more to come, raising the hopes of bulls on periodic rallies and then mercilessly dashing those hopes.

PART FIVE

THE SMELL
OF PANIC

14

Where Are the Buyers?

[APRIL 1984]

I

The long Chinese torture of a market eroding since the spring of 1983 cast a growing pall over Wall Street. While periodic rally attempts, notably in the Dow stocks, lulled the media commentators into continued reporting of a correction in an ongoing bull market, the general public was in an increasingly impaired position, most people holding stocks at a loss. The public was disillusioned, attesting to the fact that very few had received good investment advice. This disenchantment spread like a virus to the brokerage firms who had dispensed the ruinous advice in the first place, generally placing the importance of their commission business over that of profitable service to their investing clientele. What did all this mean? It implied that, mostly sporting losses, the public would not be able to propel any market rally beyond the parameters of bear market rallies.

Undaunted by having misled the public for many months, the financial media were ready to have another go at enticing the badly mauled public back into the Wall Street arena.

PARALLEL 105

Historical
Revival Looked For in Next Quarter

After the weak first quarter of 1984 in the stock market, there was a general consensus that the second quarter would be much better. *The Wall Street Journal* on April 2 headlined its market page: "Managers Detect More

Confidence As 2nd Quarter Gets Underway." While earlier hopes had been dashed, hope would always spring eternal on Wall Street. In "The Trader" column in *Barron's* that week Floyd Norris wrote: "What a relief. It's over. The first quarter of 1984 we mean. Couldn't be happier to see it go, even if it did end on a sour note." The Dow had closed out the first quarter at 1,164.89, down 93.75 points.

The parallel with 1929 was particularly specific. Inasmuch as most people did not expect the market decline of September 1929, they assumed, hoped, and prayed that October would usher in a stronger market and a stronger quarter.

In the *Journal* of September 24, 1929 the "Broad Street Gossip" column stated: "A revival is looked for in the last quarter. The consensus among traders is that it is still a bull market and that prices of the selected issues will work higher in the last quarter."

At this time the market was declining rapidly, heading for a new bear market low.

PARALLEL 106

Market
Market Declines on No News

On the heels of high hopes for April 1984 and the new quarter, the market on April 2 reversed sharply to the downside following a brief early-morning rally of over 5 points, the Dow closing down almost 12 points. The key feature of the sell-off was that it occurred *on no news*. Thereafter, the slide was precipitous.

The "Broad Street Gossip" column in *The Wall Street Journal* of September 25, 1929, tried to account for the sharp declines of the day before on no news:

> The market ran into a substantial slump in the late trading, with Steel common at one time off nearly 11 points from its high of the day. Other active stocks fell from 5 to 10 points. There was no explanation for the wave of selling; some said it was due to liquidation and others to a bear drive. Evidently it was a little of both. Some said there was investment trust selling, but no doubt some investment trusts were also buyers. The automobile shares were under pressure, General Motors selling below 70. If brokers' loans do not show a substantial shrinkage this week brokers cannot be blamed, as it has been a liquidating week.

Like trains all approaching a central terminal from different directions, major market energies were being channeled into a crash pattern. Ronald Reagan was riding a wave of extreme popularity due to the persistence of the strength in the economy and the virtual absence of inflation. There was very little question as to who the next president was going to be. So this was one train that was not going to be derailed. President Reagan was due to be in charge when the other trains came hurtling into the terminal.

Another train was the deficit problem. The Reagan administration witnessed the largest deficits in U.S. history, dwarfing all previous deficit figures combined. Markets were able to wrestle with this problem—but only up to a point. Sooner or later everyone would realize that the Reagan optimism was ill founded. The deficits were to remain, forcing the Treasury to borrow at an unprecedented pace. Interest rates were rising, raising questions as to how much longer the Reagan recovery could last. Interest rates were at the highest level in history for this low a rate of inflation. One could conclude only that the recovery had been bought at a terribly high price. Yes, like 1929, these were unprecedented times.

Another train was the all-time record-breaking trade deficit, the U.S. economic strength supporting many foreign economies.

Still another train was the historic strength of the dollar. It led to currency depreciation elsewhere and a tremendous capital inflow to the United States. But all this was a sword of Damocles, because later events would reverse the flow.

Speeding on another rail was a train labeled bank failures, now running at the highest level since 1939. All the bad loans of yesteryear were coming home to haunt the banks. The Penn Square failure in 1982 had merely set a chain of circumstances in motion that threatened the extinction of the Continental Illinois bank in Chicago in 1984. That, in turn, would jar the confidence of depositors elsewhere in our largest banks, those which had loaned out billions to Third World countries and were threatened by giant defaults.

Nobody really took all these things too seriously because there was always the Federal Deposit Insurance Corporation to serve as a bulwark of confidence. Nevertheless, the FDIC was about to take its biggest hit with the collapse of the Continental Illinois and, with relatively limited capital, could not afford a repetition of this drain. And if the FDIC were forced to obtain more money, the deficit problem would be exacerbated still further. The oldest rule of economics was coming to the forefront: "There ain't no such thing as a free lunch."

Two of those trains were looming into view by April 1984. The first of these was the foreign debt problem and the second was the increasing probability of a growing banking crisis.

Historical
International Debt Repayments

In order to prevent Argentina's imminent default on its massive debt, the United States put together a last-minute stopgap loan package of $500 million on March 30; included in the package were Mexico, Colombia, and Venezuela.

In 1929 defaults on private debts were increasing and *international repayments continued only because America supplied further loans.* This papering over of the increasing number of debt defaults simply made the problem worse.

Yes, the problems of the 1920s were being repeated. A few years before his death in a plane crash in Kansas City in September 1981, Morgan Maxfield penned a small book entitled *1929 Revisited.* It was published in 1977 by the National Youth Foundation of Kansas City. In that book he cited some 1929 parallels that existed at the time the book was written:

1. Currency depreciation after World War I.
2. Peak movement of dollar loans occurred during 1927 and 1928.
3. Large counterflow of foreign funds into the United States.
4. Large U.S. capital outflow prior to the crash.
5. 1929–30 falling commodity prices and a debt moratorium.
6. The collapse in commodities placed the debtor mineral and agricultural countries in an impossible payments position, countries such as Argentina, New Zealand, and Australia.
7. All the South American countries which had been borrowing so unwisely and so well from the United States investors found themselves in difficulty.
8. Eight South American countries defaulted in 1931, partially or in full; three more countries followed two years later.
9. Debt situation in Europe was equally unhealthy.
10. Bank failures were to follow.
11. Payments stopped on short-term credits.
12. Unparalleled era of frozen assets had set in.
13. Moratorium on debts led to series of central bank runs.
14. British budget out of balance.
15. This was followed by fears for Bank of England solvency.
16. English pound under great downward pressure after September 1931.
17. The U.S. dollar provided relative safety for short-term investors.
18. The inability to pay foreign debts led to increased protectionism.
19. Exchange controls set in to regulate imports.

This was only a partial blueprint, but it provided a working outline of a series of events to follow. Already a number of 1929 parallels were added to the list.

PARALLEL 108

Historical
Currency Depreciation

The demand for U.S. dollars all over the world seemed to be inexhaustible. In terms of the pound, the mark, the franc, the lira, the Canadian dollar, the 1929 parallel was clear. There was worldwide currency depreciation.

PARALLEL 109

Historical
Peak Movement of Dollar Loans

The peak movement of dollar loans occurred during the early 1980s and, in parallel, the peak movement of dollar loans occurred during 1927 and 1928.

PARALLEL 110

Historical
Counterflow of Foreign Funds
into the United States

As long as foreign money was coming into the United States, there would be no panic and crash. The lure of the dollar was irresistible, the high U.S. interest rates acting as a tremendous suction. Ironically, Wall Street was looking for and hoping and praying for lower interest rates. But the lower rates, when they came, would see foreign money being repatriated, the best signal for the crash soon to follow. This influx of foreign funds was well in evidence at this time and constituted an exact 1929 parallel.

━━━━━━━

PARALLEL 111
Historical
Falling Commodity Prices

The collapse in the price of gold and silver was the precursor to a collapse in commodity prices all over the world. This was in keeping with the Kondratieff deflationary wave. It was this collapse that made the problems of paying off loans so difficult for countries depending on the export of their leading commodities. High interest rates against this background showed the extraordinary aspects of the problem as did similar problems in 1929 just prior to the collapse in rates.

Truth, never out of date, was well expressed in early textbooks which had sought to explain what went wrong in 1929. The evidence was all there, all the nineteen characteristics just cited. In 1984 all those trains were speeding toward the central terminal and in the months ahead there was to be little or no deviation from a master historical blueprint duplicating that of the late 1920s.

II

The market was living on borrowed time. Nobody expected serious difficulties in an election year that would see an incumbent president riding a wave of extreme popularity based on an expanding economy; on the other hand, the case was growing that April 1984 was not a great deal different from April 1929. I felt that market rallies had definable limits and that the market was no place for investors, as time was rapidly running out on the grand cycle.

Going into April, it looked like the bottom was about to fall out of the market, but my trading barometer once again said: not yet . . . not yet. As in 1929, there were to be trading rallies to disguise the major internal sickness which had been so well documented as having set in back in the spring of 1983.

In approaching the April 5 bottom, John L. Keeley, Jr., an investment adviser in Chicago, was quoted in the April 4 *Wall Street Journal* as saying: "People are starting to get emotional, and as they endure the slow water torture of continued price erosion they are torn between hoping the fragile 1,145 support area will hold and wanting some kind of purge to get the correction over with."

In the same issue of the *Journal,* Robert Farrell of Merrill Lynch stated that institutions having high cash positions of more than 15 percent jumped to 35 percent in number and were "the most with high cash since June 1982." Contrary to popular opinion, these numbers were not bullish at all. With no change in opinion, a portfolio cash percentage will *automatically* increase as stock prices generally decline. Such high cash percentages proved to be very poor bullish evidence in a major bear market.

PARALLEL 112

Psychological
Severe Correction in a Bull Market

On April 6 Carter Randall, a regular panelist on the *Wall Street Week* TV program, stated that he thought this was a severe correction in an ongoing bull market. The difference here is that the word "severe" had been added to previous similar widespread feelings about the market.

The famous "Turn in the Tide" editorial by William Peter Hamilton, which had appeared in the October 21, 1929, issue of *Barron's*, had described the market action up to that time as a *severe* secondary reaction. He couldn't bring himself to say bear market any more than could the majority of market commentators in 1984.

Every time it looked like the bottom was going to fall out, the magicians of Wall Street always seemed to conjure up enough strength to produce still another trading rally. The April 5 bottom at Dow 1,130 was but another one of those white rabbits, designed to maintain investor complacency, mesmerizing and entertaining an increasingly nervous audience. But nobody saw anything like a crash coming, that, of course, being simply one of the signs that one *was* on the way.

Peter Eliades, a well-known cycles analyst in California, had stated that there was absolutely no way that the Dow would break under the 1,115 level. The early April upturn seemed to support such confident statements, but, like 1929, these were not normal times. Those who were following a curious mixture of planetary movements, sunspots, and Elliott Wave analysis had no clues as to what was actually going to happen. They were all operating on the assumption that 1984 was like any other kind of year, a year that would see the normal parameters of cyclical highs and lows fulfilled. It was no different in the decade culminating in the 1929 crash. There were cycle analysts back then. Edgard Lawrence Smith, an advocate of the ten-year cycle, was one of these. His two major works were *Common Stocks As Long Term Investments* (1926) and *Tides in the Affairs of Men* (1939). He did not see the 1929 crash coming and yet was as adamant in his cyclic projections as were the Elliott Wave theorists in 1984.

Prior to the brief April trading rally, the Dow Theory had once again reconfirmed the presence of a major bear market, both the industrial and transportation averages going under the earlier February 1984 lows.

A few days after the trading barometer's buy signal, the Dow exploded higher on April 12 in one of those one-day wonders that had pockmarked the charts in 1984. In this case it was based on a turn in the bond market, a market not in a strong position to extend any rally. Another parallel was seen on that day.

━━━━━━━

PARALLEL 113

Psychological Correction Seen to Be Ending

Most technicians thought the move in the Dow to a double bottom at 1,130 on April 11 saw the end of the 1984 "correction." Bullish sentiment soared as the Dow scored an explosive late rally on the twelfth. Every analyst quoted in *The Wall Street Journal* on April 13 was bullish. Typical of the quotes was the following:

> "The downtrend in the financial markets of the last three weeks has been reversed," said Norman Frey, analyst with Dean Witter Reynolds. "With extremely bullish retail sales and M1 numbers, very impressive technical formations and lower interest rates, this is a very big move."

The Wall Street Journal, September 18, 1929:

> Many observers interpreted this action to mean that the general list had completed the recent period of correction and was embarking on another substantial upturn. This conclusion brought vigorous demand into representative stocks during the first hour, and new highs on the recovery were reached by General Motors, Steel, General Electric, Johns-Manville, Timken Roller Bearing, and National Cash Register.

The *Journal*, September 26, 1929:

> It is generally thought the market now has reacted to a point where there should be some sign of resistance to any further selling after the forced liquidation has been exhausted. Many still contend the recent reaction has been a technical affair to correct an over-bought position and to bring over-exploited stocks to more reasonable levels. If this view is correct it is likely that, *with a so-called secondary reaction completed,* the market will be in a position to move forward again [emphasis added].

PARALLEL 114

Psychological
Cover Story for a Resumption of Interest
on a Large Scale

When the bulls got restless for a turn in the market after a serious decline, they pounced on a number of reasons to rationalize their view. Those reasons then constituted the cover story for a rise. It was all very logical and neat. Being a cover story, it had to be quite plausible and easily accepted by the majority. In April 1984 such a cover story was provided by the bulls. The Dow had sharply tumbled from the 1,286.64 level of January 6 to the 1,130.55 level of April 5, an annual rate of decline exceeding 600 points. The market was desperately ready to clutch at any plausible bullish cover story.

Part of that cover story was given in the April 10 *Journal:*

> "For the next few days the market probably will trade in a narrow range," contended Fred Dietrich, vice president of Dickinson Co., Chicago. "But by next week the market could be ready for a technical rally because the tax season will be over, good earnings reports will be coming in and Congress will be adjourning."

The cover story grew a little bigger in the April 18 *Journal:*

> "The market's short-term outlook has improved because of institutions' greater liquidity," asserted Andrew Kern, executive vice president of Avatar Associates. He added that this has resulted from *selling during the past few months, from recent tender offers and from IRA contributions* [emphasis added].

Memories being short, no reference was made to what happened the year before when IRA contributions were generally expected to give a tremendous boost to the market; yet the market topped out soon thereafter. But it was a good and plausible reason to be hauled out of the past, dusted off, and used again. Surely the public had forgotten all about April 1983.

An equally neat cover story was used in *The Wall Street Journal* on September 24, 1929, to drum up interest in a market that had already uncomfortably dropped more than the bulls expected:

> While many conservative observers are of the opinion that nothing more than irregularity can be looked for during the remainder of the current month because of the uncertainty created by the market recently, it is felt in many quarters that October is likely to be a month of considerable market activity. *Factors which could induce a resumption of interest on a large scale include prospects of*

remarkably favorable earnings to be reported for the third quarter, and possible split-ups in various stocks. Another influence might be investment trust funds available for the purchase of standard stocks at favorable prices" [emphasis added].

Market action coming off the April low was full of disturbing crosscurrents. Most people viewed the 1,130 level in the Dow as the bottom. The April 13 *Wall Street Journal* was replete with bullish comments:

"The money-supply news was anticipated and people also were encouraged when the industrial average held above its 1984 low," commented James C. Andrews, first vice president at Janney Montgomery Scott, Inc., Philadelphia. "The IBM earnings news also helped turn the market around. It appears we'll have a run on the upside for a while."

"The IBM announcement bolstered the opinion that most first-quarter earnings reports are going to be very good and some are going to be substantially better," asserted Alfred W. Harris, Jr., senior vice president of Josephthal & Co., St. Louis. "The industrial average has approached 1,130 several times in recent months, but each time weakness seemed to evaporate. Thus, people now view the 1,130 level as a near-term bottom."

He added that "investors also were encouraged by the House's action in passing the bill to raise $47.2 billion over three years, which means some effort is being made to reduce the federal deficit."

But the most revealing *Journal* revelation on April 13 was a reference to *corporate insiders*. This brought into play a very important 1929 parallel:

███████

PARALLEL 115

Market
Corporate Insider Buying Was Not Bullish

Norman G. Fosback, editor of *The Insiders*, of Fort Lauderdale, Florida, said that for the first time since mid-1982 corporate insiders had turned bullish. He said his March survey showed 48 percent buyers and 52 percent sellers, which was up from 31 percent buyers in February and above the "normal" 40 percent insider buying percentage.

Before one got carried away with the Fosback "bullish" pronouncement, one had to keep in mind that this advisory service had cost its followers dearly for many months prior to its announcement that insiders were buying. Being fundamentally oriented, this service remained 100 percent fully invested on the assumption that the market remained in a major bull market.

What *The Insiders* did not say was that insider activity is *an extremely uncertain indicator* because it is subservient to the underlying real trend of the market. Insiders had been selling for many months prior to the spring 1983 market top, and their stepped-up buying in the spring of 1984 meant absolutely nothing in terms of the true trend of the market because there were parallels to similar insider buying in 1929. Insiders are human beings and they are subject to making mistakes in judgment. Here is but one small example of the sagacity of insiders who thought their stock was a bargain. The following paragraph appeared in *The Wall Street Journal* on August 14, 1929:

> Buying of Sears, Roebuck in thousand-share lots by officers of the company was reported last Saturday. Sears closed at 156. Since no new developments in the company's affairs are in the wind, the only supposition that remains is that Sears' officers considered the stock a *bargain at that price* [emphasis added].

The insiders thought it was a bargain at 156, only to see it tumble to 80 on November 13, 1929.

But the public was not averse to the ways of Wall Street. The public could not separate fact from fiction and thus was a sitting duck for any proposition that was concocted to part the unwary from their money. Of course the public would get excited when told that the insiders were stepping up their buying. The public was not about to check the record of those who reported such information, let alone the history of such insider buying in crisis markets such as 1929.

These were critical times. Despite the early April buy signal, the market changed direction many times on April 13. It was what I called a Jesse Livermore day, totally confusing to the uninitiated. Such frequent changes of direction in a single trading day denoted a *confused* market, one not capable of maintaining an uptrend for very long. Yet if one were to read all the articles appearing in *Barron's, The New York Times,* and *Financial World* by mid-April, one would be impressed by their extreme bullishness.

Many advisers trying to make a name for themselves were caught up on the relatively brief April strength. Robert Nurock, a regular panelist on *Wall Street Week,* in mid-April said that this was the time to buy stocks because the market was making a rounding bottom. It sounded sexy, but subsequent action was to prove unglamorous.

In mid-April I returned to Duke University to deliver a lecture to the economics department, documenting the many parallels I had with the fateful year of 1929. It did not surprise me at all that my remarks went completely against the grain of the current feeling. After all, universities teach economics, not technical analysis.

III

For some months the market had been making a mockery of so-called technical support levels. It would be just a matter of time before the Dow 1,130 support level would be violated. There was a notable absence of buyers in the market, perfectly understandable in view of the 156-point decline since January which had locked in so many with wide losses. The market was saying as clearly as it could that when a normal degree of selling encountered an abnormal absence of buyers, a dangerous situation prevailed, much like that of 1929 just prior to the great crash. The market would drop on light volume and keep dropping.

It was difficult for people to understand why the stock market could go down in the face of glowing corporate earnings. Mary Ann Keller, a renowned auto analyst, stated at this time that it was ironic that the auto shares had gone down in the face of such a fantastic first quarter. That statement illustrated an incredible misunderstanding of what the stock market was all about. All good fundamental news was thoroughly discounted by the market in 1983. Since most people followed fundamentals, it became obvious why most people were holding stocks at a loss in 1984. The stock market game, of course, would never end because most people would insist on following such things as earnings, dividends, p/e ratios, etc. They will insist on following economists and not stock market technical analysis. Pierre Rinfret, a well-known economist, said that he saw no problems *before* 1986. Apparently he thought that a $200 billion loss in stock values up to this time was no problem.

The April trading rally was suspect for another reason. Foreign markets began to look as if they were soon to make a dive. The London and Tokyo stock markets had traced out what looked like parabolic rises. Many analysts were unconcerned about the bear market in U.S. stocks as long as markets like London and Tokyo were rising. Now all this seemed about to change. One by one, the bullish arguments were disappearing.

As in the 1929 formation, the Dow traced out a broad decline from 1,286.64 on January 6 to a low of 1,134.21 on February 22. It then traced out a *bear market rally* to 1,184.36 on March 16 and then descended to a new bear market low closing of 1,130.55 on April 5, fully confirmed by a new low in the Dow Jones Transportation Average. At this point, a reconfirmed classic Dow Theory bear market signal was recorded. Dow, in his theory, was not concerned with *intraday levels* or anything else that might have complicated the simplicity of the pure Dow Theory signals, signals that were totally dependent on simply the closings of the industrial and transportation averages. Amateur technicians had expounded the bullishness of the rising bottoms in the Dow, stressing the 1,134.21, 1,139.76, and 1,152.95 levels. At that time, they never mentioned intraday levels. They were "certain" of that bullish formation. The minute the Dow broke to a new low on April 5 at 1,130.55, the amateur technician, with one quick stroke of amnesia, forgot all about the bullish conviction based on the rising bottoms which had so quickly aborted. Now the attention shifted immediately to the intraday levels, striving to make a case that the February lows were still holding. It pointed up the fact that a drowning man will clutch at anything which might keep him afloat.

Every time the crash scenario looked imminent, some mysterious support seemed to materialize. On April 12 the market exploded, the Dow rocketing up over 26 points. While surprising in the force and suddenness of the late turnabout, for me it was not unanticipated, thanks to the April 6 barometer buy signal. The bear market had seen enough explosive one- or two-day extravaganzas for me to accept them and take them in stride. One of them, of course, would be the real thing and keep going, but the barometer would catch it. But for now, the market had to be taken one day at a time. There was still too much unsold stock hanging over the market to allow for anything more than bear market rallies at best.

The rationale behind the April rally was simple and, I thought, far too obvious. As the Dow weakened on April 12 after an opening rise, *it was apparent that the bond market was getting stronger.* Since Wall Street was hooked on the idea that the stock market was simply hostage to the bond market, the late explosive rise was a knee-jerk reaction. Having anticipated a temporary turn for the better in the bond market, I had called attention to the expectation that the first response would be a stock market rise, just as the first response to the starting bond market rally in October 1929 was a stock market rise which was followed not long thereafter by the great crash, *a crash that took place while the bond market continued to rise!* Somewhere down the road the bond market would embark upon an extended rise which would do the stock market no good. In view of this history, rallies in the bond market would fail to signal an early ending for the great bear market in stocks.

This was not a normal market. It was to twist, extend, shorten, reverse, and stretch all normal parameters. *Barron's* ran articles by Gerald Appel and James Alphier introducing new market indicators; buy signals based on those indicators were very quickly proven to be wrong. Every technique used to produce a buy signal was to abort.

The basic reasons for owning a common stock were disappearing. One could not say that he was holding a stock because of earnings. Most stocks went down in 1929 *regardless of earnings.* One could not say he was holding a stock because of dividends. Dividends were raised across the board in 1929 and the market crashed, the drop wiping out many years of past dividends.

One could not say that he was holding a stock because it was going up. Most stocks were going down, as was proven again by the new early April lows in the advance/decline line. There was only one reason why anyone was holding a stock and that was because *it was being held at a loss.* That, of course, was no reason to hold a stock. But since most people didn't like to take a loss, they ended up with bigger losses. That is what happened in 1929. There wasn't a blessed reason left for holding common stocks, other than not wanting to accept a loss. Eventually, when that reason gave way, due to the wiping out of margins, the great crash took place.

I was stressing a point that had never been made before: WHEN TOO MANY PEOPLE ARE HOLDING STOCKS AT A LOSS, THEN THAT

BECOMES THE *ONLY* REASON PEOPLE ARE HOLDING STOCKS. THE FEAR OF TAKING A LOSS IS *THE VERY LAST SUPPORT FOR THE MARKET PRIOR TO A CRASH.* That characteristic was at the forefront on October 21, 1929, when the Dow had closed at 320.91, showing a drop of 15.8 percent from the September 3 high of 381.17. By April 1984 the Dow had dropped 12.09 percent, getting critically closer. It would remain for the Dow to get down to the 1,083 level in order to equate exactly with the 15.8 percent drop of October 21, 1929.

The bulls on Wall Street were slow to give up. Stephen Leeb of Money Growth Institute, Jersey City, New Jersey, was the most persistent in maintaining that the Dow would not fall under the 1,100 level, that being the approximate book value of the thirty Dow industrial stocks. One only had to check the record of such fundamental enthusiasts. In this case, Leeb was quoted in the *Journals* of January 4, March 9, and April 11, bullish on all three dates.

Many authorities have a dim view of book value as having any forecasting worth. "It seems an unpromising guide to possible future prices"—Teweles and Bradley.[1] "Has a very limited use as a forecasting tool"—Norman Fosback *(Market Logic).* Mr. Leeb had forgotten how far stocks went under book value in 1929–32.

IV

On April 12 the Dow Jones Industrial Average scored a sensational surge of over 26 points in a late rally credited to IBM earnings and a plunge in the money supply figures. The euphoria was apparent the next day in *The Wall Street Journal:* " 'We had buying of panic proportions,' said Mike Kijanka, director of stock indexes and options for Dean Witter Reynolds, Inc. 'In one afternoon, we made up two weeks of a move to the downside.' "

PARALLEL 116

Psychological
The Bull Is Back

Responding in predictable fashion to the April 12 market extravaganza, John Bollinger, resident technical analyst for Financial News Network, stated on April 13: "It's great to have the bull market back." Bollinger was of the opinion, like most people at that time, that the bull market that had begun

[1]Richard Teweles and Edward S. Bradley, *The Stock Market* (4th ed.; New York: John Wiley & Sons, 1982).

in August 1982 had been continuously in force, and the sharp rise of April 12 had simply reinforced that opinion. Without his realizing it, his statement was producing an oft-repeated parallel of the 1929 market, the blind belief that all market downside action had been normal corrections in an ongoing bull market.

On October 8, 1929, the identical phrase was seen in *The Wall Street Journal*'s "Broad Street Gossip" column: "The bull market is back again, for the time being at least. The same old bull leaders were again the leaders in yesterday's pronounced advance and recoveries in the case of some stocks amounted to five to ten points."

PARALLEL 117

Psychological
Complete Reversal

The bigger the advance, the more certain some people were that the rise constituted a complete reversal of the previous downtrend. Remarks to that effect in *The Wall Street Journal* on April 13 were also seen in the *Journal* of October 7, 1929: "The market underwent a complete reversal with substantial gains in all stocks" ("Broad Street Gossip").

PARALLEL 118

Market
The Market Is More Selective

Following a true internal market top, as had occurred in the spring of 1983, the bulls naturally found it increasingly difficult to select winning stocks. That was called *selectivity*. Paralleling the point in 1929 when half the market was already into a bear market, the bulls waded into 1984 not realizing how the odds had risen against them. Now fully aware that the market had been in a "correction" for many months, they expected that their "second bull market leg" would be more selective.

When Roger Babson gave his famous crash prediction of September 5, 1929, half of the market had already been in a bear market for nine months. He cited that fact, basing his crash prediction on that technical information. Livermore's staff had discovered the same thing, which today would have been revealed by the advance/decline line. However, rather than recognize the dangers of the increased market selectivity, the *Journal* on September 6, 1929, said: "However, many experienced Wall Street observers feel that this selectivity has been the market's greatest safeguard. It is argued that so long as such marked discrimination is exercised, the general list may go along for some time before any reversal of trend is seen. Shrewd students of speculation predict that a long series of five and six million share sessions will give warning of the approaching culmination of the present phase of the Coolidge-Hoover market."

PARALLEL 119

Historical
The Economy Is Slowing

Since many believed that the Washington magicians could fine-tune the economy and keep the boom going, troublesome statistics beginning to show up at this time received a favorable scenario from Wall Street, the theory being that if the economy slowed, then interest rates would come down and the bull market could go on and on. A 27 percent drop in housing starts was reported, the sharpest monthly drop since 1959, when the series began. A 12 percent drop in building permits was also reported.

Most market analysts still tried to read the market and the economy together, forgetting that the stock market generally leads the economy by six to nine months. The market peak in 1983 was stating that the economic boom had a definite time limit and the 1984 statistics were beginning to reflect that limit.

It was no different in 1929. Against the background of those times, growing problems in agriculture and textiles and a slowing in automobile sales proved that the boom was losing steam. Memories being short, nobody took the time to ascertain the true market top at that time and then to apply the six- to nine-month rule of thumb to the economy. If they had, they would have discovered that the true market top occurred in December 1928. By simply applying the rule of thumb, they would have been able to predict the end of the economic boom in the summer and early fall of 1929 and would have gotten out of the market (like Livermore, Kennedy, and Baruch) before the great crash.

Back in 1923, Edwin Lefevre stated this truth about the stock market leading the economy. He was rather definite about it: "But brokers should not dwell too strongly on actual conditions because the course of the market is always from six to nine months ahead of actual conditions."[2]

[2]Edwin Lefevre, *Reminiscences of a Stock Operator* (Dallas: Books of Wall Street, 1976), p. 295.

PARALLEL 120

Historical
Financial Emancipation of Women

Long before women got out of the home and balanced the family financial scales with the two-job family, Wall Street had already accepted their equality, at least as far as their money was concerned. Back in 1929 there were board-rooms combined with speakeasies for the sole comfort and convenience of the female speculator. Many articles were written specifically with the woman speculator in mind (see Parallel 21).

In April 1984 the Libra Mutual Fund for Women was formed. Of course, men could also buy shares in the fund, but the accent was on women. When it came to opening up as many new channels as possible, Wall Street had always been an early innovator.

PARALLEL 121

Historical
Economists Are Overly Optimistic

As blind as the economists in 1929 to what was going on, Dr. Arthur Laffer and Dr. Pierre Rinfret were in the forefront of the 1984 superoptimists. Neither saw any problems before 1986. In an interview on Cable News Network's *Moneyline* on April 2, Dr. Rinfret drew the following conclusions:

1. Boom economy—best news for the consumer in five years.
2. Interest rates will not abort the recovery.
3. Dollar confounds and confuses but is the most powerful currency in the world.
4. A $125 billion trade deficit this year.

Laffer and Rinfret were the modern-day counterparts to the famous Dr. Irving Fisher of Yale University back in 1929. The modern era demanded its Babsons and Fishers, and 1984 would not disappoint. Fisher was the 1929 apostle of the "permanent plateau of prosperity" thesis.

Historical
High Interest Rates Will Not Abort
the Economic Recovery

Dr. Rinfret had unwittingly touched upon another 1929 parallel. The belief that high interest rates would not abort the economic recovery was expressed many times in 1929.

Leonard P. Ayres was very optimistic on the stock market. According to the *Journal* of August 14, 1929, Ayres stated that corporate earnings would surmount the growing credit difficulties. In the September 4, 1929, *Journal* appeared the following:

> Gen. George R. Dyer of Dyer, Hudson & Co., sailing for Europe last week said: "I believe that anyone who buys our highest class rails, industrials, including steels, coppers and utilities, and holds them, will make a great deal of money, as these securities will gradually be taken out of the market. The field for expansion of all the better utility corporations has hardly been scratched. There apparently is no end in sight for the demand of steel, copper and lead. *We are used to high money rates and they are here to stay with us for some time, but with the activity and increasing values for securities, money rates are not so important*" [emphasis added].

This was the ultimate in blindness, the Dow having peaked the day before, not to see those levels again for twenty-four years.

Psychological
Good Stocks Becoming Scarce

General Dyer had touched on a characteristic that always seemed to show up at major market peaks: *the stock scarcity story*. It always seemed to emerge at the worst of times, when the market was rallying and mergers and acquisitions were at a peak. It was Irving Fisher's pet theme when countering the Babson crash prediction in September 1929. He felt that the higher stock prices went, the higher they were going to go, because people would increasingly hold them rather than pay the taxes on the profits. That led to his ideas about increasing stock scarcity.

The *Journal* stated on September 18, 1929, that "the better class of railroad shares are *scarcer* than they have been in a number of years" (emphasis added).

The next day they stated: "The public appetite for securities continues una-
bated. A reflection of this is found in the *scarcity* of certain popular stocks and
the oversubscription to new investment trust issues" (emphasis added).

The April 13, 1984, showing of *Wall Street Week* reflected the typical
thinking of the day. Frank Cappielo saw interest rates peaking. James Price
thought institutions were nibbling and felt that disappointing stocks should
be sold. Bernadette Murphy saw a successful test of the lows and stated that
IRA money was coming in. Ellen Harris had been a steady buyer since January
3. She said that stocks went down more than she figured. She liked American
Airlines, UAL, Sperry, and Burroughs. She recommended buying Treasury
bonds. Thought that interest rates were coming down. Was negative on
Telephone. Saw a good market somewhere in here. Confessed that she didn't
know from day to day. Impressed by good earnings and multiples. Saw a good
market over the next eighteen months. Looking for lower rates and a slowdown
in the economy. She reflected the Wall Street consensus, a pretty bad bet
when one tests the record.

V

PARALLEL 124

Historical
Volcker Resignation Rumors

Characteristic of a nervous market is how susceptible it is to wild rumors. On
April 19, *The Wall Street Journal* explained the decline in the market of the
eighteenth as follows:

> Weakness in both markets was partly laid to a rumor that Paul Volcker had
> resigned as chairman of the Federal Reserve Board. The Federal Reserve quickly
> denied the rumor.

Throughout late September and early October 1929, there were many wild
rumors quite upsetting to the stock market and among them was the one
stating that Secretary of the Treasury Andrew Mellon was going to resign. In
order to quell the rumor, which was attributed to the bearish crowd, Secretary
Mellon stated on October 9, in an official statement, that he would continue
with the Hoover administration to the end.

The market was quick to rebound late in April 1984 in keeping with my
barometer buy signal, but the technical foundation was shaky. It was a typical
bear market rally having definite upside limits. Wall Street was setting up the
public to walk right into a bull trap.

The following appeared in *The Wall Street Journal* of April 20:

Despite the continued bond-market weakness, "stocks displayed resilience," said A. C. Moore, a partner in Block Trader, an institutional service that moves in and out of the market reacting to technical factors. He said the market apparently has "run into resistance at the 1,170 level of the industrial average, but if it breaks out above that level the rally would have an initial objective of 1,220."

With the trading barometer racing toward a sell signal at this time, I generally visualized a bear market rally peak in the 1,160–1,200 area. Ironically, as the Dow moved up sharply to 1,175.25 on April 26, the sell signal was forthcoming. The stage for the second important bull trap of the year was set. The move in the Dow above the 1,170 level had produced the desired effect: It produced a dangerous complacency and allowed many technicians to drop their guard.

It was simply another illustration of how good things look at the top. A number of buy programs were announced in the *Journal* on the rise, but something that couldn't be hidden was the disturbing fact that Treasury yields had climbed back to the highest level since August 1982. Market breadth on the April rally was particularly poor.

PARALLEL 125

Historical
Collection of Events Exacerbates the Decline

It isn't necessary, and in most cases isn't possible, to predict accurately the events of a declining market, but it is possible to make an accurate technical forecast for the market. Therefore, follow the market and leave most of the commentary on events to the historians.

Nobody in 1929 could have predicted the Hatry scandal in England, which burst upon the scene in mid-September 1929, an event that served to exacerbate the severity of the stock market decline in New York. It isn't the event that counts. It is the market's *response* to the event. Jesse Livermore, most aware of this, was particularly interested in the Hatry scandal right from the outset, recognizing it immediately as a forerunner of a much weaker stock market, a market that would crash a month later.

The message of the stock market in 1984 was clear. It was telling people to get out of stocks in every way it could. It was pointing to major trouble ahead, trouble that could take the form of severe deflation, renewed inflation, higher interest rates, a financial scandal, a major default, a surprise bankruptcy, or a political bombshell. The collection of events would certainly materialize.

Since events are extremely difficult to predict, it remained for the stock market to show the way. The specific shape or form of the forthcoming trouble was really irrelevant.

Since the technical always precedes the fundamental, a new crisis was looming on the horizon at this time which was not to break out into the open until May. Continental Illinois Corporation stock had been in a bearish trend for some time, but when it broke under a double bottom at $20 a share in February 1984, it was foreshadowing a coming crisis. But the real technical tip-off was when the stock broke sharply in mid-April to $15 a share. That in itself would have told anyone that an April stock market rally had to be a very short-lived affair. The mid-April break in Continental Illinois occurred on the highest volume ever recorded, but a volume that was to prove minuscule compared with the deluge to follow. However, in keeping with my principle of volume preceding price, the volume signal alone in April was enough to predict that something extremely important was brewing on the downside for Continental Illinois. This was but one of the developments casting an important shadow over the May and June markets.

Another shadow was the peaking patterns in the London and Tokyo stock markets in the face of extreme optimism, and in the wings was the decline in commodity prices, exacerbated by the coming Continental Illinois crisis.

Attention was diverted in April by further merger and acquisition moves that captivated Wall Street while the more ominous subsurface moves should have been the first business of the day. While there were still some takeover battles going on, the brief 1982–83 bull market saw the end of the line, as far as the frequency was concerned. The takeover game in Wall Street served to deflect attention from the internal market deterioration, and most takeovers created debt problems later, the peak of merger activity tending to end up with market indigestion. While such takeovers were going on, involving in some cases many billions of dollars, they served further to blind people to what the true market trend was. Nobody thought a bear market was possible in the midst of such merger activity. Despite all the hoopla about the 1983 stock market, most stocks went down that year, and in 1984 the bear came fully out in the open.

That exactly matched the action of 1929. Mergers and acquisitions rose to a peak that year, deflecting attention from the deterioration elsewhere. Most stocks in 1929 were showing a loss that year *before* September, the month of the Dow high. Most stocks in 1983 were showing a loss *before* the November Dow high that year.

On September 18, 1929, *The Wall Street Journal*'s "Broad Street Gossip" column had the following comment:

> There may be a secondary reaction. This is anyone's guess, but the traders who have had years of experience in the Street say it is still a major bull market.

Transactions involving billions are scheduled to go through during the next twelve months and everyone knows these cannot be successfully concluded when stocks are declining and the public is in a pessimistic frame of mind [emphasis added].

A tragic note was sounded in 1984 with the Dominelli affair. Dominelli was a modern-day Ponzi. (Ponzi waxed rich in the 1920's in a scheme promising investors lush short-term returns on their investments of 40% to 50%. As fast as the money poured in Ponzi would pay off the early investors, confident that the demand for his services would stay ahead of the pack. Ultimately the entire scheme collapsed as of course it had to. Ever since then all such extremely attractive deals promising the public too much became known as Ponzi schemes.) Dominelli was simply symbolic of a new and expanding wave of financial scandals. He was the tip of the iceberg, simply the first of many scandals that were expected to surface as the major bear market took an increasing toll of losers.[3]

[3]The 1984 scandals were not restricted to the United States. At this time the list included a West German affair, a South African scandal, a big gold swindle, the J. David Dominelli affair, the controversy over Ed Meese, the "Heard on the Street" affair involving a *Wall Street Journal* columnist, an options scam, and even whispers about the sacrosanct Bechtel Corporation.

15

At Least the *Titanic* Had an Orchestra

[MAY 1984]

I

The big spills in the stock market would always follow a period of euphoria. The market euphoria in early January was followed by a 150-point smash. That was followed by a bear market rally. Going into May, the Dow broke out above the trading range highs of March and April and recorded a new bear market rally high, which I expected would produce the second bull trap of the year. I was not disappointed. The bulls grabbed at the bait with the same gusto that had hooked so many in early January. James Dines said: "An hourly close above 1,180 and you will hear the champagne corks popping in the background." Bill Griffith of Financial News Network said: "Everything looks go for stocks and bonds." John Bollinger of Financial News Network said: "The intermediate trend of the market has now turned up." Myron Kandel of Cable News Network said: "Chart watchers were delighted that the Dow closed over 1,180. . . . This time the advance looks a lot more healthy. . . . The bulls are back in Wall Street."

The psychological parallels with early January were striking. My best technical indicators were again to be found in the people quoted. If I could show that the same people who loved the market in January were the identical ones now again having a love affair, then it would reinforce my contention that this had been simply a bear market rally and would be followed by new lows in the Dow. I compared the January quotes with those made just recently, and there was the pattern I expected:

James Finucane on January 5: "Expects the market to reach the 1,340 level in February but then top out." On April 18: "He said he expects the industrial average to climb to the 1,210–1,240 area during the next six weeks."

Harry Laubscher on January 5: "He thinks the industrial average will climb to about the 1,350 level." On April 26: "We should see an overdue rally in the bond market and, in turn, the stock market."

Chester Pado on January 6: "What's impressive about this rally is that it has broadened out as it continued." On April 25: "He has been encouraged."

Newton Zinder on January 6: "The continued rise [yesterday] on increased volume proved that Wednesday's rally wasn't a one-day wonder, and the market now shouldn't have any trouble reaching a new record." On April 27: "General Motors and International Business Machines came to life and their leadership encouraged the traders."

William Goldstein on January 10: "People are back to buying stocks that represent good investment values. He also maintained that stocks which lead during the next 30 days probably will be the leaders for the rest of the year." On May 2: "It appears that all the selling that was going to be done has been completed and that the worst is over as far as rises in interest rates are concerned."

David Weber on January 10: "The market has started out the year on a strong note." On May 3: "The very good earnings reports are driving the market up despite the higher interest rates."

Frank Russo on January 11: "Perhaps the market is taking a necessary breather before lunging toward new high territory. Yesterday's consolidation, which he thinks probably will continue over the short term, should be viewed as bullish." On May 3: "Noting that recent buying decisions are being made on a long-term rather than a short-term trading basis, the bigger capitalization stocks are always the beneficiaries of this kind of approach."

John Groome on January 13: "After the needed pause that refreshes following the market's dramatic rise from August 1982 to mid-1983, it appears ready to break out of the doldrums and make an assault on the 1,400 level. He said that there is a confluence of favorable news, including rising earnings, and expectations of dividend increases, a sanguine outlook for inflation and anticipation of at least a modest dip in interest rates." On May 1: "The market is being influenced by fear of an acceleration of inflation and of still higher interest rates but this is being counterbalanced by excellent earnings reports and lack of any broad speculative excesses. He contended that it is a show-me market containing a great deal of skepticism, but the elements that signal a broad market bottom are falling into place."

Leslie Pollack on January 17: "People have become a little discouraged because the market didn't follow through on the big moves early this year. But I expect the market to move higher because some interest rates are easing and there's a very low level of speculation in the market." On April 19: "It has discounted all possible negative news and, if we get any good news on interest rates, we could see an explosive move on the upside."

Alfred W. Harris on January 24: "The market is awaiting something to send it higher and I think the catalyst will be lower interest rates. He added that the market appears to be in a period of profit-taking but there's no rush to get out." On April 19: "It was encouraging that no panic selling developed, and since the industrial average has held above the 1,130 level so many times recently, the favorable earnings reports coming in probably will supply the stimulus to send the market higher."

I could only conclude from this that *the market was readying for a straight-down move that would take it to new lows in the May–June time segment,* a conclusion carried in my May 5 letter.

As in January, it was another tug-of-war between the forces of supply and demand. John Bollinger at the highs said: "You can't find a single bull out there." But the record of the quotes in *The Wall Street Journal* showed without a doubt that there were far too many bulls but, having already put their money on the line, their sentiment couldn't lift the market a dime. The May bulls happened to be the January bulls, and if their sentiment couldn't send the market higher in January, it certainly couldn't in May.

Even the trading pattern was almost identical with that of the January bull trap. The rise produced a euphoria, three days of heavy volume advance, turned down on the fourth day and the fifth, and on that day analysts called it "consolidation."

William Goldstein was quoted in the May 2 *Journal* as follows: "The market's action for the past two weeks had been very positive with selling drying up when prices retreated and buying picking up on the advances." What was not noticed, however, was that all year this characteristic was what led into false upside breakouts, catching the bulls in a continuing series of euphoristic bull traps. All the bull trap upside breakouts were done on very high volume, and thus one had to conclude that the higher the volume on the market rise, the more likely it was that the next downswing was being triggered.

The market took a headlong tumble on May 4, the Dow dropping over 16 points. The decline was blamed on a statement by Henry Kaufman, who predicted that "interest rates will move spectacularly higher, perhaps by the end of this year or in 1985, and damage virtually every sector of the economy." Backing up Kaufman, the bond market was being slaughtered and it was difficult for the bulls to justify their "second leg" concept. Ironically, on the very day of the Kaufman tumble, Bob Nurock's "elves" turned bullish, the buy signal from that source being announced that evening on the *Wall Street Week* telecast. The market, however, was not listening, as it embarked on a slide to new 1983–84 bear market lows.

The bulls were adamant not only in their misplaced optimism on the early

May bear market rally high, but in their continued belief that the January–February slide had been a normal correction in an ongoing bull market and that the February intraday low would hold on all market reactions. Bob Gross of the *Professional Investor* stated that the Dow would hold above the 1,130 level and then top 1,200 and then come down sharply to a maximum low at 1,090. Peter Eliades, writing a cycles letter from the West Coast, maintained that no matter what happened the Dow would not break under the 1,115 level on any reaction. Gross was convinced that from June on the Fed would help the incumbent president to be reelected.

Despite the better than 50-point rally since April 5, the advance/decline line had recorded *a pitifully weak showing,* adding only a net gain of 2,130 on the rise. It stood 1,070 under the March 2 showing. Yet the April–May rise in the Dow resurrected the old argument that the long-awaited "second leg" of the bull market was at hand.

As the Dow was just starting a new 100-point plunge, syrupy phrases showed up in the *Journal* which placated an increasingly nervous public and encouraged them to continue holding stocks: "There was an absence of sellers as equity managers seemed to feel better about holding stocks," observed Thomas Ryan, vice president in charge of block trading at Kidder Peabody & Co. "The better psychology and lack of pressure to raise cash seemed to have been prompted by a resumption of takeover activity."

Such complacency was further encouraged when, lacking downside follow-through to the Kaufman-inspired slide, the market ignored a prime rate boost and rallied sharply almost 10 points on May 8, closing about 10 points under the May 2 rally peak. Peter J. DaPuzzo, senior vice president at Shearson/American Express, Inc., remarked that "the Treasury financing appeared to be going well, and the interest-rate news apparently had been discounted." He added that "there's lots of cash on the sidelines," including the funds that institutions received from the takeover of Gulf Corp. by Standard Oil Co. of California. Such statements concerning cash on the sidelines had a way of mostly being uttered just prior to important market slides.

True to form, and completely discrediting the published comments of the day before, the Dow broke over 10 points on May 9 and the *Journal* headline told the story well: "Rate Worries after Treasury Sale Send Stocks Tumbling in Heavy Day." But the bulls wouldn't be quieted. The following was seen in the May 10 *Journal:* "We are excited at this juncture, not because the market should go up, but because the vast majority of our indicators are telling us that it will go up," contended Robert Nicholson, an investment adviser in Coral Gables, Florida.

At this time General Motors was flashing the famous bellwether bear market confirming signal, having refused to close at a new high for four months. While the company had just announced the highest first-quarter earnings in its history, the price of the stock had declined throughout most of the first quarter, the earnings gain totally discounted by the price of the stock. The stock was tracing out a classic bear market formation, topping out in the second week of January while all the auto analysts were joyfully anticipating the great quarter that lay ahead. The declining trendline stood at 72 and all tops were declining ones.

There was a great stock market lesson again being taught in 1984, a lesson that Wall Street apparently would never learn and, if they did, would never pass on to their clients. The lesson was simply this: *Corporate earnings comprise the very worst of all stock market indicators.* Corporate profits surged in the first quarter of 1984. Those who relied on this information were among the hardest hit in the 1984 downturn.

II

I cautioned my readers in the May 12 market letter to stay away from call options, optimists, and elves. In a bull market the bulls are right and in a bear market the bears are right. One of the shortest bull markets in history took place between August 1982 and June 1983. In that period, the bulls were right, as they *always* are in a bull market. Since June 1983 the bears were right, as they *always* are in a bear market. At this time 71 percent of all market advisory services were either bearish or looking for a correction. Some viewed those sentiment figures as being bullish because there were too many bears. On the contrary, those sentiment figures were potentially very bearish because, as just stated, the bears are *always* right in a bear market. Whenever such arguments arose regarding sentiment, I always stressed the important fact that 75 percent of all market letters in September 1929 were bearish a few weeks before the great crash. Such one-sided bearish sentiment was a very bearish indication, because, being in a proven bear market in September 1929, the bears would have to be right. None of them, however, was looking for a market crash. They were all *short-term* bears. But their sheer numbers and the fact that the public was constantly told to sell into all rallies and buy only on a scale-down bore bitter fruit. The September 1929 persistent slide, interrupted by one brief rally, produced a growing avalanche of margin calls, and the magic moment was reached in late October of that fateful year, when virtually everybody sold simultaneously.

In the spring of 1983 I saw the peak of the brief bull market looming ahead and the transition to a bear market. Not only did I see a bear market starting in 1983, but I saw one which would include a stock market panic and crash rivaling that of 1929. I felt that there couldn't be many more months left.

Everything was the *opposite* of a bull market. Coming off the bottom back in August 1982, consumer confidence had been low and corporate earnings were falling, the bond market was rallying, and interest rates were falling. President Reagan's popularity soared and the rising Dow was viewed by the White House as a solid endorsement of the Reagan policies. As the economic recovery went into high gear, lofty projections of super-high Dow levels were being made. Paul Volcker was reappointed by the White House and the machine appeared to be in place that would keep Reagan in the White House after January 1985. At the very peak of the 1983 runaway market speculation, Secretary of the Treasury Donald Regan, on June 16, 1983, stated that the stock market would remain on high ground for the next eighteen months and that stocks were a lot better buy than any we had had in two decades. Most stocks had already peaked out by early May 1983 and the advance/decline line had peaked on June 16, the very day that the ex-Wall Streeter had made his buoyant forecast.

Then things began to go wrong. By May 1984 conditions were the opposite of what they had been during the brief 1982–83 bull market. Consumer confidence was high, corporate earnings were outstandingly strong in the first quarter of 1984, the bond market was getting killed, and interest rates were moving up. The White House, no longer bristling with super-confidence, was angry with Federal Reserve policy, blaming the high interest rates on Paul Volcker. Already one of my earlier predictions was coming to pass. In July 1983, when Paul Volcker was reappointed by President Reagan, I had stated that it was a shrewd political move and an insurance policy. If anything went wrong, and my prediction was that things were going to go wrong, the Reagan administration had a fall guy in Paul Volcker, somebody they could put the blame on.

Things were going wrong by May 1984 and the White House wasted no time in placing the full blame on Volcker. The White House knew that escalating interest rates and the plunging financial market threatened the president's reelection chances and they vented their full anger on Volcker, a man who had done a super job and did not rate the role of fall guy. Like the little Dutch boy, Volcker had gone to Chicago in early May to put together a plan to save the Continental Illinois bank from going under, putting his finger in the dike to stem what could become a threatening flood. The president of the Chemical Bank of New York was quoted at this time as stating that interest rates were going up because of the *irresponsible policies* of the Reagan administration. But the White House pinned the blame on Volcker for threatening the recovery *that was politically required for reelection.* As inevitable as was the collision course of the *Andrea Doria* and the *Stockholm,* markets had to eventually clash with budget deficits which had gotten completely out of control. Paul Volcker had nothing to do with engineering those deficits; the blame rested with the Reagan administration and the Congress, each passing the buck to the other. The stock market was simply beginning to put the blame where it was deserved, and that made the administration angry. It began to look as if economic recovery was bought at a very dear price.

Dr. Martin Feldstein, head of the Council of Economic Advisers, announced his long-expected resignation at this time; he would leave in July to return to a teaching post at Harvard. Since he had a diametrically opposite view from that of Treasury Secretary Regan, the unavoidable friction between them was difficult to disguise, and Feldstein was a thorn in the side of the administration. Whether he was pressured out or whether, seeing what lay ahead, he chose to leave, remained to be seen. Personally, I thought Dr. Feldstein saw very clearly what lay ahead, didn't want to be a part of it, and sought the safer haven of a return to teaching. Sensing the rockier road ahead, one by one they were leaving.

III

One could not help but notice the widening trend of scandals, bank closings, bankruptcies, and embezzlements. When the market was in a bull trend, those things were at a minimum and mostly swept under the rug. Now, however, in a proven bear market they were coming out into the open, a key characteristic of worsening conditions.

In rapid succession, new scandals involved U.S. Synthetic Fuels, AG Becker Paribas, and a huge tax shelter fraud. The break in the bond market sent Lion Capital into Chapter 11. There was a hint of a new scandal involving ex-CIA head William Casey. But all these things paled into insignificance compared with a new financial bombshell—the collapse of the eighth-largest bank in the United States, Continental Illinois of Chicago. This shocking news grabbed all the headlines in early May.

PARALLEL 126

Historical
Blunders and Follies Repeat Themselves

When people are blinded by greed and the times are good, the probability of blunders and follies becomes very high. The Continental Illinois fiasco simply stood as one of the higher monuments to human stupidity and greed in a cemetery of dead hopes. I had exhorted my subscribers to remove their deposits from Continental Illinois many months prior to the collapse, such advice based on the sound evidence that the bank had the highest loan/deposit ratio of any bank in the country, standing at 110 percent.[1] Depositors, thanks to the Federal Deposit Insurance Corporation, were protected as long as the FDIC poured billions into the defunct institution. Shareholders, on the other hand, were at the mercy of the marketplace, and there was very little mercy. In the late scramble to get out, the stock was knocked down to under $5 a share.

To placate the public, the bank at first denied reports it was filing for bankruptcy-law protection. As the rumors of liquidity difficulties spread, there were other rumors that the bank would be acquired by a bigger U.S. bank or a consortium of foreign banks. Such rumors, however, had no substance and the government had no acceptable recourse other than to apply the strong arm of the FDIC. But the strength of that arm began to come into question for the first time in the fifty-year history of that institution. So many billions were required to rescue Continental that it seriously impaired the resources of the FDIC. More was expended in administering financial adrenaline to save the bankrupt bank than in all previous FDIC operations combined. If one had taken the trouble to measure the FDIC's strength in relation to total U.S. bank deposits, one would have discovered that the FDIC had enough on hand to insure only one cent out of every dollar on deposit in the country. But to let Continental go under was unthinkable. The U.S. taxpayer, who had nothing to do with the stupid loans made by Continental, was ultimately going to have to pick up the tab. The public, never polled on such things, was to be the ultimate sucker. The government would never allow the FDIC to run out of funds, and this was but another burden to be placed on an already out-of-control Reagan budget.

<hr />

PARALLEL 127

Historical
Highest Loan/Deposit Ratio Since 1929

According to Warren Weagant, the U.S. banking system had come full circle by 1984 in perfect rhythm with the Kondratieff long wave: "Before the banking system failed in the 1930's, most commercial banks had loaned out approximately 75% of all money deposited by customers. The loan/deposit ratio chart shows that banks were now more exposed to the dangers of possible loan defaults and an outflow of deposits than during the time prior to the stock market crash of 1929."

[1]See Warren Weagant, *Safe Banks* (San Francisco: Command Productions, 1983), p. 55.

LOANS/DEPOSITS

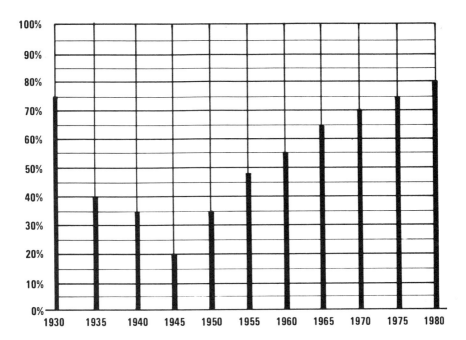

The bond market continued to worsen and took an increasing toll on both the guilty and the innocent. In addition to the collapse of Lion Capital, a government securities trader pleaded guilty to the largest tax shelter fraud on record; RTD Securities, a small government securities trading company, went under, threatening the assets of seven school districts; and the city of San Jose, California, lost $60 million in the bond market decline. The decline brought about the reshuffling of the $4.8 billion Teamster Central States pension fund, ousting poor management with such prestigious names as the Massachusetts Financial Services and the Equitable Life Assurance Society.

The situation got so bad in the bond market by May 11 that *The New York Times* headlined the financial page on May 12 as follows:

PANIC SALES
HIT BOND MARKETS

Late Rebound Erases
Losses;
Dow Off 10.05

Even then, the bond market still had almost three weeks left on the downside.

IV

Arthur Ammann, vice president of Boettcher & Company, Denver, adequately summed up the current thinking, quoted in *The Wall Street Journal* on May 11: "The market is locked in a tight trading range between 1,120 and 1,185, as a tug-of-war takes place between good earnings and continued economic growth on one side and federal deficit difficulties and high interest rates on the other."

Ammann's equation, however, was already out of balance. The stock market had already discounted good corporate earnings and the economic slowdown was already underway, as attested by the bellwether slide in housing starts announced several weeks before. So what Ammann believed to be an equation of $2 = 2$ was actually $0 = -4$. The deficit problem was not getting any better and the Wall Street-anticipated slide in interest rates was very slow in coming.

But *The Wall Street Journal* was not to be deterred as the eternal purveyor of good news, headlining their stock page of May 14: "Stock Averages Holding Their Own Despite Recent Interest-Rate Rise," John Andrew beginning the column with the question: "Who says the stock market is afraid of rising interest rates?" (See Parallels 66 and 122.)

Such optimism was shared the next day as Terry Diamond of Steiner Diamond & Company of Chicago was quoted in the *Journal* as stating that "given the level of gloom currently prevailing on Wall Street any surprise is likely to be on the positive side." But such hopes were proved to be premature. The bond slide had poisoned the short-term outlook for stocks. With investors still slow to be parted from their long holdings, the Dow had dropped to the 1,125 level by May 21, and the next day in the *Journal* Eldon A. Grimm, senior vice president at Birr Wilson & Company, stated: "It was encouraging that no big rush to get out developed when the industrial average dropped below its previous 1984 low of 1,130.55." Such bullishness was still premature.

PARALLEL 128

Technical
Blue Chips Camouflage True Market Weakness

Some market analysts were astute enough to recognize the fallacy of using the Dow as a reliable reflection of the true stock market. The Dow had been on a "solitary walk" since June 1983, the most telling characteristic forecasting the great bear market that followed. This dichotomy was recognized by Peter

Glanville, senior vice president and research head at Dain Bosworth, Inc., of Minneapolis. He saw the extent of the market's weakness as being camouflaged by some of the popular market averages. He noted that with the Dow at this time being off less than 13 percent from its all-time high, the over-the-counter market was down about twice that. He also recognized that the leveraged buy-outs, acquisitions, and restructurings were also camouflaging the hostile market environment. He contended that the best place for venture capital was the public market because many stocks with bright futures were being offered at going-out-of-business prices.

The financial media, rather than warning the public of the disturbing market parallels with 1929, bored the public day after day with the repetitious reporting of the leveraged buy-outs and acquisitions. What the public desperately needed and wasn't getting was good reporting on the stock market as a whole, not the irrelevant dangling of worthless goodies about stocks which in the main were simply sucking innocent investors into a doomed paper chase.

Any good market technician was quick to recognize the extreme dangers of the 1984 stock market, but apparently there weren't too many. What Glanville touched upon was exactly what had so disturbed Roger Babson in 1929 and had moved the astute Jesse Livermore to expect that the stock market was readying for a crash. It was the same old story of the true market versus the Dow.

After it was too late to turn the clock back on the dying 1929 bull market, it was stated in *The Wall Street Journal* on September 30, 1929: "We are now beginning to hear queries as to whether this is the start of a bear market. The people who ask this question seem to forget that 60% of the issues on the Stock Exchange have been in a bear market for nine months. We have no idea when the pressure will lift because at this stage it is largely a matter of mob psychology. However, we do think that nothing alarming is in prospect and some time in the next few days some sort of intelligent base should be established."

So there it was, the admission that the market had been bearish for most stocks for the first nine months of 1929. The blue chip camouflage could no longer disguise that fact and this technical fact of life, more than anything else, is what had most influenced Joe Kennedy, Jesse Livermore, and Roger Babson.

PARALLEL 129

Historical
Wall Street Overexpanded

It had become increasingly clear that Wall Street, counting on the 1982–83 brief bull market to last forever, continued to expand at the worst of times. E. F. Hutton had opened fifty new offices right at the top. Robert Fomon stated that operating expenses rose sharply because of this and were largely responsible for their net income dropping 65 percent in the first period. Their hiring policies had changed to freeze. The final cycle would go from hire to freeze to fire. It was only a matter of time.

The Pacific Stock Exchange was expanding to new quarters at this time and other exchanges continued to expand.

In 1929 new regional exchanges continued to be opened and brokerage houses continued to expand the number of their regional offices long after the true stock market had peaked.

The merger mania which had been so in evidence as the market was peaking in 1983 began to die down by 1984, but there were still enough leveraged buy-outs and acquisitions to keep the financial news commentators busy. Most telling at this time was a remark made before a congressional committee that "this was like the late 1920s."

PARALLEL 130
Historical
Normal Cycles Weren't Working

It was becoming increasingly apparent that normal cycles were no longer working, just as they had not in 1929, and painfully so to all those who bought into the 1982–83 upswing, expecting a normal bull market that would see stocks sharply higher by 1984 and 1985. Instead, most stocks had peaked in the spring of 1983 and by 1984 most people were holding stocks at a loss. It was argued that the decline in most stocks since the spring of 1983 was simply the digestion period prior to the resumption of the bull market, but by this time a year had passed since the technical peak in stock prices, and that had gone far beyond the normal waiting period for a bull market second leg.

I could not help but believe that those looking for levels of 2,000 to 3,000 in the Dow based on Elliott Wave analysis and other cyclical theories would err.

PARALLEL 131
Psychological
Permanent Plateau of Prosperity

Economic strength and low inflation gave birth to the increasingly accepted idea of the economists that perhaps the economy was on a permanent plateau of strength. Such optimistic thinking had caught on early in the cycle. The

February 1983 issue of *Horoscope* stated: "Remember, a Dow Jones average of 1,600–1,700 is the magic number if it is to keep pace with the growth of other economic indicators. According to some leading analysts, *we will never again in our lifetimes see the lows of 1982—when the market was considered to be 50 percent or more undervalued.*"

When asked on September 3, 1929, where the market was headed, the famous astrologer Evangeline Adams said that the Dow was headed toward heaven. Since it turned out to be the Dow peak, one might have interpreted her words to mean that the Dow was about to die.

PARALLEL 132

Historical
Stock Market and Astrology Very Popular

By 1984 practically every astrology magazine had a stock market column. Arch Crawford had reached some prominence in his issuance and sale of *Crawford Perspectives,* an amalgamation of astrology and technical analysis. This type of market coverage had been legitimized to the extent that Mr. Crawford would be called fairly regularly to make a market prediction on the Financial News Network based on his astrological work.

May was deemed to be particularly important because it focused attention on a number of problems which were not consistent with the widely advertised Reagan recovery. The collapse of Continental Illinois drew attention to the growing banking problems, but the big picture included also a number of major 1929 parallels which had surfaced this month.

Consistent with the Maxfield blueprint in 1977, we had clicked off currency depreciation, peak movement of dollar loans, the large counterflow of foreign funds into the United States, and falling commodity prices. The collapse in commodity prices was particularly in evidence this month just as it had been in May 1929, several months before the great stock crash.

PARALLEL 133

Historical
Increasing Number of Defaults

Late in the month, Bolivia suspended interest payments and Ecuador also defaulted. This pattern of defaults and near-defaults had not as yet gotten out of hand because the United States papered over most of the loans just as it had been doing in the late 1920s. But the pressure on a rising number of defaults was increased by the fall in commodity prices which was affecting so many South American countries. Ironically, rather than cut back on production, production was expanded, and that simply put further downward pressure on commodity prices.

PARALLEL 134
Historical
America Papered Over the Loans

But American banks, despite the dismal failure of earlier foreign loans, continued to paper over new loans coming due rather than bite the bullet and write off tremendous losses. This was an exact parallel with 1929 and the practice would be continued until such huge loans could no longer be rescued.

PARALLEL 135
Historical
Record Trade Deficit

Since the dollar was getting stronger and stronger, it would buy more abroad and thus our foreign imports ballooned to record levels while our exports could not keep pace. The trade deficit grew month after month and was headed for an annual record figure of $130 billion.

PARALLEL 136
Historical
Protectionism

This naturally led to an increase in protectionism, especially in the steel and textile industries.

V

I had stated the month before that both the London and Tokyo markets appeared to be at the peak of parabolic rises. Up to that time, the bulls continued to cite the strength in the foreign stock markets. I saw that as all about to change. The May 7 issue of *Barron's* had a twelve-page spread on "Investing in Japan." Things always look most attractive at the top, and thus the focus at this time on investing in Japan served as a very reliable signal that the Japanese stock market was about to take a dive. The same could be said about the London stock market. British voters had given Margaret Thatcher a sharp political reversal at the polls. The Tories lost control of the councils in Birmingham, Edinburgh, Southampton, Exeter, and elsewhere. The handwriting was on the wall for a change of government in England, one more parallel with the late 1920s. Against that background and the overvalued London market, British Telecom was going public with the largest public share offering in British finance, another symptom of the peak of the market. The U.S. media had been underscoring the good performance of the foreign stock funds, still another symptom that the big move was soon to be over.

Prices started to plummet on the exchanges in London and Tokyo. Up to this time, the media had been explaining the strength in the foreign stock markets as due to the strength in the dollar and high U.S. interest rates. The sharp drop in the Tokyo market was attributed in the May 11 *Wall Street Journal* to "trader nervousness about the increase in U.S. interest rates." That was as confusing as when earlier in the year a slowdown in the economy was worrying Wall Street. Many rumors were flying now, and there seemed to be a growing new sense of concern. I expected to see bearish sentiment continue to increase, with the more optimistic recommending buying on a scale-down as they did in 1929. There was much hedging now among analysts, who typically stated that the market wanted to go up but could go down first. They were covered both ways.

By this time, every indicator covered in my 1976 *Strategy* book was confirming the bear market, and now the most important of all indicators had gotten in line: time. Because of the time indicator, nobody thought a bear market would start in 1983. Now we were seeing even that indicator getting in line. Quoting from page 231 under "Bear Phase One": "Time Indicator: Twenty-two to 24 months have gone by since the last major bear market bottom. A market top having all the earmarks of a major bull market peak must have been seen within the past one to five months." June 1984 marked the twenty-second month since the August 1982 bottom, and at this time it was rather obvious that we had seen a major bull market peak within the previous few months.

There was increasing talk about changing the currency. Representative Ron Paul was the source of this talk and the idea was given increasing credibility by a spread in *Barron's*. I saw another 1929 parallel brewing. *The $1 bill in* *your pocket today was born in 1929* when the Treasury withdrew the large-size notes and switched to bills of the current size. Off and on, intelligent sources related plans to change our currency sometime in the next few months in order to exert stricter controls over currency leaving the country and to invalidate cash funds on which no records are kept and no taxes paid. It was a move in keeping with the budget problem, which appeared to have no immediate solutions. Such a move was expected to coincide with a rise in the price of gold as a beneficiary, the illegally held old currency being shifted into gold to await a transfer later back into the new currency.

There was no question in my mind that 200-million-share days lay ahead as well as 50-point daily declines in the Dow. It was easy to show the mechanics underscoring these increasing probabilities. Stock splits had been announced for Allied Corp., United Technologies, and Westinghouse. Those moves would drop the Dow Jones industrial divisor close to the 1.00 level, or lower, meaning that a fractional move of ⅞ in the price of a Dow stock would equate with a 1-point move in the Dow Jones Industrial Average. If each Dow industrial stock fell ⅞ of a point, then the Dow would drop 30 points. If each stock in the Dow 30 dropped 1¾ points, then the average would fall 60 points in one day. These were new highs in volatility. Psychologically, future breaks in the Dow would be difficult to contain by virtue of the expanded downside potential brought about by the new record low in the divisor.

Stock splits and dividend increases were all ploys to keep people in the market. Somebody has to hold the stocks in every bear market, and to make them want to hold stocks, the stocks have to be made to look more attractive. The same ploys were used in 1929. Remember all the hoopla about the breakup of American Telephone? The powers that be knew what was going to happen to the telephone stocks, so the public had to be lured into wanting to hold them. I blew the whistle on those stocks in November 1983, revealing why Merrill Lynch had set up the Humpty Dumpty fund in order that people wouldn't worry and would stay with the telephone stocks. I had viewed the entire Telephone operation as a giant smoke screen that deflected attention away from the stock distribution going on elsewhere.

VI

Like the *Titanic*, the market in May 1984 had been tilting dangerously and was taking on water. The call had gone out to don the life jackets and lower the boats. On May 2 there had been a brief champagne party, the Dow breaking out on the upside to 1,186.56, but it was the last bit of gaiety before the S.S. *Dow* hit an iceberg. The captain of the ship was anxiously eyeing the advance/decline line, and his years of nautical experience told him that a move under the April 11 low meant that he could not save his ship. His crew and passengers had viewed the relatively placid waters since late February, but had recently been alerted that there was another ship in the foggy vicinity bearing down on them, a ship later identified as the S.S. *Bond.* There was no party on board the *Bond.* It was the first to hit an iceberg. It was sinking fast, sending out distress signals to any ships nearby. While contemplating the *Bond*'s fate, the *Dow* also hit an iceberg, and from that point on, it was every man for himself.

The relatively limited 56-point trading range since late February represented the placid waters which hid the giant icebergs from view. The passengers and crew on the *Bond* were as unaware of those dangers as were the passengers and crew on the *Dow.* Their charts failed to disclose the location of those huge floating masses of ice. Already the advance/decline line was about to open up a gaping hole in the hull of the *Dow* and the captain had few illusions about the chances of staying afloat thereafter.

Obviously, something was very wrong. While bearish sentiment continued to grow, it could not be considered to be a bullish omen. If enough people rushed to one side of the boat, it could capsize. The market was charting a dangerous course, and the rising bearish sentiment was simply speeding it toward its ultimate moment of destiny.

By holding to the current course, the Dow would be at new lows in a few days, smashing by the end of the month and charted to go still lower in June. The rate of fall at this time was greater than it had been on the January–February slide.

In reviewing the big picture, I saw that the stock market in the spring of 1983 had begun to flash serious warnings of the troubles that would lie ahead. The number of new individual stock price highs had peaked on May 6 of that year. That meant that from that day forward the bull market was no longer technically genuine. A genuine bull market must see a constantly expanding number of new highs. It had now been over a year since one could make that observation. That was followed up by the advance/decline line peaking on June 16, 1983. At that time the entire forward momentum of the market had been technically checked. From that day, the Dow Jones Industrial Average was on a "solitary walk," most of the new buying concentrated in a handful of blue chip stocks. That was followed by the peak in the Dow on November 29, 1983, fulfilling my earlier prediction that the bear market would start in 1983. That was followed by the great bull trap double top in early January 1984, the bear market coming fully out into the open. That, in turn, was followed by the February–May bear market rally that saw the true rally peak on March 16. I termed the bull trap of May 2 the "champagne" rally because when the Dow returned to the 1,180s so many analysts stated that one could hear the champagne corks popping in the background. Now, with the advance/decline line about to put the technical lie to the entire base formed since late February, that base was seen at the time as likely to crumble faster than the Maginot Line.

VII

On May 24 the Dow intraday low hit 1,096.31, making a mockery out of the "base" stretching back to February. Everything had now thoroughly broken the February low levels and the new slide since the "champagne" top of May 2 was outpacing the January–February slide. The greatly expanded number of new lows, together with an advance/decline line then running 100 points ahead of the Dow on the downside, attested to the millions of margin calls going out daily, something Wall Street and their customers didn't like to talk about. All the ingredients were rapidly coming together for a wholesale, concerted move out of the stock market—a panic.

Since 75 percent of all trades were institutional, the institutions were taking the brunt of the market collapse. The new record high in the monthly short interest was seen to be extremely bearish, reflecting mostly professional short-ing in line with the trend of the market.

My major prediction in 1983 of the coming bear market, panic, and crash was based initially on a very important assumption. If that assumption was wrong, then my entire prediction would have been wrong. That initial assump-tion was that *this was not a normal market.* Since my assumption was totally correct, against all the Wall Street odds, all those analysts making their projections based on normal cycles had to be wrong. One such cycles analyst had stated at this time that the odds were 100 to 1 against the Dow breaking under the 1,114 intraday low. The very fact that these cycles people were wrong simply underscored Parallel 130. Back in 1929 the economist Stuart Chase stated: "We have probably three more years of prosperity ahead of us before we enter the cyclic tailspin which has occurred in the eleventh year of the four previous periods of commercial prosperity." Chase was relying on normal cycles, but 1929 was not a normal market.

I saw things in 1984 as rapidly approaching that magic moment when everybody would want to get out of the market at the same time. Relative strength in the 91-day Treasury bills reflected the growing fear and rush for safety. The continued rise in the money market fund assets also reflected that growing fear. If the parallels held, when the actual crash was upon us *gold* would be used as one of the repositories for such funds fleeing the stock market. Gold was not popular at this time, investors waiting for the ultimate break in the dollar. Trading in a relatively narrow price range despite the vertical rise in interest rates was indicative of this growing general fear.

Give or take a few months, a crash was inevitable. I kept returning to Parallel 127, which, more than anything else, underscored the extreme dangers in the banking system. Before the great crash of 1929, the average ratio of loans to deposits for all commercial banks reached over 75 percent. Then, through the painful process of bankruptcy, liquidation of assets, more restric-tive loan policies, tougher regulations, etc., the average ratio dropped to 40 percent in the mid-1930s. During the 1940s, the economy was rolling along at full speed and the ratio dipped to 20 percent, when only 20 cents on each deposit dollar was loaned out by most banks.

Then came several decades of credit expansion. By 1980, banks had gone full circle back to the ratio levels reached before the big crash of over half a century ago. By 1983 and 1984 the average loan/deposit ratio had reached 87 percent. A full-scale banking crisis was but one of a collection of events which would serve to explain to future historians why the stock market crashed.

As Weagant wrote in his book:

> Most bankers believe that a banking crisis is not possible today. However, the safeguards covering the banks are not as clear-cut and guaranteed as most people believe them to be. If a banking crisis is not possible, then we must believe bank illiquidity is acceptable. We must believe that depositors will never ask for their account balances in cash, that all banks will be totally backed, supported and given mountains of cash to settle with depositors no matter how poorly managed or fraudulent the bank might have been.
>
> When bankers are questioned about why they have loaned to borrowers who could not pay them back, they have a wonderful answer. They answer that it does not really matter if a loan is ever paid off! They claim that such credit-worthy borrowers as the United States government are never *expected* to pay off their entire debt, and they do have a point. The U.S. government has made no serious attempt to pay off the national debt.
>
> Our government might come to the rescue of the bankers by using taxpayers' money to pay off the loans to bankrupt countries. This would delight the banks and in return give them a nice reward for making these irresponsible loans with taxpayers' money. But the number of problem loans is monstrous. It could be as high as $250 billion worldwide. If the U.S. government took $250 billion from the U.S. Treasury, the American public would certainly cry out.[2]

Treasury Secretary Donald Regan opted in favor of the U.S. taxpayer paying off the bad loans to bankrupt countries. He was also in favor of rewarding our banks for making those irresponsible loans. According to Weagant's figures, Continental Illinois loaned out $32.2 billion (a large percentage of the loans being bad). However, their total deposits were only $29.3 billion, thus showing the bank to be 110 percent loaned up!

In late May several more banks went under, banks failing in California, Tennessee, Louisiana, and Illinois. To hear the announcement on the evening news one would have thought that he was getting a weather report. It would be only a matter of time before the announcer said: *"Only* seven banks failed today." As an indication of the immensity of the growing problem, over six times the total assets of the FDIC had vanished in the stock market since the

[2]Weagant, *Safe Banks*, p. 49.

May 2 champagne rally of three weeks before. The Wilshire 5000 Equity Index showed a loss of $82 billion in stock values in that short period of time. In other words, if speculators had simply wanted to withdraw from the banks what they had just lost in the stock market, a new banking crisis would have ensued which the FDIC would have been powerless to prevent, their own assets being woefully inadequate. The Continental Illinois problem had impaired 15 percent of the total FDIC assets. That was only one bank. I had pleaded for about two years for people to withdraw their funds from Continental Illinois, since it was public knowledge that the bank had the highest loan/deposit ratio in the country. The record high loan/deposit ratio, even back then, was a red flag warning to everybody.

One by one the loose practices that generally go unnoticed in a bull market were being revealed in 1984. Promoters of these less than acceptable dealings were being progressively spotlighted and the wheels of justice were turning. May 1984 was a forecast of things to come. In a single month, embezzlements, stock frauds, Ponzi schemes, bankruptcies, bank failures, and other assorted scandals surfaced. But the public failed to see the pattern of these events, secure in their belief that nothing was going to go wrong in an election year in the midst of what they still thought was a strong economy.

In 1929 the stock market crashed in the face of what was thought to be a strong economy. The year 1984 provided a similar backdrop. Foolish optimism prevailed. The stock market fundamentalists had their heads in the sand, completely blind to what was soon to happen. This was well expressed in a double headline in the May 23 *Detroit Free Press*. This is what appeared in the business section: "Optimism Prevails for Short Term. Stocks hit 13-Month Low."

16

False Bottom

[JUNE 1984]

I

June 1 started off with an almost 20-point rally which was quickly erased by the middle of the month, the Dow breaking to a new bear market low of 1,086.90. I was on national TV the day of the rally, being interviewed live by Lou Dobbs of Cable News Network in Atlanta. I put it on the line once again, stating that we were in a major bear market that would include a panic and crash. The market having already broken sharply since late November, my remarks were met with disbelief. Two weeks later the Dow dropped to 200 points below the late 1983 Dow peak.

Internally, however, things were happening which were temporarily to alter the course of the bear market. The bond market had taken a terrible beating in May and was bottoming. Final lows were reached on June 4 and were retested on June 28. Having finally come to rest, the bond market bottom gave birth to an idea that would shortly mesmerize the Street and bring back the stock buyers. Now in a strong technical position to rally, the bond market was tapping out the message that interest rates were ready to come down. This was the siren song Wall Street wanted to hear, but the big swing was reserved for late July and early August. June was a positioning month. The seeds were being sown for a huge sucker rally and the harvest was to be still another generation of losers.

Vartanig G. Vartan of *The New York Times* did a piece on June 3 entitled "What Happened to the Stock Market?" The subheadline aptly told the story of what had actually been going on: "To date, 1984 has been a bust for equities, thanks mainly to rising interest rates. Pick your stocks carefully, experts say."

The opening paragraphs of the article were quite revealing:

> Tumbling prices have sent both the stock and bond markets into turmoil again, scarcely a year after they were finishing the most splendid recovery since World War II. As a result, a nation of perplexed investors keeps asking: "What went wrong?"
>
> It's fair to raise the question. After all, the Dow Jones industrial average rose to nearly 1,300 by the end of last year, when many forecasts called for a further increase to between 1,400 and 1,500 this year. Despite a spirited rally Friday, the Dow is far from those lofty levels and, in fact, last week traded below the 1,100 mark. In the process of a painful, drawn-out "correction," as it's called on Wall Street, many people have lost whatever profits they reaped in the bull market.
>
> And while some analysts can still find individual stocks or industry groups they like, most are being cautious, particularly since interest rates have been creeping up to levels that make a lot of people very nervous.
>
> Stock prices usually decline in May, and this month they have lived up to historical precedent. But the market also has a habit of going up in the final two years of a Presidential term. So, unless some authoritative action is taken soon to turn things around, 1984 can be a year that rewrites the record books.
>
> That can't be a comforting thought to the Reagan Administration. No one knows how voters in the Presidential election year will react if the Dow Jones industrials plunge below 1,000, say, or if yields on long-term Treasury bonds escalate to 15 percent by this summer.
>
> It is those rising yields that many experts blame for knocking equity prices into a cocked hat.
>
> Last autumn, with the recession nearing its end, Wall Street professionals and Main Street investors alike looked forward with confidence to a prosperous 1984. The economy, in fact, has recovered sharply, the unemployment rate has plummeted and inflation is still apparently being held in check. Corporate profits, meanwhile, have climbed.

What did go wrong? The answer was crystal clear. People do the obvious thing. Not being capable of random action, people followed the media, believed the economists, failed to heed the major bearish signals stemming from technical analysis, and, above all, failed to reread history at the most critical juncture in the market in fifty-four years. If they had heeded technical analysis and history, they could not have failed to observe the proliferation of the 1929 parallels. Like the 1929 lemmings, they had been had. The very people who had missed the top completely had for months been telling their followers that everything after the late November 1983 Dow peak was a normal correction in an ongoing bull market. While people waited in vain for that magical "second leg," their portfolios were deteriorating and, as Vartan had pointed out, they had lost all of their bull market profits.

II

The London economic summit meeting began on June 7. One could find a
very clear 1929 parallel.

PARALLEL 137

Historical
Foreign Leaders Baffled and Confused

Memories were very short. In 1983 President Reagan had given assurances at
the Williamsburg economic summit that interest rates were going to come
down. The summit proved to be a cruel hoax on our foreign trading partners.
They were sent home with high hopes that the Reagan administration was
going to bring down the budgetary deficits and lower interest rates, thus aiding
foreign currencies. But, instead of coming down, the dollar soared to new
highs and produced massive losses for those who bet on their own currencies.
The 1929 parallel was clear. In 1929, Montagu Norman, governor of the Bank
of England, had visited Washington early that year, hoping to be given a
clearer view of monetary conditions. Instead, he returned home "baffled,"
with an "even deeper feeling of confusion and obscurity."[1] On June 7 a repeat
performance was to be made at the London economic summit. The same
promises would be given—that interest rates were to be brought down in the
United States. This time, however, I suspected that such promises were to be
taken with a grain of salt.

True to form, the summit was a farce. President Reagan said little, leaving
most of the talking to Donald Regan, who also said little. Prime Minister
Margaret Thatcher said that everybody expected little and nobody was disappointed. Recall of the muddied vision of Williamsburg was uppermost in the
minds of the participants. The cloud of 1983's broken promises was more
newsworthy than the recorded smiles for public consumption. It was more like
a social tea party given a note of hilarity as Treasury Secretary Regan reiterated
vociferously that the high U.S. deficits had nothing to do with higher interest
rates, a statement the British press called "simple-minded." While President
Reagan in his press conference stated, for domestic consumption, that there
"is a new era in America of strong growth and stable prices," foreign leaders
at the summit were not so quick to buy that 1929-type optimism. It smacked
too much of Hoover's "permanent plateau of prosperity" statements made
several months prior to the great crash.

After the summit, David Stockman, picking up where Martin Feldstein left

[1]Gordon Thomas and Max Morgan-Witts, *The Day the Bubble Burst*, (New York: Penguin
Books, 1980), p. 179.

off, as much as thumbed his nose at Donald Regan, underscoring the link between the high deficits and the high interest rates. Whether this meant that Stockman would be the next to leave the administration remained to be seen. But one thing was clear: There was trouble in the "family" and the transmission of mixed signals, something that was scaring the daylights out of the financial markets, presented a picture of serious confusion at the top. Confusion also reigned in the Congress at this time, inasmuch as a serious snag occurred in the deficit reduction bill.

The pieces were rapidly falling into place for a series of events that historians would later seize upon to explain why the U.S. stock market crashed. Being of worldwide significance, these events were not lost upon foreign stock markets, notably London and Tokyo, which had been giving signs of topping. The proliferation of 1929 parallels could not be ignored. The 40 percent rise in protectionism in the past few years was highlighted at this time by the new quotas in the steel industry, an industry that was struggling merely to survive. More and more, the word "moratorium" was showing up in the press in the wake of the growing number of loan defaults. News in this respect coming from Bolivia, Ecuador, and Argentina suggested that there might be an official moratorium on all debts, an event that preceded the collapse of the banking system in the United States in the early 1930s. There was already a partial moratorium on the Mexican and Brazilian debt payments.

The message was not lost on the bank stocks, which plunged at this time in deep bear market patterns. Witnessing the highest number of bank failures since the early 1930s, banks turned increasingly away from nonperforming Less Developed Country (LDC) loans, which had gotten them into so much trouble. Now they were trying to shore up their declining net worth by lending money to big-time speculators who had made the leveraged buy-out the hottest game in town. A congressional committee was told at this time that the merger mania was reminiscent of the late 1920s. Ironically, the second-weakest bank in the country, according to Weagant, was Manufacturers Hanover Trust of New York. This bank was financing more of the leveraged buy-outs than any other bank. According to John Shad, the head of the Securities and Exchange Commission, if interest rates didn't come down, the current wave of leveraged buy-outs *would translate into an increased number of bankruptcies.* The ultimate loser in the leveraged buy-out was proving to be the shareholder. While the public was being raped, I had no sympathy, because nobody was twisting their arms to buy the shares of the buy-out candidates. The chart books told a grim tale of what had happened to Carter Hawley Disney and a host of others. The shareholders got the short end of the stick. And while the excitement of the earlier rises continued, the financial news networks were wasting the viewer's time by paying too much attention to the buy-out stories. Now, once again, the shareholders were caught holding the bag while a few individuals ran off scot-free with millions. The days of the plundering pirates were very much alive.

PARALLEL 138

Historical
Parabolic Curve in Leveraged Buy-outs

The most revealing thing of all about the leveraged buy-outs was that they were peaking out in a perfect parabolic curve, as was shown in the June 9 issue of *The New York Times*. The series showed (in billions of dollars) 0.6 in 1979, 0.9 in 1980, 2.3 in 1981, 2.6 in 1982, 7.1 in 1983, and 10.0 (estimated) in 1984.

This was the same parabolic curve as the New York Stock Exchange volume, the short interest, new issues, stock splits, and secondary offerings. It underscored my original contention that everything was blowing out as it did in 1929.

PARALLEL 139

Historical
Changing the U.S. Currency

The New York Times ran an in-depth article on June 6 entitled "U.S. Weighs Redesign of Currency." For some time there had been rumors that the United States government contemplated changing the design of the currency. The reasoning behind such a move was to invalidate all the black-market operations stemming from drugs and tax cheats. Claims were made that the currency had already been printed. Whether or not this actually happened, it would serve as another 1929 parallel. In 1929 the Treasury withdrew the large-size notes and switched to bills of the current size.

III

PARALLEL 140

Historical
Three-Year Slump in Agriculture

Any serious student of the economics of the 1920s was well aware that the agricultural cycle had turned down in 1926, three years before the 1929 stock market crash. To draw a parallel, one would have to know in 1984 that agriculture had been in a three-year slump.

The Wall Street Journal made the parallel official on June 14, the following stated on the front page:

Farmland prices sink further and might not recover for years.

A three-year slump deepens as new farm bankruptcies add to the supply of land for sale and as rising interest rates cut buyer demand. In Lubbock, Texas, Lewter Real Estate says some farmers recently were forced to sell at about $750 an acre, 20% or 25% less than they could have got last year. In Foley, Alabama, Larkin H. Harris Real Estate says prices in the area are 5% to 10% lower than they were a year ago. And prices are 15% below those of a year ago in parts of Iowa and Missouri that were hurt by last summer's drought, says J. J. Nolan Farm Realty in Osceola, Iowa.

Buying by non-farmer speculators is depressed, brokers say, because interest rates seem too high in relation to expected inflation in land values. And most farmers themselves are so deeply in hock that they couldn't afford to buy more land, says Raymond Upchurch, a Raleigh, North Carolina broker. "It's going to take three to five years of good crops and prices to turn this around," says Tom Lane, a broker in Osage City, Kansas.

"Sales have dropped off to absolutely nothing," complains J. Norwood Clark, a broker in Cairo, Georgia. "December 1980 is the last time I drew a salary."

That certainly didn't sound like the well-advertised Reagan prosperity, any more than similar conditions in agriculture in 1929 backed up Hoover's prosperity.

The mid-June Dow low at 1,086.90 saw an overwhelming number of analysts bullish. However, if one had taken the time to identify them all, one would have discovered that they had been bullish all year. That meant that the majority of them were losers. The market was not about to reward losers. Nevertheless, their arguments were building toward the biggest sucker rally of the year, duplicating the famous last run for the roses in the summer of 1929.

PARALLEL 141
Historical
Insider Buying

In keeping with the stock "scarcity" theory which always has a way of surfacing at the worst of times, a number of bullish arguments were brought forward by many analysts immediately after the June 15 false bottom. Leveraged buy-outs, takeovers, and reports being made at this time that insiders were again buying stocks were presented to paint the illusion that good stocks were becoming scarcer. Of course, any student of market history would run for the hills when hearing such arguments. When new stock certificates are no further away than a printing press, the "scarcity" theory has never held water. Some of the biggest names in the business were about to fall for those old baseless arguments.

Norman Fosback, publisher of *New Issues,* reported at this time that the long trend of pernicious and concentrated insider selling was ending, citing a rise in insider buying. Such reports were picked up and expanded upon by bullish analysts who fervently wished to rationalize further their baseless reasoning that the brief 1982–83 bull market was still alive, simply awaiting an overpublicized "second leg." What they failed to see, however, was that any switch to insider buying had only *short-term* implications in view of the overwhelming technical evidence that any coming rally had to be a *bear* market rally, simply another bull trap like those of early January and early May.

Many corporate officers in 1929 thought that the initial downturn in stock prices created bargains in the shares of their companies. Such insider buying back then was as misplaced as any such buying in 1984. What Fosback had failed to warn his readers was that insider buying *had no long-term implications.* Therein lay another 1929 parallel.

Insider buying in a proven bear market not only carries no weight; it is foolish. The following appeared in the "La Salle Street Comment" in the August 14, 1929, *Wall Street Journal:*

> Buying of Sears, Roebuck in thousand-share lots by officers of the company was reported last Saturday. Sears closed at 156. Since no new developments in the company's affairs are in the wind, the only supposition that remains is that Sears' officers considered the stock a bargain at that price.

Right below that was another juicy item:

> Insull Utilities Investment common made a quick recovery from its low of 95 on the Chicago Stock Exchange last Friday. Insiders rejoiced at the opportunity to get the stock below 100.

Both stocks collapsed several weeks later.

PARALLEL 142

Market
Everything Is Short-Term Trading

Ever since the great bear market started in the spring of 1983, the stock market was no place for investors. There wasn't enough time for investors to record a capital gains profit. Ironically, the capital gains period was shortened in June 1984 from twelve months to six. This was but another lure designed to attract investors back to the market. But a capital gains period of any length would be meaningless in a major bear market. Investors had no place in the market and they were going to be used once again as the major bag holders. Somebody had to hold the stocks in every down market, and the major repository chosen every time for such losses was the investors, those who fell for everything brokers, economists, the administration, and the media had been pelting them with all during the brief 1982–83 rise, which had simply served as the high diving board before the greatest plunge in fifty-five years.

Since most people buy and then hold their stocks for a long period of time, these people generally comprised the biggest market losers. That is especially true in severe bear markets because, not being short-term-oriented, such investors lack the flexibility or the technical knowledge to get out of the market in time before the worst of the slide.

In 1929 the public was consistently told to buy good stocks and put them away. Many did, to their everlasting regret. Just when the public was most desperate for intelligent market advice, *The Wall Street Journal* on October 15, 1929, related that Arthur Cutten was still bullish. The "Broad Street Gossip" column that day stated: *"Cutten Declares He's 'Still Bullish,'* said Arthur Cutten, when asked his opinion of the future trend of the market. 'Temporary shakeouts no longer interest me since my position is that of an investor and not a speculator. I used to try and make money on the short swings, but found that it could not be done consistently, and I now follow the policy of picking good companies and staying with them!" It was a stupid statement, but no more so than so many similar statements made in 1984.

So the stage was being set in June for some possible bear market detours, very similar to the situation in June 1929. The Argentina loan was again papered over, the bond market had finally built a worthwhile base, the stock market had shown support in the Dow 1,080–1,090 area, and it was an election year. What could possibly go wrong? John Bollinger, the resident technical analyst for the Financial News Network, stated that he saw new highs for the Dow this year. Robert T. Gross of *The Professional Investor* told his readers: "Go for it." Some very big hooks were being baited.

PART SIX

1929 REVISITED

17

The Rally That Fooled the Majority

[JULY 1984]

I

It was time for the end game to start, the final gambit. In order to be totally effective, it had to lull the bulls into a false sense of overconfidence. The bulls had been calling the market wrong since the spring of 1983. They were hungry for a rally. The bears, on the other hand, had enjoyed the developing bear market tremendously. They were ripe to make a mistake. Rather than follow the obvious, hewing strictly to the bearish scenario, why not give the bulls their hoped-for bull market "second leg"? In other words, *the game plan would be to deliberately sacrifice the queen in order to win the game.* The predicted market crash would win the game for the bears. I had stated many times that every market rally isn't followed by a market crash *but that every crash is preceded by a rally.* Therefore, with all the necessary evidence in place for a crash, with evidence carefully compiled and documented for almost two years, *the only missing ingredient was a rally.* But to do the necessary job, *it had to be a big rally occurring in a short space of time.*

All year the bulls were predicting lower interest rates. The May–June double bottom in the bond market looked so bullish for bonds that I could see the stage being set for this big, final rally in the stock market. Interest rates were to be the big hook. The financial community had been brainwashed for so long to believe that lower interest rates were bullish for the stock market that they would not realize until it was too late that the lower rates were actually the early warning of an economic downturn. So the stage was set for the last act. This was to be the summer of 1929 revisited.

These thoughts went through my mind as I carefully considered what lay ahead for the summer. Then I thought of something else, something so obvious that it would never be erased from market memory. I thought of August 1982. Suppose the widely looked-for summer rally was delayed, as it had been in 1982? Then, out of the blue, appeared another great August rally. The response would be electric, inasmuch as the great August 1982 upturn was still fresh in the public memory. The only thing that could trigger such a rally would be lower interest rates. The bond market was telling us that they were coming; all that remained was a July buy signal. I bided my time.

The Dow Jones Industrial Average had closed at 1,124.56 by the end of June. The June rally had not carried very far and I was very bearish as the market moved into July. But as I gradually put the pieces together, it seemed logical to expect that the most believable turn might develop from the last proven support area, between 1,080 and 1,090. I assembled this scenario in the back of my mind and resumed my day-to-day observations.

II

The month started off with a Eurobond scandal involving a suicide, the Tokyo and London markets getting bombed, and the British bank rate being upped two percentage points. The Dow worked lower, dropping to 1,104.57 on July 12.

At the close of trading on July 13, the A-Dis Trading Barometer flashed a buy signal. The Dow stood at 1,111.75. I decided to wait one day and then call our telephone subscribers the night of the sixteenth, the day the Dow closed at 1,116.83. The advice was given to cover all short positions and close out all put options. A follow-up special bulletin was always mailed to my letter subscribers after such telephone calls. The special bulletin was dated July 17 and mailed that day. The Dow closed at 1,122.90 the day the bulletin was mailed.

Most subscribers received the bulletin on July 20, the day the Dow closed at 1,101.37. That turned out to be two days before the exact bottom.

After my telephone call the night of the sixteenth, things began to happen immediately. I received a call from Milwaukee telling me that it was heard in Boston that I was predicting a 400-point rise in the market. The *Orlando Sentinel* interviewed me and ran a large article with my picture on July 20 headlined "The Bulls Are Off and Running." The *Toronto Star,* picking up those sources, also ran a piece saying I was predicting a 400-point rally.

While these rumors were rife, the market backed and filled for a while. The market provided a clue that something was different when Henry Kaufman predicted on July 17 that interest rates were headed higher and the market responded that day with a rise of over 6 points.

Thereafter, the Dow headed down toward the 1,080–1,090 support area, clicking off technical downside nonconfirmations all the way. On July 24 the Dow closed at 1,086.57, slightly below the June 15 low of 1,086.90.

Now totally convinced that the July barometer signal was a valid one, I headlined my July 28 market letter "Something Is in the Wind." Internally the market was getting better. Despite the drop on July 24 in the Dow to a new seventeen-month closing low in the bear market, fulfilling all previous signals given, the barometer doggedly stayed on the July 13 buy signal. The time had come to play my ace.

I was now convinced that the coming crash could only follow one more huge sucker rally. The July 13 signal had to be forecasting such a rally because time was beginning to run out for the major scenario. Such a rally had to come now or never.

Rallies also have a way of developing after the bulls throw in the towel. On the first day of summer (June 21) the Dow closed at 1,127.21 and by July 25 stood at 1,096.95, a summer loss of 30.26 points up to this point. The elated mid-June bulls were soon handed their heads as the Dow was being positioned to break the June low. The July low on the twenty-fourth was not greeted with the same degree of bullish enthusiasm which had been generated on the June low. The bearish position had become too popular, as was so well illustrated on the July 25 *Money Talk* show on the Financial News Network. On that show the public was being educated to the ways of the bear—how to buy put options and go short, etc. Nobody was talking summer rally any longer.

I played the ace. What I saw ahead was a replay of the huge bear market rally of 1973. That rally had taken the Dow from 851.90 on August 22 to a rally peak of 987.05 on October 26, a rise of 135.15 points. That was a rise of 15.8 percent. The same percentage rise from the July 24 low of 1,086.57 would take the Dow up to the 1,258 level. I became a short-term bull, playing what I saw as something similar to the summer of 1929.

Convinced that the blueprint for the coming rally had already been laid down in 1973, I had retained all the key *Wall Street Journal* statements made during the 1973 bear market rally. My job was clear: I wanted to prove beyond a shadow of a doubt that what lay ahead was a large rally with an exact duplication of fundamental, technical, psychological, and historical factors seen in the rally that had begun in August 1973. I presented the blueprint in my July 28 market letter:

THE 1973 RALLY THAT FOOLED THE MAJORITY

Date	Dow Closing	Wall Street Journal Quotes
8/24	863.49	"Market has more than discounted economic slowdown. Stocks are cheap."
8/27	870.71	"Market is very technical."

Date	Dow Closing	Wall Street Journal Quotes
8/28	872.07	"President Nixon says that there will be no recession next year. Market is base-building."
8/29	883.43	"Analysts are getting bullish."
8/30	882.53	"Foreign buying is in evidence. Investors are returning to the market, convinced that there will be no recession next year."
8/31	887.57	"Investment officers shucking earlier gloom. Attractive bargains."
9/4	895.40	"Market is base-building."
9/5	899.08	"Interest rates are peaking."
9/6	901.04	"Bargains for foreigners. Real growth predicted for 1974. Interest rates cresting."
9/7	898.63	"Market full of buying opportunities."
9/10	891.33	"Market is base-building. Interest rates have peaked."
9/11	885.76	"Low volume is encouraging."
9/12	881.32	"Market is acting well."
9/13	880.57	"Some fear of higher rates."
9/14	886.36	"Vice President of Chemical Bank Trust Department says that the bear market is over and sees dramatic change in the market for the better."
9/17	892.98	"Brokers are bullish."
9/18	891.26	"Merrill Lynch bullish."
9/19	910.37	"Highest volume since February. Broad-based bull market is in early stages."
9/20	920.53	"Classical signs of a bull market."
9/21	927.91	"The worst is over."

At this point, about 85 percent of the sucker rally was completed. The final day of the rally saw the maximum amount of bullishness.

Date	Dow Closing	Wall Street Journal Quotes
9/24	936.71	"Mutual funds coming in."
9/25	940.62	"Analysts getting very bullish."
9/26	949.50	"Change in psychology noted. Banks, mutual funds and other institutions think the market is going higher and there is a buying stampede under way."
9/27	953.26	"Basic upward trend appears to be firmly established."
9/28	947.09	"IBM is an excellent value."
10/1	948.82	"Extremely constructive market action."
10/2	956.81	"Interest rates have peaked."
10/3	964.40	"Investors are rushing to get back in."
10/26	987.05	"The market wants to go up. Sees uptrend resuming. We are convinced that a five-year decline ended last June."

It soon became very clear that in 1984 market psychology had not changed one iota from what it was in the summer of 1973.

III

Meanwhile, the parallels continued to grow in number.

PARALLEL 143

Market
No Precedent for the Current Situation

Seeing the market trending lower for the first half of 1984, accompanied by what was still thought to be a strong economy, many observers stated that they saw no precedent for this situation. They were puzzled. Such observers invariably were those who had been misguided bulls on the stock market all year, all devotees of the "bull market second leg" school.

With all the reports in 1929 of how business and the economy were continuing to forge ahead, conditions always described as "sound," many observers found it increasingly difficult to explain the September 1929 downturn in stock prices.

The "Abreast of the Market" column in the September 24, 1929, *Wall Street Journal* carried the following:

The important interests with large blocks of stock generally liquidate when the market is having one of its spectacular spurts during periods of great enthusiasm. However, as there is really no precedent for the current market situation, many in the financial district at the moment are decidedly puzzled regarding the outlook for the immediate future and sources of selling therefore will be watched closely.

PARALLEL 144

Market
Upturn in the Bond Market

As long as the bond market was falling, nobody was expecting a stock market rally. That had been the situation in May and June. The stock market was hostage to the bond market. However, the May–June base in bonds gave way to a July bond market upturn, thus setting the stage for the stock upturn. Stocks turned up violently after the July 24 bottom, the upturn attributed to falling interest rates as reflected in the improved bond market.

This was the parallel I was awaiting, and I was sure it now had arrived. The bond market turns up, triggers an explosive stock market rise, but then stocks peak and turn down while the bond market continues to improve. That is the situation that preceded the 1929 crash.

The psychology of the times was well expressed in the "Abreast of the Market" column in *The Wall Street Journal* of October 23, 1929:

> One of the leading commission and wire houses which turned cautious about the time the market was at its peak advising clients to take profits and which has been predicting the various turns in the market since that time with unusual accuracy is looking for a good rally to continue, and expresses the view that many stocks have reached their lows for some time.
>
> The firm pointed out that as there is nothing in the business situation to warrant further liquidation, a substantial recovery could carry stocks considerably higher. It adds that the best bargains will probably be found among the rails and oils.
>
> There has been quite a good bond market in the past two weeks and prices have moved forward. This is considered an encouraging sign, for market interests point out that stocks do not usually work into a prolonged bear movement when the bond market is showing improvement. The investment demand which has come into bonds has been larger than in some time.

This was exactly the touch I was looking for. The bond market back in 1929 touched bottom on October 4 and turned up for an entire year! The stock market responded on the upside for a brief rally and then a few weeks later recorded the greatest crash in history with the bond market still rising! They were hooked back in 1929, just as they were now, on the notion that stocks could not be in a prolonged bear market as long as the bond market was going up. How quickly the crash destroyed that popular notion. History showed that the rising bond market in 1929–30 was the first definitive sign of a *flight toward safety.* The bond market was being used as a repository for funds fleeing the stock market. However, the move back in 1929 wasn't back into corporates or municipals but into *governments,* the market which was thought to offer greater safety. Certainly the attractiveness of bonds didn't lie in high yields. Strength in bonds in October 1929 had to be seen as a warning, the same warning signs given in the upturn in the bond market in mid-1984.

Mid-1984 saw some famous analysts calling for the big "second leg" bull rally, basing their forecast on the new strength in the bond market. They, too, were slow to recognize that there was a growing flight to safety, a trend put in motion by the fears spreading since the collapse of the Continental Illinois bank. For several weeks the assets of the money market funds were rising, an additional sign that much important money was fleeing the stock market.

PARALLEL 145
Historical
Rumor of Another Rise in the Discount Rate

On July 9, 1929, there were rumors that the discount rate was to be raised. This rumor preceded the strong bond market rally and was soon forgotten.

On September 13, 1929, the "Abreast of the Market" column in *The Wall Street Journal* carried the following:

> After showing a comparatively firm tone for several hours yesterday, the stock market encountered bear pressure in heavy volume which led to renewed liquidation, during which many leading issues declined substantially. The supply came as a result of widely circulated rumors of another advance in the re-discount rate by the Federal Reserve Bank of New York.

In both cases interest rates turned down, the discount rate was not raised, and both markets enjoyed a brief technical rally which would precede the crash.

—————

Historical
Dividend and Interest Money Seeking Investment

Numerous references were made in July 1984 to the reinvestment of dividend and interest checks that would help propel the market into a bull market second leg.

Such references were as irrelevant then as they were back in 1929. People were mesmerized with fundamentals and failed to realize that the stock market at this time provided no investment opportunities. There wasn't enough time left for capital gains. Nevertheless, the die-hard bulls conjured up every excuse they could to justify their contention that the bull market that had begun in August 1982 was still alive.

Such misplaced optimism was present in September 1929 and was well expressed in the following quote from the "Broad Street Gossip" column in *The Wall Street Journal* of September 23, 1929:

> The Street will soon be talking about big end-of-the-year bonuses, hundreds of millions of end-of-the-year dividend and interest money seeking investment, things that some of the big wealthy corporations propose to put in the stockings of their shareholders. It certainly looks like the most prosperous Christmas in the history of Wall Street.

—————

Psychological
Profit-taking to Be Curbed

In July 1984 the capital gains stock-holding period was reduced from twelve months to six months. Many thought that this move, designed to bring people into the market, would be very bullish and prove to be a curb on profit-taking. I felt that it would prove to be one of the more important hooks that would lure people into buying into the rally I predicted, but it would also see them *holding their stocks too long*, awaiting a quick capital gain that would be *nonexistent* by January 1985.

The psychology was identical in 1929. It didn't matter what the specific hook was; there merely had to be something there that would appear to inhibit profit-taking, something that would keep people in the market when they should be getting out. In 1929 it was the proposed federal tax reduction.

In the "Broad Street Gossip" column in *The Wall Street Journal* of September 27, 1929, appeared the following:

> The Street regards proposed federal tax reduction as a very big bull card. It may mean an additional $200,000,000 available for investment. The bulls also say it will curb a lot of profit-taking in stocks this year.

I V

Despite the late July upturn in the stock market, things were not getting any easier on Wall Street. Merrill Lynch had laid off 2,500 to date, a move I had predicted the previous summer when the big brokerage concern's stock had been selling at $112 a share. The 2–1 stock split at that time signified trouble ahead, accurately forecasting the 1984 problems. I found it rather ludicrous that brokerage firms would be raising their commission rates at this time—not having the interests of the "little guy" in mind, but, rather, their own best interests. The rate hikes hit the smaller accounts the hardest. In a tough market, commission rates should have been lowered, not raised. I felt that it was a stupid move and would cost the industry dearly before very long. Many brokers were disturbed by the news, fearing the loss of many accounts. The discount brokers were retaining their low rates, and much business was shifted to the discount sector.

This move to raise commission rates coincided with the announced shortening of the capital gains period from twelve to six months. The change in the law definitely discriminated against the stock seller in favor of the buyer. Somebody who had been holding stocks for many months could not sell them now and qualify for the six-month holding period. One could therefore make a case that the simultaneous arrival of these two changes was a conspiracy to discourage the selling of stocks. Both of the moves were expected to backfire later on.

A few months earlier, President Reagan had been proudly pointing toward the Dow Jones Industrial Average as proof that his policies were working. Now no references to the stock market were forthcoming from the White House. *Business Week*, in the July 9 issue, pointing out that the latest rise in the prime rate was met by a deafening silence, in contrast to the criticism leveled at the previous boosts, believed that second-quarter statistics had convinced the administration that the economy was so vigorous that there was no chance of a politically damaging slowdown before the November election. I felt that the real reason for the lack of criticism was that they could not comment on the higher interest rates without refueling an argument that they finally knew they could not win: that the high recurring budgetary deficits were a direct cause of the higher interest rates. The May budget deficit had been the highest in history, over $33 billion; at the same time, the rising rates were negating the congressional budget reduction efforts. What I saw ahead for the stock market was clearly saying that the White House policies were not working.

The crux of the entire format of what lay head was the Kondratieff deflationary wave, the same wave that went into effect in 1929. This is what best explained why commodity prices were collapsing, and the message was clear. Gold collapsed at this time, breaking the January lows, further accenting the deflationary trend.

I knew that my 1929 scenario was not popular. Not in a popularity contest, however, I felt that it was my duty to protect investors from what I saw ahead and I was proud of my advice which had underscored the selling of all stocks in the spring of 1983.

The parallels with 1929 had been proliferating since January. So many things could not duplicate without the key message of 1929 also duplicating. There were far too many parallels to attribute the duplications to luck or coincidence. Every day further evidence of the deflationary cycle was being revealed. For instance, *The Wall Street Journal* on July 19 carried an item headlined: "New Zealand Dollar Falls; Trades at 50 U.S. Cents." On the same day: "OECD Warns Australia on Wider Budget Deficit." Also on the same page: "Tokyo Shares Decline as Trading in Riccar Is Suspended, Yen Falls." Also on same page: "European Nations Will Try to Refinance Billions of Debt to Lower Interest Costs."

Seeing these parallels and noting the parabolic rise in the London and Tokyo markets by early April, I had interpreted such rises as signaling an imminent downturn in both markets, the start of major bear markets. This was in keeping with a worldwide trend, the strong U.S. dollar forcing all currencies and markets to their knees. Central bank rates were being forced up to protect faltering currencies, with recent hikes in Canada and Great Britain in keeping with the 1929 parallels. Additional parallels were seen in the mounting troubles for Prime Minister Margaret Thatcher, the coal miners' and dockworkers' strikes, exports piling up on the docks, and the lowest level for the pound in history. The political implications were interesting in view of the English change of government in 1929.

V

So, while a bearish case could be made in May 1929 and a similar bearish case was evident in July 1984, both portions of the cycle did not preclude a huge rally that was to set up the mechanism for the end-game gambit. At first, the strong buy signal of July bothered me. Then, as I viewed it to be similar in nature to the final rally of the summer of 1929, I saw it in clear perspective as not contrary to the major scenario. So, despite the evidence at hand, the technical evidence for what lay ahead was clear. The market was headed straight up.

18

The Guns of August

[AUGUST 1984]

I

The guns of August went off on schedule. So explosive was the rise that most people couldn't understand why its longevity was so quickly stunted. They could not see at the time that the entire move was simply a demonstration of brainless herd instinct on the part of mutual fund managers with their hope that it would trigger a public stampede like the one in August 1982. They were the stampede and they were destined to hold the bag for a long time.

August 1 saw the Dow catapult over 19 points; August 2 saw a further rise of over 31 points; and August 3 registered a stunning gain of 36 points. These outstanding advances saw the Dow close above the 1,200 level for the first time since February 2. The August 3 rise, one of the greatest in history, set an all-time volume record of over 230 million shares, equaling the trading volume for the entire year of 1923! This blockbuster of a rise grabbed financial headlines all over the world and Wall Street fell for it hook, line, and sinker. Brokers all over the country were on the phones all day telling their clients that interest rates were coming down and that the second leg of the great bull market was underway, being particularly careful to remind them of what had happened in August 1982.

Something was very wrong, however. It had to be the same thing that gnawed in the stomach of Jesse Livermore. Technically, the fly in the ointment was the advance/decline line, the measurement of how many stocks were going up and how many were going down. The Dow Jones Industrial Average had rocketed upward from the July 24 closing low of 1,086.57 to over the 1,200 level in eight trading days and yet the advance/decline line was sharply below the May level when the Dow had peaked on a bear market rally at 1,186.56. That told me that it was the great blue chip rally I had predicted and that I had my needed summer of 1929 parallel. That was precisely the evidence that Jesse Livermore moved on in 1929, as well as the same evidence that Roger Babson based his great 1929 crash prediction on. So here it was happening again in precisely the same manner.

While I had foreseen the violent July–August rally as a necessary precursor to the panic and crash, I saw the rally as necessarily being one of short duration, the function of which was to create the biggest bull trap of the year and the most fatal if one hadn't taken advantage of it and sold every stock he owned. The chart of the Dow Jones Industrial Average gave the impression that the market was breaking out of a giant base, but to gain true perspective, one had to look at the chart for the year. There, the true picture appeared: the bull trap of early January and early May and the current approach to an extremely overbought zone.

The trading barometer flashed a sell signal on August 3, and as its record had shown it always to be a few days early (as all good indicators should be), my followers were able to dump their long positions into the August 10 final blowoff rise, which had taken the Dow Jones Industrial Average intraday high to 1,253.75.

Ironically, the producer of the *Crossfire* show, Cable News Network, called and asked me if I could fly in on August 3 and do the show with Pat Buchanan and Senator Dodd that night. Having other interview commitments, I turned them down, but did agree to do the show the following Tuesday. I knew that Pat Buchanan was going to rake me over the coals, thinking I had missed the huge July–August rally. When Tuesday rolled around, I tucked a copy of the *Orlando Sentinel* in my inside pocket and at the most propitious moment in the show pulled it out and held it up to the cameras. There it was, my story of the huge imminent rise as detailed in the July 20 edition of that paper. It proved that Buchanan hadn't been reading his mail, inasmuch as I had him as a complimentary subscriber. He still thought I was singing one theme like a broken clock. After finally realizing that I had called the entire rally, what he didn't realize was that this rally was the necessary precursor to the crash scenario which was still very much alive, more alive than ever. In a series of varied interviews, I stressed two things about the rally: (1) The Dow would not be taken to new highs, and (2) the rally constituted the biggest bull trap of the year.

Wall Street didn't see it that way. Nothing was more fascinating than watching the chemistry of the psychological juices at work as the market skyrocketed in the first three days of August. They were totally hooked on the rally.

In order for the anticipated bull trap to occur, several things had to fall in place, and they were doing exactly that. First of all, the rise had to get everyone wildly bullish. The exceedingly high-volume upside breakout above the Dow 1,140 level had accomplished this. That told other stock market technicians that the market was signaling still higher levels ahead. That was my first requirement, and it was being met on schedule. Psychologically, the timing for the trap could not have been better. This was August, and nobody was going to forget what had happened in August 1982. With such an explosive rise occurring in the month of August, everybody would get to thinking that this might be another August 1982, and such psychology in itself would be enough to propel the market higher. Besides this, the cover story was more than apparent: Interest rates had crested, the economy was slowing, and the Fed would not tighten money. The sky was now the limit. One would also hear that this was the second leg to the great bull market. The cover story was identical with the same one that hooked Wall Street in the 1973 bear market rally.

What made the strong advance all the more convincing in its early stages was the fact that the TV networks not only were stressing the bear side too strongly in mid to late July, teaching the techniques of going short and buying put options, but were rather skeptical all the way up on the rally because they suddenly remembered what happened following all previous upside volume explosions in the market in 1984. This was simply an example of human psychology. Once people think they have the key to the market, *the market changes the locks*. All the previous widely advertised predictions of a summer rally had gone sour, and thus the market was set up to record a violent move to the upside and catch Wall Street with their pants down. Now the mechanism was in place to blind everyone to the next major market move.

While the market was exploding higher in the opening days of August, I stated that this kind of upside momentum would be difficult to kill. In periods of such unbridled enthusiasm, we have to let psychology run its course. I knew this rise would resurrect all the bulls who got caught in the January euphoria and give them the *mistimed* chance to tell their clients that they *knew* the bull market would resume. This was what bull traps were all about. I told my followers that I didn't give a whit if the Dow went to 1,200, 1,225, or 1,250 or had stopped dead at 1,166. Nothing was going to keep the crash scenario more alive than a rally that looked like it was taking the market to heaven. The shorts were caught in the net of fear, sensing that this rise was something very much out of the ordinary. These, of course, were *not* normal markets, and thus it was in keeping with my scenario that the sucker rallies had to be *huge, convincing, and showing no end in sight*. But, of course, by its very nature and purpose, the upturn had a definite limit. The market is fair and it wasn't about to reward all those who had missed the January top by letting them off the hook scot-free. This rally was designed to make such people think they were about to reach safety and then, when they were all breathing with relief, suddenly sink their ship.

When nailed down by Lou Dobbs on Cable News Network's *Moneyline* show on August 2, Robert Stovall said that this was *the second leg of the bull market*. His firm, Dean Witter Reynolds, was currently advertising that position in many newspapers. In order for the developing bull trap to be validated, these were the kinds of statements that had to be made. The public had to be totally sold on that "second leg" story and to be constantly reminded that this was August, August, August, shades of 1982. If this was the rally that fooled the majority, as I firmly believed it was, it was taking place roughly seven months after the January peak, following the same timing that had occurred in the 1973–74 bear market, when the rally that fooled the majority occurred in August 1973, seven months after the market top. These turns habitually occurred during what I described as the second phase of the bear market. The 1973 bear market rally cover story was that interest rates had crested and that there would be no recession in 1974. Wasn't this the identical story in August 1984? It certainly was, and the story was being repeatedly told by all the misguided bulls.

The very fact that so many were looking for the second leg of a bull market that had died in early 1983 told me that not enough people had accepted the reality of the bear market that then prevailed. They still looked upon the downturn as a correction in an ongoing bull market. The July–August rally for them still further disguised the bear market and they were to find that by the time they realized that their entire bullish scenario had died in 1983, it would be too late. They would again be locked into a vortex of price destruction.

Back in 1973 I made a big mistake in thinking that the market that year was simply making a correction in an ongoing bull market. I had based that notion on the fact that the Dow had not retraced more than 50 percent of the preceding 1970–73 rise. The 50 percent level stood at 841 and the lowest the Dow had gotten to prior to the big bear market rally was 851.90, reaching that level on August 22, 1973. Then ensued the sharp nine-week rally of 135 points, and my complacence did not prepare me for what was to follow that rally. The same type of faulty analysis was now entrapping the bulls. Because the Dow never broke under the 50 percent retracement level of 1,032, these bulls thought that the entire 1983–84 decline was a correction in an ongoing bull market. Besides this, it was important to point out that three things happened on the 1973 bear market rally that looked very convincing from the bull's standpoint:

1. The Dow 200-day trendline was penetrated on the upside.
2. The Dow retraced more than 50 percent of the preceding decline.
3. General Motors had moved above its trendline.

Providing identical signals, the August 1984 rally saw the Dow 200-day trendline penetrated on the upside on August 2, bettering the 1,160 level, and a move above 1,187 which was immediately forthcoming showed the Dow as having retraced more than 50 percent of the preceding Dow decline. General Motors had moved above its own trendline. As bullish as those changes looked on the surface, they did not alter the big picture any more than did similar changes back in 1973.

The key to understanding the 1973 rally and designating it as a rally in a bear market was seen in the advance/decline line. By the time the rally ended, the advance/decline line was still over 10,000 short of the February 1973 level, when the Dow had last stood at 987. In the August 1984 rally, the advance/decline line was running woefully short of the May levels. Also, with the attractiveness of the bond market, the current institutional cash would not be concentrated in equities but would be divided between the two markets, with an increasingly heavier commitment to bonds. So, as the market raced toward seriously overbought levels, the handwriting was clearly on the wall that it would not last and that it had served its purpose well.

II

The A-Dis Short-Term Trading Barometer, which had caught the entire July–August rise with the buy signal of July 13, reverted to a sell signal on August 3. This enabled my followers to take their long profits and short into this churning and dangerous market above the Dow 1,200 level. In anticipation of the record-setting volume rally, I had stated that the prime purpose of the rally was to turn everyone bullish. I had anticipated the makings of the third bull trap of the year. The first bull trap had occurred in early January and the second one in early May. Now the third one was being seen, the biggest of all. For the trap to be set up, it was first necessary that the Dow cross the 1,140 level, which it did without hesitation. When it did that, other stock market technicians automatically had to become bullish. According to William Jiler,[1] the higher the volume, the greater the trap. The sensational volume, therefore, was not seen as a parallel to August 1982, the start of a great upswing, but, rather, as the necessary accompaniment to the largest bull trap of the year—an ending rather than a beginning.

In turning everyone bullish, the upswing had to produce *a change in investor psychology.* That was another prerequisite for a major bull trap. "There's a psychological shift," said David A. Lee of Robinson Humphrey American Express, Atlanta. In my July 28 market letter I had used a September 26, 1973, quote referring to the *change in psychology* near the end of that 135-point bear market rally.

---

[1]William L. Jiler, *How Charts Can Help You in the Stock Market* (New York: Commodity Research Publications, 1962), p. 149.

Bull traps always blind the bulls rather than the bears. The reason for this is also psychological. Being in a bear market, the bulls had been sitting for months with stock losses, and they were so grateful to see a huge rally that, of course, they didn't see it as a trap at all. They saw it as rationalizing their previous bad judgment.

In anticipation of the sharp rise in the Dow, I had listed all the *Wall Street Journal* quotes which had been published during the 135-point bear market rally of August–October 1973. With what I had seen thus far, it looked like the market had already done the equivalent of nine weeks' work. The *Journal* was clicking off duplicate quotes left and right. We had seen: (1) stocks are cheap, (2) analysts are getting bullish, (3) foreign buying is in evidence, (4) attractive bargains, (5) interest rates are peaking, (6) real growth predicted, (7) brokers are bullish, (8) the bear market is over, (9) change in psychology noted, and (10) investors are rushing to get back in. That should have told any student of stock market history approximately where the market stood in the continuing bear market.

The August 4 issue of *The New York Times* business page was a collector's item, worth filing away for future reference. In reading it, one would have instantly recognized the 1929 psychology. The euphoria expounded in that issue was beyond anything I had ever read about the stock market. There was a volume chart showing all the record volume days, and it looked exactly like the volume chart of the 1920s, including the parabolic blowoffs in 1928 and 1929. Some of the quotes in this issue were outstanding: "After the end of this year the Dow will never again go under 1,100" (Philip Erlanger of Advest, Hartford, Connecticut). "This is a real quality rally measured by leadership and volume" (Alfred E. Goldman of A. G. Edwards, St. Louis, Missouri).

But the quotes got even better and still more revealing: In the August 8 *Wall Street Journal,* Robert Walsh of Rotan Mosle, Houston, was quoted as saying: "A lot of people are scared. They haven't made money in so damned long they want to get out right away. . . . We've waited a whole year for this to happen, let's enjoy it."

If I were a broker, I wouldn't have wanted to state publicly that my clients hadn't made money in so damned long that they now wanted to get out. I also would not have wanted to admit that I had waited a whole year for something to happen. It proved the point that most people buy and then hold. That is why most people were holding stocks at a loss. Good brokers make money for their clients in both up markets *and* down markets; thus, when a buying opportunity comes along, such as in mid-July 1984, they have huge profits with which to play the swing, not losses which they can only hope to cut.

I had to demonstrate that these "new" bulls were the same old ones who had been wrong all year. I explained why Mr. Walsh made the comments he did in the August 8 *Journal* and why those comments stemmed from his own frustration. The proof was right there in the *Journal* issues of January 11, February 17, and March 29, 1984:

> Robert Walsh, senior vice president at Rotan Mosle, Houston, views the market as "in the early stages of the second phase of the bull market." He expects the industrial average at some point during 1984 to reach the 1,480–1,530 level. He notes that the market reached bull market peaks during three of the past four presidential election years. [January 11.]

> Robert Walsh agreed that the "market is in the process of making a slow turn, but after the steep price waterfall that the market has had in recent weeks it probably will be a U-turn rather than a V-turn." [February 17.]

> "During the past five weeks the market absorbed a lot of negativism as the industrial average moved in a trading range between 1,130 and 1,180," asserted Robert Walsh. Noting that the high technology stocks were "starting to show some life in the past couple of sessions," he said "this indicated that the worst is over because they were the first to get hit in the recent correction." He also maintained that the upturn in the utility average "indicates that interest rates aren't going to rise to any extent." [March 29.]

I cited these examples as a teaching exercise. Mr. Walsh's clients, having been told to buy stocks all year, and now registering losses, were, of course, anxious to bail out on any good rally and cut their losses. Mr. Walsh, on the other hand, finally getting a good rally, wanted to keep his clients in the market and play the rally. Any broker who had sustained losses for his clients would feel that way. The clients, on the other hand, saw it differently. It was their money and they wanted to cut losses. This psychology had a great deal to do with where the market was ultimately headed.

The institutions started the July–August rally following Paul Volcker's very bullish remarks of July 25. One had to keep in mind that the institutions were dealing with *other people's* money, not their own. They had the power to *start* things, but the job of keeping things going reverted to the public. The public was holding stocks *mostly at a loss;* thus, in order to buy something, they had to sell something. Since what they had to sell was showing them a loss, they lacked the necessary buying power after a 200-point decline *that they hadn't seen coming.* Therefore, while it appeared that the public was flocking back in, the party was ending.

I cited another quote from the August 4 issue of *The New York Times:*

> Steven R. Larson, sales manager for Richards, Merrill & Peterson, Inc., a one-office retail brokerage house in Spokane, Washington, heard from one of his clients Thursday for the first time since August 1983. The customer's stock, which had lost ground all year, had jumped seven points in the market rally, and yesterday she told him to sell it if it started to retreat.

That illustrated the fact that most people were holding stocks at a loss. These people would use the July–August rally as a selling opportunity, and it was to become increasingly apparent that the institutions had detonated an explosion that could not last.

Once again I felt that we were living through one of the most interesting of the 1929 parallels, the absence of any lasting pattern, what Jesse Livermore saw as the market seesawing under the influence of unknown forces. It was clearly a time to counsel those who had cleared out to stay out.

The week of August 6–10 was such a period. It was a week of wide swings on high volume with many things *out of gear.* It was a week of heavy public participation as the Dow extended the rally *on uncertain technical ground.* Late in the week, many observers were already talking of new bull market highs dead ahead, just as they had during the 1973 bear market rally. My overriding notion here was that regardless of where the Dow finally stopped going up, the July–August rally was *one terminating entity.* Any reasonable trader faced with such huge short-term profits would be taking them in the week of August 6–10, and the technical action in that week underscored the wisdom of that move.

III

The August 6 bulletin detailing the barometer sell signal of August 3 was received by my subscribers just in time for them to sell into the huge blowoff market of August 10, when the Dow had rocketed upward to an intraday high of 1,253.75. Ironically, this market blowoff is what turned most analysts bullish, very bullish. It was the required precursor to what was to follow.

The explosive and short-lived bear market rally that had begun in July had ended. It had been sensational while it lasted, and it died as sensationally as it had begun, flaming out in a stunning, predictable reversal of classic proportions. Obviously the rally had no long-term implications for investors, any more than did the great rally in the summer of 1929. The sole purpose was to make everybody bullish and, once that was achieved, to spring the trap— the most important of all bull traps.

The rally ended on the morning of August 10 as the public herd instinct pushed the Dow to an intraday high of 1,253.75, *only to see one of the most classic reversals to the downside on record.* By August 15, the Dow closed under the 1,200 level with no hesitation, breaking almost 50 points under the August 10 high.

Since I had outlined my expectations in July of *a possible 135-point bear market rally,* the actual rally of 137.48 points could hardly have been termed a surprise. It was a fulfillment of the prediction of "the rally that fools the majority," occurring during the second phase of a bear market. I had pointed to the 135-point bear market rally of 1973 as the most probable example to be followed. In the anticipation of this, it was easy to predict the type of comments that would be seen in *The Wall Street Journal.* One only had to review the comments made during the 1973 bear market rally and watch for similar comments on this rally.

By the morning of August 10, it had become apparent that "investors were rushing to get back in" and that "people were convinced that the long decline had truly ended," the identical sentiment that accompanied the rally peak in late October 1973. But the best proof lay in the price action itself, both the 1973 and 1984 rallies ending in precisely the same manner.

After the 1973 rally ended, the Dow was smashed to new bear market lows in a startling, almost 200-point plunge over the next several weeks. While it could not be predicted with certainty that the identical pattern would be repeated, this did point up the possibilities for huge profits to be made on the short side of the market.

But I had to go a giant step further. Yes, I used 1973 as my example for the expected bear market rally, but the current bear market loomed a great deal larger than that of 1973. I was, of course, thinking of 1929. Ever since the spring of 1983, I had been reporting the growing proliferation of the 1929 parallels. The important point at this time was that the July–August rally enhanced the crash scenario rather than diluted it. I stressed that all rallies are not followed by crashes but *all crashes are preceded by rallies.* Therefore, with the vast number of psychological, historical, market, and technical 1929 parallels existing, rallies were potentially dangerous. The one just seen smacked very much of August 1929.

Others (though in the smallest of minorities) were beginning to see some of those 1929 parallels. Julian M. Snyder, publisher of the *International Moneyline* newsletter, was well aware of these and had often cited many of them in his letters. At this time he was citing the following: *bad economic signs*

1. An agricultural depression, falling farm prices, and farm real estate collapse.
2. A huge pyramid of business debt on top of a very thin equity base.
3. A shaky banking system bulging with substandard and nonperforming loans.
4. A rising tide of protectionism.
5. A mountain of international debt owed to banks by less developed nations.
6. A record high margin debt.

I had talked about all of these at great length. Current market concerns were mostly centered on the shaky banking system and the international debts. More U.S. banks had failed in 1984 than in all of 1983, and the total since the end of 1982 was now up to 97 banks, the highest number of bank failures since 1939. In the summer of 1929, Snyder pointed out, the stock market had rallied against the identical background of events, and he termed it *sheer madness,* which, of course, was another parallel in itself.

Good times were breeding bad times. The failure of the Penn Square bank, which in turn led to the downfall of Continental Illinois, began during the fast-and-loose times of the energy boom. The threatened collapse of Financial Corp. of America stemmed from too rapid an expansion of their mortgage business when rates were low in the spring of 1983 and their mistaken assumption that rates would fall further. The stock plunge for Financial Corp. of America was thus far greater than that of Continental Illinois, having dropped from a high of 33 down to the latest closing at this time of 4⅞ in a shorter period of time. When times had been good, the stock had been split just prior to the worst part of the decline and it was cited as one of fifty companies having had the most rapid earnings growth. All during 1983 I had been citing the bearishness of all the stock splits and had revealed that the companies having the fastest earnings growth were among the stocks hardest hit in the bear market. Additional proof that the management of Financial Corp. of America didn't have the slightest knowledge of the stock market was seen in the company's holding of ten million shares of American Express, failing to have sold them in 1983 when the bear market was starting. The plight of Financial Corp. of America once again pointed up that when the market was on a down signal, the events would always occur to explain why the stock market went down.

An important highlight of the mid-August trading was the growing evidence of *a flight to safety,* the heavy shifting out of certificates of deposit and into the ultimate in safety—the 91-day Treasury bills. This was seen as seriously foreshadowing additional troubles for the big banks. Julian Snyder had pointed out in his publication that German and Japanese banks alone had some $95 billion on deposit with the big American banks. He had also noted that a major problem at a big bank, such as with an oil company, could trigger a run that would dwarf the Continental Illinois crisis. Events were moving swiftly now. The Federal Deposit Insurance Corporation was reporting a record 721 banks currently on their problem list.

I had described the August market peaking pattern as churning and dangerous—one day up, the next sharply down, the next sharply up, etc. As Jesse Livermore had noted in similar stock market peaks, it was no place for an amateur. Internally, however, a clear story was being told. The specialists were very busy arranging to lock the public in once again with huge losses.

IV

Barton Biggs was interviewed by *Barron's* in the August 13 issue. His chief claim was that stocks were as cheap the week before as they were at the August

1982 bottom and as they were in the spring of 1949. He said he thought stocks were incredibly cheap on the basis of real earnings. He thought the upsurge was going to last for a while, and at the worst would be a rally back to the old highs. He saw the 1,100 level as an outside bottom if the market came down again.

His statement that stocks were cheap was fascinating, inasmuch as it echoed another of the 1973 bear market rally quotes as carried in *The Wall Street Journal,* that precise statement having been made in the August 24, 1973, *Journal* at the outset of that 135-point bear market rally: "Market has more than discounted economic slowdown. Stocks are cheap." An important distinction, however, was that in 1973 the statement was made at the *start* of the 135-point rally whereas Biggs made his statement *after* the Dow had rallied 137 points.

Numerous references had been made about the cheapness of stocks at times when stocks weren't cheap at all. Peter Furniss, vice president of Lehman Brothers Kuhn Loeb, contended in the *Journal* of March 30, 1984, that "stocks are cheap." But, more important, during the sharp October 1929 bear market rally that saw the Dow rise 8.5 percent in only five sessions, there were numerous references in the *Journal* as to what "bargains" stocks were, how cheap they were, and how attractive. To equate exactly with the 1973 bear market rally, the Dow in 1984 would have had to rise to the 1,257 level. Stopping at an intraday high of 1,253.75 on August 10 was close enough to qualify as an excellent technical reproduction.

In combing the literature on technical analysis, I couldn't find any discussions whatsoever on Dow closing levels versus Dow intraday levels. I would think that all valid breakouts would be required to exceed the previous intraday highs or lows. A good case in point was provided by the market in August. The intraday Dow high was recorded on August 10 at 1,253.75, but the highest Dow closing up to that time was 1,224.05. Then on August 21 the Dow scored a new rally closing high of 1,239.73 and the best intraday high reading was 1,250.55 on August 22. The failure to better the intraday high of August 10 was extremely important. It had crystallized the fullest extent of the technical rally, encapsulating the maximum internal upside momentum. The Net Field Trend, a powerfully important indicator of true market strength, peaked at +19 on August 21 and 22. A reading of +19 was a very high number and had equated in the past with important historical market highs. The period was very reminiscent of September 1929. In that fateful month, the Dow had peaked on September 3, but the New York Times Index didn't peak until later in the month. Nevertheless, true technical strength had fully peaked by the earlier date.

A reconfirmed sell signal was recorded on August 22 and it took on added technical dimensions because a very brief buy signal that had occurred earlier did not take the Dow to a new intraday high, and that was an important market message.

The July–August rally had done its work well, producing widespread bullishness. Frank Cappiello, Jr., a regular panelist on the *Wall Street Week* TV program, having looked for 1,500 on the Dow in 1983 and 1984, was moved to predict 1,400 on the Dow by election day. But such bullishness wasn't being translated into portfolio gains. Only a bare handful of the stock market advisory services had made any money for their clients in 1984. Most were showing losses ranging as high as 39 percent, according to the *Hulbert Financial Digest.*

In this bear market, which most analysts had been reading as a continuing bull market, the monthly short interest rose sharply on the latest report and the market's *response* to the figures the next day (August 22) was a sharp reversal to the downside. People generally failed to realize that the short interest was a corollary to overall market volume, just as it was in 1929. The volume in 1929 was the highest in history up to that time and so was the short interest. People seldom looked at the other side of the coin. If the short interest was the highest in history, so also was the *long* interest. In terms of sheer numbers, the risk was far greater on the long side should the shorts be proven right. It was well to keep in mind that the stock market topped out in 1983 and declined in the face of the largest short interest in history.

But the new bullishness was not going to go away in a hurry. The great July–August upsurge saw advisers responding at a much faster pace than they did in 1982. According to *Investors Intelligence,* after the August 1982 upturn the percentage of outright bulls did not reach 50 percent until February 1983, but this month over 50 percent of the services became bullish in a mere two-week period. That was the sign of a rally based more on hope than substance.

One of the key characteristics of the end of the 1973 bear market rally was a growing certainty that the long decline of the preceding period was over. The *Dick Davis Digest* of August 20, 1984, confirmed the presence of that characteristic: "In my opinion, there is no need to look for hidden meanings or traps. The bell has rung. The market's frustrating 13-month downtrend has ended and, for at least a while, the direction is likely to be north."

Contrast that statement with the following one reported in *The Wall Street Journal* on October 26, 1973, when the 135-point bear market rally had peaked out the day before: "The market wants to go up. Sees uptrend resuming. We are convinced that a five-year decline ended last June." Immediately following that statement, the Dow dropped about 200 points over the next five weeks to new bear market lows.

And contrast those statements with the ones made in the *Journal* back in October 1929 when a bear market rally that saw the Dow *not* going to new highs brought out a plethora of remarks that "the bull is back." I saw the stage set for the probable replay of one of the greatest stock market dramas of all time.

An additional parallel was provided by John Bollinger, the technician for the Financial News Network, who stated on August 23 that "the market wants to go up." That precise phrase appeared in the *Journal* on October 26, 1973, the day before the 135-point bear market rally ended.

V

An important repeat of Parallel 116 was recorded at this time. Parallel 116 was a psychological one—the return of the bulls. Whenever the phrase "The bull is back" is used, the probability is very high that the market is entering a bull trap. It was seen in January 1984 just prior to a large break in stock prices. It cropped up again in April during the first rally in the bear market. It was most prevalent in late August; for example, the August 27 issue of *Barron's* ran a whole section headlined "The Bulls Are Back." A few weeks before the great 1929 crash the phrase appeared in the October 8, 1929, *Journal*.

August 1984 exhibited another 1929 parallel.

PARALLEL 148

Historical
Firm Money Policy No Longer Justified

In view of the documented slowdown in the economy and the assured upturn in the bond market reflecting a sharp downturn in short-term interest rates, it was widely expressed in many quarters that the Federal Reserve Board's firm money policy was no longer justified and that it would be abandoned in favor of lowering rates further. This belief was strengthened by the notion that the Fed would cooperate with the Reagan forces in order to help reelect the incumbent president.

This constituted a disturbing parallel with equal pressure on the Federal Reserve Board to ease rates in 1929 and abandon a firm money policy. *The Wall Street Journal* ran a piece in the October 24 issue headlined "Bank System in Healthy Shape. Reserve Board's Firm Money Policy No Longer Justified, Being Abandoned." This parallel was to take on added significance by November 1984, when the Treasury was faced with a dilemma. On the one hand, lower interest rates were urged so as to help a sagging economy, but at the same time this would weaken the dollar and drive foreigners out of dollar-denominated investments.

19

The Reincarnation of Roger Babson

[SEPTEMBER 1984]

I

As the market limped through the final dog days of August, it approached September with a degree of understandable nervousness. What the bulls had thought was a successful launch in August was not working out.

I was scheduled to appear September 4 on the Financial News Network's *Money Talk* program in Santa Monica. The next day marked the anniversary of an important event in market history. It was on September 5, 1929, that Roger Babson made his famous crash prediction. That prediction was reported in the September 6 *Wall Street Journal,* as it sought to explain why stocks had been up in the morning of the fifth and down so sharply in the afternoon:

> Considerable attention was attracted by an address before the Annual National Business Conference by Roger W. Babson in which he predicted a stock market crash that would cause a decline of from 60 to 80 points in the Dow Jones barometer. Mr. Babson declared that the majority of stocks were not following the leaders, pointing out that 614 of the 1,200 stocks listed on the New York Stock Exchange have declined in value since the first of the year.
>
> However, many experienced Wall Street observers feel that this selectivity has been the market's greatest safeguard. It is argued that so long as such marked discrimination is exercised the general list may go along for some time before any reversal of trend is seen. Shrewd students of speculation predict that a long series of five and six million share sessions will give warning of the approaching culmination of the present phase of the Coolidge-Hoover bull market.
>
> But Babson's forecast of a crash that would rival the collapse of the Florida land boom induced some frightened liquidation, which gave impetus to the

downward movement in the general list. Stop-loss orders were caught in large numbers, and the whole market was extremely weak during the last hour. Bad breaks occurred in Steel, American Can, Du Pont, Johns-Manville and other trading favorites, and the market continued under heavy pressure to the close.

Jesse Livermore, knowing that Babson was going to speak on September 5, didn't wait to launch a major bear raid. Livermore knew Babson's market position, which was largely based on the declining advance/decline line. Livermore's research had uncovered the same technical truths.[1] While *The Wall Street Journal* reported on September 5 that "nothing occurred in the outside news to account for the reactionary tendencies which swept over the general list" the day before, we can be pretty sure that Livermore had a big hand in helping to push the market down the day before the Babson speech.

As I walked into the FNN studio in Santa Monica on September 4, these things were uppermost in my mind. Inasmuch as the very thing that Babson saw in 1929 was occurring in 1984, I was compelled to issue a similar warning on that nationally televised show, and, of course, I did. I could point out that over half the stocks listed on the New York Stock Exchange had declined since the first of the year, the identical statement that Babson had made. Of course, it occurred to me that rather than being able simply to chronicle the proliferating 1929 parallels, I personally was able to embody one of the parallels:

PARALLEL 149
Historical
Babson 1929 Crash Prediction

Babson's prediction was ridiculed by *The Wall Street Journal* but it turned out to be right. The ridicule was largely based on the fact that Babson had been predicting the crash for some time. My predictions of a coming crash were published in the spring of 1983 and were equally ridiculed.

As it turned out, Babson wasn't bearish enough. The parallel would differ in that respect, but the rest of the comparison was faultless. I gave advice identical to Babson's: Liquidate all debt—sell all stocks—transfer funds into the money market funds, Treasury bills, and insured accounts in safe banks. I recommended these measures because, like Babson, I saw the increasing imminence of a stock market crash. Like Babson, I would be criticized for my advice and there would be a media effort to discredit my remarks. But, like Babson's advice, mine would also enable people to avoid the great market troubles that lay ahead.

[1]Gordon Thomas and Max Morgan-Witts, *The Day the Bubble Burst* (New York: Penguin Books, 1980) p. 191.

Robert Prechter, the popular Elliott Wave theorist, foresaw a 100-point advance from the Dow 1,223.28 level and stated that he saw no type of 1929 situation or bear market. A characteristic of the big break in 1929 was that almost nobody saw it coming. However, there was a small band of people in 1929 who were generally ignored in the wave of optimism that served to blind the majority. Babson's views were shared by Alexander Noyes, the financial editor of *The New York Times*, Joe Kennedy, and Jesse Livermore. An equally small band was noted in 1984. It consisted of Eliot Janeway, Tom Holt, Julian Snyder, Donald Hoppe, Dr. John King, Martin Weiss, Al Sindlinger, and Arch Crawford. There may have been others, but these were the better publicized of the extremely bearish views. The small band of bears was proven correct while the majority lost their shirts.

II

The sell signal of August 22 took on special significance because I expected the predicted July–August rally had been expected to equate with the 1973 bear market rally of 15.8 percent. It managed to put together a rise of 14 percent. Following that rally, the Dow in 1973 had plunged 200 points to a new bear market low. A number of advisory services had picked up on my 1973 comparison but had only seen it in retrospect. My entire bullish case in July had been based on the expectations of a duplication of the 1973 bear market rally following the barometer's July buy signal. How long it would take to duplicate that experience was debatable, but there was no question in my mind that the ultimate resolution of the technical problem had to be a smash.

The very purpose of the summer rally was to turn everyone bullish. It succeeded. *Investors Intelligence* at this time showed that 54 percent of the advisory services they monitored were bullish. The August 27 issue of *Timer Digest* showed the ten top market timers as nine bullish and one bearish. I was the lone bear, having sold into the August 10 Dow intraday high of 1,253.75. It was noted that most of those market timers had turned bullish on August 10, the worst possible day to have done so.

Like the Olympic fireworks, the early Wall Street display of pyrotechnics had lit up the early August skies as institutions led the bullish parade, with hundreds of millions of shares snatched up in what was generally thought to be the long-awaited second leg of a bull market. Forewarned that the brief July–August run-up constituted the third 1984 bull trap, the smart money had sold out their long positions at the August peak. Most people, however, attracted like fireflies to the early August explosive rise, were still in the market, awaiting a replay of the early August rally. Their patience was becoming increasingly expensive. They didn't realize that they bought right into the biggest sucker rally of the year. With most of them sitting on their hands after the August run-up, volume had shrunk to a mere fraction of the early August records.

The low volume was seen to be very bearish. Market commentators seldom stressed that point. People buy stocks, then hold them, and then eventually sell them. People bought stocks in great numbers in early August. That drove volume to record highs. Now they were holding those stocks, awaiting a big profit. But holding a stock makes no contribution whatsoever to market volume. That was why a decline following a big advance always would start out on low volume. The longer the trend lasts, the more disappointed the holders become. Eventually they start to throw in the towel, realizing that they may have made a big mistake. Then volume rises. Picture a huge building having one revolving-door entrance. A man sits at a window in a building across the street with binoculars trained on the entrance. He is on a stakeout. He reports to his boss that he saw ten million people go into the building in early August. Only people going in and out through that revolving door affected market volume. The observer saw only a handful of people come out of the door. He reports that most people were still in the building. The boss tells him that a fire has broken out on the roof and to report back on how many people are leaving the building. Still seeing only a few people leaving, the observer has to conclude that most of those ten million people are not aware that the building is on fire. Increasing awareness of the fire would cause more people to head for the exit.

That was the situation at that time. Most people were still in the market building and the exits would not become dangerously crowded until there was a general awareness that the building was on fire.

III

PARALLEL 150

Historical
Economy Slowing Down

By 1929 the superstructure of the economy had been weakening for some time. The building cycle had peaked in 1926 at the crest of the Florida land boom and an agricultural depression had set in the same year. By 1929 weaknesses were showing up in commodity prices and in the textile industry. Overproduction was more critical than at earlier stages of the economy. Durable goods were being produced at a rate considerably in excess of their use. That was most apparent in building construction. Office space became much larger than the amount used and residential vacancies reached a high figure in many areas. Excessive plant capacity was widespread.

The economic recovery in the 1983–84 period was uneven and short-lived. The steel industry remained in a virtual depression, agriculture was in the third year of depressed conditions, the decline in the prices of most commodities exacerbated the worsening conditions in copper mining, and depressed conditions prevailed in the textile industry. The backbone of the recovery had been in home building and automobiles, but when the early 1984 plunge in housing starts occurred, the only remaining strong support for the faltering economy was car buying. But, as in 1929, that, too, had been overdone and sales were to slacken. The oil industry was never able to return to the peak of the 1980 boom. And, as in 1929, there was a high degree of built-in unemployment that the Reagan boasts had never been able to reduce.

The slowing economy caused investors to become very confused. They were brainwashed to believe that when the economy slowed down, the stock market would take off, inspired by the lower interest rates. The market decline the previous January had been explained in *The Wall Street Journal* as being due to a fear of a slowing economy. Then the continued decline in February was explained in the *Journal* as reflecting a fear that the economy was getting too strong. That set the stage for the current hook—that a slowing economy would be good for the stock market. But two back-to-back 100-million-share days on the downside in mid-September ushered in a new fear—that the economy *was slowing down too fast.* In the wake of this new fear, stocks did not respond as favorably to the bond market as most had expected, this latest small break occurring in the face of bond market strength. (The identical thing had taken place in 1929 as strength in the bond market in October of that year reflected the fact that money was fleeing the stock market, seeking greater safety.) The number of housing starts took another sharp spill. Meanwhile, pension funds were reported as increasingly switching from stocks into bonds for greater safety.

IV

People were bored almost to the breaking point by the horde of analysts still preaching the doctrine of the bull market "second leg." They, of course, became perfect setups for the "second leg" trap because they had waited so long for it. Its occurrence in a pre-election period simply increased the enormity of the bull trap and what would follow.

With many analysts brainwashed in the mold of Templeton-Prechter forecasts of Dow 3,000, such pie-in-the-sky forecasts were necessary in order to set the stage for the disappointments that would follow. Templeton had stated that the Dow would never go under 776 again. In line with such statements made in the past, that simply told me that the Dow *would* go under the 776 level again. Whatever appeared to be obvious could be counted on to be a mirage. It was stated by Carter Randall only a year before that the market never goes down in an election year. "Never" was a dangerous and silly word to use.

Martin Weiss, a very intelligent and respected market observer, saw the same dangers ahead that I had my eyes glued upon. He saw all rallies as temporary and with the purpose of providing the bull traps that had to precede a coming collapse. When he told Bill Griffeth on the Financial News Network on September 27 that he was looking for such a collapse, Bill asked: "Do you think the Fed would permit that?" His question pointed up one of the most poignant of the 1929 parallels—the belief that the Federal Reserve had the power to prevent a crash. That was absolutely no different from the belief held by the president of the New York Stock Exchange in 1929.

PARALLEL 151

Historical
The President Preaches Prosperity

Under the headline "President Preaches Prosperity," the September 26 issue of *USA Today* reported: "Reagan started Tuesday with favorite themes from his campaign stump speech telling a joint meeting of the World Bank and International Monetary Fund that prosperity 'is far nearer than most of us would ever dare to hope.'" Of course, historians would recall similar statements made by President Hoover in 1929.

Hoover had promised continued prosperity. His campaign pledge had been to push "the direction of economic progress toward prosperity and the further lessening of poverty."

One had to ask ironically: Prosperity for whom? As in 1929, one of the most striking of the current parallels was rearing its ugly head:

PARALLEL 152

Historical
Maldistribution of Income

While President Reagan was preaching prosperity, claims about "prosperity being around the corner" belied the shockingly high statistics relating to 35 million people living at the poverty level and millions more living very close to it. Accusations that the Reagan administration favored the rich to the exclusion of the poor brought the parallels with the Hoover administration disturbingly close. Not only did there exist large pockets of poverty and widespread depressed conditions in 1984, but 8 million people remained unemployed. The Reagan "prosperity" was very selective.

Now examine the parallel with 1929:

Prosperity requires that consumption and production expand simultaneously, but between 1919 and 1929 the gap between them widened ominously. While manufacturing output was increasing about 42 percent real wages in manufacturing were increasing about 15 percent. The income of the masses was rising less rapidly than that of the rich, until by 1929 the one-tenth percent of American families at the top of the social scale were receiving approximately as much income as the 42 percent of the families, and their annual incomes stood below $1,500. If they could have fulfilled their desires, they would have absorbed an output many times the peak productive output of 1929, for the United States has not yet attained a productive capacity to equal what Americans would like to consume.

Moreover, since approximately 2 million persons and sometimes 4 million remained unemployed during the height of the "prosperity," the problem of finding buyers to keep factories operating must become acute. When the unemployed reached 15 million, as some estimators counted it in 1932, there would exist a market for perhaps less than half of the potential output of existing establishments. Thus was the process of economic progress retarded by impediments in wealth diffusion. A panic would reveal the desperate need for readjustments between production and consumption. The direct material loss, staggering as it was, would prove less than the almost irreparable destruction of human values.[2]

Then we read: "Hoover knew that in the end, the real people who mattered, in economic terms, were that handful of men who controlled some two hundred companies that made up about 50 percent of the nation's corporate wealth. These were the people he had carefully wooed and courted to become President. These were the people who would expect him to redeem his campaign promises of continued prosperity."[3] Hoover was well aware that 60 percent of American families were living on less than $2,000 a year, living in poverty.

In terms of the maldistribution of income in the United States, little had changed by 1984. It was still a case of the top 15 percent having as much income as the bottom 42 percent, give or take a few percentage points. So, while President Reagan talked about prosperity, the coal miners of West Virginia, the steelworkers of Pennsylvania, the copper miners of Montana, and millions of farmers were asking whether it was prosperity for the few or for the many. The more things changed, the more they stayed the same.

[2]Jeannette P. Nichols, *Twentieth Century United States—A History* (New York: D. Appleton-Century, 1943), pp. 283–84.
[3]Thomas and Morgan-Witts, *The Day the Bubble Burst*, p. 120.

PART SEVEN

THE CRISIS

20

Sitting on the Fault Line

[OCTOBER 1984]

I

One of the most intriguing aspects of the stock market is that mysterious period prior to a crash. It is difficult to define it perfectly. First of all, there has to be confusion, a period of seemingly balanced push and pull, with no clearly defined trend—up in the morning, down in the afternoon, and then, just as suddenly, down in the morning and up in the afternoon—sudden reversals out of the blue that soon vanish. This confused and trendless period often lasts many weeks. Moreover, important technical parameters are not violated during this mysterious period, thus adding to the confusion. *Such a period had stretched from August 10 through October.*

The only economist astute enough to state publicly at this time that the country was already in an economic recession was S. Jay Levy. He saw the possibility of corporate earnings dropping as much as 40 percent by the spring of 1985. When pressed further, he said that what he saw ahead would be like the early 1930s. So he was added to that small band of observers who were realistic enough to recognize that something big was brewing and were willing to walk the very narrow line of extreme minority thinking—a refreshing contrast to the Wall Street consensus which had held so long to the line that their "bull market" was in a healthy consolidation phase awaiting a second leg and that the economic slowdown was healthy.

The shocks were coming faster now. For months I had documented the growing trend of scandals involving fraud, embezzlement, Ponzi-type schemes, broker-churning cases, bank failures, etc. The market had more than a handful of excuses for a major decline, but this was all still the tip of the iceberg. I expected conditions to worsen considerably after election day, although that was the last thought in most people's minds as the calendar homed in on Reagan's certain landslide reelection.

Few would believe that a serious decline in the stock market would follow on the heels of a popular mandate for four more years of the Reagan administration. But the stock market, through its own actions, was projecting a serious extension of the major bear market. Few could accept the concept that such a bear market could contain a panic and crash. It was unthinkable, out of the question. The most common argument was that the Federal Reserve would simply not allow it to happen. The very fact that the administration and the Congress had done little to bring the raging deficit problem under control raised questions as to how effective the Fed might be in preventing an old-fashioned depression. Pre-election day rhetoric sought to mask the problem in a wave of patriotic optimism.

This was a period of watchful waiting. The Dow once again was on its way under the 1,200 level. Were it not for the approaching election, no further bull traps would have been required or forthcoming. So, despite a drop to the 1,160s early in the month, breaking the September lows, the anticipated debacle was not to be this month—not yet, not yet—but ever so close. There had to be that last hurrah. The *technical* last hurrah had occurred on August 10. The internal breakdown thereafter was more than sufficient to warn that anything on the upside had to be deemed another bull trap. The polls were so lopsided in Reagan's favor that his certain reelection, being the centerpiece of the bullish camp, had to mark the final touch in the demise of the bull. The stage was being carefully set for the final scene—the *psychological* last hurrah. I could see the market turning up at this point for no other reason, the bulls drawing their last breath prior to election day.

By staying in the 80-point trading range, the market gave the appearance of business as usual, but beneath the surface October was to see a further rise in the number of 1929 parallels.

The market technically was not able to keep pace with the Reagan optimism. My most reliable technical indicator was the Net Field Trend, which, based on on-balance volume, measured the true strength of the Dow Jones Industrial Average. It had peaked at a +19 reading in August and dropped to +4 in September. It rose pitifully to +5 by late September and never bettered that figure throughout October, instead dropping to −1 by the end of the month, a week before election day.

But the bullish sentiment continued to hold sway. Paul Dysart, Jr., Terry Laundry, and Robert Prechter were particularly bullish among the letter writers. None of them sensed that something extraordinary was brewing on the downside. Their optimism was matched by the majority of market letter writers, *Investors Intelligence* continuing to report that over half the letters they monitored were bullish. Such high percentages of optimism reliably preceded sharp market declines, but this time, such signals were to turn out to be of far greater importance than anyone realized. In the weeks ahead, I suspected that this sentiment indicator would contain a major flaw, one that would coincide with the actual crash itself. In normal markets, such sentiment indicators worked rather well—too many bulls at a market top and too many bears at a market bottom. However, this was not a normal market, as I had been repeatedly saying since 1983. Currently, there were far too many bulls, the sharp August rally having done its work well. That signaled that the sentiment pendulum would soon be on a major downswing, and the lower the averages fell, the more bearish sentiment would become. When it could be said that bears outnumbered the bulls, then *Investors Intelligence* would *become* more bullish. But there would be the flaw. If there was to be a crash (and I was certain at this time that it was very close), bearish sentiment would not only continue to build but would completely permeate market thinking as it did in 1929 and the point would be reached at which everyone would want to get out of the market at the same time, either by choice or by force. Therefore, I would await the time when it could be said that 75 percent of all market letters were bearish. When I could make that statement, the crash, I knew, would become fact. It would be too late to turn the ship around.

Few people were aware that in September 1929 bearish sentiment had reached that point. I couldn't put it down as yet as one of my 1929 parallels, because it hadn't yet occurred, but I was certain that when the downturn began in earnest, bullish sentiment would totally crumble and be replaced by this much greater degree of bearish sentiment. Such widespread bearishness would be the force capable of breaking the wineglass, marking that magic moment when everybody would rush for the exits at the same time. So, regardless of precisely where the Dow would be when the crash occurred, the Dow had to break under the previous bear market low of 1,086, such a move proving to everybody that the market hadn't been consolidating in an ongoing bull market, as Wall Street analysts had contended, but had simply been preparing for the next major leg down in the worst bear market in fifty-five years.

The latest available short interest figures covered the period from August 9 through September 7. The total had swelled to another all-time record high, 233,314,000 shares, fulfilling my earlier predictions. That large rise in the short interest corresponded almost exactly with the peak of the August bear market rally, and the conclusions were clear. Every bull trap that had occurred had been accompanied by a record high short interest, and that proved conclusively that, as always, such short selling was professional, well timed, and, above all, right. Only bears win in a bear market, and the fact that the stock market had declined following all the record high short interest figures also proved that this was a continuing bear market. No technician could divorce this technical evidence from the enormity of the historical fact that the 1929 crash came on the very heels of an all-time high in the monthly short interest.

Market responses play a major role in technical analysis. The response to this latest new high in the monthly short interest was a market decline, the Dow dropping to the low 1160s by October 9. The fact that the market declined following the announcement of the figures attested to the validity of the bear market. If it had been a bull market, a record short interest would have been squeezed mercilessly. The higher the short interest climbed, the more bearish it had become for the market. People didn't understand this because they had been taught to believe that shorting was going against the trend. In a bear market, it is going with the trend, not against it. Those who bought stocks in a bear market were going against the trend.

II

Norman Fosback of *Market Logic* had recently announced that insider selling again had the upper hand over insider buying. A brief period of net insider buying in June was cited by many as their reason for being bullish. Fosback stated that the insider figures would have little or no impact on the current market, noting that the indicator had only longer-term implications. However, he had ignored the 1983 signals stemming from the pernicious, concentrated, and unrelenting insider selling activity, signals that had clearly coincided with the start of the current bear market. Concentrated insider selling constituted one of my major reasons for having been bearish at the start of the bear market in the spring of 1983. It remained an important reason for concern.

It was a foregone conclusion that everything following the classic August 10 blowoff denoted professional stock distribution. It explained why no rally could go very far after that date. All rally attempts were doomed to failure. I had issued only two signals of primary importance prior to the fall of 1984. The first was the July buy signal that had preceded the 153-point summer rally and the second was the all-out sell signal that corresponded to the August 10 rally peak that had seen the Dow Jones Industrial Average intraday reading reach 1,253.75. There were alternating trading signals thereafter but the sell signals became stronger and the buy signals were progressively weaker.

This pattern was in keeping with expected action following the August explosion. I had predicted that the July–August upturn would at least duplicate the August–October 1973 bear market rally, and it turned out to be such a good carbon copy that it reconfirmed my earlier prediction that it would be the best rally of the year, and the last. It had been the third bull trap of the year and the most effective. I remained convinced that, as in 1973, the brief 1984 summer run-up in stock prices would shortly be followed by a major smash.

I could talk freely about this in my weekly market letters without censorship. If I had been writing a letter for a Wall Street house at this time, I wouldn't have been allowed to be so outspoken.

Convinced that the July buy signal was calling for the rally that fools the majority, I expected that the pattern of quotations in *The Wall Street Journal* during the 1973 bear market rally would be repeated. By demonstrating that it was being repeated, I showed that the July–August upsurge had without doubt been a bear market rally, not only duplicating 1973 but also indicating that what was being observed here was a simple and ominous repetition of the summer of 1929.

PARALLEL 153

Psychological
The Worst Is Over

On October 8 *The Wall Street Journal* ran a large ad by Shearson Lehman/ American Express. The first major heading in the ad stated: "Worst Behind Us; Buy on Current Weakness." The ad went on to say: "We believe that most of the negative near-term sentiment is already reflected in the market. There may be a touch more to go on the downside, but the worst is behind us. Our advice is to take advantage of this price weakness by using it as a purchase opportunity. We have recommended a fully invested position for nearly three months, 60% in stocks, 40% in bonds."

Not only did this parallel the 1929 sentiment, but it was also expressed on September 21, 1973, in the *Journal,* being a tremendous help in determining where the market stood in both cycles.

But, more important, this note was sounded in 1929 just before the great crash. Here is what was said in the *Journal* on October 25, 1929, reflecting the great decline of the day before:

> Prices were literally slaughtered. Thousands of marginal accounts were wiped out and the shrinkage in values ran into billions. It was about the most severe decline Wall Street has experienced in history, with the so-called big business interests shrinking with the rest. That Wall Street and finances generally are resting on a solid foundation no one can deny. Never has the Street gone through such a drastic decline and left such a small amount of wreckage. That the best kind of support was given to stocks yesterday was evident from the big buying orders that made their appearance when the market was at its worst. Everyone with surplus money seemed anxious to pick up bargains. This included the "big interests," the corporations and investment trusts. *At the close 90% of the Street believed that the worst was over and that stocks would not return to their low levels of yesterday* [emphasis added].

Four days after that was published, the stock market experienced the worst
crash in history. No, the worst wasn't over—*it was just beginning!* So one had
to beware when hearing that the worst was over. After it was said in 1929,
the market crashed. After it was said in 1973, the market crashed. Now it was
1984. Shearson Lehman/American Express said the worst was over.

It could be seen from the stock price charts that there had been literally
dozens upon dozens of mini-crash situations, the most publicized of these
being Continental Illinois and Financial Corp. of America. Added to these
individual disasters was a plethora of weak situations whereby earnings estimates were cut back in recognition of the weakening economy, especially in
the areas of agriculture and housing. The sharp drop in the earnings of the
First Chicago Bank stemmed from bad loans that had to be written off as
nonperforming, the majority of which were bad farm loans. The latest figures
showed farm job unemployment rising. Of course, weakness in the agricultural
sector was not new. The three-year slump had been reported in June by the
Journal. There was the parallel with the conditions of 1926–29.

III

With but a short time until election day, there was still far too much bullish
sentiment. The market would have to burn that out before there could be any
worthwhile buy signal relevant to anybody other than very short-term traders.
In other words, people weren't bearish enough. They were still too mesmerized
by political promises which had completely blinded them to what was happening under their very noses. While one side could boast of its victory over
inflation, that victory now became its Achilles' heel. All during the upswinging
Kondratieff curve, it was fashionable to incur debt because inflation eased debt
burdens. Now, starting on the long deflationary downslope, it was no longer
fashionable to be in debt. On the contrary, debt was a curse to the nation,
to business, and to the individual. The debts, without inflation, became real
and suddenly very burdensome. Eliminating inflation, therefore, was one of
the most important precursors of the coming panic, crash, and depression.

PARALLEL 154

Historical
Economists See No Depression Coming

On October 12 one of the greatest of all the 1929 parallels was noted. It
appeared as a front-page article in *The Wall Street Journal.* The headline read
as follows: "Economists Don't See Threats to Economy Portending Depres-

sion. Government Now Has Tools to Avert Any Collapse, Panel of Experts Agrees. Case of Continental Illinois."

The *Journal* had interviewed ten of the most eminent analysts. The group included three Nobel laureates and two former Federal Reserve Board chairmen. *None of them saw a depression coming.*

> Entering its third year next month, the current economic expansion ranks among the most vigorous upturns in decades. Yet, concern lingers that the economy somehow remains dangerously fragile. The worry reflects a range of well-publicized problems—from the sea of red ink in the federal budget to sour loans to Third World nations. And so, the question still is asked: Can a Great Depression happen again?
>
> The question has nagged now for about a decade, ever since the severe downturn of 1973–75. The economy has grown, endured a recession, grown again, endured another, deeper recession, recovered again and gone on to new highs of business activity. The road has been deeply rutted. Indeed, just two years ago, at the depths of the last recession, visions of bread lines and street corner apple sellers seemed almost palpable.
>
> And yet, despite recent history and current worries about how long the current expansion can last, the public should have—if anything—more confidence than before that an economic crackup like that in the 1930's won't happen again. That, at least, is the judgment of 10 eminent analysts interviewed by *The Wall Street Journal.*

Paul A. Samuelson, a Nobel laureate economist at Massachusetts Institute of Technology, stated: "Another depression on the order of the 1930's just doesn't seem possible."

The *Journal,* while reporting the unanimous opinion of the experts that no depression was in the cards, nevertheless covered themselves with the following:

> *No one can be sure, of course, that another 1930's-style collapse won't occur* [emphasis added]. Forecasters at times have been woefully wrong about the economy. In 1929, the late Irving Fisher of Yale, among the most prominent economists of his time, was pronouncing business sound. As late as 1930, some forecasters still appeared sanguine. Yet, the conviction now that this history won't repeat itself rests on some evidence. Those interviewed cite changes in attitudes, institutions and the economy's makeup, as well as a closer monitoring of business activity. Some of the analysts, in fact, seem even surer that no collapse is in prospect than when last polled in early 1982.

One can see here a combination of important 1929 parallels. Not only did the economists see no depression coming but (1) they were all overoptimistic, (2) believed that the Fed wouldn't allow it to happen, and (3) were very much a part of the general blindness, the precursor of all panics and crashes: nobody saw it coming. In light of their failure to foresee the 1983 downturn in stock prices, why would so many believe that their economic forecasting was any better? It was this very smugness among the economists in 1929 that was being repeated now. The *Journal* piece on October 12 instantly called to mind the certainty with which E. H. H. Simmons laced his many bullish speeches, stating on September 11, 1929, that the days of panics and crashes were over. He, as the president of the New York Stock Exchange, was listened to and believed, as were Arthur Laffer, Pierre Rinfret, and others in 1984. Simmons, too, earnestly believed that the Federal Reserve System would not allow a crash to happen. It proved to be an assumption without foundation, utterly dangerous because so widely believed. Such dangerous complacency dominated the 1984 thinking among the leading economists.

Typical of the total lack of feel that economists have for the stock market is the way they viewed the stock market in early 1981. On February 12, 1981, a month after my sell-everything signal of January 6, *The Wall Street Journal* ran a front-page piece headlined "Economists Don't Agree with Joe Granville." As it turned out, the economists were wrong. The economy went into a recession and the Dow dropped from 1,004 (the level at the time of the sell signal) to 776 by August 1982. That was the very month and year that the economists had been predicting a level of 1,145 in the Dow in their early 1981 forecast. The Dow did precisely the *opposite* of what the economists expected.

One of the harbingers of the 1983–84 market decline had been the buying binge the mutual funds went on in the 1982–83 rise. Most of the buying was done at the worst time—right at the top. The highest previous net purchases of $1.7 billion occurred at the mid-1983 stock market peak. I told my followers to flee for their lives right at the time of the peak mutual fund buying. The July–August 1984 buying binge showed that the mutual fund managers were once again repeating their earlier mistakes. This time they went all out, showing net purchases of $2.7 billion on the August rise, again buying at the worst time—right at the top. Such concentrated mutual fund interest in the market was a precursor of the decline that followed the mid-1983 peak. And here again even greater concentrated buying had to be seen as an equally reliable precursor to the great decline that would follow. Those young mutual fund managers did not as yet realize the seriousness of their mistaken enthusiasm, their acting in concert by herd instinct. But the damage was done. Holders of shares in mutual funds were again impaled on the hooks of the misguided enthusiasm of those young managers who thought and acted as if these were normal times.

Yes, things were very different now. People are creatures of habit. For many years, passbook savers bypassed higher yields in preference for 4 to 5 percent passbook returns, a throwback to fears created by the Great Depression and the banking collapse of the early 1930s. Now they were doing the same thing with stocks, a throwback to the long upswing of the Kondratieff Wave when inflation was good for stocks and people rightly held stocks for the long term. Now this was no longer so.

Now, as in 1929, gambling was rife. The investor in 1929 had no future. But like the investor today, he thought he did. However, the times of euphoria and the gambling fever reduced everything to the day-to-day trading game. What was happening now used to be illegal and that underscored still another of the existing 1929 parallels:

PARALLEL 155

Historical
The 1929 Bucket Shops Are with Us Again

This was well documented by an interesting quote from James Grant's biography of Bernard Baruch: "Another worry was gambling, a subject on which the constitution was silent except to prohibit the laying of bets on stock prices. (That is, betting without buying or selling the shares.)"[1] The reference was to the New York Stock Exchange constitution. According to its definition, what was described as bucket shops back in the 1920s resembled the option and stock index trading of the 1980s. Today, people lay bets on stock prices without buying or selling the shares. The bucket shops of the 1920s were back again and made fully legal.

Correct technical analysis provided the initial outline which a collection of events was now simply filling in. Virtually alone in the spring of 1983, I told investors to flee for their lives. The period constituted the true market peak. Applying the same techniques I had applied then, I had warned in April of impending peaks in the London and Tokyo markets. A few weeks later, both markets peaked and plunged, the London Financial Times Index peaking at 922.80 and plunging to a low of 770.30. Events at this time brought about the sharpest one-day plunge in the history of the London market, the Financial Times Index crashing over 27 points, dropping to 838.7, within range of breaking the 1984 low. In line with the major deflationary trend, Norway cut the price of oil and the British North Sea Consortium followed suit, shocking oil analysts who had not seen such a move coming. The British pound broke to a new low of $1.18, which would force the Bank of England in time to raise the bank rate to protect the currency. Further adding to Margaret Thatcher's problems, a threat of an October 25 strike by the pit supervisors' union promised to halt all coal mining in England.

[1] James Grant, *Bernard Baruch: The Adventures of a Wall Street Legend* (New York: Simon & Schuster, 1983), p. 48.

These events were in sharp contrast with the great optimism registered at the spring peak. So while nobody could have predicted the specific events that would bring the London market down from its bull peak, there was no question that the London market had entered a dangerous top formation in April, a time when everyone thought that foreign markets were the place to be. As in September 1929, the London market was being keenly watched for any signs that would exacerbate the developing bear market in New York. The New York market could not be impervious to what was then happening in London. The last time Britain had cut the price of oil, the 1983 bear market in stocks was about to start in the United States. A repeat performance now was expected to be more harshly reflected in American share prices after the artificial pre-election support had vanished.

The cuts in the price of oil triggered an interesting chain of events. Already under tremendous pressure to protect the pound sterling, England had no choice but immediately to follow Norway's lead. This led to a defection on the part of Nigeria from the OPEC solidarity; Nigeria, strapped with over $20 billion of external debt, was forced to maintain the most favorable selling prices for its key product. These deflationary moves immediately helped the Dow Jones Transportation Average to move up against a declining industrial average, airline stocks temporarily boosted by the oil price cuts. This also sparked excessive strength in the bond market, which had also been reflecting the drop in yields from the latest Treasury auctions. The general market got in line with this string of events and exploded in the late trading on October 18, posting the largest one-day rise in two months. In order to illustrate the seeming contradiction between the news and the market, *The Wall Street Journal* reported on October 18 that oil news weakened the industrials. The next day, however, they reported that the oil news helped the industrials.

Of course, no longer-term bullish implications were seen in the rally of October 18. On the contrary, it was definitely not a replay of July–August. It was seen as a short selling rally similar in nature to the early January and May run-ups and totally different from what I had foreseen in July. I put it down as pre-election fireworks, but not a trend changer.

The Wall Street Journal on October 19 headlined their market page: "Stocks Soar As Oil Price Reductions Signal End to Inflationary Pressure." Of course inflationary pressures were abating. That is what a trend toward deflation was all about. The entire 1983–84 bear market had been signaling the end of inflationary pressures. This was not bullish because, expecting the trend to continue, I thought it would go full circle, not stopping at mere disinflation, but going deep into deflation.

IV

The sharp rallies at this time continued to be selling opportunities. The sharp October 18 rise led into an A-Dis Trading Barometer sell signal on the nineteenth. In view of the fact that each buy signal had been weaker and each sell signal stronger, this latest sell signal carried great technical authority. Any further attempts to take the market up again would be dismissed as worthless pre-election euphoria.

This latest rally attempt that had taken the Dow briefly over the 1,240 level on October 19 was flawed by a persistent ability of the American Stock Exchange advance/decline line to score new bear market lows. Mirroring this disturbing dichotomy, money continued to leave the market. Seven consecutive weeks of rising money market fund assets attested to that fact. Growing problems lent an echo ring to Reagan's pre-election references to prosperity and an expanding economy.

By late October, the market was sitting on a number of important trendlines and the sell signal of October 19 had clearly implied that those trendlines would soon be violated. Prior to this critical time, the market, for a brief period, appeared to be confused and rudderless. What had been widely advertised as the greatest incentive to buy stocks had been operable for some time —the drop in short-term interest rates. However, the stock market was not responding to that in a bullish manner. The market would seldom discount the same thing twice. It took off in the July–August rally because of the well-documented upturn in the bond market. The fall in rates since that time was greater in September and particularly sharp in October, but instead of taking off again as it had done in the summer, the stock market stalled in a well-defined narrow price range. If the market couldn't rally on these sharply lower short-term rates, obviously something was very wrong.

The lower rates were pointing toward a worsening economy, and that was the basic reason why the stock market could not mount a meaningful rally. In other words, as I had predicted earlier, the honeymoon between the bond and stock markets was over. The July–August stock rally had shown those two markets in lockstep. That was because it hadn't yet dawned on Wall Street analysts that the economy was already in a recession. They therefore interpreted the lower rates as being bullish for the stock market. However, when the Street began to get an inkling in September and October that the Reagan expansion was all campaign rhetoric and was no longer fact, the stock market lost its interest-rate rudder, increasingly responding to the more bearish implications of the lower rates.

A lot of water had gone over the dam since January, when Wall Street firms had been telling their clients what a dream market lay ahead in 1984, that the Dow was headed toward 1,400, 1,500, and higher. People forgot to beware of what was most widely advertised. Everyone had been so bullish in January that they had already done their buying. The technical position of the market at that time was so bad that it was a foregone conclusion that the market was going to turn importantly down, and the technical trend, always preceding the economic trend, was stating then, with full authority, that the economy would then be shortly turning down. But Wall Street, so mesmerized with the bullish scenario, stuck with it all year, as proven by the downturn in the brokerage house earnings. No truly important buy signal had a chance until Wall Street analysts threw in the towel and turned bearish. At this late date, there was still far too much optimism. *Investors Intelligence* reported at this time that 52 percent of all market letters were bullish. But, with the election coming up, they weren't about to throw in the towel. There were too many forecasts of how great everything was going to be after Reagan's reelection victory. People had forgotten that the more something is believed or acted upon, the greater the disappointment if it doesn't work out. People had relied heavily on the January optimism and they paid a high price for that misplaced optimism. Now they were leaning hard on the certain Reagan victory, and the technical structure of the market at that time told me that they were leaning far too hard on it and were, like Humpty Dumpty, headed for a great fall.

Far too much stress had been placed on the cooling of inflation. What people had forgotten was that before the cycle could fully swing to deflation it first had to knock out inflation. The stock market was no longer responding well to cooling inflation, simply because it was seeing the pendulum swinging from inflation to deflation. Wall Street wanted people to believe that the pendulum would stop at disinflation, but the constant stream of numbers from the Commerce Department showed the sloping lines typical of all developing recessions. But, in light of the Kondratieff Wave, why was it so widely assumed that this recession would not turn into something far worse? Because it was a period of peace and stable prices.

PARALLEL 156

Historical
Peace and Stable Prices

Harold M. Finley, senior vice president at Prescott Ball & Turben in Chicago, was quoted on October 25 in *The Wall Street Journal* as follows: "The current business expansion is the first one in 60 years that isn't fueled by war or rising prices." What he was actually saying was: "I haven't seen these conditions since the roaring twenties."

In carefully tracking the analysts most widely quoted in 1984, I found that one could have gone short following the times of the greatest bullish pronouncements. They had been so certain that 1982–83 was kicking off a major bull market that it had never occurred to them that the stock market could drop in 1984 and 1985. President Reagan deserved great praise for cooling off inflation, but he should have quit while he was ahead. Now the bills came due. Of course inflation was going to die. In order to fulfill the Kondratieff forecast, inflation had to be cooled off prior to disinflation and then deflation. Debts could be condoned during a period of inflation. They would become very heavy in a period of deflation when world liquidity was contracting.

With the approaching anniversary of the 1929 crash, the question would always come up: Could it happen again? The *Miami Herald* interviewed me at this time and asked that question. I told them emphatically yes, it most certainly could happen again and far sooner than most people would think possible. However, it was silly to look for exact calendar parallels. Nobody knew the exact time any more than anyone knew where the Dow would be a year later. But one thing was certain, and I told them: Not only could it happen, but the probability of its happening was greater now than it had been at any time in the past fifty-five years. I stressed the total lack of correlation between the outcome of the election and the stock market. The future had already been factored into the market and the economy, and financial history would be the same regardless of whether Reagan or Mondale won. I put it this way: Would it really have made any difference in 1929 who won the election in 1928? Minor things, of course, might have been different, but a political label wasn't going to avoid the crash that was already in the cards before the 1928 election.

The 1984 election served to deflect public attention from what was actually going on. Most of the political rhetoric hinged too much on the cooling of inflation and the alleged strength in the economy while reality was looking to the future. Reality saw the cooling of inflation as leading to the mounting problems of deflation. Reality saw an economy that was no longer expanding. Reality saw lower interest rates as reflecting the worsening economy.

The market looks nine months ahead. It precedes the economy by that period of time. When the market peaked in the spring of 1983, it was heralding the end of the economic recovery nine months later. When it occurred, nobody recognized it. Wall Street called it a welcome slowdown. Nine months after the Dow had peaked, the slowdown had not only persisted but was worsening. Later on, economists would look back and state that the recession had begun in March 1984 with the very sharp drop at that time in housing starts, the sharpest drop since the figures were first reported in 1959. The economy wouldn't bottom out until nine months after the stock market bottomed, and thus, as always, it paid to watch the stock market rather than the economy.

In 1929, soft spots were showing up in the economy—notably in agriculture, textiles, automobiles, and commodity prices. Steel was the last to break from peak production. Soft spots in the 1984 economy were seen in agriculture, steel, and textiles and by the fall of 1984 were starting to be seen in the automobile sector, which was the last bulwark of economic strength. The break in commodity prices in 1984 was highlighted in October by the fresh oil price cuts.

As I looked ahead to the post-election stock market, it was safe to say that *nobody saw any real trouble ahead.* Every day one heard the *consensus view* that the market was consolidating and would make new highs in the November–December period. In view of the fact that the source of that consensus comprised the identical source that in January saw Dow levels of 1,450–1,500 dead ahead, I knew that *I had to move diametrically opposite to such a consensus and say that there was real trouble ahead and that probability pointed to some uncharted shocks instead.*

21

The Last Hurrah

[NOVEMBER 1984]

I

Opinion was so lopsided in favor of the market exploding on the upside after a Reagan sweep at the polls that I was certain such euphoria was the necessary precursor to the crash. I conveyed my contrary opinion in a short and punchy title to my November 3 market letter: "Landslide = Major Market Slide."

Had Al Smith defeated Herbert Hoover in 1928 it would have had little or no effect on the 1929 crash. The factors that brought about the crash were already in place in the market and the economy. The approaching Reagan victory would not change what would happen in the market and the economy one iota. If history and technical analysis were any guide, Ronald Reagan would rue the day he decided to run for reelection, a statement I had been making all year. The economic recovery was borrowed at a very dear price, with over half the borrowing from abroad. Now the bills came due.

Orthodox economics teaches us that deficit spending is acceptable and required in a depression and is unavoidable in time of war. But we were in neither a war nor a depression and yet the deficits exploded out of sight during Ronald Reagan's first four years in office, towering far above all those of previous years combined. Whether this was outside of anyone's control or was created by design will be left to history to decide. What remained was the stark fact that we were left with an unprecedented debt which bought an economic recovery at a terrible price. To say that this was all right and to believe that we could work out of it by maintaining policies that put us into it in the first place was, as Robert Roosa was quoted as saying at this time, "living in a dream world."

Ever since the bear market had begun in the spring of 1983, bullish market analysts had been living in that dream world, looking for impossible goals in the Dow Jones Industrial Average of 1,500 and higher each year. As recently as August, Larry Wachtel of Prudential Bache had been predicting 1,450 by election day and Lynn Elgert, author of the Elgert Report, from Grand Island, Nebraska, was predicting 1,500 by the end of 1984. There was absolutely nothing in the technical picture that could have even remotely supported such projections, but the dream world demanded those ethereal numbers to lull the public into a stupor of satisfaction.

Another important warning sign seen at this time was the current *flight toward safety.* Money had been pouring into the 91-day Treasury bills, flooding the bond market, and spilling over into the money market funds. But the important message was that it was fleeing the stock market. Additional evidence was forthcoming at this time that large pension funds were switching from stocks to bonds. For the brief period of the July–August rally, stocks and bonds had been in lockstep, Wall Street believing that strength in the bond market was going to be bullish for stocks. That, of course, was the major bull trap that I had described at the time. Now the honeymoon was over. Strength in the bond market had seen the stock market continually fail since the key internal rally peak of August 10. Ironically, strength in the bond market would also be overdone and soon both markets would be declining, the lockstep then being on the downside.

But the drop in short-term rates raised hopes that the Federal Reserve Board would abandon their tight money policy, especially with the pre-election proddings from the Reagan administration and even from the president himself, who helped kick the Dow up 16 points on October 30 by predicting that rates would fall still further. But therein lay a dangerous similarity to 1929 (Parallel 148). Everyone knows what happened to the banking system in this country following the crash of 1929. But how many people know that the banking system in 1929 was described in *The Wall Street Journal* as being in healthy shape? In fact, because of that alleged "healthy shape," the Fed's firm money policy was reported as being no longer justified and was being abandoned.

Then on October 24, 1929, in *The Journal:*

"From early 1928 up to within the past few weeks, the Federal Reserve Board has enforced a stiff money policy which has had several unforeseen results, most notable of which probably has been the steady expansion of brokers' loans supplied by lenders other than banks. Not all the results of this firm money policy have been salutary; on the other hand, it cannot be denied that it has had the effect of reducing the rate of bank credit expansion sufficiently to allow the normal growth of capital to catch up with credit extension.

"At the moment, the banking picture is so strong that there seems no justification for continuation of a high money policy. As a practical matter, all evidence points to the conclusion that the board has modified, if not altogether abandoned, this policy and embarked upon an easier money policy."

████████

PARALLEL 157

Historical
Sharp Drop in Interest Rates

The *Journal* carried the following on October 28, 1929:

INTEREST RATES DROP RAPIDLY

*Acceptances Off Sharply in Week. Relatively Easy
Call Money Probable*

The decline in all classes of money rates, which started in August, almost coincidentally with the lowering of the New York Federal Reserve Bank's buying rate for bankers' acceptances, has been accelerated by the stock market break. Only within the past few days, however, has this decline affected the bankers' acceptance market, which is, in the last analysis, perhaps the most important market as indicating the true state of credit.

Time money rates have declined nearly as spectacularly as has the call rate, with short loans now quoted at 6¾% as against 9¼% at the end of September and a year's high of 9½% in May. Even now, however, time money is lending at above the legal maximum rate in New York State. Because there is some doubt as to the legality of time loans made above 6%, no great significance is attached to current quotations except as general indication of an easing in credit.

These were the same things that were being heard by November 1984. Short-term rates were coming down, the economy was slowing, and therefore the Fed was expected to abandon the previous tight money policy. There were just too many parallels to ignore. One ignored them at great financial risk.

████████

PARALLEL 158

Historical
Rumor of a Cut in the Discount Rate

This was a striking parallel with the precise action of 1929. Following the pressure to have the Fed abandon their tight money policy and in light of the sharp drop in short-term rates, rumors were circulating that the Fed was about to cut the discount rate. The story was carried in *The Wall Street Journal* on October 24, 1929:

LOWER DISCOUNT RATE PROBABLE

High Figure Out of Line with Commercial Paper,
Banker Acceptances

The conditions which caused the Federal Reserve Bank of New York to increase its discount rate from 5% to 6% on August 9 have disappeared. At that time borrowings of member banks in this district were running in excess of $380,000,000, or roughly $50,000,000 higher than in 1928. At the present time borrowings of member banks in this district are under $130,000,000 and the reporting member banks of New York City have reduced their indebtedness from $295,000,000 on August 7 to $49,000,000 on October 16.

The same set of circumstances started similar rumors in November 1984. Rates were dropping, accelerating on the downside since September. The administration, desperate because the Reagan expansion had come to a screeching halt, was pressuring the Federal Reserve to keep pushing rates down. Rumors of an imminent cut in the discount rate became common at this time.

But memories were short. Most had forgotten that rumors of a rise in the discount rate (see Parallel 145) were being circulated in July just days before the market embarked on the 153-point summer rally. In light of that, a cut in the discount rate would spell major trouble for the market.

II

Election day arrived. Now the country was going to see what had been obvious all year—the reelection of Ronald Reagan by the widest margin of states ever recorded. There was even talk of a fifty-state sweep. For the first time in history, the New York Stock Exchange was open for business on election day, and it was easy to see that Wall Street was betting that the certain reelection of Reagan would be a big plus for the market. The Dow closed up 14.71 points, putting the average at 1,244.15. That closing constituted an upside breakout for the Dow, bettering the previous bear market rally high closing of 1,239.73 recorded on August 21.

Something, however, was very wrong. The market had known for over nine months that President Reagan was going to be reelected. In that period, contrary to what Wall Street analysts had expected at the start of the year, *stock prices on balance had fallen.* The market had been hammering out a message all year that his certain reelection would not alter the bear market in stocks that had begun in the spring of 1983. While the Dow was climbing sharply on election day, I stated in an interview on the Financial News Network that we were living on borrowed time, that traders should sell into the election day strength because I expected a sharp slide immediately thereafter. While election day strength *appeared* to be significant for the bulls, it was in reality the *exact opposite*. What people were actually seeing, and not realizing it, was the arrival of the fourth significant bull trap of the year.

I based my expectation of immediate downside action on the technical fact that the A-Dis Short-Term Trading Barometer had not given back the sell signal of October 19. Had it been on a buy signal on election day, everything would have been reversed and the November 6 upside breakout would certainly have signaled a powerful rally extension. Because time was running out so fast, I had to assume that every operable sell signal spelled out imminent doom unless it was quickly reversed. But if there was to be another rally before the year ended, it would simply be an extension of the major broadening top formation and would not be meaningful in launching any new bull trend. I was more convinced than ever that the full brunt of the Kondratieff downwave was around the corner. It was technically immaterial at which precise floor the elevator cable broke.

The key characteristics of the election day bull trap were: (1) news, (2) the market doing the obvious, (3) effecting an upside breakout through a significant resistance level, (4) high volume, and (5) technical weakness by virtue of important upside nonconfirmations. The market was moving on news—the expected Reagan landslide. Being so obvious, it was clearly wrong. The Dow 1,240 level had been so widely advertised as a key upside resistance level that the breakout above 1,240 had to constitute a bull trap when viewed in the perspective of the proliferation of other bull trap characteristics. Market volume wasn't of record high proportions but was high enough to qualify for the expected reversal which was to follow. Most important, the upside breakout was effected against a background of technical weakness. Most notable in this respect was the fact that the A-Dis Short-Term Trading Barometer not only had remained on the sell signal of October 19 but had reconfirmed the sell signal. I had previously stated that a move above the Dow 1,240 level on a closing basis with an accompanying barometer buy signal would have been very bullish. On the other hand, such a move on a continuing barometer sell signal would be extremely bearish and could have constituted only a very important bull trap.

Something else occurred on November 6 that was discouraging to the bulls. The Dow failed to better the August 10 intraday 1,253.75 high. I had previously stressed the greater importance of intraday levels as compared with closing levels.

The biggest technical failure on the election day market was seen in the high/low indicator. Only seventy-seven big board stocks recorded new twelve-month highs. Since most people were perpetually mesmerized by the Dow,

they largely turned their attention away from the overriding technical fact that
the tide was going out. The high/low indicator had been telling the big story
since the spring of 1983:

Date	Dow Closing	12-Month New Highs
May 6, 1983	1,232.59	388
June 16, 1983	1,248.30	306
November 29, 1983	1,287.20	73
January 6, 1984	1,286.64	99
October 19, 1984	1,225.93	179
November 6, 1984	1,244.15	77

III

Now for the day after. The bulls went to bed on November 6 confident that
the president's record sweep of forty-nine states and the Dow closing over
1,240 would fulfill their dreams of widely forecasted Dow 1,300–1,500 year-
end levels and much higher levels thereafter. But on the November 7 market
opening, the market immediately flashed a signal that *something was wrong.*
The market opened down and stayed down all day. In other words, *there was
absolutely no follow-through on the election eve euphoria.* With a closing at
1,233.22, the chances of bettering the August 10 intraday high became increasingly remote.

On the assumption that this post-election downturn could have been the
start of a major slide of historical importance, I had to study *The Wall Street
Journal* now for what I called the actual crash parallels, phrases specifically
culled from the September–October 1929 period. Three of them showed up
in the *Journal* on November 8: (1) it was a very orderly decline, (2) there was
no panicky selling, and (3) the use of the phrase "depressed mood." This may
appear to be grasping for straws, but it is a well-proven technique for documenting the specific characteristics of a move, step by step, especially if these
parallels proliferate.

On election day, the Dow had been roaring higher, but I had reminded my
viewers on the Financial News Network that day that *we don't get buy signals
on rising markets.* Since my turn to the bull side in July had been based on
a barometer buy signal, the higher market on election day on a continued
barometer sell signal meant that what was being seen was a repeat of what had
happened the previous January and May and was definitely not a replay of the
July–August rise.

It required iron discipline to stick with a sell signal in the face of what had
appeared to be strong up days, such as during the election day euphoria. I

thought back to the previous December 23 sell signal. On January 4 and 5 the Dow exploded higher, jumping almost 30 points in two days. I was not concerned. The Dow peaked on January 6, and over the next six weeks plunged 152 points! The significant characteristic of that sell signal was that it had been *reconfirmed* prior to the plunge in the market. On April 26 a sell signal was also recorded. The Dow peaked on May 3 and again the barometer signal was *reconfirmed.* The Dow fell 100 points thereafter. The October 19 sell signal was steadily taking on major importance. Already three reconfirmations had been recorded by this time. Therefore, with the previous experience of drops of 152 points and 100 points, I had to conclude not only that the bulls had more than enough reasons to be nervous, but that, in retrospect, those drops would be greatly understated.

It had to be remembered that the first barometer buy signal following the January peak was aborted. The developing slide in November was being closely monitored for similar signs, especially the proliferating 1929 parallels. Now that election day was out of the way, a factor which had been mesmerizing the bulls all year finally disappeared. Now we all *knew* that Ronald Reagan would be at the helm for another four years and, as far as the stock market was concerned, what everybody knows is worthless. The better part of a year had gone by while Wall Street was waiting for that great "second leg" to a bull market. The first "leg" lasted between nine and ten months, while the next eighteen months saw stock prices "consolidating" *lower.* No bull market second leg had ever taken that long to arrive. But Wall Street analysts called it *a consolidation in an ongoing bull market,* exactly what they had been saying after prices peaked in 1929. It was hard to sell the word "consolidation" to somebody who had bought in at the peak prices recorded in the spring of 1983. Any new rallies weren't going to help too many people, so many hopelessly locked in with huge losses because they had bought the story that this was still an ongoing bull market.

What had ruined the gold speculators was their keen anticipation of a second leg to the rise that had started in the summer of 1982. When that was not forthcoming, gold collapsed. The pattern in gold was followed in the stock market. Those who recognized the aberration in the gold bull market should have seen it as a warning that the stock market would follow an identical pattern. It did. While everyone had been looking the other way, I had documented the 1982–83 brief stock market rise as a completed entity, replete with all three bull market phases, what I had underscored at the time as *encapsulement.*

The honeymoon for stocks and bonds was ending at this time. Ironically, but predictably, Merrill Lynch ran a full-page ad in *The Wall Street Journal* telling people that this was the time to buy bonds—right at what I felt was the peak. The bond market bottomed in May and June, breaking out forcefully in July. That coincided with the explosive July–August stock rally. Since

August, however, the continued strength in the bond market began to draw considerable strength from the stock market and was the major factor in holding the market to a relatively narrow 80-point trading range. Heavy pension fund shifting from stocks to bonds inevitably had to take its toll on stock prices, the recent election euphoria notwithstanding. But, like all moves, these tended to outrun themselves, and at least over the short term, both markets were expected to run downhill. Relatively speaking, there was far more strength in the bill market than in the long end of the bond market, and that suggested a continued *flight toward safety*, rather a strange phrase in a market atmosphere that was so widely touted as effervescent. The ninth consecutive weekly rise in the money market assets was reported at this time, a massive jump of $4.4 billion, three times the amount added the week before. As long as those figures were rising, one had to conclude that money was fleeing the stock market. Now the figures were rising at a far more rapid rate, thus putting an additional strain on the stock market.

Adding to the nervousness and confusion at this time, an increasing case could be made that the dollar had peaked or was soon to do so. So many times in the past that had appeared to be the case, only to be followed by a resumption of strength and another series of new highs. I linked any such conclusion to the price of gold. As long as the spot price for gold remained under the major trendline, I did not expect the currency markets to rally for long. Until gold went above its trendline, a strong case for a peak in the dollar could not be made. I saw only one thing that would seal the fate of the dollar —a stock market crash. Only then would gold become a repository for funds, funds fleeing the stock market. Thus the sharp drop in interest rates at this time was fast becoming a double-edged sword. If they dropped too fast, so would the dollar, and that would threaten a serious repatriation of foreign funds so heavily invested in the American economy. All these possibilities were adding to the current confusion.

IV

While the post-election confusion was coming to a boil, technical analysis clearly saw the situation. Something happened that signaled a near-term breakout from the tedious 80-point trading range, and there was no doubt that the breakout was to occur on the downside. The market flashed the ominous signal the very day after election day. The sharpest one-day drop in the Climax Indicator for all of 1984 occurred on that fateful day, dropping from +22 to zero.[1] Such significant CLX daily changes served as rather reliable forecasters of very important market moves, and technical analysis demanded that one should go with the flow following such technical shocks. As when a stone is

[1]The Climax Indicator is the net count of on-balance volume breakouts among the thirty Dow Jones industrial stocks. I considered it a technical indicator of primary importance.

dropped into a pond, these wide CLX moves set up a series of shock waves in advance, and such moves were far too important to disregard. The sharpest one-day rise in the CLX had occurred on June 18, when the indicator rose from −15 to +9, a spread of +24. That move came off the June 15 Dow bottom at 1,086.90. It turned out to be a worthy technical precursor of the July–August rally that followed a few weeks later. Now the *reverse* picture was being seen, the sharpest one-day drop in the CLX for the year, a downside spread of −22, *a profound change signaling a series of shock waves to come.*

It neatly fit my scenario that something was very wrong with the bullish case at this juncture. I didn't recall anyone expecting a market collapse following a Reagan landslide at the polls. But the minority view was almost always the most reliable one to adopt, and I saw this to be especially true when everybody had been expecting a bullish response to the November 6 election.

I had stressed the bearishness of all high Climax Indicator readings when recorded against the background of low Net Field Trend readings, the necessary precursor to a later sharp drop in the NFI.[2] That implied that the on-balance volume upside breakouts largely constituted lower up readings, reflecting a great loss of technical strength. The greater the spread between the high CLX readings and the NFI, the greater was the bearish signal. Looking back through all the CLX readings of over +20 in 1984, I found that the widest spread between the CLX and the NFI had occurred in early August and now. Early August was the internal technical precursor of the trouble now about to take place and the November signal was interpreted as saying that *major trouble was increasingly imminent.*

If one had constructed an advance/decline line and removed all the interest-sensitive stocks, it would have been seen that the line *wasn't very far away from the July low.* This was very important to know. It showed that the drop in interest rates had only been good for the interest-sensitive stocks but had not had much bullish impact on the general list.

Now that the A-Dis Trading Barometer had reconfirmed the October 19 sell signal three times, it bought additional time before any buy signals could be flashed at lower levels. It also stressed the fact that future rally attempts would be every bit as suspect as the previous ones. Any rally attempts now would also be encountering a series of CLX upside nonconfirmations.

V

Now, Four More Years. The President outlines his priorities and plans. On Election Day, with indications of his landslide victory already apparent, Ronald Reagan spoke with *Newsweek* White House correspondents Eleanor Clift and Thomas M. DeFrank on his plans for the next four years. Excerpts:

---

[2]The Net Field Trend Indicator I considered to be of outstanding importance. It is simply the net count of the field trends of each of the thirty Dow Jones industrial stocks. A field trend is determined by the volume trends—rising, doubtful, or falling.

Newsweek: What are we going to see in a second term?

Reagan: The course we charted from the beginning—trying to bring about growth without inflation that will provide the jobs that our people need and build greater revenues without adding to the individual tax rates, and thus get at the deficit. Plus reforms that we still want: balanced budget amendment, line-item veto, things of that kind.

Newsweek: So tax simplification is an acceptable vehicle to reduce the deficit?

Reagan: That is acceptable. But the main thing is the growth in the economy.

Reagan was a supply-sider. The nation had been led to believe during the first term that supply-side economics was the "new" economics, the solution that would roll back the malaise which had been blamed on the Carter administration. For a while it seemed to work. The 1981–82 recession ended, interest rates fell, inflation was all but eliminated, and the stock market enjoyed a brief bull market, a market often referred to by the president while it was going up. Almost from the beginning, the budgetary deficits began to soar far above the levels Reagan had blamed Carter for. But while people saw the stock market rise, saw more people going back to work, saw interest rates coming down, and felt that the president was adamant in his promise to bring down tax rates, they couldn't and wouldn't bring themselves to relate the deficits to their own personal lives. To most people, a budget deficit was meaningless. Unless it showed up in their paycheck or on their tax return, they remained oblivious. So Ronald Reagan was returned to office, promising to do something about the deficits which had been spawned during his first administration.

Supply-side economics was as old as the hills. It was not the brainchild of such neophytes as Arthur Laffer, who, while dubbed by the media as the "father of supply-side economics," wasn't even alive to see the 1929 crash and depression destroy the use of supply-side economics under the Hoover administration.

Supply-side economics owed its birth to the French economist Jean Baptiste Say (1767–1832). Say contended that supply automatically created its own demand and that, when in balance with demand, overproduction could not logically exist. All the classical economists were supply-siders and, despite their almost religious adherence to the supply-side principles, they failed to relate it in any way to the recurring boom and bust cycle. Now we have come full circle. Supply-side economics returned to vogue in 1981 under Reagan and again would be set back by the coming panic, crash, and depression. This constituted an amazingly exact parallel with 1929.

PARALLEL 159

Historical
Supply-Side Economics Back in Vogue

Paul Erdman[3] unwittingly touched upon the *cyclicality* of supply-side economics. The swing from that classical theory to Keynesian economics (accenting the demand side of the equation) and now back again to the classical theory ironically relates to the length of the Kondratieff long wave. In other words, the return of supply-side economics brought the country back to the economic policies of the late 1920s and therein lay the great parallel.

Both eras showed problems without precedent and supply-side economics provided no relief. Erdman put his finger on the very nub of the problem: not whether Say or Keynes was right but the fact that neither of their theories would work at this time. He left the door open to an untried brand of neo-economics which he left nameless.

Let him say it in his own words:

> Until the 1930's the "science" of economics was dominated by what was thought to be a basic, immutable law of nature: supply creates its own demand. It was logical. You make something (say a pair of shoes), you get paid for it and now you use that money to buy something of equivalent value from somebody else (say food from a farmer). Supply created and also equaled demand. Right? For a century and a half everybody thought so—with the exception of a few crackpots like Karl Marx.
>
> To be sure, even noncrackpots in the nineteenth and early twentieth centuries could not help but observe that at times this "law" seemed to be temporarily suspended. There were constantly recurring economic crises and financial crashes when an "oversupply" appeared to develop. The result was that companies and whole industries would flounder because they couldn't sell what they had made. But such crises never lasted very long. Usually within a matter of months, such "oversupply" would disappear as the people who had lost their jobs in bankrupt companies found new jobs in new enterprises producing new products, and with their incomes restored as they once again got paid for contributing to the "supply" of new products, they would start buying. This renewed demand would sop up the "oversupply" that had been hanging over the market—and *voilá*, order, balance, equilibrium and thus full employment for anybody who wanted to work. According to the theory current at the time, such equilibrium *had* to return. Say's law said so: supply always creates its own demand. And although Jean Baptiste Say, who decreed this law, was a Frenchman, his formulation summarized the core teaching of the Scot who was the father of classical economics, Adam Smith.
>
> All of this seemed to make sense, more or less, until the crash of 1929, after

[3]Paul Erdman, *Paul Erdman's Money Book* (New York: Random House, 1984), pp. 1–15.

which a situation developed that had no precedent, one whose explanation you could seek in vain in the writings of any of the classical economists from Adam Smith through his great successors—Ricardo, Hobson, Marshall. It was a depression in which such an oversupply developed that farmers burned their crops and abandoned their land; tens of thousands of factories stopped production, never to start again; in the United States alone, ten thousand banks closed and never reopened; 10 percent, then 15 percent, then 20 percent of the labor force was out of work. It started in earnest in 1931, and as the years went by, the crises seemed to deepen. What's more, it was worldwide: the same malaise in Britain, in Germany, in Switzerland. It seemed as if nobody could sell anything to anybody. Where, you might ask, was Say when we needed him?

Along came John Maynard Keynes, who stated that Say was wrong. He stressed the other side of the equation. Since nobody had anything at the depth of the Great Depression and thus couldn't buy anything, he said that the time had come to create demand by *deliberately encouraging large deficits.* It was up to government, artificially or otherwise, to create demand and that would put people back to work. But the 1930s was a sad commentary on that theory because by 1939 over 10 million were still out of work and it took a war to create full employment, not Keynesian economics. But Keynesian economics could and did make a deep impact upon the thinking at that time because it could make a logical case for deliberate government deficits. Its time had come, *but a return of Keynesian economics was not possible following a failure of supply-side economics under Reagan.* This was the crossroads the country confronted by November 1984, with no historical precedent for which road would now be taken. It was a major crisis, unique in economic history. It pointed up the very worst of the 1929 parallels.

PARALLEL 160

Historical
An Unprecedented Situation

Paul Erdman, referring to 1929 and its aftermath, had called it "a situation . . . that had no precedent"; likewise, the problem confronting the economy and the stock market by late 1984 was also without precedent. One would seek in vain for a period in history when the country was at peace and enjoyed stable prices but had a budgetary deficit problem of the scope of what was developing under the Reagan administration.

This problem was totally unexpected by the supply-siders. For example, Bruce Bartlett implied in 1981 that massive budgetary deficits would not occur with the application of Reaganomics.

In a real sense, Keynesian economics died during the recession of 1974–75. In 1975 the unemployment rate hit its highest level since the depression—8.5 percent—despite a $45 billion federal budget deficit (at that time, the largest since World War II) and a soaring inflation rate. According to conventional Keynesian theory this could not happen. The Phillips Curve, a basic Keynesian component, states that there is an inverse relationship between inflation and unemployment—the higher one is, the lower the other should be. Thus, the Keynesians were completely baffled about what policy prescription to offer for the situation. Normally, unemployment calls for a budget deficit, while inflation calls for a budget surplus. Since they already had the largest peacetime deficit in American history, they could hardly call for more deficit spending, and a reduction in the deficit to battle inflation would exacerbate the already bad unemployment situation. The Keynesians were therefore left without anything to offer to rectify the situation. Soon, many were proclaiming the death of Keynesian economics.[4]

That was a supply-sider talking. *He was ridiculing a Carter deficit of $45 billion.* Now, the unprecedented situation of an economic recovery and a budget deficit more than equaling the total of all government deficits combined in our entire history pointed up the absurdity of now switching back to a Keynesian solution. *Keynes did not envisage a 1984 situation nor had any other economist who ever lived.* Like 1929, it was a totally *unprecedented* situation. For now, rather than a growing economy. which Reagan desperately needed, a new recession was underway and Keynesian solutions of deliberately increasing deficits on top of what already existed were not only absurd, but, despite their inappropriateness, ominously inevitable.

Meanwhile, back to Erdman:

> If despite the largest deficit spending in the history of the universe—which is as good a description as any of Reagan's supply-side policies and the vast deficit that resulted—the American economy, while recovering robustly, still leaves almost ten million Americans out of work; if the same holds true for the Canadians and the Germans and the French and the Scandinavians, what will get us and thus the world moving back to full employment and prosperity for all?
>
> Have we reached a point now where both Say and Keynes are dead?
>
> If so, where lies salvation?
>
> If nobody knows, is it then inevitable that the system is going to blow up for sure this time?
>
> If not now, then when?
>
> Read on and find out. A hint: the end may be nearing, but it's not here yet.

My only criticism of Erdman was that he didn't go far enough. He saw the unprecedented problem but failed to see the overriding importance of the

---

[4]Bruce R. Bartlett, *Reaganomics: Supply Side Economics in Action* (New York: Quill edition, 1981), p. 3.

historical parallels. If he had, he wouldn't have stated: "I do not see a Crash
of '86 along Joe Granville lines, but I do see an end to the current investment
honeymoon."[5] He, too, would have seen that the crash could not be that long
delayed.

VI

The lightning-like change in investor psychology the day after election day was
almost total. It was as if everyone knew the lines to a prerehearsed script—
knew that an important scene had ended on November 6. It was either a
brand-new cast in the drama coming onstage, or the old players had completely flipped, now speaking lines completely out of character. But the audience didn't need the script. They silently sensed a deep change, the post-
election day market stripping away the façade of the pre-election rhetoric. All
the dilemmas had been there before. But with the votes counted and the
winner declared, no time was wasted in rolling back the rug to reveal the extent
of the mess that had been swept under it.

   The Wall Street Journal spelled out the sudden change. On November 13
the opening paragraph on the front page stated the following: "Economic
advisers to Reagan face a dilemma in preparing the fiscal 1986 budget. With
nearly two-thirds of the budget untouchable and with a tax boost regarded as
a last resort, there is growing doubt that the deficit can be reduced." The stock
market, having seen election day as the last hurrah, responded with a drop of
12.59 points, dropping the Dow to 1,206.60 for the fifth consecutive post-
election decline. The *Journal* story had simply and clearly implied the dis-
honesty of the pre-election rhetoric.

   This time it would be difficult to hold the market in the narrow trading
range of the past two months. In that period the market had stayed locked
into a narrow 80-point trading range, giving no great rewards to either the bulls
or the bears. The bulls claimed that the period was marked by bullish consolidation while the bears noted it as a period of stock distribution. The bullish
argument, which was an outgrowth of the optimism generated by the July–
August 153-point rally, was that interest rates were headed lower, an observation given an extra fillip in late October when President Reagan also forecasted
a continued drop in rates. Added to the bullish argument was the widespread
belief that upon Reagan's expected landslide reelection the stock market
would take off on the upside. That's about all the bulls had going for them
—lower interest rates and the election. They weren't looking at all at the other
side of the interst rate coin, which made the more classic argument that lower
rates were reflecting a worsening economy and the threat of a weaker dollar,
which in time would see a disturbing foreign repatriation of funds. They chose

[5]*Paul Erdman's Money Book*, p. 171.

to ignore completely the great 1929 example of collapsing interest rates which proved to be no boon for the stock market or the economy. With a peaking of stocks on election day and a near-term peak in bonds, the bullish boat had lost its rudder. The bulls lost their last reasons for buying stocks.

They now wouldn't be buying stocks because of yield. Bonds yielded more. They now wouldn't be buying stocks because of earnings. Earnings were definitely trending lower. Jay Levy saw earnings down by 40 percent by the spring of 1985. They now wouldn't be buying stocks because of a booming economy. The economy was in a slowdown which was likely to worsen. They now wouldn't be buying stocks because of Reagan's reelection. The market had been saying since election day that Reagan's reelection was bearish. They now wouldn't be buying stocks because interest rates were going to come down. The bond market was saying that rates were soon to stabilize and go back up. There remained, however, one reason for buying stocks, bizarre as it might seem. *People were now buying stocks because they wanted to lose money!* It was the only possible remaining reason, illogical as it sounds.

But it wasn't illogical at all! Sigmund Freud had done much of the pioneering work in all phases of self-guilt and had touched on the evidence that a large number of gamblers unconsciously want to lose so as to atone for some hidden guilt. James Dines stressed that conclusion in the opening chapter in his large work on technical analysis.[6] I took it a step further by identifying in terms of market volume where the dividing line stood between investment and speculation (gambling). Once it was determined, *one could then conclude that large stock market losses would follow the latter period.* That was based on the well-documented assumption that most gamblers lose and unconsciously want to lose.

A simple comparison of the volume figures in the 1920s and the past decade illustrated a very interesting point. The violent departure from normal trading volume proved *the disturbing transition from investment to short-term trading.* In other words, the investor didn't stand a chance in 1929. In 1984 virtually everybody was in the market for the short haul, which, of course, injected a highly disturbing degree of *instability.* Everybody became impatient for quick profits. The radical departure from normal trading volume could only mean that people were turning over their stocks at an alarming rate. In our own decade, instead of telling their clients that the Dow was headed for 1,500 and 3,000 at the end of the decade, stockbrokers should have been calling attention to the fact that *the current volume curve was a dead ringer for what it was in 1929.*

Here are the figures:

[6]James Dines, *How the Average Investor Can Use Technical Analysis for Stock Profits* (Dines Chart Corporation, October 1972), pp. 1–14.

Market Trading Volume (in millions of shares)

1918	143.3	1972	4,138.2
1919	318.3	1973	4,053.2
1920	227.6	1974	3,517.7
1921	172.8	1975	4,693.4
1922	260.9	1976	5,360.1
1923	236.5	1977	5,273.8
1924	284.0	1978	7,205.1
1925	459.7	1979	8,155.9
1926	451.9	1980	11,352.3
1927	581.7	1981	11,853.7
1928	930.9	1982	16,458.0
1929	1,124.6	1983	21,589.6

We certainly hadn't doubled our population in the years 1982 and 1983 or doubled the number of stockholders in that period. The violent change (as between 1927 and 1929) could have come only from *the rapid transition from investors to traders.* According to the above figures, the market entered such a period of extreme instability and the end of the bull market in 1983.

So I derived several parallels from these volume figures. Parallel 3 showed that the volume pattern was identical to that of 1929. Parallel 142 underscored that everything had become short-term trading. Now I add still a third parallel derived from these volume figures:

———

PARALLEL 161

Psychological
Excess of Trading Correlated with
Masochistic Urge to Lose

With the excessively large trading contingent, coupled with the documented evidence that an excess of trading is invariably followed by a market collapse, the volume comparison now showed three exact 1929 parallels.

While there were no defensible reasons for buying stocks at this time, prior to election day stocks had been bought for the wrong reasons. First of all, the investor was gone. This was strictly a trading market and there was no future in it for investing. Even with a shortened six-month capital gains period, *there wasn't enough time left in this market for capital gains.* The sand in the market hourglass was running out very fast now. Buying long seemed masochistic.

Inasmuch as the institutions now were responsible for 75 percent of total market volume, the growing market instability and the poor shot at capital gains rested largely at their doorstep. Institutions had increasingly become market timers. There was no long-term stability in the makeup of their portfolios. Against this background of volatility, the increasing shift from stocks to bonds as well as the evidence of nine consecutive weeks of rising money market fund assets showed the market increasingly weighted down by a rising and unwanted supply of shares. The long-term investor was not there to pick up the institutional slack, because that individual had already done his buying back in early 1983 and had gotten locked in with large losses. The stock market was thus rushing toward that magic moment when everybody would want to (or be forced to) sell at the same time.

At this very late date, far too many advisory services were bullish. *Investors Intelligence* showed that 57 percent of the services were bullish. That implied that the buying had already been done, with the bulk of it probably done in early August. Such earlier buyers offered no market support at this time. Thus, any future rally attempts would be followed by an avalanche of selling. Whether one more rally attempt could be squeezed in was not an important consideration. The big picture predominated. There could be brief periods of relief for the traders, but there was no sunshine whatsoever for the investors.

The brief bull market of 1982–83, which had lasted only nine to ten months, provided the illusion of long-term strength, and it was in that brief period that most people did their buying. Their reasons entrapped them. They bought because of the improving economy. They bought because corporate earnings were rising. They bought because they were sure Ronald Reagan would be reelected. And they bought (the last hurrah) because interest rates were coming down. But a new generation of stock buyers did not exist because there were no defensible reasons to buy stocks. Thus, the earlier buyers were stuck. All new buyers would be losers over the next few months because there was nothing to support stocks that long against the developing crash conditions.

In the face of such developing conditions, Arthur Laffer was saying at this time not to worry. His supply-side position was simply that we would work out of the deficit straits automatically with an expanding economy. *But he had been equally optimistic in the spring of 1983 when the great bear market in stocks began.* The steady stream of statistics coming in showed that the economy was not expanding. Producer prices fell for the third straight month, the first time that had happened since 1967. Corporate profit growth slowed abruptly in the third quarter, largely because of a cutback in economic expansion. Retail sales dropped and auto sales began to fall, that being the last bulwark of economic strength. Further aggravating the situation, world harvests of all major crops were setting highs, portending problems for U.S. farmers who were major producers of those crops. The collapse in commodity prices which had dated back to May had paralleled a similar decline in 1929 which had started in the same calendar month.

VII

The drop in the Dow after election day had been precipitous. From 1,244.15 on November 6, the highest closing level in the entire bear market rally phase which had started in July, the post-election slide carried the average swiftly down to 1,185.29 by November 19. That almost 60-point slide was accomplished in nine sessions.

On November 16 the Dow had fallen sharply by 18.22 points, cracking the coveted 1,200 level to close at 1,187.94. There were over a thousand declining stocks. On the nineteenth, however, something was wrong. The advance/decline line recorded a worse drop than on the sixteenth but the Dow Jones Industrial Average fell only by 2.65 points. I interpreted this to mean that the specialists found themselves embarrassingly in a long position. This meant that they had to take the market up one more time so as to disengage themselves from that long position. Sure enough, the Dow rose sharply for the next three sessions, rising 9.83 on November 20, 6.40 on November 21, and 18.78 points on November 23, the Dow returning to 1,220.30 that day.

This was the day I appeared on *Wall Street Week* with Louis Rukeyser and a panel consisting of Frank Cappiello, Robert Nurock, and Robert Stovall. In the limited amount of time on that show, seen by ten million viewers, I stressed a few of the technical indicators that were portending an approaching market crash. The advance/decline line was underscored, drawing the parallel with 1929 action. I reminded Nurock that despite the huge rally in the Dow from 1,086.57 to 1,244.15 between July and November, the advance/decline line never returned to the May 2 level when the Dow had shown a rally peak then at 1,186.56. I also underscored the documented bear market action of the high/low indicator as well as the constant daily bear market lows being recorded by the American Stock Exchange advance/decline line. I summed up this technical evidence as proving that the Dow Jones Industrial Average was and had been on a "solitary walk" since June 1983. I stated that this was what had been seen in 1929 and what was being seen in 1984.

Of course I did not expect to be believed. Bob Nurock on the same show stated that he would be an aggressive buyer at Dow 1,220.30. But I wanted it to be solidly on the record that I was stating the same things that night that Roger Babson had stated in September 1929 and that both of us based our remarks on the identical technical evidence. I predicted a slide to the 600–700 area in the Dow for 1985.

The sharp drop in the Climax Indicator from +22 to zero the day after the election virtually guaranteed that any subsequent rally attempts would see a clear picture of declining tops, setting the market up for what I called the giant downward zigzag. With a Climax Indicator reading of +14 on the November 23 sharp rally, I had all the technical evidence I needed to walk into the Public Broadcasting studio in Owings Mills, Maryland, that night and predict a near-term crash.

At the very least, the signals which had preceded the January–February downturn were being repeated. The crash could start anytime now or, if a Santa Claus rally attempt intervened, no later than in the January–February 1985 period.

I was impressed by the fact that the assets of the money market funds had risen for ten consecutive weeks. That had been one of the outstanding characteristics of the January–February 1984 slide.

Still more impressive, the post-election day slide had taken the Dow below the 1,209.64 level, that being the halfway point of the rally that had taken place between October 9 and November 6. According to the 50% Principle, that technically implied that the larger 50% Principle level of 1,165.36 would be tested, the halfway point of the entire upswing stretching from July 24 to November 6. Should that give way, the last test would be the July low of 1,086.57, a breaking of which would see the market in crash action.

After fulfilling my role of Roger Babson on the November 23 telecast, my third appearance on the *Wall Street Week* show, I was aware of the historical probability that I wasn't bearish enough. Cognizant of the small band of Cassandras who, in 1928 and 1929, foresaw the horrendous trouble ahead, I considered myself in a similar role. The "little band" was laughed at, totally disbelieved—but right. But even then, they weren't bearish enough. While I did forecast a drop to 600–700 in the Dow for the next year, I would not have been the least surprised if the drop went much further. Nobody knew the day or the hour when the great crash would occur, any more than Noah knew the exact moment of the flood. But Noah was forewarned to build the ark, and for the umpteenth time, I sent out another warning. It was late, very late.

Technical weakness was being best illustrated at this time in terms of the weekly highs and lows. The week before I was on *Wall Street Week* the Dow had declined 31 points. For that week there were 76 stocks recording new 12-month highs and 62 recording new lows. However, for the week ending November 23, a week seeing the Dow rise 32 points, there were 76 stocks recording new highs and 96 recording new lows. In other words, the important high/low indicator was *worse* on a 32-point Dow up week than it had been the week before on a 31-point down week.

Bob Nurock asked me what would have to happen to make me turn bullish. I said that I would want to see all markets in gear on the upside. Richard Russell had accented that point many years ago. There has to be a *harmony* of price movement. Without harmony, there can be no happy tunes.

VIII

An increasing number of 1929 parallels were accompanying the last hurrah.

PARALLEL 162
Historical
Corporations Rich in Cash

A book was published in 1982[7] which stated at the outset: "A Dow Jones Industrial Average of 3,000 by December, 1989." It claimed no extraordinary foresight, but merely the acceptance of the fact that corporations kept more of their profits than they paid out in dividends, what the authors called the R factor. On the basis of that factor, they claimed that stocks would always ultimately reflect their constantly higher liquidating value, known in the trade as the book value. To back their contention, the authors presented a chart of a two-hundred-year uptrend in stock prices in the United States. It was all very impressive, but as full of holes as a piece of Swiss cheese.

In one short paragraph they completely negated their entire thesis:

> The Great Crash of 1929 created tremendous values. Those investors who purchased stocks in the early Thirties and held them were rewarded with gigantic increases. We believe that the crash of the Seventies has created a similar situation. Tremendous values are now available in the stock market. Investors who purchase stocks in the early Eighties should be rewarded with a dramatic advance.

The authors sidestepped the very embarrassing fact that their theory offered absolutely no defense against a stock market crash. Any six-year-old would understand that there are tremendous values after a market crash. But suppose one bought their theory before a crash? There was nothing new about an R factor or anything else it was called. People in 1929 bought the same fallacious concept and were later wiped out. One can always make a generality about corporations being rich in cash, but to base a market theory of buy-and-hold on this completely ignores the presence of market cycles, especially the long-term Kondratieff Wave calling for a major stock market crash in the 1980s.

This argument came up constantly in the 1983–84 period, soon to be completely invalidated by a great crash in stock prices.

In October 1929 several references were made to cash-rich corporations:

On October 2, 1929, *The Wall Street Journal* carried the following in the "Broad Street Gossip" column:

> But no one can say that industry is not on a very solid foundation, in better condition, in fact, *than at any time in history. Corporations and individuals have more cash than ever before* [emphasis added].

[7]Thomas Blamer and Richard Shulman, *Dow 3000* (New York: Harper's Magazine Press, 1982).

Then on October 24, 1929, in the *Journal:*

> The big corporations now have more cash than they need and are lending it
> in Wall Street. With *corporations rich in cash,* having small inventories and being
> stronger than ever physically, it would require more than a big market slump to
> disturb their equilibrium. And the same applies to the thrifty individual who has
> saved [emphasis added].

In the same ill-fated month, Irving Fisher, the top-rated economist in the
United States, pointed to factors making for expansion in market volume and
prices. He fell into the same trap back then that impressed Blamer and
Shulman in this decade. Here are his own words as carried in *The Wall Street
Journal* on October 24, 1929:

FISHER DISCUSSES STOCK PRICES

*Points to Factors Making for Expansion in
Market Volume and Prices*

In an address before the District of Columbia Bankers Association here
Wednesday evening, Irving Fisher, Professor of Economics, Yale University,
discussing the question "Is the Stock Market Too High?" gave reasons why the
market has doubled since 1923. Rise in the market after the war above the pre-war
level by from 50% to 100% was due to war inflation, Professor Fisher said.

Since then it has doubled, he said, for the following reasons: Because of
increasing prosperity from: Less unstable money. New mergers. New scientific
management. The new labor policy of waste saving. New inventions. Prohibition.
The magnification of effects of all the preceding causes to the extent that bonds
and other senior securities do not share in the increased earnings. Investors' new
confidence in common stocks through diversification, through investment trusts,
investment managers and mergers. The investors' recent loss of confidence in
bonds because, in being in terms of dollars, they impose on the investor a risk
of a loss in the purchasing power of the dollar. An income tax which has been
perverted into a capital tax, and a public speculative mania.

Professor Fisher expressed the opinion that of these dozen or so causes the
public speculative mania is among the least important.

He pointed out that during the past three years of bull movement every
reaction of the stock price level downward has been hailed as the beginning of
a major bear movement, but thus far, he said, this major downward movement
has not materialized; instead, there has been a series of fluctuations up and down.

Stocks Versus Bonds

Commenting on the suggestion that the stock market is "inflated" because,
for example, utilities are selling at 25½ times their earnings . . . it is asked why
the prices of their stocks are so "inflated" as compared with the larger yields of

bonds in the same companies. Professor Fisher pointed to the fact that bonds will not share in future great savings and economies, such as are reasonably expected from the recent mergers in the utilities field. Stocks, he declared, "will get all of these greater earnings, for the bond return is fixed."

So if the stock market is now inflated, he continued, it would be only because the earnings apportioned to the account of stocks, both distributed and undistributed, have not increased or shown any likelihood of increasing in the ratio of the increase of the price level of stocks. But the contrary is the case, he added.

Reasons for Larger Earnings

A number of reasons were given by Professor Fisher why expected earnings in the future should bulk larger than a few years ago, among which is the fact that we are living in the age of mergers. That the old trust-busting sentiment has lapsed almost completely is shown, he declared, by the inability of the opponents of the Coolidge and Hoover administrations to get the public excited on the subject. "These mergers," Fisher said, "have effected great economies, and have therefore increased the profits of corporations to a great extent. Every merger boosts the stock of the merged companies because of this expectation. A considerable part of the rise in stock prices in the last two years has been due to the increased rate of formation of these mergers and the anticipation of future economies arising from them."

In conclusion Professor Fisher termed as "silly" our present taxation system which counts realized capital gain as income.

"A holder of Allied Chemical and Dye stock told me," he said, "that he acquired it at 35 and now would like to sell it at over 300 but avoids doing so because he would be soaked in his income tax if he shifted the investment to something else. This means that the stocks which advance the most will not be sold, or sold the most reluctantly, or only on a still greater advance. That is, *the more they advance the more they tend to advance still further.*"

Fisher's entire thesis, which proved totally false, was repeated by Blamer and Shulman in the 1980s. It was a particularly dangerous form of idol worship, bowing down before the god of corporate earnings, in the baseless assumption that the cash-rich corporations would inevitably generate increasingly higher earnings without serious interruption.

The famous October 1929 Fisher speech offered a source of several additional parallels which were now quite evident (I use Fisher's exact terms):

Historical
Less Unstable Money

Under the Reagan administration the U.S. dollar had become the most coveted currency in the world. Inflation had been reduced to about 4 percent and one could say for the first time in a long while that we were enjoying less unstable money.

Historical
New Scientific Management

Fisher did not specifically define what he had in mind when he included this as a reason for prosperity, but I feel it is pretty certain he was referring to the Henry Ford-inspired production line and the great advances in automatic and semiautomatic machinery. Business was the business of America and scientific management was the guiding hand of increased business efficiency.

Corporate America in the 1980s also saw a parallel scientific management —the keen young executives streamlining their huge operations with the computer. Business was truly a science.

Historical
New Labor Policy of Waste Saving

Due to the 1981–82 recession, many corporations were reduced to a lean-and-mean status and became increasingly conscious of waste saving.

PARALLEL 166
Historical
New Inventions

Matching the industrial revolution of the 1920s, new inventions in the 1980s had made a significant contribution to the business of America. The age of the computer had fully arrived. Of equal importance, the world had grown increasingly smaller through the use of satellites, revolutionizing communication.

PARALLEL 167
Historical
Job Loss High Due to Automation

Streamlining the business of America in the 1920s was not without its problems. "Mass production meant hard times for millions of workers. Once its techniques had been mastered, *up to 200,000 workers a year were replaced by automatic and semiautomatic machinery.* A new phrase entered the language —'technological unemployment.' For the first time in a hundred years employment in manufacturing struck a plateau, then turned down. Yet the labor force as a whole was rising in the Twenties much faster than the rate of population growth, from 41.5 million to 48 million"[8] (emphasis added).

The parallel with the present is striking. The automatic and semiautomatic machinery today has graduated to the new world of robotics, a cousin of our computer-directed industry. It, too, has caused a disruption in the work force, making a contribution toward a comparative high level of unemployment.

PARALLEL 168
Historical
Labor Force Rising Faster Than the Population

As in the 1920s, the growth in the labor force has far outstripped the rise in the population. Between 1970 and 1980 the population of the United States rose approximately 11.3 percent while the employed work force grew by 23 percent.

[8]Geoffrey Perrett, *America in the Twenties* (New York: Simon & Schuster, 1982), p. 321.

PARALLEL 169

Historical
Relatively High Unemployment

Long before the 1929 crash, unemployment had been a nagging problem, remaining above normal despite the overall rise in the work force. Right in the heart of the boom (February 1928), unemployment was more serious than at any time since immediately after the war.

The same trends were noted during the first Reagan administration. Despite the overall rise in the work force, unemployment remained high, standing at approximately 7 percent, right where it was when President Reagan took office in 1981. The economic recovery was as suspect in 1984 as it had been in 1929. This, too, was an era of permanently high unemployment.

PARALLEL 170

Historical
Diversification

Professor Fisher had stressed the safety aspects of diversification in his pre-crash speech. He was referring to the reduction of risk available in the investment trust shares that were then so popular. His "safety net" thesis disintegrated a few days later as the investment trust shares tumbled along with everything else.

Similar arguments today pointing up the advantages of diversification via mutual funds contain as much substance as Fisher's mistimed statement. The market was no longer anchored in long-term concepts, now being tossed on the waves of short-term timing as documented by the doubling of trading volume between 1981 and 1983. With institutions accounting for 75 percent of the daily volume, diversification offered a poor shield against the predicted downturn in the 1983 and 1984 market and the panic and crash seen looming in the weeks and months ahead.

PARALLEL 171

Historical
Downward Movement Has Not Materialized

To say that the major downward movement of the Kondratieff Wave has thus far not materialized is to offer as much solace as did Fisher's complacency a few days before the great crash. All the warning voices of 1928 and 1929 were justified in one fell swoop when the collapse did occur. To say that something won't happen because it hasn't happened yet is such a weak argument that it is seen to be no argument at all.

PARALLEL 172

Historical
Realized Capital Gain Counts as Income

Fisher termed the tax system "silly" but used it as a cornerstone for his argument that stocks which advance the most will not be sold because the holders of those stocks do not want to pay that capital gain tax. The net result was that people generally would hold their stocks too long, which is the same general failing today. Fisher's "perpetual motion" theory of advancing stock prices, put forward at the very worst of times, was given great credibility by his stature as the best-known economist in the United States at that time.

PARALLEL 173

Historical
Overcrowded Industries to Be Reduced

The proliferation of the automobile companies in the 1920s created an overcrowded and fiercely competitive industry. That industry was decimated by mergers and bankruptcies, and the ensuing crash and depression did the rest. The industry was eventually reduced to what became known as "the Big 3."

The parallel today is the computer industry. When somebody comes up with a good thing, everybody wants to jump into it. Thus the field becomes overcrowded and fiercely competitive and will be decimated by mergers, bankruptcies, and eventually the crash. The computer field and everything related to it overproduced to meet what was thought to be an unlimited demand. Like the 1983 new-issue market, the field became glutted. No sooner was one model put on the market than it became obsolete. The stocks collapsed, and only a handful remained relatively unscathed, a few leaders such as International Business Machines and Digital Equipment. So, like the automobile industry of the 1920s that at one time numbered over a hundred different companies, the computer industry was headed toward the ultimate "Big 3."

PARALLEL 174

Historical
Hoover and Reagan Tax Cuts

In the best supply-sider tradition, both the Hoover and Reagan administrations cut taxes early in their terms.

PARALLEL 175

Historical
Rising Value of the Dollar

Prior to the great crash of 1929, an outstanding phenomenon was the rising value of the dollar. For example, the dollar was worth 8 francs in 1919, 16 in 1923, and 25 by 1926.

The phenomenon of 1983–84 was the towering dollar. It seemed that nothing could bring it down. It had attracted a tidal wave of foreign money flowing into the United States. Foreign currencies were collapsing. The once-mighty British pound had collapsed to new all-time lows.

PARALLEL 176

Historical
Pockets of Poverty

The 1927–29 period was marked by pockets of poverty. Many unskilled workers were not enjoying the benefits of the Coolidge-Hoover prosperity.

It was no different during the widely advertised Reagan "recovery." Across the land there was still too much unemployment, stemming from the collapse in commodity prices, the three-year agricultural depression, near-poverty in the steel industry.

The unfavorable U.S. trade balance by late 1984 had reached the worst level in the country's history. This was costing us another 200,000 jobs a year.

PARALLEL 177

Historical
Buy Bonds

In 1929 Hoover prevailed on Mellon to tell the people to buy bonds. Fearing the stock speculation and its ultimate consequences, Hoover wanted people to convert their stock holdings into bonds.

In the spring of 1984 President Reagan recommended the purchase of bonds, predicting that interest rates would come down. Interest rates would come down, but not for the reasons the president had in mind at that time.

PARALLEL 178

Historical
Construction Boom Ending

Tracing out an almost identical curve, the building boom of the 1920s was matched by that of the late 1970s and early 1980s, both upswings terminated some months prior to the crash in the stock market.

PARALLEL 179

Historical
Farmlands in Turmoil

When Herbert Hoover took office, our farmlands were in turmoil. Land prices were dropping precipitously, the trend having started with the Florida land bust in 1926.

When Ronald Reagan took office, our farmlands were also in turmoil, farmland prices also dropping precipitously. In 1984 alone farmland prices dropped 20 percent.

IX

As of November 29, the market was put into an easy position to fully confirm the breaking under the November 19 low of 1,185.29. Both the high/low indicator and the advance/decline line were expected to give powerful confirmations of further weakness to come. This time it looked as if it would be very difficult for the Dow to avoid going under its trendline. The market was seen to be fast approaching the most critical of all periods, and there would be a double bearish influence of irresistible downside pressure. Not only was the market approaching the end of the six-month capital gains period but it was not entering the period of normal topping out of the four-year cycle.

The expected huge post-election rally had failed to materialize. Another month had gone by without those widely advertised new highs in the Dow. Despite the seasonal probability of some rally attempts in December, I saw the following month as a treacherous minefield in which anything could happen, with the probabilities heavily weighted against the bull.

A brilliant summation of the problems at this point was written by Hodding Carter III in the November 29 edition of *The Wall Street Journal:*

WASHINGTON STAGGERS TOWARD A FISCAL ABYSS

What's going on in Washington isn't a serious exercise in budget making. It's the Reagan administration's version of the proverbial Chinese fire drill. The problem, however, is that *the deficit is an ominous reality,* not a circus make-believe, and the president's refusal to come to grips with its implications is not so much humorous as *frightening.* Add to the president's willful *irresponsibility* the additional ingredient that no one—underscore no one—in Washington today seems willing to venture a workable solution that stands the twin tests of fiscal responsibility and political feasibility, and *you have the makings of renewed economic misery* [emphasis added]. . . .

The dimensions of the problem must be restated repeatedly, if only to concentrate our attention. First, *there is no chance that the deficit will be brought much below $200 billion a year without radical surgery* [emphasis added]. Second, no one of any political persuasion in mainstream America believes that the economy can sustain persistent massive deficits without buckling. Third, the program areas that Reaganite and Democratic electoral politics have put off limits total more than $700 billion of the trillion-dollar budget. The remaining $290 billion or so represents the money spent on everything except defense, interest payments and Medicare. There is no way to squeeze enough money from those remaining programs to lower the deficit by any meaningful amount. . . .

The unpleasant is now the unavoidable, unless we are to court disaster. The untouchable labels must be removed from defense spending and middle-class entitlements. A selective tax increase, preferably accompanied by reform of the sort proposed by the Treasury Department, must be passed. The buck stops at the White House, but also at Congress as well. What's required is bitter medicine for Keynesians and supply-siders alike, but the patient can't recover without it.

Here was the fitting epitaph to the last hurrah.

22

The Bhopal Shock

[DECEMBER 1984]

I

As December began, the market was left in a weakened technical position. The disappointing market response to the sweeping reelection of Ronald Reagan lowered the resistance of the market and left it vulnerable. Implying in my December 1 letter that the stock market appeared on the very brink of probable crash action, I could, of course, have had no knowledge of the great tragedy that was about to hit the people of Bhopal, India, a major disaster directly affecting a major U.S. industrial corporation, Union Carbide, representing 3.33 percent of the Dow Jones Industrial Average. When such an unpredictable event hits a stock that is already extremely weak, it exacerbates the decline that follows. Union Carbide had temporarily bottomed in the 48 area in July against the background of a persistently declining trendline. The July–August rally had seen the stock price temporarily come up above its trendline but that rally had never turned the trendline itself up. By early September, the price had dropped back under the trendline again and by October the flattened trendline again turned down. The election day euphoria saw the price rally to 52, exactly touching the declining trendline. On the day before the Bhopal tragedy, the stock had declined to 49, close to breaking under the July low. The December 3 tragedy had come like a thief in the night, a nightmare that killed 2,500 and affected upward of 100,000 to 200,000 others through the leakage of deadly methyl isocyanate gas at the Union Carbide plant. The negative implications of the expected lawsuits were awesome, amounting to many times the entire value of the company. The December 3 tragedy sent out market shock waves and struck a near-mortal blow to the well-known chemical company, putting the finishing touches to a stock that was near collapse anyway.

This again raised the interesting question that constantly confronts those who must choose between technical analysis and fundamental analysis. A successful case can always be made that *the technical must precede the fundamental.* The technical cannot predict *events,* but it can and does predict areas of vulnerability before such areas can be detected and reported fundamentally. Therefore, the *persistent technical weakness* in Union Carbide preceded a new fundamental weakness and had made the stock particularly vulnerable to any piece of bad news. In a particularly damaging article in *The Wall Street Journal* on December 6, the Union Carbide disaster was related to what happened to the Manville Corporation in 1982, that company having to file for bankruptcy to protect itself against a rash of lawsuits stemming from deaths and injuries related to asbestos. Manville, then a member of the sacred Dow 30, crashed from $40 a share to under $5 a share between 1975 and 1982, with the bulk of that decline occurring in the 1981–82 market slide. The stock was ultimately removed from the Dow Jones Industrial Average in August 1982. The Manville crisis occurred when the 1982–83 brief bull market was just starting, and thus the disaster there failed to upset the general market. The shock to Union Carbide, however, occurred at a different time and against a completely different market background. Unlike August 1982, the general market was in a weak technical position. I strongly felt that the Union Carbide crisis would exacerbate a weak trend already in motion, any near-term market technical rallies notwithstanding.

PARALLEL 180

Historical
The Unpredictable Shock

In keeping with the proliferating 1929 parallels, the Union Carbide crisis related to the Hatry scandal which had suddenly exploded on the London scene in mid-September 1929. It didn't cause the 1929 crash that occurred a few weeks later, but it exacerbated a weak trend *that had already been in force.* It was in keeping with the times. Therefore, the U.S. stock market in late 1984, being in a fully documented classical and major bear market trend, was telling me that the events would be there so as to rationalize in retrospect why the market went down. Nobody could have predicted the Hatry scandal in August 1929, but any good technician would have seen that the 1929 summer rally was all in the blue chip stocks against the background of most stocks going lower and against the background of a weakening economy. Fundamental shocks coming later could then have been no surprise because they had given a technical forewarning of their occurrence. I had underscored the similarity between the July–August advance and the 1929 summer rally and thus shocking surprises following that similarity fit the disturbing pattern. The Union Carbide disaster dropped a huge boulder into an already choppy pond.

The Bhopal tragedy, like the Hatry scandal, came out of the blue and immediately decimated the value of Union Carbide stock. Unmentioned by other technicians, however, *there was a disturbingly high number of other stocks in the Dow Jones Industrial Average having chart patterns similar to that of Union Carbide just before the December 3 shock.*

Union Carbide's stock price was *cut in half* in 1984. Nobody had thought that was possible. Likewise, nobody could possibly envisage the Dow average being cut in half in the year ahead.

At this late date, there were still so many looking for that "second leg" to a bull market that had died in early 1983. While they were waiting, *the secondary markets were getting killed.* This was the most definitive technical evidence one could have preceding the worsening of a bear market. It was the peaking in those secondary markets in early 1983 that best foreshadowed the developing bear market. The same thing had happened in the 1928–29 period while most people had been mesmerized by the Dow Jones Industrial Average. Now, as then, *nobody was seriously taking safety precautions.* In 1929 the thinking was that the Federal Reserve would prevent any downturn of significance. The same thinking prevailed in late 1984. The collapse of the Hatry securities on the London Stock Exchange in September 1929 created a shock from which the market never recovered. *That was minuscule compared to the 1983–84 collapse of most stocks on the American Stock Exchange and in the over-the-counter market.* So there could be no second leg while these secondary markets were crashing. Robert Farrell of Merrill Lynch stated at this time that "we can't have the next leg of the bull market until people start giving up." Ironically, Wall Street was *not* recommending that people give up, and thus Wall Street was delaying their hoped-for "second leg."

II

The probabilities at this time were that most people who held stocks bought on the 1982–83 brief upsurge were holding them at a loss. Belatedly seeing that brief rise for what I had said it was at the time it was occurring, Alan Abelson, in *Barron's* issue of December 24, 1984, saw it in retrospect a full eighteen months after the 1983 peak:

> We also would like to give an award, even, alas, if it's rather in the nature of a posthumous one, to the individual investor. He bravely entered the stock market

in the fall of 1982 and was shamefully mugged by Street gangs without let or mercy for the next eight months. When last seen, he was buried beneath a mass of fallen stock prices. Perhaps his widow and orphans can draw some solace from the knowledge that the Forgotten Investor (a tombstone ad in his memory is being planned for the 1984 New York Stock Exchange Annual Report) was exploited in a new world record time. The last comparable episode, during the 'Sixties, took nearly 10 years. This time, the foul deed was done in barely eight months.

The fact that the Dow Jones Industrial Average was down only 8.1 percent under the all-time closing high of 1,287.20 recorded on November 29, 1983, hid the fact that hundreds of stocks had suffered losses since the 1983 highs far greater than those recorded in the great crash of 1929.

A brief sampling of well-known stocks attested to the great internal damage being inflicted upon the stock market:

Stock	1983 High	December 1984	Percentage Decline
Allis Chalmers	19 3/8	7	−63.8
Amax	32 3/8	16 1/2	−49.0
Am. Hosp. Supply	49	30	−38.7
Am. Motors	11 1/4	3 3/8	−70.0
Anacomp	23 1/8	2	−91.3
Apache Oil	16 1/2	11	−33.3
Arkla	30	18	−40.0
Armco Steel	21	9 1/8	−56.5
Asamera	14 1/2	7	−51.7
Asarco	44	21	−52.5
Augat	47 1/4	21	−55.5
Avon Products	37	20	−45.9
Aydin	62	18	−70.9
Bally Mfg.	28	12 5/8	−54.9
Bard, C. R.	47	20	−57.4
Baxter Travenol	31 3/8	12	−61.7
Best Products	27	12	−55.5
Bethlehem Steel	26	15 1/8	−41.8

Now, keep in mind that the great crash of 1929 saw the Dow industrials decline 47.8 percent, the railroads down 32.1 percent, and the utilities down 54.5 percent. However, prior to the crash, the stock market was in approximately the same position it was in December 1984. The general market had peaked and the averages were reflecting blue chip strength which was soon to give way. That is precisely what Roger Babson saw in September 1929 and what caused the legendary Jesse Livermore to go short across the board.

The devastating price comparisons made in late 1984 were a small sample of many hundreds of stocks which had already equated with the worst of the 1929-type declines, matching and exceeding the percentage drops shown here. Because those secondary markets had acted so poorly, most people now held stocks at a loss. A great many people were largely attracted to low-priced stocks, always dreaming of that "killing" in the market that such stocks seemed to offer when they were going up. They ended up getting killed, the way so many had since the spring of 1983.

Historically, such extreme internal market deterioration does not right itself with the secondaries suddenly getting well and climbing back to get in gear with the blue chips. On the contrary, it is the blue chips that collapse and join the secondaries. This is why it was so important to track those secondary areas all the way down from the early 1983 peak. The secondary issues, as they had in 1929, were putting the handwriting on the wall for what was ultimately going to happen to the blue chips.

This is why I had placed a great deal of emphasis on the bellwether stocks, those stocks having the most reliable records of leading the market. It is in those areas where the biggest and most reliable market stories are told.

III

In September it had been heard on the Financial News Network that Teledyne was a very important bellwether stock. The stock at that time was racing higher, approaching the $300 level. In a special bulletin dated September 18, I had included a chart of Teledyne accompanied by its important major trendlines together with an arrow indicating that the stock was almost at the peak of its upward channel. Following that bulletin, the stock peaked at 302⅜ and started down. The downtrend cut through all general market rally attempts, including the brief election day euphoria. The stock was trying to say something and, being an accepted bellwether stock of the first water, *it was warning of stormy weather ahead for the general market.* The key test for the stock was the approach toward the 200-day moving average trendline at the 250 level. On December 12 the stock broke sharply, dropping 10⅛ points to close at the very low of the day at 248⅞. It was important to see whether there would be any downside follow-through the next day. There was—the stock broke another 3 points. What was particularly strange was that *The Wall Street Journal* did not refer to the sharp break in the stock in the December 13 market commentary. Just as odd was the lack of reference to the Teledyne bellwether on the Financial News Network following the better than 60-point plunge after the stock had been bullishly referred to in September, when it was then racing toward the 300 mark.

Having had no signals indicating anything more than frustrating two- to three-day failing rally attempts, the bears confidently held their short positions and their put options. Their patience was that of contentment, lacking the frustration the bulls were exposed to in their fruitless search for those mythical "new highs by the end of the year," a phrase that had been incessantly pounded into the ears of the public all year. Now it could be seen that those widely disseminated forecasts, which had ranged all the way from 1,350 to as high as 1,500, were not based on technical knowledge but apparently rested on the fragile foundation of hope, an ethereal something that had never succeeded in changing the price of a stock.

But hope was slow to die. Despite the shabby technical condition of the market, *Investors Intelligence* reported in December that the percentage of bulls among the advisers they monitored rose to a new high of 59.8 percent. In the face of a worsening technical posture, such bullishness had to be seen as worthless as was the general Wall Street forecast of "new highs by the end of the year." Until that worthless bullish sentiment was destroyed, the market would find it very difficult to mount any meaningful rally. *Only a major market break could reverse the sentiment picture,* and thus any future buy signals of any importance had to stem from lower prices rather than higher ones. If the majority of market letters had been followed, then it had to be assumed that most people had already done their buying. The market could not enjoy any new areas of demand. The frustrated buyers who came in on the August rally could now only affect the supply side of the market equation, a fact that was increasingly confirmed in terms of the technical indicators.

Over the previous year, I had referred to my "confusion index." It is simply a cumulative count of the number of times the word is used in *The Wall Street Journal* on the inside back page. At this time it had broken out to a new high for the bear market, and December 1984 showed the most frequent use of the word during any recent period in memory. Since the market hated confusion, the high index readings had always been bearish and record highs were that much more negative.

In the midst of this confusion, however, there was a comforting clarity in the traditional technical indicators, those of major importance. Some technicians, in attempting to build independent systems of their own, often downplay the traditional indicators because they feel that technical analysis has become so popular that the traditional indicators may not work anymore. That is always a highly dangerous concept. Any departure from such time-tested indicators as the advance/decline line, the high/low indicator, the 200-day trendline, and the 50% Principle is foolhardy. Such was the case in late 1984.

It was necessary to ground one's strategy on this solid foundation: when this was done, the conclusion had to be bearish. While I was well aware of a number of technical downside nonconfirmations at this time, the posture of the other major indicators in their steady decline underscored the temporary nature of the early December low in the Dow at 1,163.21. Several things took place on the way toward that low.

The 50% Principle states that when a swing in the Dow retraces more than half of the previous swing, the probabilities are very high that the entire swing will be retraced. Applying it to the market at this time, I came up with the following:

1. Halfway between 1,175.13 and 1,244.15 = 1,209.64
   That level was broken on November 13. Dow will now test the 1,175.13 level.
2. Halfway between 1,086.57 and 1,244.15 = 1,165.36
   That level was broken on December 7. Dow will now test the 1,086.57 level.
3. Halfway between 776.92 and 1,287.20 = 1,032.06
   A breaking of that level would signal the crash, testing the 776.92 level.

So, at this point, the scenario looked unassailable. However, what can go down can also go up. In order to break this bearish pattern, the Dow would have to come back up and close above the 1,203.68 level, the halfway point between the 1,244.15 high and the 1,163.21 low.

I was very bearish at this point. I believed that the advance/decline line had been telling a bearish story, recent rally attempts failing to budge the line off the current critical zone. And never, ever would I turn away from the American Stock Exchange advance/decline line. It was making new bear market lows every day. The Amex Market Value Index broke the trendline on the November slide and was not too far away from the July low. The high/low indicator had been persistently negative, the way it was expected to act in a bear market. The 200-day trendline on the Dow Jones Industrial Average was cracked and that never was an event that could be treated lightly. Another bear market characteristic was the better than 60-point decline immediately following the highest short interest on record.

For the fourteenth consecutive week, the money market fund assets had risen, bringing the total to the highest level seen since December 1982. With the drop in short-term rates, the steady rise in assets could only mean that money was fleeing the stock market for safety rather than chasing less attractive rates. This was the key characteristic accompanying the sharp January–February 1984 stock slide. Now we were seeing a more extended picture of money leaving the stock market.

But then something happened. On December 18 the Dow exploded, the average rocketing almost 35 points, rising from 1,176.79 to close at 1,211.57. While the 50 percent retracement level of 1,203.68 had been bettered, there had been too many false rallies up until this time. I demanded more proof that things had changed. I labeled it as the last bull trap of the year.

I went through the ritual again of explaining the characteristics of a bull trap: (1) news, (2) the market doing the obvious, (3) effecting an upside breakout through a significant resistance level, (4) high volume, and (5) technical weakness by virtue of important upside nonconfirmations. In this case there was no disputing the obvious news pertaining to interest rates following the sharp drop in the money supply. It was too obvious, but by that time the A-Dis Short-Term Trading Barometer was racing toward a reconfirmed sell signal, and so it was clear that any upside explosive response would be of very short duration and would coincide with the new sell signal. The upside move did cut through the overhead resistance area between 1,185 and 1,200 in the Dow but encountered much stronger resistance on a momentary crossing above the 1,220 level on December 19. Certainly the volume was there, as it had been on all previous 1984 bull trap upward explosions. While there was room for some argument pertaining to what upside nonconfirmations existed, the Climax Indicator and Net Field Trend readings were all too familiarly reminiscent of the previous important 1984 bull traps. The Climax Indicator had soared to a +25 reading on December 18. That was similar to the +23 reading of January 5, the +28 reading of August 3, the +22 reading of August 21, and the +22 reading of November 6. As for the sharp rise in the Net Field Trend Indicator, that characteristic had been in force in January 1984, when it had risen to +14, and in August, when it had risen sharply to +19. Up to this time, every one of the brief upward explosions since August had shown lower intraday highs.

IV

What was the market saying at this point? I maintained that the general market would not rise to meet the blue chips but that the blue chips would descend to the general market. Historically, the market would always find a rationale, later to be documented fundamentally. The market was saying that something was wrong with the economic recovery. If it had been a normal recovery, one would have expected that the mortgage delinquency rate and the foreclosure rate would have been trending downward. On the contrary, *The Wall Street Journal* ran an article on December 19 with the following headline: "Mortgage Payments and Foreclosures Rose to Record Levels in the Third Quarter." The 1984 third-quarter rate *topped the highest delinquency rate recorded at the depths of the 1982 recession.* The *Journal* report stated that industry analysts said the third-quarter spurt in delinquencies—despite the decline in joblessness—reflected regional pockets of continued high unemployment, a nationwide increase in delinquent payments of other consumer loans, and the slower rate of increase in the prices of houses. That was *not* a reflection of a normal economic upturn. It smacked of the 1929 economy, when there were also pockets of poverty, a maldistribution of income, a three-year agricultural depression, far too much unemployment, and a growing malaise in the housing industry.

End-of-the-month reports showed a huge buildup in consumer debt. That fact, coupled with the report on delinquencies and foreclosures, signaled a dangerous pattern of precarious overextension of debt.

Against this background of rising trouble, the administration was seeking to pressure the Federal Reserve to ease money rapidly to offset these growing economic potholes. But the stock market sensed a much larger problem that would have to be faced in 1985. Unlike the period when we could shift from the supply-side economics of Herbert Hoover into the Keynesian economics of Franklin Roosevelt and then inflate budgetary deficits with impunity, today we do not have the luxury of Keynes to fall back on because we would be starting at the highest budgetary deficits in history, deficits history will record as having been totally out of control. The danger was that the minute our foreign investors sensed that the shift was going from supply side to Keynes, they would pull every nickel out of the U.S. stock market, and fast.

Alan Abelson of *Barron's,* in speaking of the Street gangs who shamefully mugged the public for eight months after the fall of 1982, said that the public was now buried beneath a mass of fallen stock prices. So there it was: recognition of the fact, a year and a half after the market peak, that the 1982–83 buyers got buried. But, of course, hope would always spring eternal. The bulls had sermonized for eighteen months on the bull market "second leg." However, when one has to wait that long for something to happen, then the odds mount rapidly in favor of its not happening. The cause for delay was hinted at in the Abelson piece. Abelson was careful with his language so that he couldn't be accused of directly pointing a finger at the brokerage firms and the specialists. But who else could he possibly be referring to when he talked about *the Street gangs shamefully mugging the individual investor?* Sharing the guilt with the brokerage houses and the specialists, the media certainly were part of the Gang, enticing the public to buy at the worst of times. To be fair, the economists had to take a good part of the blame also, since they provided the inflammatory statements that the brokers loved to quote when getting clients into the market at the top in early 1983. And the administration had key personnel as members of the Gang, notably Secretary of the Treasury Donald Regan, who told the country right at *the exact market peak in June 1983* that stocks were "a lot better buy than we've had in two decades."

That is the market game in a nutshell: the Gang versus the Public. If people were underwater in the market at this time (as they were), it was because they let the Gang run their affairs instead of letting the market itself dictate their strategy.

The Gang is powerful, make no mistake about that. It has the power to brainwash, mesmerize, attract one to the obvious like a powerful magnet.

However, it is not powerful enough to control the advance/decline line. It is not powerful enough to control the high/low indicator. In other words, the only thing it cannot control is technical analysis. Thus, technical analysis is the only weapon people have at their disposal to ward off the influence of the Gang.

The Gang has a strong motive, and *it is to maintain what it is doing.* The name of the game in the brokerage industry is *commission.* Since brokers know people generally don't like to sell or go short, they are automatically biased in favor of a higher market. Their pronouncements are therefore *designed to make one want to buy something.* This is why brokerage firms don't flash sell signals, but are always ready for a buy signal. So the moral question is always there: Do brokerage firms work first in their own interests and sidestep the public welfare? The evidence speaks for itself. Remember how quick Wall Street was to kill the fatted calf in December 1982? At that time, it was the biggest party in the history of the Street. Brokerage houses passed out the biggest Christmas bonuses ever, rewarding their producers for their part in bringing the public back into the market. They couldn't wait to divide the spoils. But where was the public's party? What happened to their bonuses?

Wall Street underwriters.   What was their motive? Profit. Get the new stock into the hands of the public as quickly as possible while the public had the appetite for it. Who cared what happened to the prices after that? They didn't own the stock. The public did. And thus the public walked in blindly to the biggest new-issue craze in Wall Street history, the underwriters glutting the public appetite. The public thus became buried in a sea of paper, much of it virtually worthless. But the underwriters made their profit.

The media.   What do they want? They want news. And when it comes to the market, they know more people are interested in bullish news than in bearish news. This means that they blow the horns louder on an up market because they know people like that kind of news. So the media are biased in favor of the favorable. Going into a bear market, that can, and did, have a devastating effect.

The administration.   Their motive is to stay in power. Thus all favorable events will be puffed up out of proportion and negative events will be downplayed.

The economists.   They are unwitting members of the Gang. They are sincere, but they are following something that *lags the market*—the economy. This is why an optimistic statement based on the economy was at loggerheads with the stock market after mid-1983.

Wall Street was optimistic. They wanted people to buy. That would be good for business, their business. Examining the identities of the sources of this optimism, one would have discovered that the people who were now telling the public how great 1985 was to be were the same people who told them a year before about how great 1984 was going to be. Such optimism was well reflected in *Investors Intelligence* figures which showed a very high 62.6 percent of all stock market letters they monitored as being bullish. Economists, except for a very few, like Jay Levy, *saw no recession in 1985.* They all said that President Reagan was dedicated to deficit reduction, but memories were so short. They had already forgotten the debt reduction package a year before and how optimistic the general outlook was. It was only two months into the new fiscal year and the November figures boosted the two-month budgetary deficit to $57.25 billion, just for openers. The slowing economy had contributed to those high figures.

Besides the Abelson piece about the Street gangs, *Barron's* on December 24 bore some heavy fruit. In the "Mailbag" section, the Henry Schloss letter cited the proliferation of financial futures and options, the excessive speculation taking place in the index futures, the 40 percent rise in the volume of trading in these instruments, and his cogent closing statement: *"It looks more and more like shades of 1929."*

Perhaps the most significant paragraph in the "Mailbag" letters came from Charles P. Stetson, vice president of the Stock Index Futures Group, Dean Witter Reynolds, Inc., of Greenwich, Connecticut: "As for the abnormal volatility of the stock index futures, it's caused by excessive fear and greed, exacerbated by the fact that stock index futures and index options are *the only way investors can participate in the stock market with less than 10% margin"* (emphasis added).

PARALLEL 181
Market
10 Percent Margins

Part of the dangerous market complacency was the notion that we would never return to the days of 10 percent margins. Actually, the 10 percent margins were a myth as far as the New York Stock Exchange was concerned. *Margins averaged 50 percent in 1929* and immediately following the great crash were lowered from 40 percent to 25 percent. But the introduction of the phrase "10 percent margins" accentuated the shades of 1929. It was the bucket shops that had offered the 10 percent margins back in 1929, considered illegal in terms of the New York Stock Exchange constitution. *Today bucket shops are legal.* (See Parallel 155.) In terms of the New York Stock Exchange constitution, option trading and trading in stock index futures are *bucket shop operations,* bets on stocks without taking ownership of those stocks. Again, shades of 1929.

V

Thus 1984 was to end looking like a patchwork quilt. Pre-election rhetoric had sought to smooth over the rough spots of the economy. A number of problems had not only refused to go away but were worsening in keeping with the gradual, but persistent, transition of the Kondratieff Wave from inflation to deflation.

Commodity prices continued to trend lower, thus worsening the position of those countries that most depended on a stable or rising market. They found their debt burdens barely manageable only because U.S. banks continued to paper over the loans, thus postponing a day of reckoning.

Nobody wanted gold or silver, both those metals having traced out radical extensions of the bear market trend they had been in for many months. As long as the dollar stayed strong, it was the kiss of death for the precious metals.

PARALLEL 182

Historical
Silver Price Collapse

In 1929–30 the price of silver collapsed, in keeping with the collapse of all commodity prices. One had to draw a parallel with the collapse in the price of this metal between 1980 and 1985.

The future price of oil was in doubt as 1984 ended. The many OPEC meetings had failed to calm the growing fears that cooperation was breaking down as falling crude prices began to make a joke out of the OPEC benchmark price. Eyes were glued on the February crude oil contract because chartists were aware of the implications of any move under the $25-per-barrel price. A break below that level showed a real technical possibility of a total collapse which OPEC could do nothing to stop. The projection underscored a drop to as low as $10 to $12 a barrel sometime in the months ahead. Such a move would drive the Saudis to repatriate billions in U.S. investments almost overnight in a desperate effort to refill their dwindling coffers.

There was great unrest in the U.S. farming community as the third year of depressed conditions came to an end, marking an almsot four-year recession in the agricultural segment of the economy. Peter T. Kilborn of *The New York Times* wrote a front-page piece on December 30, underscoring some of the basic problems which were not going away. He pointed out that farm policies had failed both the farmer and the taxpayer. Existing policies were seen to be distorting production, prices, and the federal budget. Looking ahead to 1985, the budget office wanted to eliminate many of the government's loan programs and abandon the system by which the government tries to maintain farm prices and farmers' incomes. Government spending on agriculture had doubled since 1977 to $34 billion, but in spite of this aid most farmers had remained mired in an almost four-year recession. High budgetary deficits had hurt the farmer more than the rest of the economy. The squeeze on profits was so bad that farmers' debts had jumped from $80 billion a decade ago to $155 billion in 1980 and $214 billion in 1984. Farms were failing at a rate of 36 per 1,000, more than triple the rate of other businesses.

"There is something happening out there that is very scary," said Senator-elect Tom Harkin, Democrat of Iowa. In the depth of the Depression, from 1931 to 1937, he said, the state lost 7.8 percent of its farmers. "In Iowa this year we are estimating we'll lose 10 percent. In one year! We're dying. There's no other way to put it."

"Contraction," said Secretary Block, a corn and hog farmer from Gilson, Illinois. "That's what we're looking at today."

Tariffs and quotas on imports were considered in 1985. Shades of 1929. Critics of the free market proposals said that such a policy would still force many farmers off the land, leading to the collapse of many farming communities.

This was the essence of the Kilborn piece in the *Times*.

Everywhere one looked the bottom line continued to scream out for attention: the government was running out of money and was seeking to plug up all existing loopholes. Obviously that meant, among other things, getting rid of farm supports which had added so much to the budgetary deficits.

In December it was reported that U.S. cuts had stunned the city of Chicago. That city was at the center of a study in national hunger, and Chicago reflected the effects of the continuing 9–12 percent unemployment in the Midwest.

The steel industry was also in a bind as the year ended. It was reported that a steel embargo could spark a trade war.

Scattered layoffs continued, with Honeywell and Texas Instruments laying off workers.

Rising short-term debt was becoming a greater problem.

Frauds and embezzlements continued to be reported. The FBI arrested New Mexico's deputy state treasurer, white-collar crime becoming an almost routine report.

Despite the continuing drop in interest rates, housing starts dropped, reflecting the continued squeeze stemming from an increasing portion of the population taking on far too much debt.

Prudential Bache reported a loss of $104.8 million for the first nine months of 1984, the largest loss ever for a full-service brokerage firm. Obviously such a loss documented the inescapable fact that the firm was calling the stock market wrong. This fulfilled a prediction I had made in 1981 when Prudential acquired Bache. They didn't want Bache when the stock was selling at $8 a share but loved it above $30 a share. Insurance companies are famous for falling in love with projects at the top. I had predicted that Prudential would find Bache to be a burden. There were rumors that Prudential was looking for a way to dump their ill-fated acquisition.

Pitfalls were showing up in the unregulated market areas. Trier Investments in Amsterdam collapsed. Trier's investors, many of them American, showed losses that ran as high as $250 million. The Amsterdam Exchange was trying to crack down on the bucket shops which had typified the unregulated Dutch securities market.

Unemployment in Europe was a continuing problem despite all the reports of the "healthy" U.S. economy. At this time, unemployment in England was at 12 percent and in Spain was reported at 19.6 percent.

But there was that one something that refused to relinquish hope. Despite the legitimate causes of concern, people wanted to gamble. Option trading was now the big game, that and betting on the ups and downs of the market via stock futures. This spiraling wave of off-track betting was luring billions away from the New York Stock Exchange and the trend was going international. Exchanges were being linked into a network in such a way that it could honestly be said that the stock market was a casino that never closed, open for business twenty-four hours a day. As 1984 ended, hundreds of new option and futures products were being planned on exchanges all over the world.

In May 1929, all the problems existed that were to bring down the stock market in the fall of that fateful year. Alexander Noyes, the financial editor of *The New York Times,* was calling for a crash. But instead, the Dow turned around at 293.42 on May 27 and soared all the way to 381.17 by September 3. That was a sharp percentage gain of almost 30 percent. The Dow Jones Industrial Average closed out 1984 at 1,211.57. A 1929-type blowoff of similar proportions would take the Dow to 1,573.82.

What was there to worry about?

Everything.

23

Fly Now—Pay Later

[JANUARY 1985]

I

Always cognizant of the many 1929 parallels, I was bothered by one specific thing as the new year commenced. The one missing ingredient was that final blowoff to the upside, some replica of what had happened in the summer of 1929. I needed that final fake-out in order to place the final jigsaw piece into a completed puzzle. Without it, I felt that my scenario was incomplete. With it, however, I would know that my case was virtually airtight.

I had carefully prepared my hole card for that scenario in my November 3 letter:

> Therefore, I cannot wholly dismiss the possibility of a huge fake-out on the upside occurring just prior to the crash itself. In calling the sharp July–August rise in the Dow, I had cited the technical importance of bettering the 1,140 level. When the Dow crossed that level, the market exploded on the upside. Comparing such possibilities now with an equally critical level in the Dow of 1,240, the difference is currently that we are on a sell signal. However, a case could be made that the next buy signal together with a confirmed breakout above the 1,240 level could be the precursor to a wild swing as high as 1,400 in the Dow. What I am saying here is that we are going through a time of 1929 backgrounds and, being a 1929, anything crazy is possible. Such a swing would cause wide anti-Granville sentiment and there would be much pressure to make me admit that my entire crash scenario was wrong. But liken the case to history. A handful of astute market observers in 1928 and 1929 were calling for a crash, including the financial editor of *The New York Times*. Yes, the Dow turned at 293.42 on May 27, 1929, and soared all the way to 381.17 on September 3, 1929. A few weeks later came the

great crash. Did the editor of the *Times* tear up his scenario? Of course not.
Conditions were worsening and the speculative blowoff in the summer of 1929
simply exacerbated the great decline that followed.

Now I felt ready for anything that 1985 had in store. With or without a
concluding blowoff, I saw no satisfactory resolution of the many 1929 parallels
that had been compiled other than an inevitable collapse. It was like viewing
the 1928–29 scene and being aware of the dangers and the signals but unaware
of the precise timing. I felt that the year ahead would never be forgotten.
Virtually nobody expected a collapse and thus the stage was set for major
shocks with no further warnings required. All bullish forecasts were suspect
because the majority of these were coming from those who had completely
missed the 1983 peak and thought that 1984 was going to be a great stock
market year. Now they were all caught up on the "5 syndrome," citing the
great record all years ending in 5 have had in the stock market. Something
widely believed has to be present in order to be a reliable precursor of a crash.
I saw the "5 syndrome" as the major market hook of 1985. Regardless of how
good the stock market might look at some time during the year, the entire year
is what would count as far as that syndrome was concerned. In 1984 the
"election year syndrome" entrapped the majority into believing that it had to
be a great year in the market. The longer something works, the greater the
odds are that it will eventually not work, and the failure then becomes a major
shock. Countering the "5 syndrome," years following presidential elections
have generally been down years, especially those following Republican victo-
ries. Then the four-year market cycle had to be considered, which called for
a low in 1986, implying a general 1985–86 slide. I was also aware of the
dangerous time period coinciding with the six-month indicator, which affected
both stocks and bonds. That important indicator measured the six-month
capital gain period and applied the timing to previous important bottoms in
both the stock and bond markets, implying that at the end of that period there
should be important selling pressures in both markets. Measured from previous important lows, that had set up the December 17–January 24 period as
being extremely volatile and dangerous with a heavy bias to the downside.

I had stressed the importance each year of the January indicator. In 1984
that indicator was correct, predicting a down year for most stocks. This time
I would not stress that indicator as being inviolate. While it is generally wise
to let the market traverse the entire month before drawing any premature
conclusions, I felt that my 1985 scenario was sound regardless of what the
January indicator did.

The current mix of technical indicators left little doubt of what was ultimately ahead. A break below the December low of 1,163.21 would be an
important bearish omen, especially if it occurred fairly early in the year, during
the first three months. The record had fairly reliably shown that the sooner

the December low is broken, the more bearish the outlook for the entire year.

Over and over the question kept coming up: What would it take to turn me bullish? My answer was always the same. I would give a list of indicators and would simply say: Change these things and I will change. At this time they hadn't changed. When they did, I would change.

What was it that most bothered me? First and foremost was the Kondratieff Wave, and that wasn't going to change. The chart showed that the cycle was entering the 1929 slope in the 1985–86 period. The wave at this point was underscoring the word "deflation" and the incoming data were increasingly fitting that major scenario—notably the collapse in most commodity prices, thus explaining the collapse in gold and the developing collapse in the price of oil. I told my readers especially to watch the crude oil price futures each day, a break below the critical price of $25 a barrel signaling an ultimate collapse to as low as $10 to $12 a barrel in the year ahead.

All the evidence I had in the spring of 1983 called for a major bear market, one that would contain a panic and crash. None of that evidence had been reversed. The year just ended had shown the bearish indications of the 50% Principle, which had called for a testing of the July 1984 low, the horrendous action in the advance/decline lines, especially those of the Amex and over-the-counter markets, the very poor action of the high/low indicators, the overabundance of bullish sentiment as measured by *Investors Intelligence,* the heavy insider selling, low institutional cash, the poor performance of the bellwether stocks, the six-month indicators, many weeks of money flowing out of the stock market and into the money market funds despite the drop in interest rates, the bearish response to the high short interest, and all of this against the background of the A-Dis Trading Barometer sell signal. So my answer was clear: Reverse all these things and I would become a major bull.

What was weighing on the market was not just the horrendous short-term technical indications, but, of course, the proliferation of the 1929 parallels, which implied that we were getting dangerously closer to a financial Armageddon that would soon rumble around the world. Nobody knew which decline would trigger the big one, and thus every decline against this historical background could have been the start of the big one. Every short-term sell signal also had to be treated as a potential major sell signal. That was the position I had taken in the spring of 1983, and the record showed that the stock market had been declining since that time for a year and a half as 1985 got underway. Similar action had preceded the 1929 stock market crash against a similar background. Back then, gambling was rife. Gambling is rife today, as demonstrated by the overall volume figures and the tremendous interest in the options and futures markets. Billions of dollars were bypassing the New York Stock Exchange, the disturbing parallel with the bucket shops of the 1920s. This was largely speculative money—gambling money. It had no long-term objectives and thus it was not investment at all.

Most of that money would go down the drain as it did in 1929, satisfying the masochistic urge to lose.

───

PARALLEL 183

Historical
Crimes Against Property

As pointed out in Robert Beckman's *The Downwave*,[1] during the upward movement of the Kondratieff Wave most crimes are against people. As the downwave develops, there is a shift to crimes against property—fraud, embezzlement, arson, etc. Current crime figures showed that this was happening, just as it had in the late 1920s.

Many of the problems were generally swept under the rug as the Dow struggled to maintain a degree of respectability around the 1,200 level. But when the U.S. stock market collapses at these levels or even much higher, the shot will be heard around the world, with a devastating effect on all markets. Then all the weaknesses which were now in evidence would suddenly be revealed to their fullest.

Most people took comfort in the widespread belief that the Federal Reserve would save the day. But this presupposed that we were in a normal cycle. A collapse in the price of oil could bring about an overnight withdrawal of short-term Arab deposits and create a very serious imbalance. The bond market had shown signs of peaking in late November, and losses in both bonds and stocks seemed to be looming ahead. The Federal Reserve does not control the stock market. If interest rates come down and stocks fall at the same time, there is little the Fed can do.

But virtually nobody saw a repeat of the 1930s coming. People generally disregarded any disturbing parallels. On December 30, 1984, *The New York Times* ran the following piece:

REMINDERS OF THE 1930's

Growth in the United States is expected to slip back to 3 percent or 4 percent next year from this year's hectic 8 percent and unemployment is likely to stop falling. In Europe, where the recovery brought no new jobs at all, it is predicted that unemployment will edge on up beyond 11 percent in 1985.

Ever since the Great Depression of the 1930's, pessimists have been predicting an encore. In a recent study of those years, subtitled "the lessons for the 1980's,"

[1]Robert Beckman, *The Downwave* (New York: E. P. Dutton, 1983), pp. 260–61.

Christian Saint Etienne, a French economist at the OECD, contends that the downturn was basically a normal cyclical decline that got out of hand because of growing protectionism, an international debt crisis and a drastic contraction of the world money supply. Mr. Saint Etienne points to "obvious" similarities with today. But there are also important differences.

Today's growth of protectionism is more gradual than the brutal Smoot-Hawley Tariff Act of 1929, which raised American tariffs 50 percent and is widely blamed for starting the world decline. Bt the huge expansion of world trade since then also means the world economy is more vulnerable to trade restrictions now.

An international debt crisis also threatens to deepen any economic slowdown now as then. In the 1930's dwindling export markets forced Germany, Austria and Hungary to default on their World War I debts, sending a wave of panic through the international financial system. Slowing world growth will make it harder for Latin America to keep up its debt repayments next year. Along with Japan, Spain and South Korea, Mexico and Brazil, two of the biggest debtors, agreed earlier this month to cut their steel shipments to the United States, consequently reducing their ability to repay their debts.

The big difference with the 1930's, however, is that the Federal Reserve shows no sign of allowing the United States' money supply to contract by 25 percent as it did between 1929 and 1933, aggravating the squeeze on the world economy. For many economists it is this fact, together with the growth of international economic cooperation, *that rules out a repeat of the 1930's* [emphasis added].

The president of the New York Stock Exchange, E. H. H. Simmons, was equally sure in 1929 that nothing was going to go wrong as long as we had the Federal Reserve (the "great business stabilizer"). He had ruled out the panics and the crashes of the past just as certainly as the case was being made now that "it couldn't happen again." And then, when least expected, it happened.

II

January started on a weak note. Just before the start of the new month, one of the most often heard comments around the Street was: "Once this tax selling is out of the way, watch this market take off." Well, the market didn't waste any time in "taking off." The new year started off with the largest decline in almost a month.

The daily Climax Indicator had clearly indicated this new weakness. On the December 18 sharp rally of over 34 points, the CLX had posted a reading of +25, which, for all practical effects, blew out the entire year-end rally period as a technical farce, fooling nobody except those who wanted to be fooled. The Dow had closed at 1,211.57 on December 18. Following a brief drop thereafter to 1,198.98 on December 21, the Dow attempted one last fling to the upside, closing on the last day of the year at 1,211.57, exactly equaling the December 18 closing. This time, however, the Climax Indicator stood at only

+11. There was a clear indication of important weakness dead ahead.

The Cumulative CLX was also telling an important story. It was now tracing out a major triple top. The first peak had occurred in November 1983 with matching peaks in January 1984 and now. This stated that all technical failures could be serious ones from this level.

While it may have appeared to be a minor thing, the important advance/decline line had failed to better the December 19 reading on the year-end 7.40-point Dow rise. That added technical conviction to the decline that immediately followed.

The high/low indicator continued to turn in a bearish performance, dredging up no more than 57 new highs on the year-end rally attempt, a far cry from the 127 new highs on December 19, or the 179 new highs recorded on October 19.

In the old days, it used to be an accepted, foregone conclusion that January was the great time for reinvestment demand. It used to come every year like clockwork. But this was no longer so. The longer-term investment-oriented markets were now a thing of the past. Everything was now short-term. Brokers were pushing their short-term products on TV, suited to the trader, the gambler. The investor had been roughly treated for the past eighteen months and his patience had been sorely tried. He was sick and tired of buying stocks for the long pull only to see them get trampled in a bear market his advisers didn't warn him about. That had so disillusioned the public that Wall Street had effectively removed the very agent necessary to launch a new bull market.

I couldn't see any upswing, no matter how large, as having any longer-term significance until all bullishness was removed from the scene. The only way current growing bullish sentiment figures could be reversed was by a major break.

III

Since technicians always reserve the right to change their minds on instant notice, my bearish stance became increasingly uncomfortable as the Dow briefly pulled back to 1,184.96 on January 4. Several things had taken place which could spark a strong rally. Norman Fosback's "Two Tumbles and a Jump" indicator had flashed an important buy signal on December 21. Fosback's rule is a simple one: "The 'Two Tumbles and a Jump' rule states that when the Federal Reserve eases the monetary climate by decreasing one of the three basic policy variables (Discount Rate, Margin Requirement, or Reserve Requirement) two times in succession, conditions are favorable for an ensuing 'jump' in stock prices."[2] While this rule was not strictly within the

[2]Norman G. Fosback, *Stock Market Logic* (Fort Lauderdale, Fla.: Institute for Econometric Research, 1984), p. 41.

realm of pure technical analysis, its record was so impressive that any technical signals for a higher market would have to be doubly respected.

I had watched the Net Field Trend Indicator jump from zero to +9 in late December, most of the jump occurring on the December 18 explosion. The early January weakness had seen that important indicator pull back to only a +2 reading. By January 9 it had jumped to +7, threatening an upside breakout above the +9 reading. Seeing that the Dow was about to abort the 50% Principle in a strong bull move, this observation coinciding with a strong upside breakout by the Climax Indicator above the December 31 reading of +11, I felt certain that a January 10 strong buy signal by the A-Dis Short-Term Trading Barometer could not be avoided.

It was time to act. At noon on January 10, with the Dow around 1,202, I announced the buy signal on a special update on my Daily Option Service. Within less than half an hour the word had been quickly disseminated among trading circles. The Dow soared for the balance of the day, closing up 20.76 points at 1,223.50.

I then told my readers that it is not for a technician to ask why, but simply when. Regardless of any feelings I might have had, a number of changes had begun to seep into the technical picture that considerably brightened the immediate outlook. The market was setting the stage for a far better than average rally, not unlike what I had seen in July 1984 just prior to the August explosion.

Whether this was to be a brief display of pyrotechnics crossing the market heavens like a comet or was to produce a more lasting glow remained to be seen. In any case, the direction for now was up and that would remain my position until my barometer said otherwise. The most impressive technical changes came in on January 9. Up to that date, rally attempts were well within the parameters of previous failing starts. However, on the ninth the Climax Indicator showed a power it hadn't shown in some time, not only shooting well above the +11 level of December 31, when the Dow had closed at 1,211.57, but igniting at the same time the very impressive upside breakout by the Cumulative Climax Indicator, the latter moving above the 1983 and 1984 highs. Coupled with that, the Net Field Trend Indicator gained four fields, positioning that indicator for a key upside breakout above the +9 December high. The persistent positive readings by the high/low indicator now took on added bullish significance, especially with the great recent improvement in the Amex high/low figures.

The buy signal radically changed the outlook for the January Indicator. While the first three trading days in the month were deemed to be negative, and the first five trading days also deemed negative (both time periods closing well under the December 31 Dow closing of 1,211.57), the technical probabilities now were very strong that the middle of the month would show higher readings as well as the end of the month if the A-Dis Trading Barometer could stay on this buy signal. That would produce a net bullish signal based on my 5-point analysis—two negatives and three positives. A break below the December closing low of 1,163.21 during the month could be ruled out completely, thus producing the bullish balance for the January Indicator.

On January 9 the big board advance/decline line broke out above the previous interim high of December 31. Volume attested to an unstoppable upside momentum this time. The rally posture suggested that the institutions and all the Wall Street powers that be were going to pull out all the stops to get the public to come back into the market. Whether they succeeded or not remained to be seen. There was a very convincing case that this upswing could turn out to be the beginning of the biggest rallying movement of the year— and the last. As it got started I sensed it as perhaps the final run for the roses, the missing ingredient I needed to make the most important of the 1929 parallels become a reality, although it was not a strict requirement.

Adding technical credence to the move, the Dow had stopped going down right at the rising 200-day trendline. The Dow Jones Transportation Average had never given back what it had previously gained on the July–August explosion but, like the industrials, had kept trending higher. Persistent strength in the transports in the face of the sideways industrial movement was the longer-term technical evidence that there was to be at least one more large rallying movement in 1985.

Did this negate the six-month indicator? Not necessarily. An explosive rise still fit the six-month parameter following the explosive early August run-up. Thus nobody knew how far this run would carry, but I had to recognize the technical case here that could take the Dow right back up to the top and new highs. It was at this point that I used the key paragraph from my November 3 letter. For, after all, I now had the next buy signal that had been referred to in that key paragraph.

I had used a similar technique in July 1984, predicated on the buy signal received at that time as well as the correctly anticipated upward explosion that had been designed to make everyone bullish at the wrong time. Thus I saw all important moves as *endings*, definitely not beginnings. While to the novice that might have seemed to be a paradox, I saw such endings as either final upside blowoffs or serious upside failures. In either case, they were to be *terminal* moves. This is the way I interpreted the buy signal.

As proven in July, all important buy signals were respected, and this one seemed to deserve a great deal of respect. Did it change my crash scenario? No more than did the final run for the roses in 1929. Keen observers of the world scene, including the administration in Washington, saw the troubles closing in upon us and were expected to use every tool at their disposal to buy some time before the inevitable hit. Thus, the final denouement might be put off until the fall of 1985 or early 1986 but it took nothing away from the constantly observed proliferation of 1929 parallels.

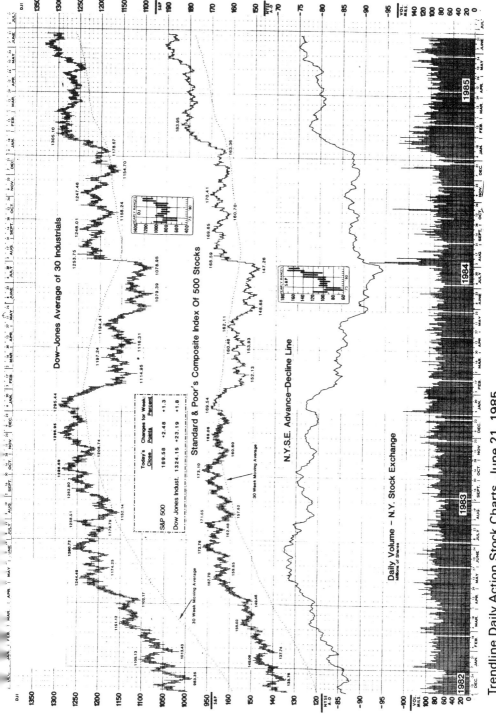

Trendline Daily Action Stock Charts, June 21, 1985

There was a disturbing *lack of equilibrium* in the steady exodus of players from the stage of the Reagan administration, one by one leaving the ship. One could recall the complete shake-up in the Carter administration in the summer of 1979 preceding the October massacre in the stock market. In any case, something wasn't right. They would have been awfully blind not to see the storm clouds on the horizon and their actions spoke louder than their words. Nobody knew the real reason why Treasury Secretary Regan was changing jobs. History would write the final chapter. But something wasn't right. There was too much shuffling around, suggestive of a crew that wanted to jump ship but didn't want to be accused of open mutiny.

While all the events couldn't be linked together, there was a very definable trend going on at this time. That trend, traced to the ballooning budgetary deficits, was moving in the direction of the government's closing up every hole, threatening the complete elimination of all tax shelters. It also tied in with the contemplated change in the currency. That subject, whenever it came up, struck a very sensitive nerve. For one thing, it was another of the 1929 parallels. The U.S. currency was changed in 1929 from the big bills to the currently used small bills. As the Grace Commission pointed out, Uncle Sam was missing out on the tax revenues from some $130–$150 billion in the "underground economy," much of this financing the illicit drug traffic which by this time had reached the proportions of a national epidemic. That money had to be neutralized, declared invalid. In keeping with the current trend of the government's running out of money, a change in the currency certainly appeared to be in the wind.

When I first introduced the subject, there were those who said that the underworld would simply switch from the old currency into gold and sit on it until the new currency change came into effect. They would merely feed the gold back into the new currency. But the government was not stupid. Foreseeing that obvious dodge, it changed the law. All gold purchases had to be registered. The very fact that that law was changed gave credence to the contemplated currency change. The law on gold registration wouldn't have been changed without the advance knowledge of the currency change. There were no perfect answers. Some speculated that the underworld would put their money into the stock market instead of gold, but that was questionable because of the exposure to record-keeping.

The bottom line at this time seemed to be a *desperation* to make things better. A deflationary depression could not come about until all the dollars produced by the previous inflationary cycle were sent to money heaven. This would be done in three ways: (1) Billions are lured into the stock market with a huge rally and sent to money heaven with a crash; (2) billions are lured into the banking system via high real interest rates and then lent out to paper over the bad loans to the developing countries, which default anyway, causing a banking collapse, thus sending that portion to money heaven;

and (3) the currency is called in, eliminating the underground dollars and sending that portion to money heaven. These were the major events coming, in keeping with the long-term shift in the Kondratieff Wave from inflation to deflation.

IV

Unlike the previous one-day wonders, the January 10 explosion packed some lasting wallop. It emphatically broke the pattern of declining tops, demanding the covering of all short sales. The power was there in terms of the Climax Indicator, the Net Field Trend, the high/low indicator, and the advance/decline line. These all made for bullish changes totally unlike the previous bull trap moves on previous sharp rallies. While the Cumulative Climax Indicator readings had been at a triple top, that meant that any failure to come down from that level effected a triple top upside breakout, exactly what was now occurring. That provoked an upside momentum that would be difficult to stop. The first order of technical business now was to see a runaway on the upside. There could be no turning back without having to explain unscheduled technical difficulties. This looked like the beginning of the last extended run to the upside. The stage was set to bring the public back into the market.

The outstanding difference this time was the strength in the secondary markets. The upturns in the over-the-counter market and the American Stock Exchange figures were the best in a long time. What had been previously bothering me was now being reversed. It was that persistent weakness in the secondary markets which had finally come to a halt and was now reversing. All the technical work was spelling out a strong go. Now I could go back to the drawing boards and make a case for the final run for the roses. In interpreting what phase the market was in, the important thing at this point was the Time Indicator. The market was entering the thirtieth month since the August 1982 bottom. Therefore, it was very late in the cycle. As the rally was to develop steam, it would be easy to lose sight of where the market stood in the 4- to 4½-year cycle, let alone the Kondratieff Wave. The record had shown no staying power past the thirty-third month in the cycle, and thus the ultimate peak of any power plays at this time would most probably be achieved no later than May.

The great reservoirs of potential buying power weren't tapped on the previous rally attempts. Now the technical posture of the market suggested that this time they would be. The two major sources of such power were the money market funds and the record high short interest. Added to this was some expected switching from bonds back into stocks.

The market was under tremendous bullish compression at this point, the advance/decline line moving out to the upside while the Dow was still well short of the 1,244.15 closing of November 6. That implied an easy upside breakout of that level coming, which in turn could spark a huge extension of the rally as short sellers would panic on that important upside breakout. Technically, the market was now well armed easily to digest any day-to-day pullbacks.

Something big was happening. Unless proved otherwise, the buy signal flashed at noon on January 10 was of major import. On January 15, however, the A-Dis Short-Term Trading Barometer was flashing a sell signal. I dispensed the following message:

> A-Dis Trading Barometer has flashed a sell signal. This is deemed to be a minor signal and would take on no significance on the high side of Dow 1,180. However, a straight line upward move now above 1,250 without any further correction would constitute an important sell signal, calling for closing out all long positions. Unless that happens, hold all existing long positions.

The message was clear. I believed that the January 15 sell signal called for nothing more than normal pullbacks within the parameters of a strong upward trend and that all gyrations above Dow 1,180 were normal unless the Dow barreled above 1,250 without the benefit of a corrective move first. Believing that this upward move (with the benefit of corrections) had quite a way to go, I felt that the powers that be would ultimately want to take the market lower in order to accumulate more stock. However, being back on a barometer sell signal, even though I believed it to be temporary, I had to bottle up my enthusiasm over the very near term pending the next barometer buy signal.

What brought about this striking change of posture? Of course, aware of the Fosback signal of December 21, I had had to be on guard for any technical evidence that would trigger an upswing in keeping with the forecast of the Fosback indicator. In fact, my November 3 market letter had already taken this into account, stating that the next buy signal could spark a huge fake-out on the upside that could take the Dow even as high as 1,400. The buy signal of January 10 could not be taken lightly.

The 50% Principle was triggered on January 10 with the Dow moving back above the halfway point between the November 6 high and the December 7 low for the fourth time. Up until then, a case could be made, based on that measurement, for an eventual drop to the 1,086.57 level. But now that signal was aborted. The first move above the halfway point on December 18 and subsequent dates lacked upside follow-through until the explosion of January 10. Subsequent action proved that the time of the one-day wonders had passed. This move certainly seemed to be real.

The move was to have a profound effect on the January Indicator. The first three days of January were deemed to be negative. The first five days of January were also deemed to be negative. The middle-of-the-month reading, being well above the December 31 closing of 1,211.57, was deemed to be positive. That left only two steps to go—the end of the month and the ability to hold above the December closing low of 1,163.21. It could be safely assumed that there would be no return to the December low in this time frame and thus the January Indicator would give a positive reading—two negatives and three strong positives.

A key question arose at this point: Would a positive January Indicator change my scenario of an ultimate market crash? No, not at all. I was viewing the entire year of 1985. I saw here, as in 1929, a generally big rallying phase currently in force and later in the year a probable smash. The higher the market would go on this rally, the greater were the odds favoring a sharp drop later in the year. While I considered the January Indicator important, it was certainly not all-prevailing. For the record, the January Indicator in 1929 gave a *bullish* reading! The December 1928 Dow low stood at 257.33 and closed that month at 300.00. The first three trading days of 1929 were positive, the Dow closing at 304.75 on January 4. The first five trading days were negative, the Dow closing at 297.70 on January 7. I recorded the mid-month as negative because the Dow closed at 297.66, although if one had measured by January 14 or January 16, the reading would have been positive, the Dow closing on those dates at 304.06 and 302.66, respectively. The end of the month saw the Dow close at 317.51, which was the high closing for the entire month, and so that was definitely positive. At no time did the Dow remotely threaten the December 1928 low of 257.33, and thus the January Indicator in 1929 was bullish. *But that was the year of the great crash!*

For an exact 1929 parallel in 1985, the Dow would have to rise very sharply first. In 1929 the final upward push started from a low point of 293.42 on May 27 and went all the way to 381.17 by September 3. That was a very sharp rise of 29.9 percent in only a little over three months. If such a percentage increase occurred now, the Dow would soar to 1,511.00, based on the December 7 closing of 1,163.21, or 1,573.82, based on the 1,211.57 December 31 closing.

It was the only missing ingredient. I had to make allowance for it in my November 3 letter when projecting the impact of the next buy signal. Now several important observations had to be made:

1. *The upswing had no bullish long-term investment implications.* (Could one imagine people coming into the stock market in late May 1929 buying stocks as a long-term investment?)

2. *The public had to be attracted back into the stock market.* Nothing would do this other than *rising* prices. The action of the secondary markets, the Amex and the over-the-counter markets, attested to a growing *public* interest.

3. Anything past thirty-three months off the August 1982 bottom was beyond the time parameters laid down in my 1976 *New Strategy* book for a normal completion of the overall up phase of the 4- to 4½-year market cycle.

Thus any huge rise occurring between January and May 1985 would have to be seen as a *major ending*, not a beginning.

Rather disquieting, however, was the rapid dissemination of market knowledge. The advance/decline made a big move and the whole country knew about it immediately. Back in the 1950s, nobody knew what the advance/decline line was. Richard Russell discussed it in *The Dow Theory Letters* back then but he was practically alone.

V

The well-defined collapse in commodity prices, notably affecting gold, silver, sugar, and oil, was underscoring the persistent deflationary moves. The steady drop in the spot price for crude oil had been exerting strong downward pressure on the British pound and this month it had dropped to still another all-time record low of $1.10. While the earlier decline had caused no undue alarm, the persistent strength in the U.S. dollar and the weakness in the pound was pointing toward increasing difficulties ahead for the British economy. This was foreshadowed by the parabolic curve to all-time new highs in the English stock market, the Financial Times Index hitting the 1,024 level in January. Now it could be said that the English stock market was looking very much the way the price of gold had in January 1980, when it had peaked at $875 an ounce. London stocks had been in a steady, unbroken climb for six months and the market was technically very vulnerable to collapse. This was another missing piece of the jigsaw puzzle that wasn't there earlier. Thus the vulnerability of the English stock market was casting disquieting shadows ahead.

The largest of the disquieting factors was the persistent rise in the U.S. dollar. But this also had traced out a parabolic curve, implying that when the rise terminated, the decline thereafter would not be a gentle one. Ashby Bladen, writing in the January 28 issue of *Forbes*, stated: "As long as the dollar stays up, the federal government will have to borrow and spend more to ward off a domestic slump." He went on to say: "A more likely cause of trouble will be a self-reinforcing downward spiral of international confidence in the U.S. as a falling dollar rekindles domestic inflation, while our international loans progressively turn sour but our foreign debts continue to escalate." There were far too many parabolic curves at this time, implying that the ultimate downturn would be a major smash, creating shock waves for years to come.

Fitting in with the trend toward increased short-term speculation, Treasury Secretary Regan was pushing toward removing the control of margin requirements from the Federal Reserve and returning such controls to the New York Stock Exchange. This had to be disquieting to any student of history.

But most disquieting of all, a shocking report appeared on the front page of *The Wall Street Journal* on January 22: "Banks are intensifying efforts to enter the stock mutual-fund business. U.S. Trust plans to start a fund next month. Marine Midland plans to follow within six months and FMR's Fidelity Investors is planning one to be managed by a major bank." This was a major area forbidden to the banks under laws passed after the stock market crash of 1929. Banks couldn't go so far as to organize, sponsor, or sell mutual funds but they could now act as a fund's investment adviser. The brokerage firms would launch the new bank mutual funds. The caveats were apparent. Existing mutual fund firms warned of these. The danger was that some customers would be impressed by the general feeling that such bank operations were federally insured, forgetting that they could lose money in the stock market, an uninsured risk.

What was not being underscored at this time was the great parallel with 1929, the proliferation of the investment trusts in the period just prior to the 1929 stock market crash. Moreover, most new mutual funds have a tendency to be formed at or near major stock market peaks. This was but another example of "everybody getting into everybody else's business." The trend was saying that the Glass-Steagall Act, which had separated the banking and securities industries, was all but dead. By 1985 one could detect very little separation. The investment kitchen was getting dangerously overcrowded, just as it had in 1929.

But these disquieting signs failed to dampen the ardor of speculative enthusiasm bubbling over on the January upturn. Economists said that 1984 was the best year in over two decades. However, most market analysts said that 1984 was an extremely difficult year to call, the *Hulbert Financial Digest* compilations of the many advisory services they follow attesting to this, most having lost money for their clients in the "best year in two decades." The lesson, of course, was clear: market timing had little or nothing to do with the economy.

The Golden Age of Ronald Reagan's second term was casting a glow of bright promise as January 1985 began. Robert Prechter of the *Elliott Wave Theorist* saw 1985 as probably the best year of the decade for the stock market. According to the tape, the sky now appeared to be the limit. The key word was "appeared." Unquestionably the power was there but could disappear with little advance notice. January 1929 had also started as a year of great promise, Herbert Hoover inaugurated on a "plateau of permanent prosperity."

If anything was going to go wrong in 1985–86, nobody could ever say that January 1985 didn't set out to fool most people. Every possible entrapment was present. The January Indicator was bullish, 1985 was a year ending with a 5, and even the now famous Super Bowl indicator was bullish. The public was coming back into the market, as evidenced by the great strength in the secondary issues. Interest rates were coming down and the first order of business in the new Congress was to attack the budgetary deficit. Inflation had been tamed and the economic outlook, according to most economists, was optimistic. But I saw all this as setting the stage for a tremendous upset.

PARALLEL 184
Historical
The Parabolic Curve of Debt

Debts of individuals, businesses, and governments soared to an estimated total of $7.2 trillion in 1984, up from $2.4 trillion ten years before and $1 trillion twenty years before. This was a parabolic curve of debt that could no longer be comfortably sustained. The debt explosion had gotten to such a dangerous point that it had put the government in a perilous position by 1985. Leonard Silk of *The New York Times* described the dilemma on January 18 as follows: "The paradox of our time is that we are so heavily in debt that we cannot afford a recession now. So both monetary and fiscal policy are being aimed at keeping the expansion going. This will not stave off the dangers flowing from an overburdened public and private debt structure forever."

The world is sinking in a sea of debt and Uncle Sam's days as the "ultimate lender" are numbered. Not only could there be another 1929 but my evidence overwhelmingly points to its *inevitability*. The luxury of time is gone. What was once years has dwindled to a matter of months and what little time there is left is ticking away. Reagan's "borrowed" recovery sooner or later would have to backfire. The coming stock market crash will send a warning all over the world that things will never quite be the same again.

Epilogue

The higher the diving board, the bigger the splash. In a paradoxical fashion the stock market, temporarily oblivious to the proliferation of 1929 parallels, mounted an important rally to new, all-time, unprecedented highs in May 1985, in what promised to be a run at the final parallel with 1929—the concluding sharp run-up in the Dow Jones Industrial Average. The cover story for this terminal run was that a slowing economy would prod the Federal Reserve Board into opting in favor of driving interest rates lower thus, driving the stock market higher. But there was no long-term comfort in the scenario. The 1982-1985 bull market was knocking on the door of cyclical recession which, were these parallels to guide, would make "recession" a weak term, indeed.

Here then is the document of parallels between 1927-1929 and the 1983-1985 period. There are simply too many parallels to ignore—too many to be simply consigned to luck. Coincidence has been overwhelmed by data.

In the 1983-85 markets this writer was proved to be premature in his bearishness. Without copping a plea for myself, in 1928 and 1929 a small group of stock market observers warned of an impending crash. Their voices, unheard beneath the self-fulfilling din of general optimism were considered premature. And, not in small part, un-American.

But even if these pessimistic voices were sounded too early—I think they were sounded just in time. To ignore THE WARNING and the historic fundamentals I bring from the experience of 1929 is foolhardy—perhaps, even willful ignorance.

Index

| T2 | 108108 Mo | S |

Customer:
Elizabeth Louise A. Love

The Warning: The Coming Great Crash in the Stock Market

Joseph E. Granville

5E-00-02-E4

R1-CMJ-584

No CD
Used - Good
9780881910346

Picker Notes:
M _____ 2 _____
WT _____ 2 _____
CC _____

64524275

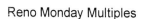